T0212960

Lecture Notes in Computer Science   9903

Commenced Publication in 1973
Founding and Former Series Editors:
Gerhard Goos, Juris Hartmanis, and Jan van Leeuwen

More information about this series at http://www.springer.com/series/7408

Naoya Maruyama · Bronis R. de Supinski
Mohamed Wahib (Eds.)

OpenMP: Memory, Devices, and Tasks

12th International Workshop on OpenMP, IWOMP 2016
Nara, Japan, October 5–7, 2016
Proceedings

Editors
Naoya Maruyama
RIKEN AICS
Kobe
Japan

Mohamed Wahib
RIKEN AICS
Kobe
Japan

Bronis R. de Supinski
Lawrence Livermore National Laboratory
Livermore, CA
USA

ISSN 0302-9743   ISSN 1611-3349   (electronic)
Lecture Notes in Computer Science
ISBN 978-3-319-45549-5   ISBN 978-3-319-45550-1   (eBook)
DOI 10.1007/978-3-319-45550-1

Library of Congress Control Number: 2016948816

LNCS Sublibrary: SL2 – Programming and Software Engineering

Printed on acid-free paper

This Springer imprint is published by Springer Nature
The registered company is Springer International Publishing AG Switzerland

Preface

OpenMP is a widely accepted, standard application programming interface (API) for high-level parallel programming in Fortran, C, and C++. Since its introduction in 1997, OpenMP has gained support from most high-performance compiler and hardware vendors. Under the direction of the OpenMP Architecture Review Board (ARB), the OpenMP specification has evolved up to the release of version 4.5. This latest version includes several refinements to existing support for heterogeneous hardware environments, many enhancements to its tasking model including the taskloop construct, and support for doacross loops.

The evolution of the standard would be impossible without active research in OpenMP compilers, runtime systems, tools, and environments. OpenMP is both an important programming model for multicore processors and a critical component of the most commonly used hybrid programming model for massively parallel, distributed memory systems. Since most of the growth in parallelism in Exascale systems is expected to arise within a node, these systems will increase the importance of OpenMP.

The community of OpenMP researchers and developers in academia and industry is united under cOMPunity (www.compunity.org). This organization has held workshops on OpenMP around the world since 1999: the European Workshop on OpenMP (EWOMP), the North American Workshop on OpenMP Applications and Tools (WOMPAT), and the Asian Workshop on OpenMP Experiences and Implementation (WOMPEI) attracted annual audiences from academia and industry. The International Workshop on OpenMP (IWOMP) consolidated these three workshop series into a single annual international event that rotates across Asia, Europe, and the Americas. The first IWOMP workshop was organized under the auspices of cOMPunity. Since that workshop, the IWOMP Steering Committee has organized these events and guided development of the series. The first IWOMP meeting was held in 2005, in Eugene, Oregon, USA. Since then, meetings have been held each year, in Reims, France; Beijing, China; West Lafayette, Indiana, USA; Dresden, Germany; Tsukuba, Japan; Chicago, Illinois, USA; Rome, Italy; Canberra, Australia; Salvador, Brazil; and Aachen, Germany. Each workshop has drawn participants from research and industry throughout the world. IWOMP 2016 continues the series with technical papers, tutorials, and OpenMP status reports. The IWOMP meetings have been successful in large part due to the generous support from numerous sponsors.

The cOMPunity website (www.compunity.org) provides access to the talks given at the meetings and to the photos of the activities. The IWOMP website (www.iwomp.org) provides information on the latest event. This book contains the proceedings of IWOMP 2016. The workshop program included 24 technical papers, two keynote talks, and advanced tutorials on OpenMP. All technical papers were peer reviewed by at least two different members of the Program Committee.

October 2016

Naoya Maruyama
Bronis R. de Supinski
Mohamed Wahib

Organization

Conference Organization

General Chair

Naoya Maruyama   RIKEN AICS, Japan

Program Committee Co-chairs

Naoya Maruyama   RIKEN AICS, Japan
Bronis R. de Supinski   LLNL, USA

Publicity Chair

Masahiro Nakao   RIKEN AICS, Japan

Publications Chair

Mohamed Wahib   RIKEN AICS, Japan

Local Chair

Shinichiro Takizawa   RIKEN AICS, Japan

Program Committee

Eduard Ayguadé	BSC and Universitat Politecnica de Catalunya, Spain
James Beyer	NVIDIA, USA
Taisuke Boku	University of Tsukuba, Japan
Mark Bull	EPCC, University of Edinburgh, UK
Nawal Copty	Oracle, USA
Luiz DeRose	Cray Inc., USA
Alex Duran	Intel, Spain
Deepak Eachempati	Cray, Inc., USA
Nasser Giacaman	The University of Auckland, New Zealand
Chunhua Liao	LLNL, USA
Larry Meadows	Intel, USA
Masahiro Nakao	RIKEN AICS, Japan
Stephen Olivier	Sandia National Laboratories, USA
Alistair Rendell	Australian National University, Australia
Mitsuhisa Sato	RIKEN AICS, Japan
Dirk Schmidl	RWTH Aachen University, Germany
Thomas Scogland	LLNL, USA

Eric Stotzer   Texas Instruments, USA
Christian Terboven   RWTH Aachen University, Germany
Priya Unnikrishnan   IBM Toronto, Canada
Mohamed Wahib   RIKEN AICS, Japan

IWOMP Steering Committee

Steering Committee Chair

Matthias Müller   RWTH Aachen University, Germany

Steering Committee

Dieter an Mey   RWTH Aachen University, Germany
Eduard Ayguadé   BSC and Universitat Politecnica de Catalunya, Spain
Mark Bull   EPCC, University of Edinburgh, UK
Barbara Chapman   University of Houston, USA
Bronis R. de Supinski   LLNL, USA
Luiz DeRose   Cray, USA
Rudi Eigenman   Purdue University, USA
William Gropp   University of Illinois, USA
Michael Klemm   Intel, Germany
Kalyan Kumaran   Argonne National Laboratory, USA
Federico Massaioli   CASPUR, Italy
Larry Meadows   Intel, USA
Stephen L Olivier   Sandia National Laboratories, USA
Ruud van der Pas   Oracle, USA
Alistair Rendell   Australian National University, Australia
Mitsuhisa Sato   RIKEN AICS, Japan
Sanjiv Shah   Intel, USA
Josemar Rodrigues   SENAI Unidade CIMATEC, Brazil
  de Souza
Christian Terboven   RWTH Aachen University, Germany
Matthijs van Waveren   CompilaFlows, France

Contents

Extensions

Tools

Accelerator Programming

Performance Evaluations and Optimization

Applications

Estimation of Round-off Errors
in OpenMP Codes

Pacôme Eberhart[1], Julien Brajard[2,3], Pierre Fortin[1(✉)],
and Fabienne Jézéquel[1,4]

[1] Sorbonne Universités, UPMC Univ Paris 06, CNRS,
UMR 7606, LIP6, 75005 Paris, France
{pacome.eberhart,pierre.fortin,fabienne.jezequel}@upmc.fr
[2] Sorbonne Universités, UPMC Univ Paris 06,
CNRS-IRD-MNHN, LOCEAN, 75005 Paris, France
julien.brajard@upmc.fr
[3] Inria Paris, 2 rue Simone Iff, Paris, France
[4] Université Panthéon-Assas,
12 place du Panthéon, 75231 Paris, Cedex 05, France

Abstract. It is crucial to control round-off error propagation in numerical simulations, because they can significantly affect computed results, especially in parallel codes like OpenMP ones. In this paper, we present a new version of the CADNA library that enables the numerical validation of OpenMP codes. With a reasonable cost in terms of execution time, it enables one to estimate which digits in computed results are affected by round-off errors and to detect numerical instabilities that may occur during the execution. The interest of this new OpenMP-enabled CADNA version is shown on various applications, along with performance results on multi-core and many-core (Intel Xeon Phi) architectures.

Keywords: CADNA library · Discrete stochastic arithmetic · Floating-point arithmetic · Numerical validation · Multi-core architectures · Many-core architectures · OpenMP · Round-off error

1 Introduction

The power of computational resources tends to increase and so does the number of floating-point operations performed in numerical simulations. Unfortunately each floating-point operation may generate a round-off error. These errors can accumulate and significantly affect the computed results. In parallel applications, more computations can lead to more round-off errors, and the order of computations can change with respect to the sequential execution or to another parallel execution: this can cause different round-off error propagations and hence different numerical results

The CADNA library[1] [4,8] that implements DSA (Discrete Stochastic Arithmetic) [16,17] enables one to estimate round-off errors in numerical simulation codes. In this paper we present a CADNA version for the numerical

---

[1] URL address: http://cadna.lip6.fr.

N. Maruyama et al. (Eds.): IWOMP 2016, LNCS 9903, pp. 3–16, 2016.
DOI: 10.1007/978-3-319-45550-1_1

validation of codes using the OpenMP standard which is widely used for parallel numerical simulations. We describe how this new CADNA version has been
developed taking into account constraints related to both OpenMP and DSA.
We show the benefit of CADNA and analyse its cost in terms of execution time
for various OpenMP programs: several benchmark codes and also a real-life
application.

As far as related work is concerned, DSA is sometimes compared to interval
arithmetic [1,10] that takes into accout round-off errors and computes, instead of
each floating-point result, an interval with guaranteed bounds. However, with a
naive implementation of interval arithmetic in a code, these bounds may overesti-
mate the effective error. Therefore the use of interval arithmetic in an application
requires specific algorithms and methods. Interval versions of linear algebra kernels have been proposed for multicore architectures [5,11,14,19] and have been
implemented using OpenMP pragmas or a standard POSIX threads [6] library.

The rest of the paper is organized as follows. Section 2 presents the CADNA
library and its use for the numerical validation of sequential codes. Section 3
describes the new OpenMP-enabled CADNA version developed to control the
numerical quality of OpenMP codes. Section 4 presents, for various OpenMP
applications, the interest of this CADNA version, as well as some performance
and numerical results. Finally concluding remarks are given in Sect. 5.

2   The CADNA Library

2.1   Principles of DSA (Discrete Stochastic Arithmetic)

The CADNA (Control of Accuracy and Debugging for Numerical Applications)
library [4,8] that implements DSA (Discrete Stochastic Arithmetic) [16,17]
enables one to estimate round-off errors in any scientific code written in C, C++
or Fortran. CADNA uses a random rounding mode: at each elementary operation, the result is rounded up or down with the probability 0.5. The computer's
deterministic arithmetic, therefore, is replaced by a stochastic arithmetic where
each arithmetic operation is performed N times before the next one is executed,
thereby propagating the round-off error differently each time. For each computed
result, we obtain N samples $R_1, \ldots, R_N$. The value of the computed result $\overline{R}$ is
chosen to be the mean value of $\{R_i\}$ and, if no overflow occurs, the number of
exact significant digits in $\overline{R}$, $C_{\overline{R}}$, can be estimated as

$$C_{\overline{R}} = \log_{10}\left(\frac{\sqrt{N}\,|\overline{R}|}{\sigma\tau_\beta}\right) \text{ with } \overline{R} = \frac{1}{N}\sum_{i=1}^{N} R_i \text{ and } \sigma^2 = \frac{1}{N-1}\sum_{i=1}^{N}\left(R_i - \overline{R}\right)^2.$$

τ_β is the value of Student's distribution for $N - 1$ degrees of freedom and a
probability level $1 - \beta$. In practice $\beta = 0.05$ and $N = 3$. Thus we can get a 95 %
confidence interval on the number of exact significant digits of the computed
result. DSA is based on an hypothesis on the distribution of round-off errors.
It has been shown that in case this hypothesis is not rigorously satisfied the

accuracy estimation is not altered if it is considered as exact up to one digit. The complete theory can be found in [16].

The validity of $C_{\overline{R}}$ is compromised if the two operands in a multiplication or the divisor in a division are not significant. Therefore CADNA performs a so-called *self-validation* that consists in controlling all multiplications and divisions during the execution of the code. This self-validation has led to the parallel computation of the N samples R_i and also to the concept of computational zero [15] defined as either a mathematical zero or a number without any significance, i.e. numerical noise. From this concept, relational operators that take into accout round-off error propagation have been defined [16].

2.2 Numerical Validation of Sequential Codes Using CADNA

The CADNA library allows one to use new numerical types: the stochastic types. In practice, classic floating-point variables are replaced by the corresponding stochastic variables, which are composed of three floating-point values and one integer to store the accuracy. The library contains the definition of all arithmetic operations and order relations for the stochastic types. Only the exact significant digits of a stochastic variable are printed or "@.0" if it is numerical noise. Because all operators are redefined for stochastic variables, the use of CADNA in a program requires only a few modifications: essentially changes in the declarations of variables and in input/output statements. CADNA has been successfully used for the numerical validation of academic and industrial simulation codes in various domains such as astrophysics, atomic physics, chemistry, climate science, fluid dynamics, geophysics [9].

We rely here on the latest CADNA version [4], which performs better with sequential codes and also enables the numerical validation of vectorized codes. Unlike in the previous CADNA version, the rounding mode is not explicitly changed in this version. It is set to rounding towards $+\infty$ once, in the `cadna_init` initialisation function that must be called at the beginning of the user program. The random rounding mode is then emulated by taking advantage of arithmetic properties of rounding towards $+\infty$.

CADNA can detect numerical instabilities which occur during the execution of the code. These instabilities are of several types.

- Self-validation: both operands in a multiplication, the divisor in a division, or the first argument of the power function are not significant.
- Instability in an intrinsic or a mathematical function: non significant argument in such a function.
- Branching instability: indeterminism in a branching test.
- Cancellation: sudden loss of accuracy on an addition or a subtraction.

At the end of the run, the total number of instabilities and each type of instability together with their occurrences are printed. If instabilities have occurred, their source need to be identified and, if necessary, the code changed. The user can specify the instabilities to be detected. One may choose, for instance, to activate only self-validation, to detect all types of instabilities or to deactivate the detection of instabilities.

3   CADNA for OpenMP Codes

We detail here how we have designed an OpenMP-enabled CADNA version for C/C++ codes, although up to our knowledge such a version could also be developed for Fortran codes.

Compatibility Check. Our CADNA implementation requires the rounding mode of each thread being set to rounding towards $+\infty$. But to our knowledge, there is no guarantee in the OpenMP standard that the worker threads have the same rounding mode as their master thread (though vendor specific extension may ensure this such as the KMP_INHERIT_FP_CONTROL environment variable for the Intel compiler [7]).

We thus have to check the compatibility between each OpenMP implementation used and CADNA. Within the cadna_init call (considered as not performed inside an OpenMP parallel region), we hence first set the rounding mode of the master thread to rounding towards $+\infty$, and then check in an OpenMP parallel region that all worker threads have inherited their rounding mode from the master thread. This is performed thanks to a software test: in double precision, only rounding towards $+\infty$ ensures that $1.0 + 1.0e - 20\ != 1.0$

This enables us to check OpenMP implementations that fork new worker threads at each OpenMP parallel region. If the parallel region within the cadna_init call is the first one in the program, this test enables us to also check for OpenMP implementations that create worker threads once at the first OpenMP parallel region, and then retrieve worker threads from a thread pool.

However, when partially analyzing a large OpenMP code with CADNA, it is convenient to be able to consider that the cadna_init call is performed after some parallel regions. In such case, and considering that all parallel regions (the ones within the cadna_init call and the ones in the CADNA instrumented code) have the same number of threads (condition hereafter referred to as (*)), we check thread pool based OpenMP implementations with the following test within the cadna_init call: we set to rounding towards $+\infty$ the rounding mode of all threads in a second parallel region, and we check in a third parallel region that the rounding mode of each thread has been correctly saved. If this second check fails, we consider that the OpenMP execution environment is not compatible with CADNA.

In our tests, both GOMP and Intel implementations have found to be compatible with CADNA, whether cadna_init is called prior to any OpenMP parallel region or not.

Random Rounding Mode. The next issue lies in the random number generation. Thanks to the new version of CADNA (see Sect. 2.2) used here, we now rely on a random number generator that was designed to be easily replicated in each execution flow; this was indeed required for a SIMD execution of CADNA where the random generator was replicated for each scalar lane of the SIMD unit. It is thus straightforward to have a distinct random generator in each

OpenMP thread: the three required variables are defined as `threadprivate` and are initialized in a parallel region within the `cadna_init` call.

However, in order to ensure that the values of these threadprivate variables will persist from one parallel region to the next one, we have to check the conditions listed in Sect. 2.14.2 of the OpenMP 4.0 reference [2], which we hereafter denote as (**) and which we summarize here as: same number of threads and same affinity policies for all parallel regions, no nested parallelism and no dynamic adjustment of the number of threads. It can be noticed that the conditions (**) encompass the condition (*).

Instability Detection. In an OpenMP application instrumented with CADNA, the counters dedicated to the numerical instabilities (see Sect. 2.2) can be concurrently incremented by multiple threads, which can lead to data race conditions. We have thus protected the updates of these counters with OpenMP `atomic` constructs.

OpenMP Reductions. When an OpenMP application includes an OpenMP reduction on floating-point variables, instrumenting such a reduction with CADNA implies to perform the corresponding reduction operation with stochastic variables. This is possible since OpenMP 4.0 thanks to the `declare reduction` construct and the redefinition of all arithmetic operators in the CADNA codes. Currently the `+`, `-` and `*` operators are supported.

Atomic Constructs on Stochastic Variables. If an OpenMP application contains `atomic` constructs, the code cannot be instrumented as is with CADNA. As specified in the OpenMP 4.0 reference [2], an `atomic` statement should involve scalar types, and cannot thus be applied on the CADNA stochastic types.

A CADNA-redefined arithmetic operation implies three floating-point IEEE operations, some bit manipulations (depending on the type of the arithmetic operation and on the rounding mode), and some instability detections (depending on the user specification). During this sequence of operations, we have to ensure that the variables are accessed by only one thread. The instability detection depends indeed on the result of the three floating-point computations. We have therefore chosen to include such CADNA-overloaded operation in a `critical` block. In practice, each `atomic` construct is replaced by a `critical` construct in the user code, and one can use distinct `critical` regions (with distinct names) when accessing distinct variables or arrays.

Provided that the conditions (**) are ensured, CADNA can now be used in OpenMP codes. We emphasize that, except for the `atomic` constructs, the OpenMP-enabled CADNA version does not require additional modifications to the user code other than those required by the sequential CADNA library.

4 Performance Tests and Application to OpenMP Codes

For our tests, we use two different HPC servers. The first one, named *CPU-server*, is composed of two Intel E5-2660 CPUs (each having 8 cores with 2-way SMT at 2.20 GHz) and 32 GB of memory. The second one is a 5110P Xeon Phi (Knight Corner), used in native mode as a distant server and named *Xeon-Phi*, with 60 cores (4-way SMT at 1.053 GHz) and 8 GB of dedicated memory.

In all our tests, the number of threads in each parallel region is determined according to the OMP_NUM_THREADS environment variable. Moreover, the same affinity policies are set for all parallel region, and no nested parallelism as well as no dynamic adjustment of the number of threads are used on both servers in order to meet the conditions (**) (see Sect. 3).

Unless otherwise mentioned, we use here CADNA with only self-validation activated, since this is its classic usage. It has to be noticed that all runs are scalar ones (no vectorization used): as shown in [4] it is possible to use CADNA for SIMD codes but this requires to access the SIMD lane identifier. To our knowledge this is currently not possible with OpenMP directives, and we therefore rely on the SPMD-on-SIMD programming paradigm (e.g. with the Intel SPMD Program Compiler - ispc[2]). In this paper we only focus on OpenMP programming: we thus consider scalar IEEE (i.e. not instrumented with CADNA) codes and scalar CADNA codes in order to precisely measure the performance impact of CADNA for OpenMP multi-threaded applications.

4.1 A Reduction Code

This first experiment shows that a sequential code and its parallel version may exhibit a very different numerical quality.

The sum S of all elements of an array A of size $2n$ with $n = 10^6$ is computed in single precision. For $i = 0, ..., 2n - 1$, each element $A[i]$ is initialised as $A[i] = -i$ if i is even, and $A[i] = i$ otherwise. Therefore the exact sum is 10^6. The sum S is computed using an OpenMP for loop construct with a reduction clause and two possible scheduling clauses: (static) so as the loop is divided into chunks of size $2n$ over the number of threads, and (static,1) so as the chunk size is 1. Results obtained for 1, 32, and 240 threads, with and without CADNA, are reported in Table 1. As already mentioned in Sect. 2.2, CADNA prints only the exact significant digits of results and @.0 if they are numerical noise.

Using the (static) scheduling option, whatever the number of threads, the result S is 1.000000E+06 with or without CADNA. Therefore the result has the maximum possible accuracy in single precision, i.e. 7 exact significant digits. Indeed, in this case each thread has in charge contiguous elements of A and alternatively sums positive and negative values: all computed results are accurate.

Using the (static,1) scheduling option, with 32 or 240 threads, the result has no correct digits and is provided by CADNA as @.0. Without CADNA the result depends on the number of threads and one can notice that for 240 threads

---

[2] http://ispc.github.io.

Table 1. Results S obtained with and without CADNA using two possible schedulings.

	(static)		(static,1)	
# threads	without CADNA	with CADNA	without CADNA	with CADNA
1	1.000000E+06	1.000000E+06	1.000000E+06	1.000000E+06
32	1.000000E+06	1.000000E+06	1.892352E+06	@.0
240	1.000000E+06	1.000000E+06	1.617920E+05	@.0

it has a wrong order of magnitude. Each thread sums indeed values of the same sign, the absolute value of the sum thus keeps on increasing, and its accuracy regularly decreases due to the limited floating-point precision. The reduction involves inaccurate results with close absolute values and different signs and thus provides numerical noise. In this case, CADNA detects cancellations, i.e. losses of accuracy due to the subtraction of close inaccurate results.

One advantage of this simple numerical example is that its exact result can be easily compared to the computed one. It points out that the accuracy of results may change from a sequential to a parallel execution of a code and also among several parallel executions with different schedulings. This numerical example emphasizes the need for a CADNA version available for OpenMP codes.

4.2   Performance Tests

We now focus on the performance impact of CADNA on OpenMP codes by studying different micro-applications or benchmarks. In order to handle NUMA effects on *CPU-server*, we use the following OpenMP settings for thread affinity policies:

- when the number of threads is lower or equal to 8, OMP_PLACES is set to sockets(8) and OMP_PROC_BIND to master in order to have all threads on the same socket as the master thread;
- otherwise (i.e. for 16 or 2 × 16 threads) no thread affinity policy is used (OMP_PROC_BIND set to false): we let the OS scheduler run the threads on all physical CPU cores (with 16 threads, i.e. without SMT) or on all logical CPU cores (with 2 × 16 threads, i.e. with 2-way SMT).

On *Xeon-Phi*, no thread affinity policy is used. By default, we use gcc/g++ version 4.9.2, and Intel icc/icpc version 2017 (beta).

Figures 1 and 2 first present performance results for a Mandelbrot set computation (4096 × 4096 pixels, with a maximum number of 4096 iterations per pixel) and for a 3D finite difference (FD) stencil (6 iterations over a 256 × 256 × 256 grid with a six-order central stencil). First, for serial runs the CADNA over IEEE overheads match the ones previously obtained [4]. When considering OpenMP runs with only one thread, one can see an important additional overhead with gcc (see Figs. 1(a) and 2(a)). This seems to be related to the handling of threadprivate variables by gcc. Such a problem does not exist with icc (see Figs. 1(b) and 2(b)).

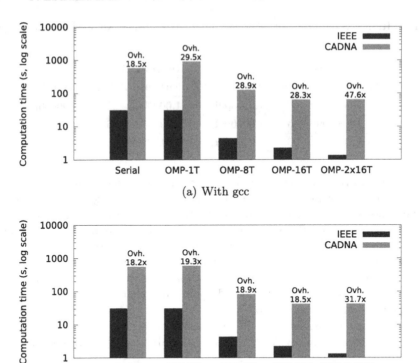

Fig. 1. Performance results for Mandelbrot computations, along with CADNA over IEEE overheads (Ovh.). OMP-XT denotes OpenMP runs with X threads.

As far as Mandelbrot computations are concerned (see Figs. 1(a) and (b)), the CADNA overheads remain stable when the number of physical CPUs used increases. This shows no scaling overhead with CADNA for compute bound applications. One can however notice that, contrary to the IEEE version, the CADNA version shows no performance gain with the SMT capability.

As far as 3D FD stencil computations are concerned (see Figs. 2(a) and (b)), the CADNA overheads remain stable (or decrease somewhat) when the number of physical CPUs used increases. This also shows no scaling overhead for CADNA for such an application which is memory-bound. Here again the CADNA version shows no performance gain with the SMT capability, but this is also the case for the IEEE version since this application is memory-bound.

Figure 3 presents results for the + reduction. The decrease in CADNA overheads between the serial execution and the OpenMP with 1 thread is only due to a slower computation for the IEEE code with 1 OpenMP thread compared to the serial IEEE code without OpenMP. When using multiple threads, one can see that the CADNA overheads are lower. This is due to the fact that the arithmetic intensity of the benchmarks is modified by the use of CADNA. Using CADNA,

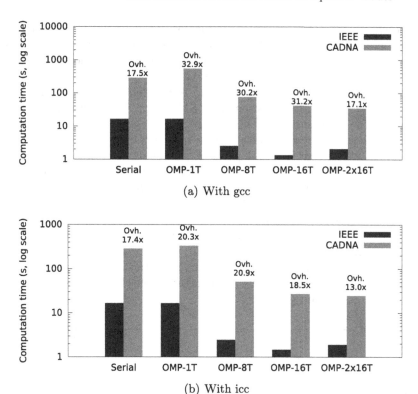

(a) With gcc

(b) With icc

Fig. 2. Performance results for FD stencil computations, along with CADNA over IEEE overheads (`Ovh.`). `OMP-XT` denotes OpenMP runs with X threads.

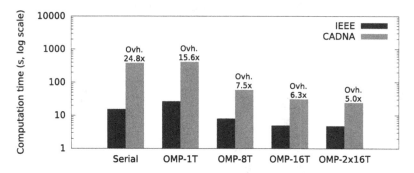

Fig. 3. Performance results (using icc) for reductions (+ operator on 2^{28} elements), with CADNA over IEEE overheads (`Ovh.`). `OMP-XT` denotes OpenMP runs with X threads.

we have indeed at least 3 times more computations (for each sample, and for the extra operations associated with the rounding mode emulation and the random number generation), while requiring 4 memory accesses. But these memory accesses can be performed at once with the same cache line (as the members of the stochastic types are contiguous in memory): the arithmetic intensity thus increases with CADNA. Since this reduction benchmark presents an even lower arithmetic intensity than the 3D FD stencil one, its performance is even more limited by the memory bandwidth. Using CADNA thus leads to performance less limited by the memory bandwidth and to greater speedups when increasing the number of threads and when using SMT. Similar conclusions have been obtained for the ∗ reduction.

In order to study the impact of `atomic` constructs required by the instability detection, we present in Fig. 4 performance results for the Mandelbrot set computation with detection of no instability and of all instabilities. The increase of CADNA overheads between serial and 1-thread OpenMP executions is thus 4.5 % for no instability (hence no `atomic` construct) in Fig. 1(a) and 6 % for self-validation only (some `atomic` constructs used) in Fig. 1(b): the `atomic` construct impact is thus not significant for 1 OpenMP thread. When detecting all instabilities (all `atomic` constructs used) in Fig. 1(b), this increase is even lower (2.1 %) since the CADNA overheads are much more important. Moreover, the `atomic` construct impact does not increase for multiple OpenMP threads as shown in Figs. 1(b), 2(b), 4(a) and (b).

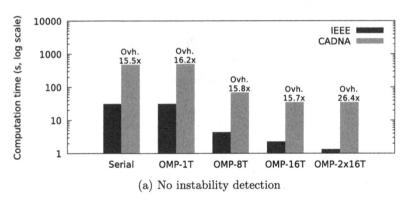

(a) No instability detection

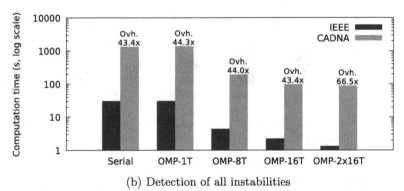

(b) Detection of all instabilities

Fig. 4. Performance results for Mandelbrot computations (using icc), along with CADNA over IEEE overheads (`Ovh.`). `OMP-XT` denotes OpenMP runs with `X` threads.

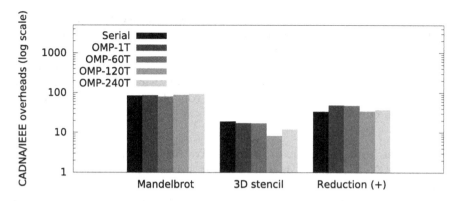

Fig. 5. CADNA over IEEE overheads for various benchmarks on the Xeon Phi, using icc and the same parameters than on *CPU-server* (except for the reduction here with 2^{27} elements due to memory constraints).

Finally, Fig. 5 presents the CADNA over IEEE overheads of our benchmarks for serial and OpenMP executions on *Xeon-Phi*. The CADNA overheads are greater on this architecture for Mandelbrot and reduction computations due to the use of the `strict` and `no-except` floating-point models (required by CADNA with `icc`): contrary to *CPU-server*, such models imply an important overhead on the Knight Corner architecture (e.g. 5.1x for Mandelbrot computations). Nevertheless these tests confirm the previous conclusions (obtained on *CPU-server*), here for a higher number of cores and threads: no scaling overhead for CADNA (and even lower overheads for memory-bound applications with SMT), and no extra overhead due to the `atomic` constructs used for the instability detection.

The overhead associated with the `atomic` constructs on stochastic variables will be studied in the next section.

4.3 A Shallow-Water Application

Presentation. The CADNA library is finally applied to a "real-life" application: a Shallow-Water model (denoted SW). A SW model is a numerical integration of the SW equations [18] that describe the flow in a fluid. The application presented here describes the evolution of the water height and velocities in a two-dimensional oceanic basin (the water velocity is constant on the water depth). Fundamentally, a SW computation can be viewed as a combination of finite difference stencils.

In our application, the model is integrated for 500 time steps on a 256×256 grid. There are two integration modes: the direct model (denoted *forward*) that computes the output of the model, and the adjoint model (denoted *backward*) that computes the sensitivity of the output to the initial conditions. Both modes (forward and backward) involve the same set of computations, the only difference lies in the direction of the time loop: from past to future in the forward mode, from future to past in the backward mode. As a consequence, the forward mode implementation is fully parallel in space using a space domain decomposition, whereas the backward mode requires the use of numerous `atomic` operations.

The successive computations of the forward and backward modes allow the estimation of a scalar quantity called the "residual" which is a key parameter for validating adjoint codes [3]. The code was compiled using `icc/icpc` version 2015, and run on *CPU-server*.

Performance and Numerical Results. We first present the performance impact of CADNA on this SW code. Figure 6 presents performance results of the forward mode. It shows that there is no scaling overhead in CADNA. The overhead is even lower with multiple threads (9.9x for 16 threads) than for one thread (15.0x) as it was already explained in Sect. 4.2 for such memory-bound application.

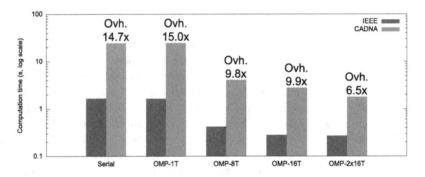

Fig. 6. Performance results (using icc) for Shallow-Water (forward mode), with CADNA over IEEE overheads (`Ovh.`). `OMP-XT` denotes OpenMP runs with `X` threads.

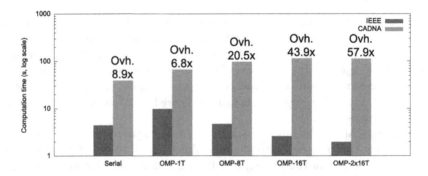

Fig. 7. Performance results (using icc) for Shallow-Water (backward mode), with CADNA over IEEE overheads (`Ovh.`). `OMP-XT` denotes OpenMP runs with `X` threads.

Table 2. Comparison between IEEE and CADNA computations of the Shallow-Water residual for serial and parallel executions.

	IEEE	CADNA
Serial	3.446611873236805E-06	3.4461E-06
OpenMP - 16 treads	3.446619149194419E-06	3.446E-06

Figure 7 presents performance results of the backward mode. In this case, parallel speedups are limited by the use of numerous `atomic` operations on floating point numbers, as already discussed in [13]. With CADNA, these operations must be converted into `critical` regions as shown in Sect. 3 (in this SW model, we use three distinct `critical` regions). As a consequence, the computation time and therefore the overhead are increasing with the number of threads, because of increased lock contention. It should thus be noticed that the numerical validation of a parallel code using (numerous) `atomic` directives remains possible using CADNA but with a higher cost.

Finally we focus on the numerical stability of the residual of the SW model (see Table 2). For clarity only the serial and 16-thread OpenMP results are presented. It can be noticed that there are only 6 common digits between the results computed without CADNA by the serial and parallel versions. CADNA estimates that 5 digits in serial and 4 digits in parallel are correct. These digits (except the last one in serial which may not be reliable in CADNA) are consistent with the IEEE versions. Thanks to CADNA, we can therefore state that the OpenMP version of this SW application is reliable with a 4-digit accuracy. Moreover, by comparing the serial and parallel numerical results, we can deduce that the differences in the IEEE results are likely due to round-off error propagations and not to a bug in the OpenMP parallelization.

5   Conclusion

In this paper, we have presented a new OpenMP-enabled CADNA version that can be used to validate parallel codes by providing the number of exact significant digits of their results, and that presents similar or lower CADNA overheads with respect to the serial ones. This library can also help to explain differences in the numerical results between serial and (multiple) parallel executions.

It is worth noting that the control of accuracy can also be performed on MPI codes [12]. Therefore the work presented on this paper could be extended to enable the numerical validation of large scale applications using both MPI and OpenMP. Besides, the CADNA instrumentation of codes could be eased thanks to OpenMP-like compiler directives that would avoid the insertion and modifications of C/C++ instructions in the user program. A preliminary study has been performed on such directives. However work has still to be carried out to propose a complete set of directives that enable all CADNA functionalities and can control the numerical quality of any C/C++ program.

Acknowledgments. The authors thank Pierre-Emmanuel Le Roux (LIP6) for managing the compute servers, and Philippe Thierry (Intel) for providing the Intel compiler (2017-beta). They also thank the reviewers for their helpful comments.

References

1. Alefeld, G., Herzberger, J.: Introduction to Interval Analysis. Academic Press, New York (1983)
2. OpenMP Architecture Review Board: OpenMP Application Program Interface, Version 4.0, July 2013
3. Brajard, J., Li, P., Jézéquel, F., Benavidès, H.-S., Thiria, S.: Numerical validation of data assimilation codes generated by the YAO software. In: SIAM Annual Meeting, San Diego, California, USA (2013)
4. Eberhart, P., Brajard, J., Fortin, P., Jézéquel, F.: High performance numerical validation using stochastic arithmetic. Reliable Comput. **21**, 35–52 (2015)
5. Hölbig, C.A., Do Carmo, A., Arendt, L.P.: High accuracy and interval arithmetic on multicore processors. Comput. Appl. Math. **32**(3), 425–434 (2013)
6. IEEE and The Open Group: The Open Group Base Specifications, 7th edn. (2013). http://pubs.opengroup.org/onlinepubs/9699919799
7. Intel: User and Reference Guide for the Intel C++ Compiler 15.0 (2015). https://software.intel.com/en-us/compiler_15.0_ug_c
8. Jézéquel, F., Chesneaux, J.-M.: CADNA: a library for estimating round-off error propagation. Comput. Phys. Commun. **178**(12), 933–955 (2008)
9. Jézéquel, F., Lamotte, J.-L., Said, I.: Estimation of numerical reproducibility on CPU and GPU. In: Proceedings of the 2015 Federated Conference on Computer Science and Information Systems. Annals of Computer Science and Information Systems, vol. 5, pp. 675–680. IEEE (2015)
10. Kulisch, U.W.: Advanced Arithmetic for the Digital Computer. Springer, Wien (2002)
11. Milani, C.R., Kolberg, M., Fernandes, L.G.: Solving dense interval linear systems with verified computing on multicore architectures. In: Palma, J.M.L.M., Daydé, M., Marques, O., Lopes, J.C. (eds.) VECPAR 2010. LNCS, vol. 6449, pp. 435–448. Springer, Heidelberg (2011)
12. Montan, S., Denis, C.: Numerical verification of industrial numerical codes. In: Proceedings of ESAIM, vol. 35, pp. 107–113, March 2012
13. Nardi, L., Badran, F., Fortin, P., Thiria, S.: YAO: a generator of parallel code for variational data assimilation applications. In: International Conference on High Performance Computing and Communication, pp. 224–232. IEEE (2012)
14. Revol, N., Théveny, P.: Parallel implementation of interval matrix multiplication. Reliable Comput. **19**(1), 91–106 (2013)
15. Vignes, J.: Zéro mathématique et zéro informatique. Comptes Rendus de l'Académie des Sciences - Series I - Mathematics **303**, 997–1000 (1986)
16. Vignes, J.: A stochastic arithmetic for reliable scientific computation. Math. Comput. Simul. **35**(3), 233–261 (1993)
17. Vignes, J.: Discrete stochastic arithmetic for validating results of numerical software. Numer. Algorithms **37**(1–4), 377–390 (2004)
18. Vreugdenhil, C.B.: Numerical Methods for Shallow-Water Flow. Springer, The Netherlands (1994)
19. Zimmer, Z.: Using C-XSC in a multi-threaded environment. Technical report BUGHW–WRSWT 2011/2, Universität Wuppertal, Germany (2011)

OpenMP Parallelization and Optimization of Graph-Based Machine Learning Algorithms

Zhaoyi Meng[1,2](✉), Alice Koniges[2](✉), Yun (Helen) He[2], Samuel Williams[2], Thorsten Kurth[2], Brandon Cook[2], Jack Deslippe[2], and Andrea L. Bertozzi[1]

[1] University of California, Los Angeles, USA
mzhy@ucla.edu, aekoniges@lbl.gov
[2] Lawrence Berkeley National Laboratory, Berkeley, USA

Abstract. We investigate the OpenMP parallelization and optimization of two novel data classification algorithms. The new algorithms are based on graph and PDE solution techniques and provide significant accuracy and performance advantages over traditional data classification algorithms in serial mode. The methods leverage the Nystrom extension to calculate eigenvalue/eigenvectors of the graph Laplacian and this is a self-contained module that can be used in conjunction with other graph-Laplacian based methods such as spectral clustering. We use performance tools to collect the hotspots and memory access of the serial codes and use OpenMP as the parallelization language to parallelize the most time-consuming parts. Where possible, we also use library routines. We then optimize the OpenMP implementations and detail the performance on traditional supercomputer nodes (in our case a Cray XC30), and test the optimization steps on emerging testbed systems based on Intel's Knights Corner and Landing processors. We show both performance improvement and strong scaling behavior. A large number of optimization techniques and analyses are necessary before the algorithm reaches almost ideal scaling.

Keywords: Semi-supervised · Unsupervised · Data · Algorithms · OpenMP · Optimization

1 Introduction

We detail the OpenMP parallelization of two new data classification algorithms. A classification algorithm sorts the data into different classes such that the similarity within a class is stronger than that between different classes. This is a standard problem in machine learning. Recently, novel algorithms have been proposed [1] that are motivated by PDE-based image segmentation methods and are modified to apply to discrete data sets [4]. Serial results show that these algorithms improve both accuracy of solution and efficiency of the computation and can be potentially faster in parallel than various classification algorithms such as spectral clustering with k-means [6]. In this paper we describe parallel implementations and optimizations of the new algorithms. We focus on shared

© Springer International Publishing Switzerland 2016
N. Maruyama et al. (Eds.): IWOMP 2016, LNCS 9903, pp. 17–31, 2016.
DOI: 10.1007/978-3-319-45550-1_2

memory many-core parallelization schemes that will be applicable to next generation architectures such as the upcoming Intel Knights Landing processor. After analyzing the computational hotspots, we find that an optimized implementation of the Nyström eigensolver is the computational challenge. We implement directive-based OpenMP parallelization on the most time-consuming part and implement steps of optimizations to speed up and achieve almost ideal performance.

The rest of this paper is organized as follows: Sect. 2 presents the background of the image classification algorithms and the Nyström extension eigensolver. In Sect. 3 we discuss Math library usage and optimization for the serial code. We show our OpenMP parallelization strategies, optimization steps and arithmetic intensity analysis in Sect. 4. Finally, Sect. 5 presents some conclusions and future work.

2 Graph-Based Classification Algorithms

2.1 Introduction

We approach the classification problem using graph cut ideas. The novel classification algorithms consider each data point as a node in a weighted graph and the similarity (weight) between two nodes Z_i and Z_j is given by formula:

$$w_{ij} = exp(-dis(Z_i, Z_j)/\tau), \tag{1}$$

where τ is a parameter [5,6]. The weight matrix is $W = \{w_{ij}\}$. In this paper, we use cosine distance since we use the hyperspectral imagery as the test data set and cosine distance is standard in this field. So

$$dis(Z_i, Z_j) = \frac{<Z_i, Z_j>}{||Z_i||_2 ||Z_j||_2}. \tag{2}$$

The classification problem is approached using ideas from graph-cuts [2]. Given a weighted undirected graph, the goal is to find the minimum cut (measured by a summation of the weights along the graph cut) for this problem. This is equivalent to assigning a scalar or vector value u_i to each ith data point and minimizing the graph total variation (TV) $\sum_{ij} |u_i - u_j| w_{ij}$ [3]. Instead of directly solving a graph-TV minimization problem, we transform the graph TV to graph-based Ginzburg-Laudau (GL) functional [8]:

$$E(u) = \epsilon < L_s u, u > + \frac{1}{\epsilon} \sum_i (W(u_i)) \tag{3}$$

where $\dot{W}(u)$ is a double well potential, for example $W(u) = \frac{1}{4}(u^2 - 1)^2$ in a binary partition and multi-well potential for more classes. L_s is the normalized symmetric graph Laplacian which is defined as $L = I - D^{-\frac{1}{2}} W D^{-\frac{1}{2}}$, where D is a diagonal matrix with diagonal elements $d_i = \sum_{j \in V} w(i, j)$.

In the vanishing ϵ limit a variant of (3) has been proved to converge to the graph TV functional [7]. Different fidelity items are added to GL functional for semi-supervised and unsupervised learning respectively. The GL functional is minimized using gradient descent [9]. An alternative is to directly minimize the GL functional using the MBO scheme [11] or a direct compressed sensing method [12]. We use the MBO scheme in this paper in which one alternates solving the heat (diffusion) equation for u and thresholding to maintain distinct class structure. Computation of the entire graph Laplacian is prohibitive for large data so we use the Nyström extension to randomly sample the graph and compute a modest number of leading eigenvalues and eigenfunctions of the graph Laplacian [10]. By projecting all vectors onto this sub-eigenspace, the iteration step reduces to a simple coefficient update.

2.2   Semi-supervised and Unsupervised Algorithms

We outline the semi-supervised and the unsupervised algorithms. For the semi-supervised algorithm, the fidelity (a small amount of "ground truth") is known and the rest needs to be classified according to the categories of the fidelity. For the unsupervised algorithm, there is no prior knowledge of the labels of the data. We use the Nyström extension algorithm beforehand for both algorithms to calculate the eigenvalues and eigenvectors as the inputs. In practice, these two algorithms converge very fast and give accurate classification results.

Semi-supervised Graph MBO Algorithm. [11]

1. Input eigenvectors matrix Φ, eigenvalues $\{\lambda_k\}_{k=1}^M$ and fidelity.
2. Initialize u^0, $d^0 = \mathbf{0}$, $a^0 = \Phi^T \cdot u_0$.
3. While $\frac{||u^{n+1} - u^n||_2^2}{||u^{n+1}||_2^2} < \alpha = 0.0000001$ do
    a. Heat equation
        1). $a_k^{n+1} = a_k^n \cdot (1 - dt \cdot \lambda_k) - dt \cdot d_k^n$
        2). $y = \Phi \cdot a^{n+1}$
        3). $d^{n+1} = \Phi^T \cdot \mu(y - u^0)$,
    b. Thresholding
        $u_i^{n+1} = e_r, r = \arg\max_j y_i$
    c. Updating a
        $a^{n+1} = \Phi^T \cdot u^{n+1}$

Unsupervised Graph MBO Algorithm. [13]

1. Input data matrix f, eigenvector matrix Φ, eigenvalues $\{\lambda_k\}_{k=1}^N$.
2. Initialize u^0, $a^0 = \Phi^T \cdot u^0$
3. While $\frac{||u^{n+1} - u^n||_2^2}{||u^{n+1}||_2^2} < \alpha = 0.0000001$ do
    a. Updating c
        $c_k^{n+1} = \frac{<f, u_k^{n+1}>}{\sum_{i=1}^N u_{ki}}$
    b. Heat equation
        1. $a_k^{n+\frac{1}{2}} = a_k^n \cdot (1 - dt \cdot \lambda_k)$

2. Calculating matrix P, where $P_{i,j} = ||f_i - c_j||_2^2$

3. $y = \Phi \cdot a_k^{n+\frac{1}{2}} - dt \cdot \mu P$

c. Thresholding

$u_i^{n+1} = e_r, r = \arg\max_j y_i$

d. Updating a

$a^{n+1} = \Phi^T \cdot u^{n+1}$

2.3   Nyström Extension Method

In both the semi-supervised and unsupervised algorithms, we calculate the leading eigenvalues and eigenvectors of the graph Laplacian using the Nyström method [10] to accelerate the computation. This is achieved by calculating an eigendecomposition on a smaller system of size $M << N$ and then expanding the results back up to N dimensions. The computational complexity is almost $O(N)$. We can set $M << N$ without any significant decrease in the accuracy of the solution.

Suppose $Z = \{Z_k\}_{k=1}^N$ is the whole set of nodes on the graph. By randomly selecting a small subset X, we can partition Z as $Z = X \bigcup Y$, where X and Y are two disjoint set, $X = \{Z_i\}_{i=1}^M$ and $Y = \{Z_j\}_{j=1}^{N-M}$ and $M << N$. The weight matrix W can be written as

$$W = \begin{bmatrix} W_{XX} & W_{XY} \\ W_{YX} & W_{YY} \end{bmatrix},$$

where W_{XX} denotes the weights of nodes in set X, W_{XY} denotes the weights between set X and set Y, $W_{YX} = W_{XY}^T$ and W_{YY} denotes the weights of nodes in set Y. It can be shown that the large matrix W_{YY} can be approximated by $W_{YY} \approx W_{YX}W_{XX}^{-1}W_{XY}$, and the error is determined by how many of the rows of W_{XY} span the rows of W_{YY}. We only need to compute W_{XX}, $W_{XY} = W_{YX}^T$, and it requires only $(|X| \cdot (|X| + |Y|))$ computations versus $(|X| + |Y|)^2$ when the whole matrix is used. For the data set we use in this paper, $M = 100$ and $N = 13,475,840$.

Nyström Extension Algorithm

1. Input a set of features $Z = \{Z_i\}_{i=1}^N$.
2. Partition the set Z into $Z = X \cup Y$, where X consists of M randomly selected elements.
3. Calculate W_{XX} and W_{XY} using formula (1).
4. Calculate $d_X = W_{XX}1_L + W_{XY}1_{N-L}$ and $d_Y = W_{YX}1_L + (W_{YX}W_{XX}^{-1}W_{XY})1_{N-L}$.
5. Calculate $s_X = \sqrt{d_X}$ and $s_Y = \sqrt{d_Y}$.
6. Calculate $W_{XX} = W_{XX}./(s_X s_X^T)$ and $W_{XY} = W_{XY}./(s_X s_Y^T)$.
7. Calculate eigendecomposition $W_{XX} = B_X \Gamma B_X^T$ (using the SVD).
8. Calculate $S = B_X \Gamma^{-1/2}B_X^T$ and $Q = W_{XX} + S(W_{XY}W_{YX})S$.
9. Calculate eigendecomposition $Q = A\Theta A^T$ (using the SVD).

10. Form eigenvector matrix $\Phi = \begin{bmatrix} B_X \Gamma^{1/2} \\ W_{YX}B_X \Gamma^{-1/2} \end{bmatrix} B_X^T(A\Theta^{-1/2})$.

11. Output Φ and $\{\lambda_i\}_{i=i}^N$, where $\lambda_k = 1 - \theta_k$ with θ_k the kth diagonal element of Θ.

3   Math Library Usage and Optimizations

All the data are in matrix form and there are intensive linear algebra calculations. We apply a Singular Value Decomposition (SVD) to two small matrices. We make use of the LAPACK (Linear Algebra PACKage) and BLAS (Basic Linear Algebra Subprograms) libraries in the codes. The LAPACK provides routines for the SVD and the BLAS provides routines for vector-vector (Level 1), matrix-vector (Level 2) and matrix-matrix (Level 3) operations. BLAS and LAPACK are also highly vectorized and multithreaded using OpenMP.

We use the Intel Performance Tool VTune Amplifier to analyze the performance and to find bottlenecks [21]. The hotspots collection shows some computationally expensive parts are related to calculating the inner product of two vectors. In the unsupervised graph MBO algorithm, this operation occurs when calculating the matrix P and takes 84 % of the run time. Also, it occurs when calculating the matrix W_{XY} in the Nyström extension algorithm and takes 90 % of the run time. We optimize this procedure by forming all the vectors into matrices and doing the inner product of two matrices. In this way, we make use of BLAS 3 (matrix-matrix) instead of BLAS 1 (vector-vector). The part of calculating the matrix P in the unsupervised algorithm is 22.5× faster using BLAS 3. This optimization is based on the fact that BLAS 1,2 are memory bound and BLAS 3 is computation bound [14,15].

4   Parallelization of the Nyström Extension

Parallelization of these two classification algorithms involves a parallel for. It is critical to further optimize the OpenMP implementation to get nearly ideal scaling. We detail this process using more complex features of OpenMP such as SIMD and vectorization. Then we use the uniform sampling and chunk of data to get the best performance.

We consider the data set, described in more detail in [16], composed of hyperspectral video sequences recording the release of chemical plumes at the Dugway Proving Ground. We use the 329 frames of the video. Each frame is a hyperspectral image with dimension $128 \times 320 \times 129$, where 129 is the dimension of the channel of each pixel. The total number of pixels is 13,475,840. Since we are dealing with very large data set we choose binary form for smaller storage space and faster I/O. Our test data is 13.91 GB in binary form and the I/O is 36.8× faster than the txt format when testing on Cori Phase I.

We conduct our experiments on single nodes of systems at the National Energy Research Scientific Computing Center (NERSC). Cori Phase I is the newest supercomputer system at NERSC [22]. The system is a Cray XC based on the Intel Haswell multi-core processor. Each node has 128 GB of memory and two 2.3 GHz 16-core Haswell processors. Each core has its own L1 and L2 caches, with 64 KB (32 KB instruction cache, 32 KB data) and 256 KB, respectively;

there is also a 40-MB shared L3 cache per socket. Peak performance per node is about 1.2 TFlop/s and peak bandwidth is about 120 GB/s. The resultant machine balance of 10 flops per byte strongly motivates the use of BLAS 3 like computations. Cori Phase II will be a Cray XC system based on the second generation of Intel Xeon Phi Product Family, called Knights Landing (KNL) Many Integrated Core (MIC) Architecture. The test system available to us now features 64 cores with 1.3 GHz clock frequency (Bin-3 configuration) with support for four hyper-threads each. Each core additionally has two 512bit-wide vector processing units. Additionally, the chip is equipped with 16 GB on-package memory shared between all cores. it is referred to as HBM or MCDRAM with a maximum bandwidth of 430 GB/s measured using the STREAM triad benchmark. The 512 KB L2 cache is shared between two cores (i.e. within a tile) and the 16 KB L1 cache is private to the core. Furthermore, the single socket KNL nodes are equipped with 96 GB DDR4 6-channel memory with a maximum attainable bandwidth of 90 GB/s.

4.1 OpenMP Parallelization

Analysis with VTune shows that the most time consuming phase of both two classification algorithms is the construction of W_{XY} in the Nyström extension procedure. This phase is a good candidate for OpenMP parallelization because each element of W_{XY} can be computed independently. The procedure of calculating W_{XY} is shown in Fig. 1. We form the data in a N by d matrix Z. Each row of Z corresponds to a data point and it's a vector of dimension d. In computation, we store Z in an array in row major. We randomly select M rows to form the sampled data set $X = \{Z_i\}_{i=1}^{M}$. The other rows form the data

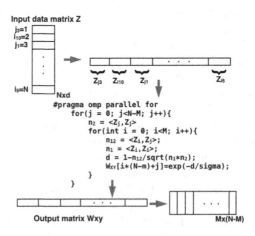

Fig. 1. The procedure of calculating W_{XY}:

set $Y = \{Z_j\}_{j=1}^{N-M}$. Then we use the nested for-loop to calculate the values of W_{XY} by the formula (1). We then put the corresponding value in an array which represent the M by $N - M$ matrix W_{XY}.

Reordering Loops. We have tested re-ordering loops as a means to optimize the algorithm. With analysis, we notice the j-loop is far larger than the i-loop. There are still two ways to do the parallelization. One way is to parallelize the j-loop as inner loop and the other way is to parallelize the j-loop as outer loop. We tried both ways and compared the results.

Step A: Parallelizing the inner j-loop

```
for  i = 0; i < M; i + +
    n_1 =< Z_i, Z_i >
    #pragma omp parallel for
    for  j = 1 : N - M
        n_12 =< Z_i, Z_j >
        n_2 =< Z_j, Z_j >
        d = 1 - n_12/√(n_1 · n_2)
        W_XY(i, j) = exp(-d/σ)
    end
end
```

Step B: Parallelizing the outer j-loop

```
#pragma omp parallel for
for  j = 1 : N - M
    n_2 =< Z_j, Z_j >
    for  i = 1 : M
        n_12 =< Z_i, Z_j >
        n_1 =< Z_i, Z_i >
        d = 1 - n_12/√(n_1 · n_2)
        W_XY(i, j) = exp(-d/σ)
    end
end
```

The results show that parallelizing the outer j-loop is much faster. The run time decreases by a factor of 7. This is because on Cori, each core has its own L1 and L2 cache. When parallelizing the outer j-loop, all the X_is can be read and reside on the L2 of each core and can be used repeatedly. If instead we parallelize the inner j-loop, there are more reads of the X_i and thus the calculation takes more time. Parallelizing the outer j loop also means each thread has more work to do, since the inner i-loop is also part of the j-loop. In this way less overhead and more load balance can be achieved. While if we parallelize the inner j-loop, not only each thread has less work and large load imbalance, but also there are multiple times of thread creation and overhead.

Vectorization and Chunk. We further optimize the OpenMP parallelization using vectorization. First, we notice, the norms of Z_is are computed repeatedly in the i-loop. So, we normalize all the Z_is in the previous step, calculating W_{XX}, and store all the normalized Z_is in a new matrix X_{mat}. Then we can calculate the inner product of each Z_j and all the Z_is (X_{mat}) all at once. This make use of BLAS 2 instead of the previous BLAS 1. Also, we can vectorize the loop when calculating W_{XY}. This optimization reduce the run time of calculating W_{XY} by a factor of 3.

Step C: Calculating W_{XY}, normalize and form all Z_is to X_{mat}

```
#pragma omp for
for j = 1 : N - M
```

$$n_2 = <Z_j, Z_j>$$
$$n_{vec} = 1 - <X_{mat}, Z_j> / \sqrt{n2}$$
\#pragma omp simd aligned
for $i = 1 : M$
$$W_{XY}(i,j) = exp(-n_{vec}/\sigma)$$
end

end

The Nyström extension algorithm is based on a random partition of the whole dataset Z into two disjoint data sets X and Y, where $X = \{Z_i\}_{i=1}^{M}$ and $Y = \{Z_j\}_{j=1}^{N-M}$ and $M << N$. Assuming we can uniformly partition the dataset, so that Z_is are evenly distributed, we can form chunks of Z_js to matrix and further optimize this calculation. The procedure is shown in Fig. 2. First, when calculating W_{XX}, we evenly sample Z_is and normalized them. We form the normalized Z_is to a matrix X_{mat}. Then all the data in between two consecutive Z_is are the chunk of Z_js. Since the chunk size is still very large, we further decompose each Y-chunk into sub-chunks. There are several considerations for choosing the sub-chunk size. If it is too small, we waste potential of combining expensive operations. If it is too large, the sub-chunk may run out of lower level cache and needs to be put into the higher cache levels, up to the point where they spill over into DRAM which may cause a substantial performance hit. The optimal value depends on the cache hierarchy, their respective sizes, their latency and so on. For a different architecture, one may consider choosing another value. We pick the the $subchunksize = 64$ when running the codes on Cori Phase I and it can be further optimized.

Then for each sub-chunk, we calculate the Euclidean norm of each row and store them in a vector $n2_{vec}$. This calculation can be vectorized since calculating the norm of each row is independent. We then calculate the matrix multiplication $X_{mat} \cdot Y_{submat}$ using BLAS 3 function DGEMM. The result is a $m \times subchunksize$ matrix $n12_{mat}$. It is the result of all the inner product of rows in X_{mat} and rows in Y_{submat}. Then we can vectorize the final calculation of values in W_{XY}.

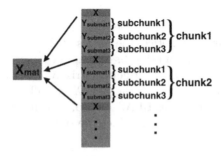

Fig. 2. Uniform sampling and dividing Y into chunks and sub-chunks

Step D: Calculating W_{XY} using uniform sampling and chunked Y matrices

```
#pragma omp for collapse(2)
for ychunk = 0; ychunk < m; ychunk + +
    for j = chunkstart; j < chunkstop; j+ = subchunksize
        #pragma omp simd aligned
        for k = 0; k < subchunksize; k + +
            n2vec[k] =< Zj+k, Zj+k >
            n2vec[k] = 1/√n2vec[k]
        end
        n12mat =< Xmat, Ysubmatj >
        #pragma omp simd aligned
        for i = 0; i < m; i + +
            for k = 0; k < subchunksize; k + +
            d = 1 − n12mat[i, k] · n2vec[k]
            WXY(i, j + k) = exp(−d/σ)
        end
    end
end
```

In this uniform sampling, the chunk size is defined as $chunksize = floor(N/M)$. When M is not divisible by N, the last chunk is larger than the other chunks. Also, $subchunksize$ may not be divisible by $chunksize$. So the size of the last sub-chunk in each chunk needs to be adjusted. The procedure of uniform sampling gives good results as compared to the random sampling and further improves the performance by a factor of 1.7.

Thread Affinity. We also consider the effect of thread affinity. We choose the thread affinity setting as "OMP_PROC_BIND=scatter" and "OMP_PLACES=cores (or threads)", because it uses one hardware thread per core. While if we use the thread affinity setting to be "OMP_PROC_BIND=close" and "OMP_PLACES=threads", it puts more threads on each physical core and leaves other cores idle, which affects scaling performance.

Experiment Results. *Cori Phase I:* We examined optimization steps on a single node of Cori Phase I. The run time decrease and scaling results of different steps of optimizing the OpenMP parallelization are shown in Fig. 3. We show the significant speed up of the Nyström loop part. In Step A, in addition to parallelizing the Nyström loop, we also use BLAS 3 optimization on the graph MBO algorithm. Since we use BLAS and LAPACK in the serial part of Nyström algorithm and the graph MBO algorithm, their run time also decrease when using multi-cores. We show the OpenMP thread scaling results on Cori Phase I in Fig. 4. Almost ideal scaling results are acheived. Each Cori Phase 1 node has two sockets (NUMA domain) and each socket has 16 cores. Although the absolute performance increases when using more than 16 threads on a single

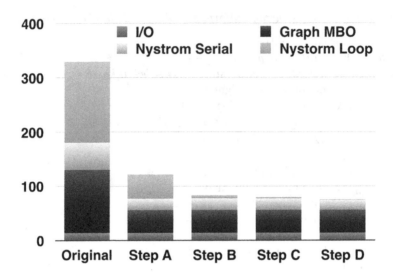

Fig. 3. The run time of different optimization steps on Cori Phase I. Step A: paralleliz-ing the inner j-loop and BLAS 3 optimization on Graph MBO. Step B: parallelizing the outer j-loop. Step C: normalizing and forming all Z_is to X_{mat}. Step D: using uniform sampling and chunked Y matrices. (Color figure online)

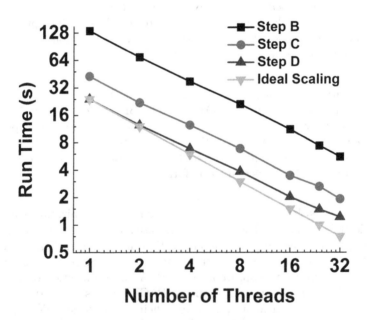

Fig. 4. The scaling results of the OpenMP parallelization of the Nyström loop on Cori Phase I. The black line with squares, the red line with circles and the blue line with triangles show the scaling results of step B, C and D respectively. The pink line with upside down triangles shows the ideal scaling. (Color figure online)

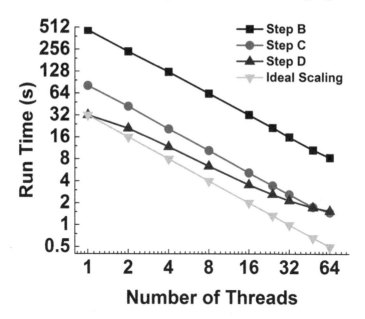

Fig. 5. The scaling results of the OpenMP parallelization of the Nyström loop on KNL white box. The black line with squares, the red line with circles and the blue line with triangles show the scaling results of step B, C and D respectively. The pink line with upside down triangles shows the ideal scaling which matches step D. (Color figure online)

node, the NUMA effect is observed. The scaling slows down due to the remote memory access to a far NUMA domain.

Knight's Landing: We employed the same optimizations already used for the Haswell optimization with three exceptions: we have compiled the code with AVX-512 support to make use of the wider vector units as well as doubled the sub-chunk size as depicted in Fig. 2 accordingly.[1] Furthermore, we have enabled fast floating point model and imprecise divides with `-fp-model fast=2` and `-no-prec-div` respectively. The (strong) thread scaling of the various sections of the code is depicted in Fig. 5 for one hyper-thread per core. We found that this configuration delivered the best performance. Utilizing two or more hyper-threads significantly decreased the performance, especially that of the Nystrom loop. We observe that our code obtains good strong scaling up to all 64 cores. We are currently investigating the hyper-threads performance and improving the scaling of step D.

4.2   Arithmetic Intensity and Roofline Model

Arithmetic intensity is the ratio of floating-point operations (FLOP's) performed by a given code (or code section) to the amount of data movement (Bytes) that

---

[1] We have explored various sub-chunk sizes but found that twice the optimal Haswell value, i.e. 128 vectors, yield the best performance.

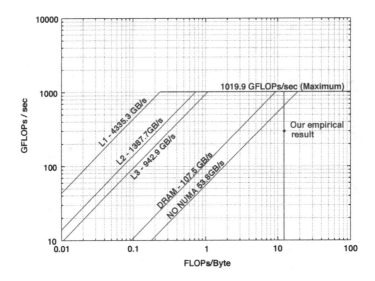

Fig. 6. Empirical Roofline Toolkit results for a Cori Phase I node. Observe, DRAM bandwidth constrains performance for a wide range of arithmetic intensities.

are required to support those operations. Arithmetic intensity in conjunction with the Roofline Model [17] can be used to bound kernel performance and qualify performance in a manner more nuanced than percent-of-peak. Figure 6 shows the result of using the Roofline Toolkit [18] to characterize the performance of a Cori Phase I node (full 32 cores). The resultant lines ("ceilings") are bounds on performance. Clearly, in order to attain high performance, one must design algorithms that deliver high arithmetic intensity. In order to characterize the Nyström loop, we used Intel's Software Development Emulator Toolkit (SDE) to record FLOP's and Intel's VTune Amplifier to collect data movement when running on 32 cores of a Cori Phase I node [19,20]. We can then compare the results to a theoretical estimate based on the inherent requisite computation and data movement.

As shown in Fig. 1, the memory access has two major components — one must read data from the matrix Z from DRAM and then write the results in to a matrix W_{XY}. The size of data matrix Z is $N \times d$, where $N = 13,475,840$ and $d = 129$ for our test data. As we store the data in double precision, the total size of the matrix (and hence volume of data read) is at least 13.907×10^9 bytes. In the inner loop, the processor must continually access M rows of the matrix Z. As the resultant volume of data (103,200 bytes) easily fits in cache, we need only read each Z_i once (data movement is well proxies by compulsory cache misses). The size of the matrix W_{XY} is $(N - M) \times M$, where $M = 100$. As each double-precision element is written once, we can bound write data movement as $(N - M) \times M \times 8 = 10.78 \times 10^9$ bytes. A similar calculation can be performed to calculate the requisite number of floating-point operations. In the optimized code, although there are dot products for $< Z_j, Z_j >$ coupled with a reciprocal

Table 1. Theoretical estimates (ignoring dual-socket nature of the machine) and Empirical measurements (using VTune and SDE) of data memory and floating-point operations for the Nyström loop.

	Theoretical	Empirical
Bytes Read	13.907×10^9	17.123×10^9
Bytes Written	10.781×10^9	12.256×10^9
FP operations	$>347.68 \times 10^9$	385.59×10^9
Arithmetic Intensity (flop:byte)	>14.1	13.12

square root and one exponential per element of W_{XY}, the DGEMM used for calculating $X_{mat} \times Y_{submat}$ should dominate the flop count. The matrix X_{mat} is 100×129, the matrix Y_{submat} is on average 64×129, and there are roughly $13,475,840/64 = 210560$ Y_{submat} matrices. Thus, the number of floating-point operations in the loop is about $210560 \times 2 \times 64 \times 129 \times 100 = 347.68 \times 10^9$ (ignoring any BLAS 2 operations, the dot products, and the exponential).

Table 1 presents our theoretical estimates and empirical measurements (using VTune and SDE) of data memory and floating-point operations for the Nyström loop. As expected, our rough theoretical model slightly underestimated each quantity. Multiple sockets (each with their own caches) may be required to read unique bytes, but in reality will access overlapping data due to the realities of large cache lines and hardware stream prefetchers. In terms of floating-point operations, it is clear DGEMM (the basis for our theoretical model) constitutes over 90 % of the total flop count with the remainder likely arising from exponentials and dot products. Overall, with a run time of about 1.28 s, the optimized code attains about 300 GFlop/s of performance and 23 GB/s of DRAM bandwidth at an arithmetic intensity of just over 13 flops per byte. At such a high arithmetic intensity, Fig. 6 suggests the full node DRAM bandwidth will not be the ultimate limiting factor. However, as we have not included any NUMA optimizations in the implementation, we expect the single socket's DRAM bandwidth (slightly less than 54 GB/s) to be a substantial performance impediment. Additional data movement in the cache hierarchy coupled with performance challenges associated with transcendental operations such as reciprocal-square-root and exponential likely impede our ability to fully saturate even a single socket's bandwidth.

5   Conclusion and Future Work

In this paper, we present a parallel implementation of two novel classification algorithms using OpenMP. We show OpenMP parallel and SIMD regions in combination with optimized library routines achieve almost ideal scaling and significant speedup over serial implementations. Although, we attain roughly 50 % of the Roofline bound (no NUMA), we expect future optimizations for the transcendentals, the cache hierarchy, and NUMA to substantially improve performance. We also expect more performance optimization results on KNL "white boxes" (pre-release hardware) and the future Cori Phase II.

Acknowledgments. This work was supported by NSF grants DMS-1417674 and DMS-1045536 and AFOSR MURI grant FA9550-10-1-0569. We would like to thank Dr. Da Kuang for his suggestions on optimizing the serial codes. This work was also supported by U.S. Department of Energy under Contract No. DE-AC02-05CH11231. This research used resources of the National Energy Research Scientific Computing Center, a DOE Office of Science User Facility supported by the Office of Science of the U.S. Department of Energy under Contract No. DE-AC02-05CH11231.

References

1. Meng, Z., Merkurjev, E., Koniges, A., Bertozzi, A.L.: Hyperspectral Video Analysis Using Graph Clustering Methods. Image Processing On Line, submitted
2. Stoer, M., Wagner, F.: A simple min-cut algorithm. J. ACM (JACM) **44**(4), 585–591 (1997)
3. Szlam, A., Bresson, X.: A total variation-based graph clustering algorithm for cheeger ratio cuts. UCLA CAM Report, pp. 09–68 (2009)
4. Bertozzi, A.L., Flenner, A.: Diffuse interface models on graphs for classification of high dimensional data. SIAM Rev. **58**(2), 293–328 (2016)
5. Chung, F.: Spectral Graph Theory, vol. 92. American Mathematical Society, Providence (1997)
6. Von Luxburg, U.: A tutorial on spectral clustering. Stat. Comput. **17**(4), 395–416 (2007)
7. Van Gennip, Y., Bertozzi, A.L.: *Gamma*-convergence of graph Ginzburg-Landau functionals. Adv. Differ. Equ. **17**(11/12), 1115–1180 (2012)
8. Bertozzi, A.L., Flenner, A.: Diffuse interface models on graphs for classification of high dimensional data. Multiscale Model. Simul. **10**(3), 1090–1118 (2012)
9. Luo, X., Bertozzi, A.L.: Convergence analysis of the graph Allen-Cahn scheme. Preprint
10. Fowlkes, C., Belongie, S., Chung, F., Malik, J.: Spectral grouping using the Nyström method. IEEE Trans. Pattern Anal. Mach. Intell. **26**(2), 214–225 (2004)
11. Merkurjev, E., Kostic, T., Bertozzi, A.L.: An MBO scheme on graphs for classification and image processing. SIAM J. Imaging Sci. **6**(4), 1903–1930 (2013)
12. Merkurjev, E., Bae, E., Bertozzi, A.L., Tai, X.C.: Global binary optimization on graphs for classification of high-dimensional data. J. Math. Imaging Vis. **52**(3), 414–435
13. Hu, H., Sunu, J., Bertozzi, A.L.: Multi-class graph Mumford-Shah model for plume detection using the MBO scheme. In: Tai, X.-C., Bae, E., Chan, T.F., Lysaker, M. (eds.) EMMCVPR 2015. LNCS, vol. 8932, pp. 209–222. Springer, Heidelberg (2015)
14. Kuang, D., Gittens, A., Hamid, R.: Hardware compliant approximate image codes. In: Proceedings of the IEEE Conference on Computer Vision and Pattern Recognition (2015)
15. Demmel, J.W.: Applied Numerical Linear Algebra. Siam, Philadelphia (1997)
16. Broadwater, J.B., Limsui, D., Carr, A.K.: A primer for chemical plume detection using LWIR sensors. Technical Paper, National Security Technology Department, Las Vegas, NV (2011)

17. Williams, S., Waterman, A., Patterson, D.: Roofline: an insightful visual performance model for multicore architectures. Commun. ACM **52**(4), 65–76 (2009)
18. Rooine Toolkit: https://bitbucket.org/berkeleylab/cs-roofline-toolkit
19. Intel Software Development Emulator. https://software.intel.com/en-us/articles/intel-software-development-emulator
20. Doerfler, D.: Understanding Application Data Movement Characteristics using Intel VTune Amplifier and Software Development Emulator tools, Intel Xeon Phi User Group (IXPUG) (2015)
21. Intel VTune Official Website. https://software.intel.com/en-us/intel-vtune-amplifier-xe
22. Cori Website: https://www.nersc.gov/users/computational-systems/cori

Locality

Evaluating OpenMP Affinity
on the POWER8 Architecture

Swaroop Pophale[✉] and Oscar Hernandez

Computer Science and Mathematics Division,
Oak Ridge National Laboratory, Oak Ridge, TN 37840, USA
{pophaless,oscar}@ornl.gov

Abstract. As we move toward pre-Exascale systems, two of the DOE leadership class systems will consist of very powerful OpenPOWER compute nodes which will be more complex to program. These systems will have massive amounts of parallelism; where threads may be running on POWER9 cores as well as on accelerators. Advances in memory interconnects, such as NVLINK, will provide a unified shared memory address spaces for different types of memories HBM, DRAM, etc. In preparation for such system, we need to improve our understanding on how OpenMP supports the concept of affinity as well as memory placement on POWER8 systems. Data locality and affinity are key program optimizations to exploit the compute and memory capabilities to achieve good performance by minimizing data motion across NUMA domains and access the cache efficiently. This paper is the first step to evaluate the current features of OpenMP 4.0 on the POWER8 processors, and on how to measure its effects on a system with two POWER8 sockets. We experiment with the different affinity settings provided by OpenMP 4.0 to quantify the costs of having good data locality vs not, and measure their effects via hardware counters. We also find out which affinity settings benefits more from data locality. Based on this study we describe the current state of art, the challenges we faced in quantifying effects of affinity, and ideas on how OpenMP 5.0 should be improved to address affinity in the context of NUMA domains and accelerators.

1 Introduction

The effects of affinity is a widely studied problem. Most programming models take advantage of the architecture and data-access patterns by providing some implicit or explicit mechanism to control data and process/thread placement. For example, Partitioned Global Address Space (PGAS) languages/APIs provide mechanisms to specify globally accessible data (with local views) that can be distributed to a thread local memory (affine memory). Unified Parallel C, a PGAS language, provides a **shared** qualifier to distinguish between data accessible to all the UPC *threads* vs. private data and distribution keywords to place the data on different affine memories. For arrays UPC provides three affinity granularities: blocked, cyclic and blocked-cyclic. In addition to these UPC provides an affinity field in **upc_forall** to schedule loop iterations to threads with

© Springer International Publishing Switzerland 2016
N. Maruyama et al. (Eds.): IWOMP 2016, LNCS 9903, pp. 35–46, 2016.
DOI: 10.1007/978-3-319-45550-1_3

local data. (A similar affinity concept [1] has been proposed as an extension to the schedule clause in the OpenMP **parallel for** construct).

OpenMP 4.0 being a shared memory programming model, it has different ways to control (implicit and explicitly) the affinity of data (first touch policy, privatization, etc.), threads, and the mapping of work to threads. Work-sharing constructs. OpenMP 4.0 also provides a mechanism to map data to and from accelerators using *target data* regions. The new OpenMP 4.5 release provides a substantial improvement on the support for programming of accelerator and GPU devices and to control how data is being mapped to/from a target device by unstructured data regions and a new *firstprivate* default for scalars.

1.1   Memory Placement

Most systems provide implicit data placement control through policies like *first-touch* and *next-touch*. First-touch is more appropriate for applications where the first access to data is representative of the applications' data accesses throughout the life of the application. This policy has been adopted as default on many systems. For applications that have a more dynamic access pattern, the *next-touch* policy may be more appropriate. Here the data is marked to be placed on the node of the next CPU that accesses it. For OpenMP, *first-touch* translates to data being placed near the thread that first accesses it. Even without any other affinity mechanism this can cause significant impact, for e.g., if the data is initialized by thread 0 only, but later is accessed by all the threads, the *first-touch* policy would locate memory on the node where thread 0 is placed thus resulting in remote memory accesses costs for threads not placed on the same node.

1.2   Thread Affinity

OpenMP 4.5 provides OMP_PROC_BIND ICV to set the thread affinity policy. The legitimate value for this environment variable is either true, false, or a comma separated list of master, close, or spread. When the values are specified in a list, they correspond to the thread affinity policy to be used for parallel regions at the corresponding nested level. In combination with the OMP_PLACES ICV, users may have complete control on the thread affinity and their placement on a given hardware. OMP_PLACES ICV can be one of two types of values: either an abstract name describing a set of places or an explicit list of places described by non-negative numbers. Pre-defined abstract names include *threads, cores,* and *sockets*. A hardware thread is the smallest execution unit that a thread can be bound to with OpenMP 4.5.

When expressed as numbers, places represent the smallest unit of execution exposed by the execution environment, which is typically a hardware thread. In conjunction to places represented by non-negative numbers, intervals is another handy way to express *places* in OpenMP. They are specified using the <*lower-bound> : <length> : <stride>* notation. For example, a user could specify exact cores to place the OpenMP threads or a range of cores based on the application characteristics to best utilize the underlying hardware.

1.3   POWER8 System

The POWER8 processor is a RISC (Reduced Instruction Set Computer) micro-processor from IBM and the first processor supporting the new OpenPOWER eco-system. The POWER8 processor has three possible configurations of either 6, 10 or 12 cores per processor chip. Each processor contains two chiplets of 3, 5 or 6 cores. A typical 12 core processor, as shown in Fig. 1 has 512 KB SRAM L2 caches per core, 96 MB eDRAM shared L3 and an off chip L4 cache that provides up to 128 MB eDRAM space. The L4 cache is supported via an external Centaur memory buffer chip. The Centaur chip is connected via a high-speed link to the POWER8 processor, eDRAM, DDR interfaces, and control logic. This is shown in Fig. 2.

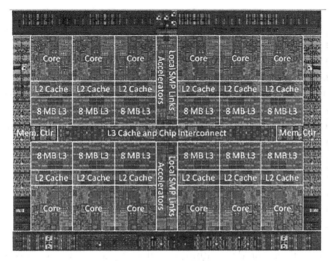

Fig. 1. IBM POWER8 processor architecture [2].

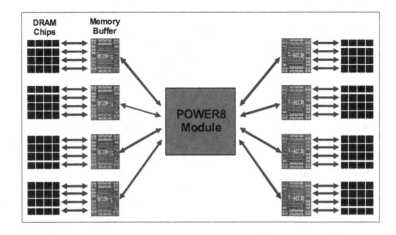

Fig. 2. IBM POWER8 memory subsystem [2].

Nodes	1	2	3	4
1	10	20	40	40
2	20	10	40	40
3	40	40	10	20
4	40	40	20	10

Fig. 3. NUMA distances on a two socket POWER8 processor system as reported by *numactl*

The POWER8 processor has a Non-Uniform Cache Architecture (NUCA) Cache Policy within the chip, this allows a shared L3 cache with scalable bandwidth and latency, allowing migration of most used cache lines to the local L2 cache and then to the local L1 cache [2]. This is a big improvement over the POWER7 processor.

When we run the *numactl* command on a two socket POWER8 system with Ubuntu 14.04, the utility reports four NUMA domains: one domain per each POWER8 chiplet. *numactl* also reports the NUMA distances between domains, which is the ratio of the latency of accessing a remote numa node memory and local memory access. Figure 3 shows the values of different NUMA distances on a two socket POWER8 system, that we use for our experimentation, as reported by *numactl*.

1.4 POWER8 Hardware Counters

To quantify the effects of data affinity and data locality, we look closely at the different hardware counters available on the POWER8 memory subsystem, including **data cache** stall cycles. Long cache latencies and cache misses usually indicate poor placement of data with respect to the executing thread in a OpenMP program. Performance instrumentation in POWER8 is provided in two layers: the **Core Level Performance Monitoring** (CLPM) and the **Nest Level Performance Monitoring** (NLPM). CLPM allows for monitoring of the core pipeline efficiency of the front-end, branch prediction, schedulers etc., along with behavioral metrics such as stalls, execution rates, thread prioritization and resource sharing, and utilizations of resources etc. On the other hand NLPM provides a way to instrument the L3 cache, interconnect fabric and memory channels/controllers. POWER8 has an enhanced Cycles Per Instruction (CPI) Accounting Model. The POWER8 CPI Stack accounts for stalled, waiting to complete, thread blocked, completion table empty, completion and other miscellaneous cycles. The stalled cycles are further classified based on the cause of the stall. Newly added to this group for the POWER8 architecture is the finer granularity of *Stall cycles due to Dcache Misses*. Since we want to quantify cycles wasted due to NUCA and NUMA latencies, we focus on the sub-set

Table 1. Explanation of the data cache miss stall counters on POWER8

*DCACHE_MISS	Stall by data cache (L1) misses
*DMISS_L2L3	Stall by Dcache miss which resolved in L2/L3
*DMISS_L2L3_CONFLICT	Stall due to cache miss due to L2 L3 conflict
*DMISS_L2L3_NO_CONFLICT	Stall due to cache miss due to no L2 L3 conflict
*DMISS_L3MISS	Stall due to cache miss resolving missed the L3
*DMISS_LMEM	GCT empty by branch mispredict + IC miss
*DMISS_L21_L31	Stall by Dcache miss which resolved on chip
*DMISS_REMOTE	Stall by Dcache miss which resolved from remote chip
*DMISS_DISTANT	Stall by L1 reloads from distant interventions and memory

* = PM_CMPLU_STALL_

Table 2. Relationship between different data cache miss stall counters on POWER8

PM_CMPLU_STALL_DMISS_L2L3	PM_CMPLU_STALL_DMISS_L2L3_CONFLICT
	PM_CMPLU_STALL_DMISS_L2L3_NO_CONFLICT
PM_CMPLU_STALL_DMISS_L3MISS	PM_CMPLU_STALL_DMISS_LMEM
	PM_CMPLU_STALL_DMISS_L21_L31
	PM_CMPLU_STALL_DMISS_REMOTE
	PM_CMPLU_STALL_DMISS_DISTANT

of hardware counters mentioned in Table 1. The collection of the counter values are enabled by a system provided script. This allows for access to counters that may not be represented as literal strings and accessible via other application profiling tools. In turn PM_CMPLU_STALL_DCACHE_MISS and PM_CMPLU_STALL_DMISS_L3MISS are a summation of stall cycles listed in Table 2. Although we record all the hardware counter values we only report those that are significantly affected by data affinity.

2 Motivation

The new Exascale system at ORNL, Summit, will be an OpenPOWER system with NVIDIA GPUs. To provide a better understand of the working of OpenMP programs on this novel architecture we look at the most impactful aspects of the programming model. By examining the POWER8 hardware counters while testing the OpenMP 4.0 affinity features implemented in GNU, we hope to measure effects of affinity at scale. Based on this study, we describe the challenges that we faced in quantifying effects of affinity, limitations in the current OpenMP programming model and how some of these may be addressed in OpenMP 5.0 to provide a **portable** notation to define better data affinity that works across different architectures. We also discuss the different hardware counters offered by the POWER8 system and highlight those which can help users identify bad data locality within their programs.

3   Experimentation

To understand the relationship between OpenMP affinity and data locality in the POWER8 architecture we want to quantify the effect of data locality under different combinations of OMP_PROC_BIND and OMP_PLACES settings and quantify their effects using the available POWER8 hardware counter information.

3.1   Experimental Setup

3.1.1   Test System
Four our experiments we use a dual socket POWER8 system with 256 GB of main memory. This system contains four POWER8 chiplets (two on each socket) that map to four NUMA nodes. The system contains a total of 20 cores over two sockets (10 each) that have the capacity to runt 8 hardware threads per core, thus providing a total of up to 160 threads for computation.

3.1.2   The Experiment
To able to identify the correlation between OpenMP affinity features, performance and the hardware counters, we use the Jacobi iterative method program to solve a finite difference discretization of Helmholtz equation (here on referred to as *Jacobi program*). We experiment with the locality of the data by controlling the initialization of the parallel loop at the start of the program. When all threads initialize the sections of data arrays in parallel using the omp_parallel construct, this allows for the *first-touch* policy described in Sect. 1 to place data closer to the physical CPU executing the OpenMP thread thus resulting in good data locality. We use the *num_threads(1)* so that only the one thread will initialize the data causing data to be placed only near the physical NUMA domain executing the single thread. This results in bad data locality. We then test combinations of OpenMP *bindings* and *places* for both these versions to compare and contrast their performance and the values of the hardware counters mentioned in Table 1. Based on this information we want to measure the effect of data locality under different OpenMP affinity setting. We also demonstrate the use of the POWER8 hardware counters to measure the data placement effects on the memory subsystem.

4   Results

As explained in Sect. 1 OpenMP 4.0/4.5 provides two environment variables OMP_PROC_BIND and OMP_PLACES to help users define the thread placement and bindings for their OpenMP application which we refer to as *OpenMP Affinity*. We experiment with two version of the Jacobi program: a version that is optimized for data locality via correct memory placement using the first touch policy and another version where all the data is close to where thread 0 is.

We use a Jacobi problem size of (60000 X 60000) to make to stress the memory subsystem, specifically to utilize the entire L3 and L4 caches. We run both programs with 10, 20, 40, 80 and 160 number of threads with different OpenMP affinity settings and record the POWER8 hardware counters. Figure 4 shows the performance of 20 OpenMP threads with different OpenMP Affinity settings. We observed that after 20 OpenMP threads the speedup does not vary significantly. The best speedup and efficiency combination (16 speedup, 80 % efficiency) is achieved with 20 OpenMP threads with the OpenMP Affinity configuration of *(spread, threads)*. Figure 5 shows the improvement of the locality-aware optimized version (with good data placement) of the Jacobi program over the unoptimized locality-unaware (all data local to thread 0) version when using different OpenMP Affinity settings for different OpenMP thread counts. We observe that for the *(master, threads)* OpenMP affinity configuration all threads execute on a single hardware thread (CPUID 0).

When using *(master, core)*, all threads execute on the different hardware threads that belong to the core where the master thread is running (the P8 processor has eight hardware threads per core), similarly for *(master, socket)* all threads execute in the hardware threads of the socket where the master thread is running. In this case we observe that all threads bind to any of the CPU ids from 0 to 79. When OMP_PROC_BIND set to master we see in Fig. 5 that there is no improvement on the locality aware over the non-locality aware versions (using first-touch policy) because all the threads are running over the same NUMA domains. For *(close, threads)*, we observe that all OpenMP threads run on hardware threads close to each other (on CPU ids: 0–19). All of these cases don't suffer from memory locality issues because they access memory that belongs to the same NUMA domain or memory that is local to the socket (our P8 system has two NUMA domains per socket).

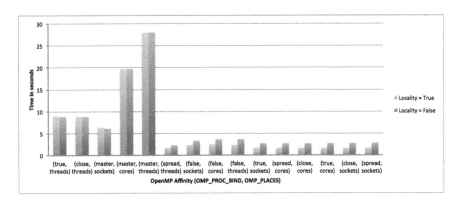

Fig. 4. Performance with 20 OpenMP threads on a two POWER8 socket system for the two versions of the Jacobi program.

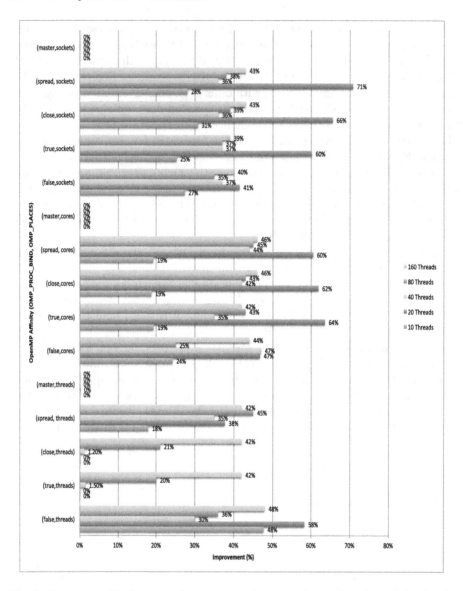

Fig. 5. Comparing Performance Improvement between the two version of the Jacobi program using different number of OpenMP threads and thread affinity settings on a two POWER8 socket system

In the *(spread, sockets)* and *(close, sockets)* configuration threads are spread across sockets but may be mapped to hardware threads running on same core. We observed that the *(true, threads)* configuration is equivalent to the *(close, threads)* according to the GCC OpenMP runtime thread mappings. For all OpenMP affinity settings with OMP_PROC_BIND set to false, threads can migrate and are not bound to a specific thread, core or socket. This migration makes it less impactful on the data placement, but suffers from degraded performance.

From the above discussion it is clear that not all OpenMP Affinity configurations are equal, moreover currently it lacks the ability to specify affinity based on NUMA **and** NUCA domains of emerging architectures like POWER8. This is the first step in understanding the need for new OpenMP affinity features to successfully deploying OpenMP on POWER machines.

Next we look at the hardware counters on the POWER8 system corresponding to the different configurations to explain the improvement we observed in Fig. 5. We select the three cases of OpenMP Affinity tuple that represent the best, mid, and worst improvement as seen in Fig. 5. Selected cases are *(spread, sockets)*, *(spread, cores)*, and *(master, thread)*. For these cases we record the hardware counters for the locality aware and locality unaware versions and calculate the improvement as the value of their difference as a percentage of the value of the locality unaware hardware counter value. From Fig. 6 we see that the two hardware counters that show the effects of data locality the most are DMISS_DISTANT, DMISS_L3MISS. We would have expected to see more significant variation in the value of DMISS_REMOTE, but we found that in some cases, these remote accesses can be cached. For example, the case of *(spread, sockets)* has better DMISS_REMOTE improvement than *(spread, cores)* which is counterintuitive. This is because in *(spread, sockets)* some threads (not all) are running on the same core sharing local cache lines for (L1, L2) and thus taking advantage of cache reuse for remote data access. This can also be seen by the significant improvement in DMISS_DISTANT which quantifies the stalls by L1 reloads from distant interventions and memory. The improvements we see in *(spread, cores)* are more due to DMISS_L21_L31, which shows a better utilization of the L2/L3 cache as this hardware counter measures the stall cycles by Dcache miss which are resolved on chip. In the case of *(spread, cores)* we are effectively increasing the amount of L2 cache available to each OpenMP

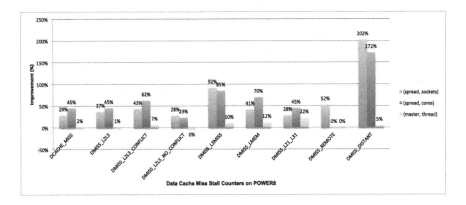

Fig. 6. Comparing hardware counter change

thread, as each thread has access to its own L2 cache on a given core. For the *(master, thread)* case, there is very little improvement in the memory subsystem utilization as everything is running on the same thread (or CPU id) and the most of the data is local to the socket. In this case the data-locality version does not make any difference because all the threads are time-sharing the same hardware thread. This is also true for the case *(close, threads)* where we don't see improvements on the data locality aware version since data is local to the threads. POWER8 provides these unique set of hardware counters to distinguish OpenMP configurations that have less useless cycles on the memory sub-system. Specifically, DMISS_REMOTE and, more importantly, DMISS_DISTANT are key in identifying if the program suffers from bad data locality as indicated in Fig. 5.

5   Related Work

Thread placement can be judiciously managed by runtime systems by monitoring hardware counters and maximizing total local memory accesses across all threads for an OpenMP region [3] by factoring in the critical path. Other strategies include examining the communication patterns to discover different thread placement strategies, so that they may benefit from shared caches, through either brute force or heuristic methods [4].

Solaris, Windows and Linux use the first-touch policy by default. To address applications that are not suited for the first-touch policy, that is, where the access patterns are not the same throughout the life of the threads [5] developed the next-touch policy where the data is marked to be moved to the vicinity (core or node) of the next thread accessing the data. Unfortunately this policy comes with its own set of performance issues and has not been widely accepted for scalability reasons even with improvements [6] such as kernel based next-touch strategy which migrates only selected pages. For many systems, it may be prudent to replicate data, instead of migrating it. This was demonstrated in [7] where the cost of replication was less than migration, through they conceded that some combination of replication and migration can achieve comparable performance. Studies in [8] focus on geographical locality for applications with dynamic access patterns and shows that migration can lead to better performance and the need for directive level migration-on-next-touch support for OpenMP applications. Data mapping suggestions and page placement for different architectures has been explored in [9,10]. Up to 20 % improvement in the benchmarks performance was observed [10] when page placement was directed via feedback about the memory accesses and dynamic memory allocation. Though this study is specific to Itanium-2 general principles are applicable to all ccNUMA systems.

Dynamic thread distribution as studied by [11] allows multi-level thread scheduler combined with a NUMA-aware memory manager to provide hints by the runtime to be able to either re-distribute threads or migrate data upon next-touch. For providing better ccNUMA locality of data, dynamic distribution of tasks through locality aware queuing software has shown promise [12].

6   Conclusions and Future Work

In this paper we evaluated OpenMP affinity support as well as memory placement on the POWER8 architecture. Data locality and affinity are key concepts to exploit the compute and memory capabilities to achieve good performance by minimizing data motion across NUMA domains. The main contribution of this paper is to evaluate current affinity features of OpenMP 4.0 on the POWER8 processors, and on how to measure its effect on data locality on a system with two P8 sockets. In some OpenMP affinity test cases, we show that the POWER8 architecture, using its NUCA L3 caches, can hide the cost of accessing remote memory (as shown in the experiment *(spread, cores)* when running a thread per core since it maximizes local caches that are available per thread. In other cases, when threads share some of the cores, there is a benefit of cache reuse in the non-shared L2 and L1 caches thus improving data locality in the application. In this paper we show that optimizing an application for data locality, the improvements will depend on the kind of affinity used.

Future version of OpenMP affinity model need to support better the concept of NUMA domains. This can be made possible by supporting another *place* option called *Numa* can be added to OpenMP 5.0 via the *OMP_PLACES* ICV so that threads can be mapped more efficiently to NUMA domains. Although the same effect can be achieved by using OS supported bindings (*taskset* on linux platforms), it is not a portable mechanism. By introducing the support of NUMA domains at the OpenMP level, we can keep the implementation details opaque from the programmer while providing a portable solution across all architectures.

Another type of extensions is to integrate the concept of OMP_PLACES with the OpenMP target directive and device_num. Our next step would be to explore ways of mapping OpenMP *target* and *target data* regions to NUMA domains to control data and thread placement.

Acknowledgements. This material is based upon work supported by the U.S. Department of Energy, Office of Science under the Advanced Scientific Computing Research (ASCR) program. This research used resources of the Oak Ridge Leadership Computing Facility at the Oak Ridge National Laboratory, which is supported by the Office of Science of the U.S. Department of Energy under Contract No. DE-AC05-00OR22725.

References

1. Nikolopoulos, D.S., Artiaga, E., Ayguadé, E., Labarta, J.: Exploiting memory affinity in OpenMP through schedule reuse. ACM SIGARCH Comput. Archit. News **29**, 49–55 (2001)
2. Caldeira, A.B., Haug, V., Kahle, M.E., Maciel, C.D., Sanchez, M.: IBM Power Systems S812L and S822L Technical Overview and Introduction (2014)
3. Su, C., Li, D., Nikolopoulos, D., Grove, M., Cameron, K.W., de Supinski, B.R.: Critical path-based thread placement for NUMA systems. In: Proceedings of the Second International Workshop on Performance Modeling, Benchmarking and Simulation of High Performance Computing Systems, PMBS 2011, pp. 19–20. ACM, New York (2011)

4. Diener, M., Madruga, F., Rodrigues, E., Alves, M., Schneider, J., Navaux, P., Heiss, H.U.: Evaluating thread placement based on memory access patterns for multi-core processors. In: 2010 12th IEEE International Conference on High Performance Computing and Communications (HPCC), pp. 491–496 (2010)
5. Terboven, C., an Mey, D., Schmidl, D., Jin, H., Reichstein, T.: Data and thread affinity in OpenMP programs. In: Proceedings of the 2008 Workshop on Memory Access on Future Processors: A Solved Problem? MAW 2008, pp. 377–384. ACM, New York (2008)
6. Goglin, B., Furmento, N.: Enabling high-performance memory migration for multithreaded applications on Linux. In: Proceedings of the 2009 IEEE International Symposium on Parallel & Distributed Processing, IPDPS 2009, pp. 1–9. IEEE Computer Society, Washington, DC (2009)
7. Bull, J.M., Johnson, C.: Data distribution, migration and replication on a ccNUMA architecture. In: Proceedings of the Fourth European Workshop on OpenMP (2002)
8. Nordén, M., Löf, H., Rantakokko, J., Holmgren, S.: Geographical locality and dynamic data migration for OpenMP implementations of adaptive PDE solvers. In: Mueller, M.S., Chapman, B.M., de Supinski, B.R., Malony, A.D., Voss, M. (eds.) IWOMP 2005 and IWOMP 2006. LNCS, vol. 4315, pp. 382–393. Springer, Heidelberg (2008)
9. Smeds, N.: OpenMP application tuning using hardware performance counters. In: Voss, M.J. (ed.) WOMPAT 2003. LNCS, vol. 2716, pp. 260–270. Springer, Heidelberg (2003)
10. Marathe, J., Mueller, F.: Hardware profile-guided automatic page placement for ccnuma systems. In: Proceedings of the Eleventh ACM SIGPLAN Symposium on Principles and Practice of Parallel Programming, PPoPP 2006, pp. 90–99. ACM, New York (2006)
11. Broquedis, F., Furmento, N., Goglin, B., Namyst, R., Wacrenier, P.-A.: Dynamic task and data placement over NUMA architectures: an OpenMP runtime perspective. In: Müller, M.S., de Supinski, B.R., Chapman, B.M. (eds.) IWOMP 2009. LNCS, vol. 5568, pp. 79–92. Springer, Heidelberg (2009)
12. Wittmann, M., Hager, G.: Optimizing ccNUMA locality for task-parallel execution under openmp and TBB on multicore-based systems. CoRR abs/1101.0093 (2011)

Workstealing and Nested Parallelism in SMP Systems

Larry Meadows$^{(\boxtimes)}$, Simon J. Pennycook, Alex Duran, Terry Wilmarth, and Jim Cownie

Intel Corporation, Hillsboro, OR, USA
{lawrence.f.meadows,john.pennycook,alejandro.duran,
terry.l.wilmarth,james.h.cownie}@intel.com

Abstract. We present a workstealing scheduler and show its use in two separate areas: (1) to enable hierarchical parallelism and per-core load balancing in stencil codes, and (2) to reduce overhead in per-thread load balancing in particle codes.

Keywords: Stencil · Nested parallelism · Runtime support

1 Introduction

Modern symmetric multiprocessors (SMPs) have cores with multiple hardware threads per core and share caches at multiple levels. Effective programming for such systems requires that code be structured so that threads and cores cooperate rather than compete for these shared resources.

Section 2 introduces some terminology. Section 3 motivates the need for the workstealing scheduler using a simple two-dimensional loop and discusses its implementation. In Sects. 4 and 5 we introduce the ISO-3DFD stencil code, show several implementations exploiting hierarchical parallelism and the workstealing scheduler, and give performance results. Section 6 describes possible extensions to OpenMP* that are motivated by the stencil implementations. Section 7 shows how the workstealing scheduler can be used in particle codes. Finally we conclude with Sect. 8.

2 Terminology

In our terminology, a core is a single hardware processor. Each core can execute multiple independent hardware threads ("hyperthreads"), which are interleaved in the core's pipeline. Threads on a core share all of the core's resources, including all levels of cache. We assume that OpenMP threads are tightly bound to cores so that the operating system cannot move them, and that there is no over-subscription. Therefore if we have a core that can execute four threads (e.g., on an Intel® Xeon Phi™ processor or coprocessor), the OpenMP runtime will create at most four threads bound to that core.

© Springer International Publishing Switzerland 2016
N. Maruyama et al. (Eds.): IWOMP 2016, LNCS 9903, pp. 47–60, 2016.
DOI: 10.1007/978-3-319-45550-1_4

3 Static Workstealing Scheduler

3.1 Motivation

Consider a code that loops over a two-dimensional iteration space:

```
for (int i = 0; i < N; ++i)
  for (int j = 0; j < M; ++j)
    work(i, j);
```

If the iterations of the nested loop are independent, then we can easily parallelize the loop nest and exploit parallelism in both loops using the OpenMP `collapse` directive:

```
#pragma omp parallel for schedule(static) collapse(2)
for (int i = 0; i < N; ++i)
  for (int j = 0; j < M; ++j)
    work(i, j);
```

The combined iteration space of length $N * M$ is divided among the OpenMP threads according to the schedule clause. If required, the compiler generates code to recover the i and j indices for each iteration using % and / operators.

In many cases we would prefer to distribute the iterations by core, rather than by thread. This can improve locality and load balancing. It also enables cooperation among the threads on a single core, as we will see in a later section. Since OpenMP does not provide such an iteration distribution, we simulate it by hand like this:

```
#include "omp_sched.h"
Percore cores[maxCores];
#pragma omp parallel
{
  Sched sch(N*M, cores);
  int block;
  while ((block = sch.nextiter()) != -1) {
    int i = block / N;
    int j = block % N;
    coreWork(i, j);
  }
}
```

Here the function `coreWork` will be called with the same i and j values in all of the threads on a given core. It must therefore internally distribute the work for the i, j iteration over those threads.

The scheduler `Sched` is described in the next section.

3.2 Scheduler Implementation

The static workstealing scheduler is implemented as two C++ classes: `Sched` and `Percore`. `Percore` contains data that is shared among the OpenMP threads that execute on the same core. The scheduler uses an array of `Percore` objects, one for each core. Since the `Percore` array is shared it must be declared outside an OpenMP parallel region or allocated on the heap. A predefined constant `maxCores` is defined to simplify declaration:

```
Percore cores[maxCores];
```

The `Sched` class must be instantiated inside a parallel region, resulting in one instance per OpenMP thread. It is constructed with the number of iterations of the parallel loop and the `Percore` array:

```
Sched sch(niter, cores);
```

Every cooperating instance of `Sched` must be constructed with the same arguments.

`Sched` has two member functions: `nextiter()` and `nextiter1()`. Both of these function enumerate the iterations for which the `Sched` instance was constructed. `nextiter()` returns the same value to all hyperthreads on the same core and contains an implicit barrier on them. `nextiter1()` returns a value to only the calling thread and there is no implicit barrier. There is a third member function `corebarrier()` that barriers the threads in a core. It uses the barrier described in [5,6].

Initially iterations are distributed as they would be in a static schedule, except that they are distributed over cores rather than threads. The `Percore` object for a given core contains the start and end iteration for that core. When one of the iteration functions is called, it first checks to see if there are any remaining iterations on the core to which the calling thread is bound. If so, it atomically increments the start value and returns that iteration. Otherwise, it traverses the `Percore` array looking at each core. As soon as it finds a core that has available iterations, it atomically decrements the end value (thus stealing an iteration from the end of its range) and returns that iteration. If a thread has traversed all cores and found no iterations to steal, the iteration function returns −1, indicating that there are no more iterations to start. See Fig. 1 for the stealing algorithm.

```
iter_t _nextiter()
{
    iter_t ret = getiter(*core);       // my core
    if (ret != -1)
        return ret;

    // need to steal, start in a random place
    int startcore = _rdtsc() % ncores;
    int i = startcore;
    do
    {
        if (i != mycore)
        {
            ret = stealiter(base[i]);
            if (ret != -1)
                return ret;
        }
        i = (i == ncores-1) ? 0 : i+1; // wraparound
    } while (i != startcore);
    return -1;
}
```

Fig. 1. Stealing algorithm

3.3 OpenMP Scheduler Constraints

Prior to OpenMP 4.5, the description of a dynamic schedule in OpenMP was subject to interpretation. In particular it was not immediately apparent whether code liks this should always succeed, or whether schedules which would cause it to abort are legal.

```
#pragma omp parallel
{
    int myHighestIteration = -1;
#pragma omp for schedule(dynamic)
    for (int i=0; i<1000; i++)
    {
        if (i < myHighestIteration)
            abort();
        else
            myHighestIteration = i;
    }
}
```

Fig. 2. OpenMP scheduler monotonicity test

This is an important question for the static workstealing scheduler, since under load-imbalance it will generate schedules that would cause this test to abort. (Consider the thread whose static schedule includes the serially final iteration; if it ever steals from another thread the iteration it steals must be lower than one it has already seen.)

In OpenMP 4.5 control of this property of the scheduler (known as "monotonicity") can be explicitly expressed by the programmer using the new schedule modifiers (`monotonic` and `nonmonotonic`). In addition, OpenMP 4.5 includes the statement of intent that in OpenMP 5.0 an unmodifed dynamic loop schedule can legally be treated as though it had the nonmonotonic qualifier. These improvements to the OpenMP standard make it clear that a static workstealing scheduler, like that described here, can be used inside the OpenMP runtime, and, therefore, that its performance should be of interest to people who will never rewrite their code to include their own scheduler (Fig. 2).

4 ISO-3DFD Test Code

The ISO-3DFD stencil code (hereafter referred to as *ISO-3DFD*) is a 16th order stencil in space (second order in time) finite difference implementation used to solve the isotropic acoustic wave equation. The baseline code is shown in Fig. 3.

We can use a roofline model [2] to estimate the performance of ISO-3DFD. Each iteration of the loop as written above has 27 multiplies, 51 adds, and 51 4-byte loads, for an arithmetic intensity of 78/4*51 or 0.38 flops/byte. We use five different systems in this article:

SNB Intel® Xeon® Processor E5-2680 v1

```
int dimn1n2 = n1*n2;
for(int iz=0; iz<n3; iz++)
  for(int iy=0; iy<n2; iy++)
    for(int ix=0; ix<n1; ix++) {
      float value = ptr_prev[offset]*coeff[0];
      for(int ir=1; ir<=8; ir++) {
        value += coeff[ir] * (ptr_prev[offset + ir] +
                              ptr_prev[offset - ir]);
        value += coeff[ir] * (ptr_prev[offset + ir*n1] +
                              ptr_prev[offset - ir*n1]);
        value += coeff[ir] * (ptr_prev[offset + ir*dimn1n2] +
                              ptr_prev[offset - ir*dimn1n2]);
      }
      ptr_next[offset] = 2.0f* ptr_prev[offset] - ptr_next[offset] +
                         value*ptr_vel[offset];
    }
```

Fig. 3. ISO-3DFD pseudocode

HSW Intel® Xeon® Processor E5-2697 v3
BDW Intel® Xeon® Processor E5-2699 v4
KNC Intel® Xeon Phi™ C0PRQ-7120
KNL the Intel processor codenamed Knights Landing in a preproduction system, B0 stepping, 1.4 GHz, 68 cores, 16 GB MCDRAM, 96 GB DDR in quadrant/flat mode.

We collectively call SNB, HSW and BDW big cores, and KNC and KNL small cores.

Table 1 shows the five systems, their Stream benchmark [7] figures, the projected performance from the roofline model, and the actual, measured, performance. Note: Only one socket is used on the big core systems to avoid complications from NUMA effects.

From Table 1 we see that the actual performance exceeds that predicted by the roofline model. This is because, by using bandwidth from main memory, the roofline model is implicitly assuming that all the loads miss cache. In fact, as we can see from the stencil pattern, there is a lot of potential temporal and spatial reuse from one iteration to the next in all three dimensions. In particular the X dimension has a lot of spatial reuse because of accesses to the same few

Table 1. Roofline prediction vs. measured performance

System	Stream bandwidth (GB/s)	Roofline prediction (GF/s)	Measured performance (GF/s)
SNB	39	15	25
HSW	59	22	44
BDW	52[a]	20	39
KNC	177	67	137
KNL	490	186	275

[a] The memory configuration on this system is non-optimal, with optimal configuration the stream bandwidth is around 70 GB/s per socket.

Table 2. Roofline using LLC BW

System	LLC bytes/ clock/core	# Cores used	Freq (MHz)	LLC BW (GB/Sec)	Roofline prediction (GF/Sec)	Measured performance (GF/Sec)
SNB	11	8	2700	237	90	25
HSW	11	14	2600	400	152	44
BDW	11	22	2200	532	173	39
KNC	14	60	1238	1040	395	137
KNL	32	64	1400	2867	1089	275

cache lines offset by between 1 and 8 4-byte floats in both positive and negative directions.

We can refine the roofline model to get a more accurate performance estimate by looking at bandwidth from the last level cache. On the small cores the last level cache is the L2 cache, while on the big cores it is the L3 cache. Table 2 shows the roofline performance using this alternate bandwidth metric (LLC bandwidth was measured by a simple test program performing a vectorized single-precision summation). This roofline assumes that all accesses hit in the last-level cache. Tables 1 and 2 bound the expected performance of ISO-3DFD.

5   ISO-3DFD Optimization

As we have seen, there is a lot of temporal reuse in ISO-3DFD and we would like to capture that reuse to improve performance. The usual way to do this is to tile the loops so that reused cache-lines are closer together in time and thus more likely to stay in the LLC. This is fairly easy in ISO-3DFD, as shown in Fig. 4. The tile sizes `tilex`, `tiley`, and `tilez` are chosen by experimentation. Tile sizes should be fairly small so that the collapsed loop has significantly more iterations than threads to improve load balancing (dynamic scheduling or static workstealing can also be used as we will see later).

5.1   Nested Parallelism vs. Hand Threading

The collapsed loop in Fig. 4 distributes iterations by thread, not by core. To obtain iteration distribution by core, we can use either the static workstealing scheduler described previously, or nested parallelism. The two methods are shown side-by-side in Figs. 5 and 6.

Both implementations distribute the tiles among the cores and then distribute the work for the tile over the threads in the core. The code in Fig. 5 uses nested OpenMP. It assumes that the threads in the outer team are placed one per core, and that the threads in the inner teams are on the same core as their master thread. The code in Fig. 6 accomplishes the same effect by precomputing

```
#pragma omp parallel for collapse(3)
for(int iiz=0; iiz<n3; iiz+=tilez)
for(int iiy=0; iiy<n2; iiy+=tiley)
for(int iix=0; iix<n1; iix+=tilex) {
  int zmax = std::min(iiz+tilez, n3);
  int ymax = std::min(iiy+tiley, n2);
  int xmax = std::min(iix+tilex, n1);
  for (int iz=iiz; iz<zmax; ++iz)
  for (int iy=iiy; iy<ymax; ++iy) {
    #pragma omp simd
    for (int ix=iix; ix<xmax; ++ix) {
      int offset = idx(ix, iy, iz, n1, n2, n3);
      float value = ptr_prev[offset]*coeff[0];
      #pragma unroll(8)
      for(int ir=1; ir<=8; ir++) {
        value += coeff[ir] * (ptr_prev[offset + ir] +
                              ptr_prev[offset - ir]);
        value += coeff[ir] * (ptr_prev[offset + ir*xn1] +
                              ptr_prev[offset - ir*xn1]);
        value += coeff[ir] * (ptr_prev[offset + ir*xn1n2] +
                              ptr_prev[offset - ir*xn1n2]);
      }
      ptr_next[offset] = 2.0f*ptr_prev[offset] - ptr_next[offset] +
                         value*ptr_vel[offset];
    }
  }
}
```

Fig. 4. ISO-3DFD tiled pseudocode

the core and hyperthread for each OpenMP thread. Hand threading assumes that OpenMP thread affinity is set properly to mirror the internal mapping to cores and hyperthreads. The distribution of the work within the core is done explicitly in the Y loop using the thread number within the core.

```
#pragma omp parallel for collapse(3)
for(int iiz=0; iiz<n3; iiz+=tilez)
for(int iiy=0; iiy<n2; iiy+=tiley)
for(int iix=0; iix<n1; iix+=tilex) {
#pragma omp parallel
  {

  int myht = omp_get_thread_num();



  int zmax = std::min(iiz+tilez, n3);
  int ymax = std::min(iiy+tiley, n2);
  int xmax = std::min(iix+tilex, n1);
  for (int iz=iiz; iz<zmax; ++iz)
  for (int iy=iiy+myht; iy<ymax; iy+=nHT) {
    #pragma omp simd
    for (int ix=iix; ix<xmax; ++ix) {
      ...
    }
  }
  }
}
```

```
Percore cores[maxCores];
#pragma omp parallel
{
int nblocksz = (n3 + tilez - 1) / tilez;
int nblocksy = (n2 + tiley - 1) / tiley;
int nblocksx = (n1 + tilex - 1) / tilex;
nblocks = nblocksz * nblocksy * nblocksx;
Sched sch(nblocks, cores);
int myht = sch.myht;
int block;
while ((block = sch.nextiter()) != -1) {
  int iiz = block / (nblocksy * nblocksx);
  int rem = block % (nblocksy * nblocksx);
  int iiy = rem   / (nblocksx);
  int iix = rem   % (nblocksx);
  iix *= tilex; iiy *= tiley; iiz *= tilez;
  int zmax = std::min(iiz+tilez, n3);
  int ymax = std::min(iiy+tiley, n2);
  int xmax = std::min(iix+tilex, n1);
  for (int iz=iiz; iz<zmax; ++iz)
  for (int iy=iiy+myht; iy<ymax; iy+=nHT) {
    #pragma omp simd
    for (int ix=iix; ix<xmax; ++ix) {
      ...
    }
  }
}
}
```

Fig. 5. Nested OpenMP   **Fig. 6.** Hand threaded

5.2   Performance Results

Table 3 compares the different implementions of ISO-3DFD. The implementations are:

Baseline   The baseline implementation in Fig. 3.
Tiled   The tiled implementation in Fig. 4.
Nested   The nested implementation in Fig. 5.
Hand   The hand-threaded implementation in Fig. 6.
Scheduler   Three implementations used to evalua te the worksteal ing scheduler. The code is hand-tiled and the loop over the tiles is parallelized in one of three ways:
Static - Use OpenMP `#pragma omp for schedule(static)`
Worksteal - Use static workstealing scheduler
Dynamic - Use OpenMP `#pragma omp for schedule(dynamic)`

Table 4 gives the performance results for the different implementations on the test platforms.

On big cores, tiling alone gives a significant improvement over the baseline. This is because the large L3 cache is able to hold almost all of the reused data. Small cores do not have an L3 cache and the smaller L2 cache is not able to enable much reuse, so tiling does not generally help here.

Turning to the scheduler columns, we see that OpenMP dynamic scheduling is generally superior to either OpenMP static scheduling or static worksteal-ing on big cores (though this might change if we looked at a multi-socket big-core case). The shared L3 improves the performance of the atomic opera-tions needed in dynamic scheduling, and the static workstealing implementation introduces additional overhead. However on the small cores, Static workstealing is clearly superior to either OpenMP static or OpenMP dynamic scheduling since it requires many fewer atomic operations.

This also helps to explain why nested parallelism (which uses `#pragma omp parallel for schedule(dynamic)`) performs better than hand threading (which uses static workstealing) on the big cores.

On the small cores we were able to improve the performance of nested par-allelism by adjusting the tile size. The small cores have reduced single-thread performance and many more cores which combine to increase the overhead of

Table 3. ISO-3DFD implementation comparison

	Baseline	Tiled	Nested	Hand	Static	Worksteal	Dynamic
Outer loop structure	collapse(2) Z,Y	collapse(3) Z,Y,X	hand-collapse Z,Y,X	hand-collapse Z,Y,X	hand-collapse Z,Y,X	hand-collapse Z,Y,X	hand-collapse Z,Y,X
Inner loop structure	simd X	serial Z,Y simd X	serial Z,Y simd X	serial Z,Y simd X	serial Z,Y simd X	serial Z,Y simd X	serial Z,Y simd X
Cooperative threading	none	none	Y loop	Y loop	none	none	none

Table 4. ISO-3DFD performance (GF/s)

System	Threads	Indep threading		Coop threading		Scheduler		
		Baseline	Tiled	Nested	Hand	Static	Worksteal	Dynamic
SNB	1	25	55	59	57	61	57	55
	2	21	47	59	57	49	56	52
HSW	1	39	109	109	106	113	113	118
	2	35	107	119	108	96	107	109
BDW	1	39	155	156	119	117	121	154
	2	45	158	167	122	108	120	156
KNC	1	49	40	38	51	48	52	40
	2	76	70	79	82	67	89	70
	4	93	86	101	107	64	115	86
KNL	1	256	119	159	264	250	274	122
	2	179	132	148	291	245	318	135
	4	166	169	209	274	196	196	173

nesting, so the amount of work per tile needs to be larger to compensate. However, even with this change, the hand threaded implementation with static workstealing outperforms nested parallelism.

6   OpenMP Extension to Loop Scheduling

As we have seen, the current OpenMP support is limited when trying to map the iterations of loops to modern hardware and forces programmers wanting the maximum performance to code their own loop scheduling policies by hand. To improve OpenMP support we propose two sets of extensions to the loop scheduling mechanisms: hierarchical loop scheduling and multi-dimensional chunking.

6.1   Hierarchical Loop Scheduling

In existing and future architectures not all hardware threads are peers. Hardware threads are organized in a hierarchy in which threads in the same level share some resources together. For example, in many architectures several hardware threads are part of the same core (sharing some part of the cache hierarchy) and these cores are part of the same NUMA domain (sharing a privileged access to some system memory). These logical groupings create a hierarchy of groups of threads.

Exploiting this hierarchy when distributing the iterations of a given loop nest is becoming increasingly important to obtain the best performance. Current OpenMP provides the mechanisms (e.g., OMP_PLACES and OMP_PROC_BIND) that allow the programmer to lay out the different OpenMP threads across the hardware thread hierarchy. But it has no provisions to ensure that the scheduling of iterations from a loop can exploit these carefully planned layouts.

Furthermore, the scheduling decisions at each level of the hardware hierarchy are likely to be different. For example, a programmer might want to dynamically distribute relatively large groups of iterations between the different cores but then statically distribute the iterations of each group between the threads of each core, or to statically distribute large groups of iterations across NUMA domains while dynamically scheduling those iterations inside a NUMA domain.

While it is possible to code these patterns today in OpenMP using nested parallelism the unnecessary fork-join overheads make it impractical in many cases. We argue that these patterns should be supported as loop scheduling options that do not require nested parallelism. We therefore propose two extensions to the existing OpenMP loop construct:

- add a new `schedule-groupsizes` clause. This clause contains a list of positive integer expressions that are group sizes. The first group size defines how the threads of the team are divided into groups. Each subsequent group size specified defines how the previous group is divided. This creates a hierarchy of groups that will be used for scheduling the iterations of the loop. The usage of this clause must be coordinated with the thread affinity mechanism to obtain good results.
- extend the current syntax of the schedule clause from a single `schedule-kind` to a list of `schedule-kind`s. The `schedule-kind` that will be applied to each level of the group hierarchy is implicitly defined by the order in the list (i.e., the first schedule kind applies to the root group, the second schedule kind applies to the next group level, etc.).

6.2   Multi-dimensional Chunking

Another common OpenMP limitation is that in a nest of loops OpenMP only offers the options to either schedule the iterations of the outer loop of the nest or collapse the iteration space of some outer subset of the nest and schedule the resulting iterations of the collapse operation. In the first case, the loop scheduling is akin to a one-dimensional tiling of the loop nest, while in the second case the created tiles can have irregular shapes that do not favor locality.

What a programmer would frequently like is to distribute multi-dimensional tiles between the threads that cooperate in the worksharing construct. Today programmers are required to manually modify their code to apply tiling optimization and then apply a loop worksharing with the `collapse` clause as shown in Fig. 4.

Because by creating chunks of iterations for loop scheduling purposes OpenMP is implicitly supporting 1D tiling, we propose to extend loop scheduling semantics to support multi-dimensional tiling. This requires that the chunks of iterations assigned to threads contain not just a subset of iterations of the outer most loop, but a tuple of iteration subsets for other loops in the nest.

To express this we propose to extend the existing `schedule-kinds` to accept not just one chunksize expression but a list of them. The first chunksize is applied to the first loop in the nest, the second chunksize to the next loop in the next, etc. The special value * is allowed in one dimension to imply that chunksize is equal to the number of iterations in that dimension. This is important in combination with the previous hierarchical scheduling proposal as the number of iterations below the root level might be unknown.

Given a certain nest of m loops and a `schedule` clause with chunk sizes $C_1, ..., C_m$ the iteration space of the loop nest is $N_1 x..x N_m$ where N_i is the number of iterations for the i loop in the nest (1 being the outermost loop and m the innermost). This iteration space is partitioned in chunks of size $C_1 x...x C_m$ except for the uppermost boundaries where they can have less iterations. Then these chunks are distributed to the threads in the team following the schedule-kind specified in the schedule clause (i.e., statically or dynamically).

A new static (without chunksize) schedule-kind that has the same semantics as the existing `static` schedule-kind but can be applied to multiple loops (i.e., create tiles of approximately the same size for each thread) could also be added to OpenMP. It is unclear to us how useful this would be, as in practice a programmer usually wants to create these tiles to match the size of a specific hardware resource (e.g., the L2 cache).

6.3 Example

Combining the two proposals we can apply them together to the ISO3DFD code as show in Fig. 7. We use the multi-dimensional chunking to create 3D tiles of size $tilex*tiley*tilez$. Then we use the hierarchical scheduling to distribute them dynamically across groups of HT threads (which correspond to cores assuming a close thread placement and that HT is the number of threads per core used). Then threads inside each core cooperate to execute the iterations of the tile. Note that the `static(*,*,1)` expresses that only those iterations of the ix loop (which are also SIMDized) are distributed among threads of each core using a static schedule with chunksize 1. The code generated from this new version should be equivalent to that of Fig. 6, but is significantly easier to write!

```
#pragma omp parallel for schedule-groupsizes(HT) \
                schedule(dynamic(tilez,tiley,tilex),static(*,*,1))
for ( iz = 0; iz < zmax; iz++)
    for ( iy = 0; iy < ymax; iy++)
        #pragma omp simd
        for ( ix = 0; ix < xmax; ix++ )
        {
            ...
        }
```

Fig. 7. ISO-3DFD parallelization with the proposed OpenMP extensions

7   Static Workstealing and Particle Codes

Particle codes often include some interaction between the particles and a mesh (i.e., a discretized version of the space in which they are travelling). For example, the Particle Mesh Ewald (PME) method accumulates charges at mesh points in order to approximate long-range interactions, and in particle transport codes each particle will update several "tally" values for any cells that it encounters while traversing the mesh.

The simplest way to implement these particle-mesh interactions in parallel is to loop over particles, using some method of guaranteeing atomicity (e.g., hardware atomics, locks or transactions) to handle write-conflicts during updates to a single (shared) mesh data structure. Although in some cases it is possible to use some algorithmic restructuring (e.g., using coloring [8]) instead, such approaches are more complicated to implement and may incur other runtime overheads or decrease the amount of available parallelism. We restrict our discussion to the simplest implementation.

In order to improve cache locality, it is desirable to have some way to group and then iterate over particles spatially, and this is commonly achieved by sorting all of the particles at some fixed frequency [9]. However, the number of particles in each region of space is not guaranteed to be uniform, and in some simulations the amount of computation per particle is not fixed (e.g. particles may represent different atoms, or different regions of space may have different material properties). As a result it is often necessary to use dynamic scheduling of some sort to overcome the load imbalance.

7.1   Application of Static Workstealing

A purely static schedule ensures that threads are working on particles from disjoint sections of the mesh (thus reducing the probability of write-conflicts), but does not account for load imbalance; at the other extreme, a purely dynamic schedule handles load imbalance well, but makes no guarantees about scheduling (potentially increasing the probability of write-conflicts). The static workstealing schedule proposed here strikes a good balance between the two: each thread is initially assigned work from one region of the mesh, but is able to steal work from another region if/when necessary.

Distributing work per core instead of per thread provides additional benefits, by ensuring that the threads executing on each core are (initially) working on particles from the same region. The primary effect of this is decreased latency for mesh data accesses through cache re-use. A secondary effect is improved atomics throughput, since an atomic update to a cache line is fastest when the line is already held in modified/exclusive state by the updating core [10].

Table 5 compares the performance of static, dynamic, guided and static workstealing schedules for a Monte Carlo particle transport benchmark developed by the French Alternative Energies and Atomic Energy Commission (CEA) [11].

Note that all of these schedules had to be implemented by hand (i.e., without using OpenMP pragmas) due to the structure of the loops involved; however,

Table 5. Monte Carlo particle transport benchmark performance (Mega events/second)

System	Threads	Scheduler			
		Static	Dynamic	Guided	Worksteal
SNB	2	84	108	87	113
HSW	2	112	163	125	185
BDW	2	211	281	244	327
KNC	4	191	315	225	378
KNL	2	278	413	335	588

every effort was made to ensure that the implementation was representative. Static workstealing provides a clear performance benefit across all of the architectures tested, and should be expected to provide greater benefits where inter-core communication is more expensive (e.g., in dual-socket systems).

8   Conclusions and Future Work

We have shown that static workstealing performs well across the board on the small core platforms and on imbalanced problems on big cores. With the introduction of the `nonmonotonic` modifier for dynamic schedules in OpenMP 4.5 (and the statement that `nonmonotonic` will become the default dynamic schedule in OpenMP 5.0), the static workstealing implementation is now legal in OpenMP implementations. Given the performance it shows on our examples, we expect that it will become the default implementation for dynamic schedules in many runtimes.

We have also proposed simple extensions to OpenMP which would allow the expression of loop tiling and the choice of appropriate schedules at each level of a closely nested OpenMP loop-nest. These extensions would allow the benefits which we have demonstrated from these techniques to be more easily achieved by OpenMP programmers.

While our stencil performance falls short of the roofline model, especially on the small cores, absolute stencil performance is beyond the scope of this paper. We expect to include in-depth analysis of the performance shortfall in a future publication.

References

1. Andreolli, C.: Eight Optimizations for 3-Dimensional Finite Difference (3DFD) Code with an Isotropic (ISO). https://software.intel.com/en-us/articles/eight-optimizations-for-3-dimensional-finite-difference-3dfd-code-with-an-isotropic-iso. Accessed 21 Oct 2014
2. Williams, S., Waterman, A., Patterson, D.: Roofline: an insightful visual performance model for multicore architectures. CACM **52**(4), 65 (2009)

3. Jeffers, J., Reinders, J.: Intel Xeon Phi Coprocessor High-Performance Programming. Morgan Kauffman, Boston (2013)
4. Dempsey, J.: Plesiochronous phasing barriers. In: Jeffers, J., Reinders, J. (eds.) High Performance Parallelism Pearls, pp. 87–115. Morgan Kauffman, Boston (2015)
5. Briggs, J., et al.: Separable projection integrals for higher-order correlators of the cosmic microwave sky: acceleration by factors exceeding 100, Cornell University Library. http://arxiv.org/abs/1503.08809
6. Meadows, L., Kim, J., Wells, A.: Parallelization methods for hierarchical SMP systems. In: Terboven, C., et al. (eds.) IWOMP 2015. LNCS, vol. 9342, pp. 247–259. Springer, Heidelberg (2015). doi:10.1007/978-3-319-24595-9_18
7. McCalpin, J.D.: Memory bandwidth and machine balance in current high performance computers. IEEE Computer Society Technical Committee on Computer Architecture (TCCA) Newsletter, December 1995
8. Sbalzarini, I.F., Walther, J.H., Bergdorf, M., Hieber, S.E., Kotsalis, E.M., Koumoutsakos, P.: PPM a highly efficient parallel particlemesh library for the simulation of continuum systems. J. Comput. Phys. **215**(2), 566 (2006)
9. Madduri, K., Im, E.-J., Ibrahim, K.Z., Williams, S., Ethier, S., Oliker, L.: Gyrokinetic particle-in-cell optimization on emerging multi- and manycore platforms. Parallel Comput. **37**(9), 501 (2011)
10. Schweizer, H., Besta, M., Hoefler, T.: Evaluating the cost of atomic operations on modern architectures. In: Proceedings of Parallel Architectures and Compilation (2015)
11. Dureau, D., Poëtte, G.: Hybrid parallel programming models for AMR neutron Monte-Carlo transport. In: Joint International Conference on Supercomputing in Nuclear Applications and Monte Carlo (2013)

Description, Implementation and Evaluation of an Affinity Clause for Task Directives

Philippe Virouleau[1,2]([✉]), Adrien Roussel[1,2,3], François Broquedis[1],
Thierry Gautier[1,2], Fabrice Rastello[1], and Jean-Marc Gratien[3]

[1] Inria, Univ. Grenoble Alpes, CNRS, Grenoble Institute of Technology, LIG,
Grenoble, France
{philippe.virouleau,francois.broquedis,
fabrice.rastello}@inria.fr, thierry.gautier@inrialpes.fr
[2] LIP, ENS de Lyon, Lyon, France
[3] IFPEN, Rueil Malmaison, France
adrien.roussel@inria.fr, jean-marc.gratien@ifpen.fr

Abstract. OpenMP 4.0 introduced dependent tasks, which give the programmer a way to express fine grain parallelism. Using appropriate OS
support (such as NUMA libraries), the runtime can rely on the information in the *depend* clause to dynamically map the tasks to the architecture topology. Controlling data locality is one of the key factors to reach
a high level of performance when targeting NUMA architectures. On this
topic, OpenMP does not provide a lot of flexibility to the programmer
yet, which lets the runtime decide where a task should be executed. In
this paper, we present a class of applications which would benefit from
having such a control and flexibility over tasks and data placement. We
also propose our own interpretation of the new *affinity* clause for the *task*
directive, which is being discussed by the OpenMP *Architecture Review
Board*. This clause enables the programmer to give hints to the runtime
about tasks placement during the program execution, which can be used
to control the data mapping on the architecture. In our proposal, the programmer can express affinity between a task and the following resources:
a thread, a NUMA node, and a data. We then present an implementation
of this proposal in the Clang-3.8 compiler, and an implementation of the
corresponding extensions in our OpenMP runtime LIBKOMP. Finally,
we present a preliminary evaluation of this work running two task-based
OpenMP kernels on a 192-core NUMA architecture, that shows noticeable improvements both in terms of performance and scalability.

Keywords: OpenMP · Task dependencies · Affinity · Runtime systems · NUMA

1 Introduction

OpenMP has become a major standard to program parallel applications on a
wide variety of parallel platforms ranging from desktop notebooks to high-end

© Springer International Publishing Switzerland 2016
N. Maruyama et al. (Eds.): IWOMP 2016, LNCS 9903, pp. 61–73, 2016.
DOI: 10.1007/978-3-319-45550-1_5

supercomputers. It provides keywords to express fine grain task-based parallelism that boosts the applications performance and scalability on large-scale shared memory machines. In particular, tasking in OpenMP helps the programmers parallelize applications with an irregular workload, letting the runtime system be in charge of performing load balancing through task scheduling in a dynamic way. However, very little support exists to express and to control the affinity between tasks and data on systems with a decentralized memory layout, like *Non-Uniform Memory Architectures* (NUMA). On such systems, the memory is physically split into several banks, also called *NUMA nodes*, which leads to different memory latencies and throughputs depending on the location of the memory bank a core is accessing data from. To get the most performance out of such architectures, OpenMP runtime systems thus need to be extended to make the task scheduler aware of both the underlying hardware and the relation that exists between a task and the data it accesses.

We relate in this paper our experiences to reach high performance out of OpenMP numerical applications on a 192-core NUMA machine. The recently-added *places* concept in the OpenMP 4.0 specification provides ways of binding OpenMP parallel regions to user-defined partitions of the machine. This basically ends up binding the threads of the corresponding region to a set of cores. Thus, relying on the first-touch memory allocation policy as a portable solution to control memory binding, OpenMP places can help to control thread affinity with respect to the memory. However, the concept behind OpenMP places needs to be extended to improve the performance of task-based applications, as tasks are most of the time scheduled over threads in a dynamic way according to a work-stealing execution model. This is why the OpenMP *Architecture Review Board* is currently discussing the introduction of a new *affinity* feature to make the runtime system aware of the affinities between the tasks and the data they access.

In this paper, we present how we control task and data placement inside our OpenMP runtime system, implementing an *affinity* clause whose syntax is very close to the one currently discussed by the ARB. We also explain how we manage such information at runtime in order to improve the execution of task-based OpenMP programs on NUMA systems, with a particular focus on the scheduling data structure and the scheduling algorithm. The contribution of this paper is threefold:

- We propose an OpenMP *affinity* extension to the Clang-3.8 compiler able to express affinities between tasks and memory and pass this information along to the runtime system;
- We describe an extension to our task-based OpenMP runtime system to guide the scheduling of tasks according to such information to reach better performance on NUMA systems;
- We present some preliminary experimental results on running OpenMP benchmarks with tasks dependencies on a 192-core NUMA system, with and without using *affinity*.

The remainder of this paper is organized as follows. Section 2 introduces some motivating examples of applications that suffer from the lack of affinity support on NUMA machines. Section 3 details our proposal from the extension to the OpenMP specification to its actual implementation inside both the Clang compiler and our own OpenMP runtime system. Section 4 presents the performance evaluation of two OpenMP kernels that were enhanced to support affinity and were executed on a 192-core NUMA machine. We eventually present some related work in Sect. 5 before concluding in Sect. 6.

2 Motivating Examples for Which Affinity Does Matter

The high memory throughput of NUMA architectures has been introduced at the price of non-uniformity in memory latency. On such architectures, accessing local memory access induces lower latency than accessing data on a remote memory bank. To get the most performance, computational units of work, like *threads* and *tasks*, should ideally only access local memory.

Many projects from the High-Performance Computing research area deal with sparse linear solvers as fundamental building blocks. For instance, let us consider the BiCGStab [13] algorithm, a classical method for solving sparse linear algebra systems. Such algorithm is structured around a main loop that iterates until convergence is reached. At each iteration, the algorithm accesses global data through the computation of some sparse matrix-vector products as well as the execution of many global reductions like dot products. Preserving data locality among iterations is crucial to reach a high level of performance, especially for the sparse matrix products arising during the algorithm execution like reported by some early experiments running the BiCGStab algorithm (Sect. 4.3).

Another class of algorithms needing special care regarding data locality is the Stencil algorithms. These algorithms consist of multiple time steps during which every element of an array is updated using the value of its neighbors. Figure 1 shows the base performances of our Jacobi kernel, a stencil algorithm, evaluated on a 192-core NUMA architecture, with both Clang's OpenMP runtime and our OpenMP runtime LIBKOMP. We can see that the performances of either task-based versions are disappointing, as the execution time of this kernel increases when the number of threads is greater than 16. The reason behind this is that tasks are not scheduled close to their data. To do so, the runtime system should be aware of which data is accessed by every task and where the data has been physically allocated. While the former could be obtained through OpenMP data dependencies, the latter would need a specific support from the runtime level. Our proposal meets both these requirements through an OpenMP portable solution presented in the next section.

3 Extending OpenMP to Support Affinities

In this section, we detail our proposal with the introduction of the *affinity* keyword and how we implemented the corresponding runtime extensions that take advantage of this new feature.

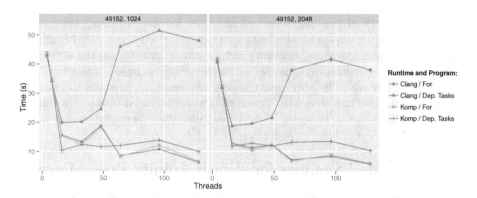

Fig. 1. Jacobi's base performances, with a Matrix size of 49152, and blocksizes of 1024 or 2048

3.1   Extension of the OpenMP Task Directive

We propose an extension to precisely control the *affinity* of a task with a specific part of the architecture hierarchy.

The two main components of NUMA architectures we consider in this work are cores and nodes. One of the key to getting performances out of NUMA architectures is to ensure tasks are executing *close* to their data. Therefore, we identified three different kinds of *affinity* the programmer may need to express, which are the following:

affinity to a thread: the runtime should try to schedule the task to be executed by a given thread.

affinity to a NUMA node: the runtime should try to schedule the task on any of the threads bound to a given NUMA node.

affinity to a data: once a task becomes ready for execution, the runtime should try to schedule it on any of the threads bound to the NUMA node on which the given data has been physically allocated.

Additionally, the programmer can specify if this affinity is *strict*, which means the task **must** be executed on the given resource, or not. In the latter case, the task scheduler may decide to execute the task on a different resource, to perform load balancing for example.

Since this extension is aimed for the tasking construct, we implemented it as a new clause for the OpenMP *task* directive. The proposed syntax for the clause is the following:

```
1 affinity([node | thread | data]: expr[, strict])
```

This proposal assumes the master thread with id 0 is executed on the first place in the place list. When *expr* refers to a thread id, it should refer to the thread id within the OMP_PLACES defined for the current team. For example, if the places for the current team are "$\{0\}, \{1\}, \{2\}$", thread with id 0 refers to "$\{0\}$". However, if the places are "$\{2\}, \{5\}, \{8\}$", thread with id 0 refers to "$\{2\}$".

When *expr* refers to a NUMA node id, it should refer to a node id within the set of NUMA nodes built from the OMP_PLACES list.

Two successive parallel regions with the same number of threads and the same places have the same set of NUMA nodes.

When *expr* refers to a data, it should be a memory address. If the NUMA node associated with the data can't be determined, it defaults to the first NUMA node of the team.

If *expr* refers to an out-of-bounds resource, the value is taken modulo the number of resources.

3.2   Extension of the OpenMP Runtime API Functions

In order to dynamically get information about the current team hierarchy, we also propose the following runtime API functions:

```
1 //Get the number of NUMA nodes in the team
2 omp_get_num_nodes(void);
3 //Get the NUMA node the task is currently executed on
4 omp_get_node_num(void);
5 //Get the NUMA node the data has been allocated on
6 omp_get_node_from_data(void *ptr);
```

These functions allow to query information about the hardware topology, and can only be called from inside a parallel region. On machines without NUMA support, we consider that all the threads are on a single NUMA node. In our proposed implementation, omp_get_node_from_data is implemented through Linux get_mempolicy interface.

We also added the following runtime API function that mimics the *affinity* clause:

```
1 //Set the affinity information to the next created
    tasks
2 omp_set_task_affinity(
3     omp_affinitykind_t k, uintptr_t ptr, int strict);
```

The scope of the function call is the next created task in the current *task region*. This function takes an omp_affinitykind_t value (either omp_affinity_thread, omp_affinity_numa or omp_affinity_data) to specify which kind of affinity control is applied. value is either an integer that represents an identifier of the NUMA node, an identifier of a thread or an address in the process address space used to select the affinity NUMA node **when** the task becomes ready for execution.

We implemented these extensions in the Clang compiler, based on the 3.8 version[1]; and we also added the corresponding entry points in Clang's OpenMP runtime[2].

Please note only the entry points have been implemented in Clang's OpenMP runtime, the actual runtime support has only been implemented in our OpenMP runtime and is described in the following section.

3.3   Extension of the Task Scheduler to Support Affinity

We implemented extensions in the OpenMP runtime developed in our team, LIBKOMP [3,5], which is based on the XKAAPI [1,9] runtime system. XKAAPI is a task-based runtime system, using workstealing as a general scheduling strategy. This section gives a brief description of some of its key internal structures and mechanisms.

The Way XKAAPI Models the Architecture. XKAAPI sees the architecture topology as a hierarchy of `locality domains`. A `locality domain` is a list of tasks associated with a subset of the machine processing units. XKAAPI's locality domains are very similar to the notion of *shepherd* introduced in [11], or ForestGOMP's *runqueues* [2]. XKAAPI most of the time only considers two levels of domains : node-level domains, which are bound to the set of processors contained in a NUMA node, and processor-level domains, which are bound to a single processor of the platform. This way, at the processor level one `locality domain` is associated with each of the physical cores, and at the NUMA node level, one `locality domain` is associated with each of the NUMA nodes.

The Way XKAAPI Enables Ready Tasks and Steals Them. The scheduling framework in XKAAPI [1,9] relies on virtual functions for *selecting a victim* and *selecting a place* to push a ready task. When a processor becomes idle, the runtime system calls a function to browse the topology to find a locality domain, and steal a task from its task queue.

Implementation of the Support for Affinity. We extended the set of internal control variables (ICV) with an *affinity-var* property, and provided some runtime API functions to get and to set this ICV. As ICVs are inherited from the generating implicit task of the parallel region to each task this region generates, *affinity-var* can be considered as a per-task variable. The variable is composed of two fields: an `omp_affinitykind_t` value and an integer large enough to encode a pointer.

When a task construct using the *affinity* clause is encountered, the runtime sets the appropriate kind of affinity and the integer value in the ICVs. During task creation, these parameters will be set in the internal task descriptor.

---

[1] https://github.com/viroulep/clang.
[2] https://github.com/viroulep/openmp.

When a task becomes ready to be executed, the function responsible for the *selection of the place* to push the task will look at the affinity and select the appropriate locality domain. The capacity to defer the evaluation of the affinity until the task becomes ready allows the runtime to rely on the get_mempolicy function to identify the NUMA node on which a data is allocated.

As described earlier, an affinity can be *strict* or not. To implement this we used a private queue per locality domain. If the affinity is strict, the task is pushed to the locality domain's private queue. During the *victim selection*, a thread may only steal from the locality domain's public queue (in case of a locality domain attached to a NUMA node, every thread on this node can steal from the private queue).

4   Examples of Use and Experimentation Results

In this section, we describe two OpenMP kernels we extended to make use of the *affinity* clause. We also give some details on the platform we used to conduct experiments, before presenting the performance evaluation of different versions of these two kernels.

4.1   Enhancing Task-Based OpenMP Kernels to Support *affinity*

This section presents how we expressed affinities inside the two task-based OpenMP kernels we described in Sect. 2.

Jacobi. We looked into our Jacobi application from the KASTORS benchmark suite [14]. The application is a 2D stencil computational kernel that is repeatedly applied until convergence is detected. We used a blocked version of this algorithm. We used both a *dependent tasks* based implementation and a *for* based implementation. Each operation on a point of the matrix depends on its neighboring blocks, therefore the blocks should be physically evenly distributed among the nodes, and the computational tasks should be located close to these data.

Knowing the number of cores in the team, the matrix size and the block size, we computed a mapping between multiple neighboring blocks and the different cores.

We used the affinity clause to achieve two goals:

- first, to ensure the physical distribution of the data during initialization: in the dependent tasks version, each memory block is touched for the first time in the initialization task, therefore pinning the task to a thread ensures the memory will be physically allocated on its NUMA node. Listing 1.1 shows an example of the blocks initialization.
- second, to ensure tasks stay close to their dependencies during computation, by putting them on their block's thread.

We implemented both a strict affinity and a non-strict affinity version.

Listing 1.1. Example of use of the affinity clause for initialization

```
1  for (j = 0; j < ny; j+= block_size)
2    for (i = 0; i < nx; i+= block_size) {
3      #pragma omp task firstprivate(i,j) private(ii,jj)\
4        affinity(thread:GET_PARTITION(i, j, block_size, nx, ny), 1)
5      {
6        for (jj=j; jj<j+block_size; ++jj)
7          for (ii=i; ii<i+block_size; ++ii) {
8            if (ii == 0 || ii == nx - 1 || jj == 0 || jj == ny - 1)
9              (*unew)[ii][jj] = (*f)[ii][jj];
10           else
11             (*unew)[ii][jj] = 0.0;
12         }
13     }
14   }
```

Sparse Matrix Vector Product. In this section, we present the *sparse matrix vector product* algorithms arising in the BiCGStab iterative algorithm. The main goal is to ensure that tasks will have local accesses to their data among the iterations. We split data following matrix graph partitioning techniques [13] while using automatic graph partitioner like Metis [7] tools.

In such a decomposition, a matrix A is split into several sub-domains of several rows: OpenMP independent tasks are responsible for computing sub-parts of the output vector. We ensure the task affinity using the common methodology in this paper: first data are allocated while taking care to evenly distribute them among the NUMA nodes while the workload is balanced among the cores; then we annotate tasks to constrain the scheduling.

To ensure an efficient data distribution on NUMA nodes, all the local data structures to a partition are allocated in parallel. Vectors are split following row permutations and splitting is dictated by partitions. Local parts of the vectors are distributed too (sparse matrix are stored in CSR format). Moreover, an output vector block associated with a part of the matrix is allocated on the same NUMA node than the partition itself.

The affinity of computational tasks are constrained by assigning them where partitions of the matrix are stored. This is very similar to the owner compute rule from HPF [8]: a task is mapped on the thread holding the output sub-vector $Y[i]$ (line 9 of Fig. 3(a)).

4.2 Experimental Platform Description

The machine we experimented on is an SGI UV2000 platform made of 24 NUMA nodes. Each NUMA node holds an 8-core Intel Xeon E5-4640 CPU for a total of 192 cores.

The memory topology is organized by pairs of NUMA nodes connected together through Intel QuickPath Interconnect. These pairs can communicate together through a proprietary fabric called NUMALink6 with up to two hops.

4.3   Experimental Results

Jacobi Kernel. We compared several blocked versions of the application with both the Clang's OpenMP runtime and the XKAAPI runtime. The *jacobi_block_for* version uses *for* constructs during initialization and computation, while the *jacobi_block_taskdep* version generates tasks with dependencies for initialization and computation. Each version comes with or without using the *affinity* extension we propose. We refer to these enhanced versions as *jacobi_block_for_affinity* and *jacobi_block_taskdep_affinity*. The last enhanced version is the *jacobi_block_taskdep_affinity_nonstrict*, which uses a strict initialization, but a non-strict affinity for tasks during computation.

The initialization part of the *jacobi_block_for_affinity* uses tasks instead of the regular *for* construct, so that we could use the affinity clause and precisely set which thread initialize which data. The computation part of the algorithm has not been changed, there is no affinity during the computation.

Matrix size and block sizes have been chosen so that partitioning easily match the number of threads up to 128. Experiments have been made with a block size of 1024 or 2048, and with a matrix size of 49152.

Base performances comparison between Clang's runtime and XKAAPI are available on Fig. 1 from Sect. 2.

Figure 2 focuses on results for XKAAPI used through LIBKOMP.

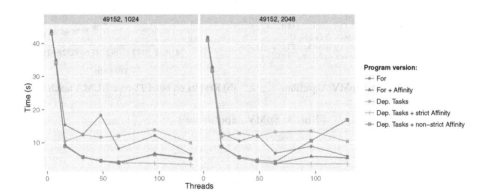

Fig. 2. Jacobi's performances overview using LIBKOMP, with a Matrix size of 49152, and blocksizes of 1024 or 2048

A general comment on these results is that the application globally does not scale well, whichever runtime or version is used. The program is memory bound and there is not much we can do besides ensuring computation occurs close to the data, in order to minimize the impact of memory bandwidth. In all these results, only the use of the *affinity* extension prevent a severe decrease in performances when increasing the number of threads.

The basic dependent *tasks* version offers really poor performances, the basic *for* version is a bit better but still has room for improvement. The two high

results for the *for* versions in Figs. 1 and 2 are obtained for a number of threads
of 48 and 96: these numbers are not powers of 2 (whereas all the other number
of threads are), and are not automatically perfectly mapped on the topology.
For these numbers the mapping of the blocks on the architecture is not a perfect
square, therefore each thread needs data from more neighbors, and a slight shift
in initial iterations placement leads to worse performances.

Interestingly, using a strict affinity during initialization is beneficial for both
for and *task* version: we can ensure a balanced mapping of the data over the
whole hierarchy, even with non-square numbers.

As described in Sect. 2, the Jacobi kernel is a stencil algorithm and is very
sensible to data locality and cache reuse. It explains why the version using dependent tasks with strict affinity achieves better performances than the non-strict
version, where tasks may be stolen from a remote node, therefore ruining the
cache reusability and the data locality (this is especially true with bigger blocks).

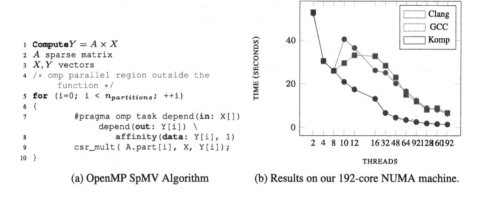

(a) OpenMP SpMV Algorithm   (b) Results on our 192-core NUMA machine.

Fig. 3. SpMV experiment

Sparse Matrix Vector Product (SpMV Operation). In our experiment,
500 iterations of SpMV operations are timed and the average times is reported in
Fig. 3(b) using various number of cores p. The matrix here corresponds to a Finite
Volume discretization of a 2D Laplace problem on a square mesh of size 2000×2000.
We run the same code compiled and executed with Clang-3.8 and its standard
OpenMP runtime (labeled Clang on Fig. 3), GCC-5.2 with libGOMP (GCC) and
our modified Clang-3.8 compiler with our OpenMP runtime libKOMP (Komp).

Up to 8 cores, all the execution times decrease in the same way for the three
configurations Clang, GCC and Komp: differences between them is not visible.
When the number of cores exceeds 8, Clang and GCC have execution times that
increase before to decrease with a growing number of cores. On our machine, a
NUMA node is composed of 8 cores. When $p > 8$ then the program has to use
several NUMA nodes. For both Clang and GCC this is due to the misplacement

of tasks on NUMA nodes where accessed memory is allocated. Data are split to fit on the local memory of each NUMA node. Vector are split into several parts, which are allocated on different NUMA nodes by using initialization tasks placement, relying on the OS first-touch policy. Matrices are split and also allocated by the use of initialization tasks so that it matches the same NUMA nodes on which the corresponding sub-vector has been allocated. Despite this tasks misplacement, the computation times are still decreasing because computations related to a domain are always done on the same core due to scheduling policies offered by Clang and GCC. XKAAPI obtains better results because of the use of affinity clauses to place tasks on specific NUMA nodes, which ensures the temporal affinity among the iterations.

5   Related Work

Many research projects have been carried out to improve the execution of OpenMP applications on NUMA machines.

The HPCTools group at the University of Houston has been working in this area for a long time, proposing compile-time techniques that can help improving memory affinity on hierarchical architectures like distributed shared memory platforms [10]. Huang et al. [6] proposed OpenMP extensions to deal with memory affinity on NUMA machines, like ways of explicitly aligning tasks and data inside logical partitions of the architecture called *locations*.

Drebes et al. [4] proposed scheduling techniques to control both the data placement and the task placement, in order to take advantage of the data locality. They implemented these techniques in dataflow programming model named OpenStream. Their approach is focused at a scheduler level and does not provide flexibility to the user regarding data placement.

Olivier et al. [12] introduced node-level queues of OpenMP tasks, called *locality domains*, to ensure tasks and data locality on NUMA systems. The runtime system does not maintain affinity information between tasks and data during execution. Data placement is implicitly obtained considering that the tasks access memory pages that were allocated using the *first-touch* allocation policy. The authors thus ensure locality by always scheduling a task on the same locality domain, preventing application programmers to experiment with other memory bindings.

The INRIA Runtime group at the University of Bordeaux proposed the ForestGOMP runtime system [2] that comes with an API to express affinities between OpenMP parallel regions and dynamically allocated data. ForestGOMP implements load balancing of nested OpenMP parallel regions by moving branches of the corresponding tree of user-level threads on a hierarchical way. Memory affinity information is gathered at runtime and can be taken into account when performing load balancing.

6   Conclusion

OpenMP 4.0 introduced dependent tasks, which give the programmer a way to express fine grain parallelism that can be dynamically mapped to the architecture topology at runtime. Controlling data locality is one of the keys to performance when targeting NUMA architectures, and on this topic, OpenMP does not provide a lot of flexibility to the programmer yet, which leaves the responsibility to the runtime to make choices regarding tasks placements.

In this paper, we presented a class of applications which would benefit from having such a control and flexibility over tasks and data placement.

We proposed an implementation of a new *affinity* clause for the *task* directive, based on the discussion within the OpenMP language committees. It enables the programmer to give hints to the runtime about tasks placement during the program execution. These hints, combined with NUMA's first touch policy for memory, can be used to control the data mapping. The programmer can express affinity between a task and the following resources: a thread, a NUMA node, and a data.

We implemented this proposal in the Clang-3.8 compiler, and implemented the corresponding extensions in our OpenMP runtime LIBKOMP.

Finally, we performed a preliminary evaluation of this work running two task-based OpenMP kernels on a 192-core NUMA architecture, that showed noticeable improvements both in terms on performance and scalability.

In future, our focus will move to compile-time techniques able to infer and attach valuable information to tasks, like an estimation of a task operational intensity, that could guide some of the runtime system's decisions regarding task scheduling, load balancing, and data placement. We strongly believe a tight cooperation between the compiler and the runtime system is a key step to enhance the performance and scalability of task-based programs on large-scale platforms.

Acknowledgments. This work is integrated and supported by the ELCI project, a French FSN ("Fond pour la Société Numérique") project that associates academic and industrial partners to design and provide a software environment for very high performance computing.

References

1. Bleuse, R., Gautier, T., Lima, J.V.F., Mounié, G., Trystram, D.: Scheduling data flow program in XKaapi: a new affinity based algorithm for heterogeneous architectures. In: Silva, F., Dutra, I., Santos Costa, V. (eds.) Euro-Par 2014 Parallel Processing. LNCS, vol. 8632, pp. 560–571. Springer, Heidelberg (2014)
2. Broquedis, F., Furmento, N., Goglin, B., Wacrenier, P.-A., Namyst, R.: Forest-GOMP: an efficient OpenMP environment for NUMA architectures. Int. J. Parallel Programm. **38**(5), 418–439 (2010)
3. Broquedis, F., Gautier, T., Danjean, V.: LIBKOMP, an efficient OpenMP runtime system for both fork-join and data flow paradigms. In: Chapman, B.M., Massaioli, F., Müller, M.S., Rorro, M. (eds.) IWOMP 2012. LNCS, vol. 7312, pp. 102–115. Springer, Heidelberg (2012)

4. Drebes, A., Heydemann, K., Drach, N., Pop, A., Cohen, A.: Topology-aware and dependence-aware scheduling and memory allocation for task-parallel languages. ACM Trans. Archit. Code Optim. **11**(3), 30:1–30:25 (2014). Special Issue on OpenMP; Müller, M.S., Ayguade, E. (eds.)
5. Durand, M., Broquedis, F., Gautier, T., Raffin, B.: OpenMP in the Era of Low Power Devices and Accelerators, pp. 141–155. Springer, Berlin, Heidelberg (2013)
6. Huang, L., Jin, H., Yi, L., Chapman, B.: Enabling locality-aware computations in openmp. Sci. Program. **18**(3–4), 169–181 (2010)
7. Karypis, G., Kumar, V.: A fast and high quality multilevel scheme for partitioning irregular graphs. SIAM J. Sci. Comput. **20**(1), 359–392 (1998)
8. Kennedy, K., Koelbel, C., Zima, H.: The rise and fall of high performance fortran: an historical object lesson. In: Proceedings of the Third ACM SIGPLAN Conference on History of Programming Languages, HOPL III, pp. 7-1-7-22. ACM, New York (2007)
9. Lima, J.V.F., Gautier, T., Danjean, V., Raffin, B., Maillard, N.: Design and analysis of scheduling strategies for multi-CPU and multi-GPU architectures. Parallel Comput. **44**, 37–52 (2015)
10. Marowka, A., Liu, Z., Chapman, B.: Openmp-oriented applications for distributed shared memory architectures: research articles. Concurr. Comput. Pract. Exper. **16**, 371–384 (2004)
11. Olivier, S., Porterfield, A., Wheeler, K.B., Spiegel, M., Prins, J.F.: Openmp task scheduling strategies for multicore NUMA systems. IJHPCA **26**(2), 110–124 (2012)
12. Olivier, S.L., de Supinski, B.R., Schulz, M., Prins, J.F.: Characterizing and mitigating work time inflation in task parallel programs. In: Proceedings of the International Conference on High Performance Computing, Networking, Storage and Analysis, SC 2012 (2012)
13. Saad, Y.: Iterative Methods for Sparse Linear Systems. Society for Industrial and Applied Mathematics, 2nd edn. SIAM, Philadelphia (2003)
14. Virouleau, P., Brunet, P., Broquedis, F., Furmento, N., Thibault, S., Aumage, O., Gautier, T.: Evaluation of OpenMP dependent tasks with the KASTORS benchmark suite. In: DeRose, L., Supinski, B.R., Olivier, S.L., Chapman, B.M., Müller, M.S. (eds.) IWOMP 2014. LNCS, vol. 8766, pp. 16–29. Springer, Heidelberg (2014)

Task Parallelism

NUMA-Aware Task Performance Analysis

Dirk Schmidl[1,2,3(✉)] and Matthias S. Müller[1,2,3]

[1] IT Center, RWTH Aachen University,
52074 Aachen, Germany
{schmidl,mueller}@itc.rwth-aachen.de
[2] Chair for High Performance Computing, RWTH Aachen University,
52074 Aachen, Germany
[3] JARA - High-Performance Computing,
Schinkelstraße 2, 52062 Aachen, Germany

Abstract. The tasking feature enriches OpenMP by a method to express parallelism in a more general way than before, as it can be applied to loops but also to recursive algorithms without the need of nested parallel regions. However, the performance of a tasking program is very much influenced by the task scheduling inside the OpenMP runtime. Especially on large NUMA systems and when tasks work on shared data structures which are split across NUMA nodes, the runtime influence is significant. For a programmer there is no easy way to examine these performance relevant decisions taken by the runtime, neither with functionality provided by OpenMP nor with external performance tools. Therefore, we will present a method based on the Score-P measurement infrastructure which allows to analyze task parallel programs on NUMA systems more deeply, allowing the user to see if tasks were executed by the creating thread or remotely on the same or a different socket. Exemplary the Intel and the GNU Compiler were used to execute the same task parallel code, where a performance difference of 8x could be observed, mainly due to task scheduling. We evaluate the presented method by investigating both execution runs and highlight the differences of the task scheduling applied.

1 Introduction

In 2007 OpenMP was extended by a new way to express parallelism through tasks. A task is an independent chunk of work in combination with an own data environment. In OpenMP tasks are executed by threads of the current team. Which thread executes which tasks is up to the OpenMP runtime and by now OpenMP offers no way for a programmer to have influence on this decision. Furthermore, there is no way for a programmer to get information about the scheduling done by the runtime.

In former work we investigated the behavior of different OpenMP runtime systems and their scheduling techniques (see [14,15] for details). It turned out, that the scheduling of tasks to threads can be extremely relevant for application performance especially on non uniform memory access (NUMA) machines.

© Springer International Publishing Switzerland 2016
N. Maruyama et al. (Eds.): IWOMP 2016, LNCS 9903, pp. 77–88, 2016.
DOI: 10.1007/978-3-319-45550-1_6

Furthermore, we found that a programmer can have indirect influence on the scheduling for some runtimes, like the Intel OpenMP runtime, by letting threads create tasks which they should preferably execute. This way of task creation is called `parallel-producer multiple-executor` pattern, since all threads create tasks in parallel and then also execute them in parallel.

Since in these cases the application performance is dependent on the scheduling done by the OpenMP runtime, it is highly desirable from a programmer's perspective to be able to observe the scheduling behavior in detail for performance analysis. We investigated the general ability of performance tools to analyze OpenMP task parallel programs in [13]. It turned out, that performance tools can deliver a lot of information for tasking programs, but no tool delivers an easy way to understand the impact of scheduling decisions done by the runtime on NUMA architectures.

Therefore, in this work we will present an approach to address this issue. Based on the Score-P performance measurement infrastructure [5] we implemented a method to combine a standard OTF2 event trace with hardware information of the system about memory nodes and with information about thread pinning. This allows to investigate if tasks were executed by the creating thread or if they were executed by a different thread. Furthermore we can analyze if the different thread was running on the same or a different NUMA node, which is useful information in case the task accesses data resident on the local NUMA node.

The rest of this work is structured as follows: First, we present related work in Sect. 2 before we will recap relevant information from our work on NUMA-aware task programming in Sect. 3, including an extended version of the benchmark we used to analyze the tasking behavior of different runtime systems. Then we present out method to analyze the tasking performance in a NUMA-aware manner in Sect. 4 and an evaluation is presented in Sect. 5. Finally, we draw our conclusions in Sect. 6.

2   Related Work

The concept of tasks [1] has been added in OpenMP 3.0 [9]. As was shown by Ayguadé et al. tasking is able to deliver comparable performance to OpenMP worksharing implementations [2]. This early performance comparison did not focus on multi-core multi-socket (NUMA) machines, but several others investigated this issue. Olivier et al. [8] and Broquedis et al. [3] both deal with the efficient scheduling of OpenMP tasks on NUMA systems. Our previous work [14,15] in contrast did not aim at changes to the scheduling, but tried to use the given scheduling mechanism which became common practice in OpenMP in the most efficient way on NUMA systems.

Performance analysis of task parallel programs is meanwhile possible with many different tools. We investigated the ability of a subset of these tools in [13]. Sampling based tools like the Intel VTune Amplifier [4] or the Oracle Solaris Studio Analyzer [10] can be used to gather a statistical overview of the execution of a task parallel program. These tools allow to identify execution time in tasks and also overhead spend in the OpenMP runtime to manage tasks or idle time because no tasks are available. But, they do not allow to identify an individual task instance in the analysis and also data on the scheduling is not presented. Event based tools like the measurement system Score-P in combination with visualization tools like the profile browser Cube [11] or the event trace visualization tool Vampir [7] allow to investigate the same information than the sampling based tools, but with a higher measurement overhead for fine grained tasks. Furthermore these tools allow to identify task instances which allows for individual tasks to locate the creation and execution region in a trace file manually. With this information the scheduling can be analyzed, but for hundreds or thousands of tasks in an application run, this leads to an enormous amount of manual work. Therefore, we will present an automated method to ease this analysis in the next sections of this work.

3   NUMA-Aware Task Creation

The performance analysis techniques presented in this work are useful under different circumstances. The major requirement is, that a programmer has created the tasks in a NUMA-aware manner. What exactly is understood under NUMA-aware in this context is wrapped up in this section and is basically a recap of the work we presented in [14, 15].

3.1   Task Scheduling in OpenMP

As mentioned before, OpenMP does not specify exactly how the runtime should schedule tasks. Even not scheduling them at all and just executing all tasks immediately would be legal according to the specification. But of course this would not lead to additional parallelism in the application and a user would be unsatisfied by the implementation. So, in the past eight years, since tasking was added to OpenMP, different scheduling mechanisms have emerged. The most relevant difference with respect to NUMA-aware scheduling is, if tasks are queued after creation in one central task queue or if they are queued in thread local task queues.

Figure 1 illustrates both approaches. On the left side a central task queue is shown. Here all threads enqueue tasks into one queue and also dequeue tasks from this data structure. On the right side of the figure thread local task queues are shown. Here, every thread has an own queue where it enqueues tasks. Every thread can also dequeue tasks from its own queue, but it can also dequeue tasks from other queues. This is then called *task stealing*. Typically stealing is only performed if the local queue is empty, since it involves more overhead.

The Intel compiler (v. 15.0) uses thread local task queues, whereas the GCC (v.4.9) compiler uses a central queue. Therefore, these compilers are used for all later experiments as representatives for one or the other approach.

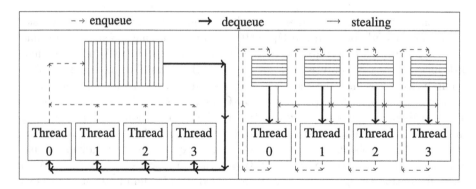

Fig. 1. Illustration of a central task queue used by four threads (left) and thread-local task queues for four threads (right).

3.2 Task Creation

NUMA-aware programming typically has to handle:

- The mapping of threads to cores on specific NUMA nodes.
- The mapping of data to NUMA nodes.
- The mapping of *work items* to threads. Work items in this context can be for example loop iterations, OpenMP sections or tasks.

The goal for NUMA-aware programming is then to execute work items by threads which run on the NUMA node where the data is located which is needed to process this work item.

Regarding the first issue, OpenMP offers support for thread pinning which allow to influence the mapping of threads to cores in any desired way. For the data mapping no support exists in OpenMP, but all common operating systems in HPC use the so called `first-touch` memory allocation policy. This policy means, that data is located on the NUMA node where it is first used. By parallel data initialization this can be used to achieve most desired mappings of data to NUMA nodes. For the mapping of work items to threads in some cases support exists, e.g. for parallel loops with a static schedule clause. But, as mentioned above, when tasks are used, the mapping of tasks to threads cannot directly be influenced by the programmer and any scheduling of tasks to threads is valid according to the specification.

In [14,15] we investigated the scheduling of tasks for different task creation patterns and for different compilers. It turned out, that the implementation of thread local task queues can be used on NUMA systems to maintain data locality to a certain amount. When the `parallel-producer multiple-executor` pattern is used, i.e. tasks are created and executed in parallel by all threads of a team, every thread fills its own local task queue. During execution all threads will then first pick tasks out of their own task queue until this queue is empty. After the queue is empty, they will start task stealing. If the programmer creates tasks by the thread which also initialized the data needed in this tasks, this results in a situation where all threads have a task queue filled with tasks which need local data. After a thread executed all tasks of its own task queue, it will start task stealing and execute tasks on remote data, if the task is stolen from a remote NUMA node's thread. But, this situation means, that no local data needs to be processed anymore, since the local queue is empty. In this case it is better to execute remote tasks than doing nothing.

3.3   Benchmark Evaluation

To highlight the performance relevance of tasking implementations under these circumstances we used a synthetic benchmark program. The benchmark emulates a situation where:

- Many work items need to be processed which all work on separate data.
- The needed data is distributed already over the NUMA nodes of the system.
- The amount of data to process on each NUMA node is different, so there is a load imbalance problem. (If no load imbalance would exist, a loop worksharing construct with a static schedule would be preferred over tasks.)

The benchmark is designed in the following way: A set of work packages (WP) to execute is created (3840 in this case). Each WP performs a vector addition as operation, where all WPs use different vectors. The size of the vectors increases

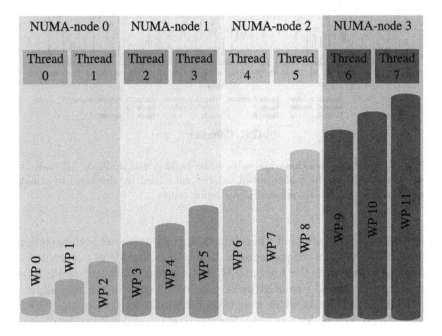

Fig. 2. Distribution of work packages (WPs) across NUMA nodes for the load balancing benchmark. Exemplary for 12 work packages (WPs) on a machine with 8 threads and 4 NUMA nodes.

linearly from the first to the last work package, resulting in a load imbalance. The vectors are distributed across the NUMA nodes evenly, i.e. the first $\frac{|WPs|}{|NUMAnodes|}$ vectors are located in NUMA node 0, the second $\frac{|WPs|}{|NUMAnodes|}$ vectors in NUMA node 1 and so on. Figure 2 illustrates the setup exemplary for a system with eight threads and four NUMA nodes and for 12 WPs to be scheduled.

During the benchmark execution the time to execute all work packages is measured individually. Furthermore we create a `firstprivate` variable for each task which is used to store the creating thread of the task. During execution of the task we use this information to find out if task stealing was applied or not.

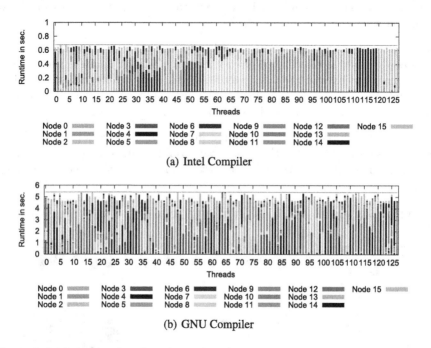

Fig. 3. Load balancing benchmark results when tasking was applied. All tasks were created by the thread which also initialized the data used by the task, to maintain locality for thread-local task queues. (Color figure online)

Figure 3 shows the results of a benchmark run on a 16-socket system equipped with Intel Xeon X7550 8-core processors. In total 128 threads were executed and the tests were done with the Intel and GNU Compiler. Each bar stands for the execution time a thread executed tasks. The colors used in the bars illustrate where the data of the tasks which were executed was located. One color for every one of the 16 NUMA nodes was used. For the Intel Compiler it can be observed, that threads with a higher ID execute mainly tasks of one color, the color of the local NUMA node. Threads with a smaller ID execute less local work and steal from different other NUMA nodes. This is because they have less data to process and after all local work was executed they start stealing tasks. When the GNU compiler is used all threads execute tasks of many different colors. This is because of the centralized task queue which cannot be used for locality aware task creation as mentioned above. The overall execution time with the GNU compiler is about 8 times higher compared to the Intel compiler. This gives evidence, that task scheduling, also it is done internally in the runtime can have a high influence on the execution of a program, so it would be good if the programmer can observe it with performance tools.

4   Task Performance Analysis

The work presented here is based on a former publication [6], where we have shown how the performance measurement system Score-P can be extended to allow event-based performance analysis of task parallel programs. This allowed us to identify different task related performance issues, like too finely or coarsely grained tasks as shown in [12]. But, it does not enable us to identify the NUMA related issues mentioned above for the following reasons.

4.1   Gathered Data

The information desirable for the analysis if tasks are executed locally or on a remote NUMA node are:

1. Information about the hardware topology, i.e. which cores are on which NUMA node.
2. Information which thread is running on which core.
3. The start and end time of every tasks execution.
4. Information which thread executed which tasks.
5. Information which thread created which tasks.

The OTF2 trace as described in [6] contains information about the start and end time of every task (3) and also information which thread executed the task (4). The second information is implicit, since the begin and end event of the task are located in the event trace of only one thread, the one which executed the task. To get information which thread created a task (5), it is necessary to have IDs for all task instances. Such IDs are not provided by OpenMP, but in [6] we presented a method to store task local IDs in a mixture of variables `private` to a task and `threadprivate` variables. These IDs are stored with every begin and end event in the OTF2 trace. Furthermore, we used the thread ID of the creating thread of a task as prefix in the task ID. This allowed us to create tasks in parallel with unique IDs without the need to synchronize between threads, as all tasks which might be created in parallel are created by different threads and thus get a different prefix for their ID. Now, we can extract this information at task begin and end events out of the task ID to obtain information (5). The information which cores belong to which NUMA node (1) of the system is static information which can be extracted before the program run from the Linux

OS. E.g. the command line tool numactl lists all cores of a NUMA node in a system. The information which thread is running on which core (2) must not be constant over the complete program run for all applications. If thread binding is not used at all, the OS might migrate threads at any time. If thread binding is used and different affinity clauses are used for different parallel regions, this also leads to changes in the mapping of threads to cores. However, in practice the majority of programs sets a fixed affinity policy, e.g. using the environment variable OMP_PROC_BIND and stick to this mapping for the whole application run. In such cases the mapping can easily be queried in the application and used later on for the analysis of the complete OTF2 trace file of a thread.

4.2 Data Analysis

To be able to visualize the gathered data in a user friendly way, we implemented a post processing tool to combine all gathered data in a new OTF2 trace file. This file can than be visualized in the Vampir GUI [7] for analysis.

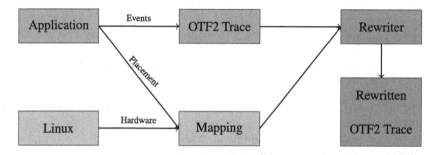

Fig. 4. Workflow of the trace rewriter tool to use hardware information to analyze NUMA related task scheduling issues.

Figure 4 illustrates the workflow for the post processing tool. During the application run the Score-P measurement infrastructure is used to generate an OTF2 trace of the application run. As usual, the trace contains begin and end events for all functions and also OpenMP events, like tasks. Every event also contains a timestamp. Also the mapping of threads to cores is written to a file during execution of the application. Furthermore hardware information on the system topology is added to this file.

After gathering this information the *Rewriter* tool reads the information on the hardware topology and the thread mapping. Then the tool reads in the original OTF2 trace and writes out a new modified trace file. If an event is not related to a task, it is copied to the new trace. If an event is a task begin event, the tool checks if the task was created by the current thread, a remote thread on the same socket or a remote thread of a different socket of the system. Furthermore, the tool adds three groups for tasks, local, same socket and remote socket. In the modified trace file tasks are sorted into these groups, depending on the location of the creating thread. On a runtime system with thread local queues, this allows to distinguish if the task was stolen from a different queue or not during the analysis with Vampir later on.

5   Evaluation

Finally, we evaluate the analysis technique with the help of the benchmark presented in Sect. 3.3. We executed the benchmark once compiled with the Intel and once with the GCC compiler on a 4 socket server with 8-core Intel Xeon X7550 processors. Remember, we observed a 8x performance difference between both versions.

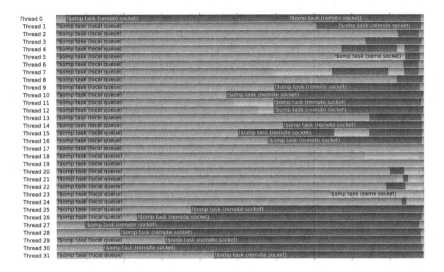

Fig. 5. Vampir screenshot showing the tasks during the execution of the load balancing benchmark with the Intel runtime. Tasks executed on the creating thread ar shown in green, stolen tasks from the same NUMA-node in orange and from remote NUMA-nodes in red. (Color figure online)

Figure 5 shows a Vampir timeline view of the execution done with the Intel compiler and Fig. 6 shows the execution using the GCC compiler. It can be observed, that the behavior with the Intel compiler is as desired. First all threads work on local (green) tasks. After some time, when no more local tasks are available, threads start doing task stealing and work on remote tasks, either on the same socket (orange) or on remote sockets (red).

With the GCC compiler and the centralized task queue, the picture is completely different. During the complete execution of the benchmark a mixture of red, orange and green tasks can be observed. But, on the very beginning, many threads also start with local (green) tasks. This is because all tasks are created

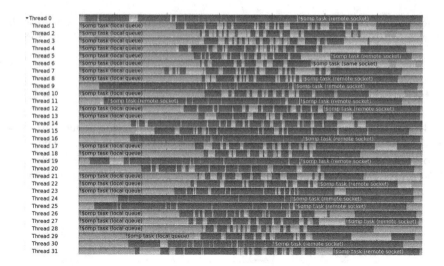

Fig. 6. Vampir screenshot showing the tasks during the execution of the load balancing benchmark with the GNU runtime. Tasks executed on the creating thread ar shown in green, stolen tasks from the same NUMA-node in orange and from remote NUMA-nodes in red. Comparing this figure to Fig. 5, a huge difference in the way tasks are scheduled in the GNU and Intel runtime can be observed. (Color figure online)

at the beginning, filling the task queue. Once the task queue exceeds a certain limit it is full and no more tasks can be queued. Then all threads execute the tasks directly instead of putting it into the queue and this of course leads to local task execution.

Overall, there are many more red tasks with the GCC compiler, which means tasks are executed by threads on different sockets than the creator of the task. Since we created the tasks with the same thread which initialized the data needed in the task, this means the executing task is also on a different socket than the data needed. So, a lot of remote memory accesses occur under these circumstances which explains the worse performance with the GNU compiler compared to the Intel compiler.

The presented technique to group the tasks in the OTF2 tracefile based on the topology information is very helpful to understand and explain performance characteristics of the benchmark program for different OpenMP runtime systems. It presents an easy to understand overview in the Vampir GUI and allow users a deeper understanding of internal task scheduling done in the OpenMP runtime. This information is helpful for application developers who want to optimize their tasking applications on NUMA systems.

6 Conclusion

Task scheduling decisions taken by the OpenMP runtime can have a high influence on the performance of task parallel programs, particularly on large NUMA systems and when the tasks work on data already distributed across the system. We summarized previous work how NUMA aware task parallel programming can be achieved for OpenMP runtime systems working with thread local task queues. Furthermore, we presented a benchmark test to evaluate the performance difference of two runtime systems, the one from Intel and the other one from GNU as examples for runtime systems with thread local queues or a centralized queue, respectively. It turned out, that on a 16-socket NUMA machine, a performance difference of 8x was observed.

To allow users understanding such a situation in a real application code, support in performance tools is desirable. Therefore, we presented a method how standard OTF2 trace data can be combined with information on the system topology and thread placement to do an in-depth analysis of the runtime scheduling with a focus on NUMA nodes. We write topology information from the system as well as information about the thread placement into a log file. Furthermore, we measure a standard OTF2 trace with Score-P during execution. Then a post processing tool was developed to combines both information and produces a trace file where tasks are grouped in either locally executed tasks, tasks executed on the same socket as the creator and tasks executed on a remote socket. As shown during the evaluation the newly generated trace can be visualized with the Vampir GUI and contains a useful overview of the tasks executed in these different groups.

As future work, this approach could be integrated into the Score-P infrastructure directly. All information needed about the system can be gathered at the application start allowing to do the grouping at runtime. This would also allow to support situations where thread pinning is changed over runtime, e.g. by different `affinity` clauses used during execution. In such circumstances it is necessary to keep track of the thread to core mapping which is easy at runtime but hard in a post processing tool.

Acknowledgement. This work was funded by the German Federal Ministry of Research and Education (BMBF) under Grant Number 01IH13001D(Score-E).

References

1. Ayguadé, E., Copty, N., Duran, A., Hoeflinger, J., Lin, Y., Massaioli, F., Teruel, X., Unnikrishnan, P., Zhang, G.: The Design of OpenMP Tasks. IEEE Trans. Parallel Distrib. Syst. **20**(3), 404–418 (2009)
2. Ayguadé, E., Duran, A., Hoeflinger, J.P., Massaioli, F., Teruel, X.: An experimental evaluation of the new OpenMP tasking model. In: Adve, V., Garzarán, M.J., Petersen, P. (eds.) LCPC 2007. LNCS, vol. 5234, pp. 63–77. Springer, Heidelberg (2008)
3. Broquedis, F., Furmento, N., Goglin, B., Wacrenier, P.-A., Namyst, R.: Forest-GOMP: an efficient OpenMP environment for NUMA architectures. Int. J. Parallel Programm. **38**, 418–439 (2010). doi:10.1007/s10766-010-0136-3
4. Intel: Intel VTune Amplifier XE. http://software.intel.com/en-us/intel-vtune-amplifier-xe. Accessed 24 May 2016

5. Knüpfer, A., Rössel, C., an Mey, D., Biersdorff, S., Diethelm, K., Eschweiler, D., Geimer, M., Gerndt, M., Lorenz, D., Malony, A.D., Nagel, W.E., Oleynik, Y., Philippen, P., Saviankou, P., Schmidl, D., Shende, S.S., Tschüter, R., Wagner, M., Wesarg, B., Wolf, F.: Score-P - a joint performance measurement run-time infrastructure for periscope, Scalasca, TAU, and Vampir. In: Proceedings of 5th Parallel Tools Workshop, Dresden, Germany, September 2011

6. Lorenz, D., Mohr, B., Rössel, C., Schmidl, D., Wolf, F.: How to reconcile event-based performance analysis with tasking in OpenMP. In: Sato, M., Hanawa, T., Müller, M.S., Chapman, B.M., Supinski, B.R. (eds.) IWOMP 2010. LNCS, vol. 6132, pp. 109–121. Springer, Heidelberg (2010)

7. Nagel, W., Weber, M., Hoppe, H.-C., Solchenbach, K.: VAMPIR: visualization and analysis of MPI resources. Supercomputer 12(1), 69–80 (1996)

8. Olivier, S.L., Porterfield, A.K., Wheeler, K.B., Prins, J.F.: Scheduling task parallelism on multi-socket multicore systems. In: Proceedings of the 1st International Workshop on Runtime and Operating Systems for Supercomputers, ROSS 2011, pp. 49–56. ACM, New York (2011)

9. OpenMP ARB: OpenMP Application Program Interface, v. 3.0. http://www.open mp.org/mp-documents/spec30.pdf. Accessed 24 May 2016

10. Oracle: Oracle Solaris Studio 12.2: Performance Analyzer. http://docs.oracle.com/cd/E18659_01/html/821-1379/. Accessed 24 May 2016

11. Saviankou, P., Knobloch, M., Visser, A., Mohr, B.: Cube v4: from performance report explorer to performance analysis tool. Proc. Comput. Sci. 51, 1343–1352 (2015)

12. Schmidl, D., Philippen, P., Lorenz, D., Rössel, C., Geimer, M., an Mey, D., Mohr, B., Wolf, F.: Performance analysis techniques for task-based OpenMP applications. In: Chapman, B.M., Massaioli, F., Müller, M.S., Rorro, M. (eds.) IWOMP 2012. LNCS, vol. 7312, pp. 196–209. Springer, Heidelberg (2012)

13. Schmidl, D., Terboven, C., an Mey, D., Müller, M.S.: Suitability of performance tools for OpenMP task-parallel programs. In: Knüpfer, A., Gracia, J., Nagel, W.E., Resch, M.M. (eds.) Tools for High Performance Computing 2013, pp. 25–37. Springer International Publishing, Basel (2013)

14. Terboven, C., Schmidl, D., Cramer, T., an Mey, D.: Assessing OpenMP tasking implementations on NUMA architectures. In: Chapman, B.M., Massaioli, F., Müller, M.S., Rorro, M. (eds.) IWOMP 2012. LNCS, vol. 7312, pp. 182–195. Springer, Heidelberg (2012). doi:10.1007/978-3-642-30961-8_14

15. Terboven, C., Schmidl, D., Cramer, T., an Mey, D.: Task-parallel programming on NUMA architectures. In: Kaklamanis, C., Papatheodorou, T., Spirakis, P.G. (eds.) Euro-Par 2012. LNCS, vol. 7484, pp. 638–649. Springer, Heidelberg (2012). doi:10.1007/978-3-642-32820-6_63

OpenMP Extension for Explicit Task Allocation on NUMA Architecture

Jinpil Lee[1]([✉]), Keisuke Tsugane[2], Hitoshi Murai[1], and Mitsuhisa Sato[1]

[1] RIKEN Advanced Institute for Computational Science, Kobe, Japan
{jinpil.lee,h-murai,msato}@riken.jp
[2] University of Tsukuba, Tsukuba, Japan
tsugane@hpcs.cs.tsukuba.ac.jp

Abstract. Most modern HPC systems consist of a number of cores grouped into multiple NUMA nodes. The latest Intel processors have multiple NUMA nodes inside a chip. Task parallelism using OpenMP dependent tasks is a promising programming model for many-core architecture because it can exploit parallelism in irregular applications with fine-grain synchronization. However, the current specification lacks functionality to improve data locality in task parallelism. In this paper, we propose an extension for the OpenMP task construct to specify the location of tasks to exploit the locality in an explicit manner. The prototype compiler is implemented based on GCC. The performance evaluation using the KASTORS benchmark shows that our approach can reduce remote page access. The Jacobi kernel using our approach shows 3.6 times better performance than GCC when using 36 threads on a 36-core, 4-NUMA node machine.

Keywords: OpenMP · Task parallelism · NUMA optimization

1 Introduction

Many-core architecture is widely used in High Performance Computing (HPC) since increasing the number of cores is an efficient way to build an energy efficient processor. Along with the trend, Non-Uniform Memory Access (NUMA) architecture has been introduced to provide high memory bandwidth. Modern CPU architecture has multiple NUMA nodes inside a chip (e.g. the latest Xeon processors with the Cluster-On-Die (COD) technology). We expect that this trend will continue and many HPC systems will have many-core processors with multiple NUMA nodes.

OpenMP has been the de facto standard for thread-level parallel programming. In the early version of OpenMP, the programming model had focused on data parallelism described by loop work sharing, which requires global synchronization in a parallel region. When the number of cores increases, synchronization overhead is getting bigger, and load imbalance among cores causes a significant performance drop. Dynamic task generation was introduced in OpenMP 3.0.

© Springer International Publishing Switzerland 2016
N. Maruyama et al. (Eds.): IWOMP 2016, LNCS 9903, pp. 89–101, 2016.
DOI: 10.1007/978-3-319-45550-1_7

In OpenMP 4.0, task dependency can be specified using the depend clause in the task construct. Task parallelism can exploit potential parallelism in irregular applications. Task dependency can reduce synchronization overhead because it generates fine-grain synchronization between dependent tasks.

To exploit memory bandwidth with the NUMA architecture, OpenMP provides thread affinity options through environment variables such as OMP_PROC_BIND. For OpenMP 4.5, the proc_bind clause is discussed to specify a thread affinity scheme for a parallel region. These can be helpful to improve data locality when performing data parallelism with loop work sharing. However, the current specification lacks functionality to do the same thing for task parallelism. A task can be tied to any thread in the parallel region. It will cause unexpected remote page access across the NUMA interconnection.

The aim of our research is to find an explicit way of improving data locality in OpenMP tasks for the NUMA architecture. In this paper, we propose an OpenMP extension to describe NUMA-aware task allocation explicitly. The extension specifies the data that the target task would access. Our compiler implementation, based on GCC, determines the NUMA node that the specified data is allocated and schedules the task to the node. The programmer can distribute data and tasks among NUMA nodes in the same manner by combining our extension and NUMA APIs. This approach can reduce remote memory access and improve memory performance.

The rest of the paper is organized as follows: Sect. 2 show related works about task parallelism and data locality optimization for the NUMA architecture using OpenMP. In Sect. 3, we propose a new clause for the task construct, which gives a hint about how to schedule tasks on the NUMA architecture. Our prototype implementation based on GNU Compiler Collection (GCC) is explained in the section. In Sect. 4, we introduce the new clause into KASTORS benchmark kernels to improve data locality of tasks. In Sect. 5, the benchmark kernels are evaluated using GCC and our implementation to show how much performance improvement can be achieved by our approach. Finally, we discuss the future work and conclude the paper and in Sect. 6.

2   Related Work

Barcelona OpenMP Task Suite (BOTS) [1,3] consists of several benchmark kernels exploiting tasks in OpenMP 3.0. The KASTORS benchmark suite (KASTORS) [4] developed by Inria is inspired by BOTS. The major difference between BOTS and KASTORS is that KASTORS utilize the task depend clause in OpenMP 4.0 to exploit dependency between tasks. Virouleau et al. [10] showed that fine-grain task dependencies can replace global synchronization of all tasks in a parallel region and improve the scalability of task parallelism in OpenMP.

The NUMA-aware task scheduler has been studied extensively [2,6–9]. Most of them focus on work-stealing algorithms in runtime to handle recursive algorithms. Muddukrishna et al. [5] showed that manual data distribution among NUMA nodes and their NUMA-aware task scheduling algorithm in runtime can improve the parallel performance. This approach is similar to ours since our approach also requires explicit data distribution. However, task allocation is done explicitly using the extended OpenMP task construct in our approach.

3 OpenMP Extension for NUMA-Aware Task Allocation

The NUMA architecture, as its name suggests, provides non-uniform memory performance, which depends on the distance between a memory location and a core. Generally, improving data locality and reducing remote memory access can exploit potential memory performance on the NUMA architecture. The same is true for task parallelism in OpenMP. A task should be executed on the NUMA node where its processing data is allocated to get the highest memory bandwidth. In this section, we propose a new clause named node_bind for the OpenMP task construct. It specifies a NUMA node that the target task should be scheduled.

3.1 Overview

Figure 1 shows the conceptual model of our approach. The software system consists of multiple task queues connected to each NUMA node respectively. Assume that an application generates a number of OpenMP task which carries out computations on a single element of array A. The figure shows how tasks and data can be allocated on NUMA nodes and matched with the help of information given by the programmer.

First, the programmer distributes the array among NUMA nodes by using existing NUMA libraries such as libnuma. Then the programmer describes OpenMP tasks with a hint about which element would be accessed in the task.

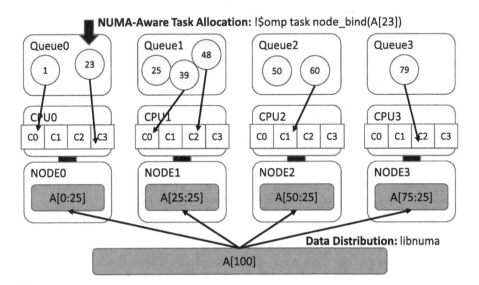

Fig. 1. NUMA-aware data distribution and task allocation

The node_bind clause used in the task construct, which we propose in this paper, gives the information to the OpenMP compiler and runtime. The OpenMP compiler can determine the node id that the specified element is allocated. The OpenMP runtime utilizes it to schedule the task to the corresponding task queue. In our implementation, a group of cores connected to the same NUMA node has a higher priority to access the corresponding task queue than others so that the cores would have more chance to access the local memory. This approach provides an explicit way of improving data locality in tasks by combining explicit data distribution.

3.2 Language Definition

Listing 1.1 shows the definition of the node_bind clause. node_bind is defined as an additional clause to the task construct. It takes one variable reference that its address can be determined by the compiler. The compiler assigns the target task on the same node that the specified variable is allocated. When multiple node_bind is given, the compiler uses the last node_bind clause.

Listing 1.1. node_bind clause definition

```
#pragma omp task [clause[[,] clause]  ...]  new_line
   structured_block
clause := untied
        | depend(dependence_type :  list)
        |  . . .
        | node_bind(variable)
```

Listing 1.2 shows an example code of the node_bind clause. The code is taken from the Strassen kernel in KASTORS. The output array C is given in the node_bind clause. When M2 and C are allocated on the same NUMA node, the task can be executed without any remote memory access. In some cases, the depend clause has enough information to specify the NUMA node to be allocated, instead of using the node_bind clause. Using output dependency for task allocation may be a good idea because usually there is one output dependency for each task, and the output array can be easily distributed among NUMA nodes compare to input arrays. However, we propose to use more explicit way of using the node_bind clause in this paper because task allocation is to be controlled explicitly and we are interested in seeing how performance changes by the initialization scheme.

Listing 1.2. node_bind clause example code

```
#pragma omp task depend(inout: C) depend(in: M2) \
           private(Row, Column) node_bind(C[0])
for (Row = 0; Row < QuadrantSize; Row++)
   for (Column = 0; Column < QuadrantSize; Column += 1)
      C[RowWidthC*Row+Column] += M2[Row*QuadrantSize+Column];
```

3.3   Prototype Implementation Using GCC

We have implemented the node_bind clause modifying GNU Compiler Collection (GCC) version 5.3.0. GCC 5.3.0 supports OpenMP 4.0 features including the task depend clause. The GCC implementation determines the address of the variable specified in the depend clause and passed it to the runtime. We used the mechanism to implement the node_bind clause. The compiler determines the address of the variable specified in the node_bind clause and add it to the argument list of the GOMP_task() function which generates OpenMP tasks.

When the address is passed to the OpenMP runtime system, our implementation calls a Linux system call, get_mempolicy() to determine the NUMA node id on which the specified variable is allocated. The node id is used to select the corresponding task queue. The GCC implementation creates a single global task queue shared by all tasks in a parallel region. Our implementation also has a global task queue and creates multiple task queues assigned to each NUMA node respectively. If get_mempolicy() returns an available NUMA id, the corresponding task queue is selected. If the function could not determine the NUMA node (it usually happens when the memory area has been allocated, but not touched by any thread), the global task queue is selected. Tasks without a node_bind clause are scheduled to the global task queue.

Task handling functions in GCC dequeue a task from the global task queue and execute it. Our implementation is modified to use NUMA task queues. As long as tasks exist in the local queue, cores dequeue tasks from the local task queue. If there is no task left in the local task queue, tasks in the global queue are scheduled. If there is no task both in the local queue and the global queue, cores take tasks from other NUMA nodes. This improves workload balance between cores at the cost of remote page access.

4   KASTOR Kernel Optimization with node_bind

In this section, we introduce the node_bind clause into the KASTOR benchmark kernels, Jacobi, SparseLU, and Strassen. Each kernel is implemented in two ways, TASK and TASK DEP. The TASK version is implemented using independent tasks in OpenMP 3.0, which is equivalent to BOTS. Depend clauses in OpenMP 4.0 are added in the TASK DEP version to replace global synchronization. We have modified both versions adding node_bind clauses. Explicit data distribution schemes using NUMA APIs have been tested on each kernel.

4.1   Jacobi Kernel

The Jacobi kernel solves a 2D Poisson equation on evenly-divided $N \times N$ grid points. Along with the TASK and TASK DEP version, KASTOR implements the FOR version for Jacobi. It uses the parallel for construct to perform loop work sharing, which is a straightforward way to parallelize stencil computation. The Jacobi kernel performs 5-point 2D stencil computation known to be memory-intensive.

Listing 1.3 shows the TASK DEP version of Jacobi. Each task calculates assigned grid points and stores the result data in the output array. The node_bind clauses are added to specify the first element of the assigned output array block in each task. Since each grid point can be calculated independently, we can distribute the calculation evenly not only among cores but also NUMA nodes. The parallel for construct was used to initialize array data so that the arrays are evenly distributed among NUMA nodes. It relies on the first-touch memory allocation policy of the Linux OS. The TASK version was also modified in the same way.

Listing 1.3. Jacobi TASK DEP Kernel with node_bind clauses

```
for (it = itold + 1; it <= itnew; it++) {
  for (block_x = 0; block_x < max_blocks_x; block_x++)
    for (block_y = 0; block_y < max_blocks_y; block_y++)
#pragma omp task shared(u_,unew_,block_size,nx,ny) \
      depend(in: unew[...]) depend(out: u[...]) ... \
      node_bind(u_[block_x*block_size*nx+block_y*block_size])
    copy_block(nx,ny,block_x,block_y,u_,unew_,block_size);

  for (block_x = 0; block_x < max_blocks_x; block_x++)
    for (block_y = 0; block_y < max_blocks_y; block_y++) ...
#pragma omp task shared(u_,unew_,f_,dx,dy,nx,ny,block_size) \
      depend(out: unew[...]) depend(in: f[...], ...) ... \
      node_bind(unew_[block_x*block_size*nx+...])
    compute_estimate(block_x,block_y,u_,unew_,f_,dx,dy,
                     nx,ny,block_size);}
```

4.2 SparseLU Kernel

The SparseLU kernel calculates the LU decomposition of a sparse matrix. Listing 1.4 shows the TASK version of SparseLU. BENCH is a 2D array of which each element is the memory pointer to the submatrix. SparseLU allocates a sub-matrix to the locations where the problem matrix has non-zero values. The LU decomposition is carried out to the non-NULL submatrices.

Listing 1.4. SpaseLU TASK Kernel with node_bind clauses

```
lu0(BENCH[kk*matrix_size+kk], submatrix_size);
for (jj=kk+1; jj<matrix_size; jj++)
  if (BENCH[kk*matrix_size+jj] != NULL)
#pragma omp task untied firstprivate(kk, jj) shared(BENCH) \
              node_bind(BENCH[kk*matrix_size+jj][0])
    fwd(BENCH[kk*matrix_size+kk],
        BENCH[kk*matrix_size+jj],submatrix_size);
for (ii=kk+1; ii<matrix_size; ii++)
  if (BENCH[ii*matrix_size+kk] != NULL)
#pragma omp task untied firstprivate(kk, ii) shared(BENCH) \
              node_bind(BENCH[ii*matrix_size+kk][0])
    bdiv (BENCH[kk*matrix_size+kk],
          BENCH[ii*matrix_size+kk],submatrix_size);
#pragma omp taskwait
```

```
for ( ii=kk+1; ii<matrix_size; ii++)
  if (BENCH[ ii∗matrix_size+kk] != NULL)
    for ( jj=kk+1; jj<matrix_size; jj++)
      if (BENCH[kk∗matrix_size+jj] != NULL) {
        if (BENCH[ ii∗matrix_size+jj]==NULL)
          BENCH[ ii∗matrix_size+jj] =
            allocate_clean_block_numa(submatrix_size, jj);
#pragma omp task untied firstprivate(kk,jj,ii) shared(BENCH) \
              node_bind(BENCH[ ii∗matrix_size+jj][0])
        bmod(BENCH[ ii∗matrix_size+kk],BENCH[kk∗matrix_size+jj],
            BENCH[ ii∗matrix_size+jj],submatrix_size);
      }
#pragma omp taskwait
```

The submatrix allocation pattern is irregular in SparseLU because it depends on the sparsity of the input matrix. Figure 2 shows the allocation pattern of the default input used in SparseLU. Each square indicates a submatrix. The submatrices allocated in the initialization routine are drawn as black squares. Submatrices allocated during the LU decomposition are drawn as gray blocks. White squares are zero matrices which are not accessed in the LU decomposition. As the figure shows, every column at even indices has non-zero elements. Given the situation, we distributed each column in a block-cyclic manner. 4 columns are grouped into a block, and blocks are distributed among NUMA nodes in a round-robin fashion. The columns are distributed among 4 NUMA nodes in Fig. 2.

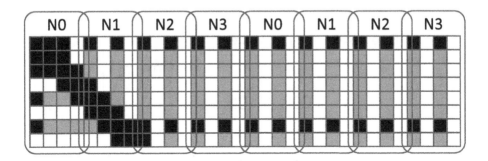

Fig. 2. Data distribution in SparseLU

The data distribution is implemented by using libnuma. numa_alloc_onnode() takes a NUMA node id as an argument and allocates a memory chunk on the specified node. Given the column index jj, the initialization routine allocates the submatrix on node $((jj/B) \% N)$ where B is the block size and N is the number of nodes to be used. Each task is scheduled to the node that the output submatrix is allocated. As Listing 1.4 shows, the first element of the output submatrix is given in the numa_node clauses so that no remote page access will occur when accessing the output. Note that the original version calls the allocation function in a task region. The modified version calls the allocation function in the single region with a target node id. The difference between these allocation schemes is explained in Sect. 5.

4.3 Strassen Kernel

The Strassen kernel calculates the multiplication of dense matrices using the Strassen algorithm. The algorithm reduces the number of multiplication operations by splitting each matrix into 4 equally divided submatrices. Figure 3 shows how the output matrix is divided in recursive function calls. The output array C is split into 4 submatrices (C0-C3 in Fig. 3) in the first matrix multiplication function call. Each submatrix is calculated in parallel using independent tasks. Each task splits the submatrix into 4 smaller submatrices and generates tasks to handle them. This recursive computation guarantees that the child tasks always compute the output elements which are allocated in the parent task, as we can see in Fig. 3.

Since the output matrix is split into 4 submatrices, the array elements can be distributed among 4 nodes at most. We distributed the array elements explicitly by using the OpenMP parallel construct and libnuma APIs. First, aligned_alloc() is used to allocate the output array with a page boundary alignment. The starting index of the corresponding submatrix is calculated in a parallel region. A thread is selected for each NUMA node in the parallel region. Then the thread calls numa_setlocal_memory() to migrate memory pages to the local NUMA node. As a result, the submatrices C0-C3 shown in Fig. 3 are allocated on multiple NUMA nodes.

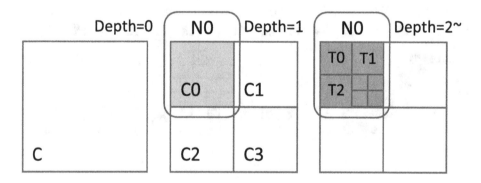

Fig. 3. Data distribution in Strassen

Listing 1.5 shows the TASK DEP version of Strassen. The kernel performs 7 multiplications and 4 of them access the output array C. node_bind clauses are specified for them. Since we wanted to use the node_bind clause at the top level of recursive calls, our modified GCC runtime performs task allocation only if the task does not have the parent task. When the parent task exists, the NUMA node id assigned to the parent task will be used.

Listing 1.5. Strassen TASK DEP Kernel Code with node_bind clauses

```
void OptimizedStrassenMultiply_par (double *C, double *A, ...
#pragma omp task depend(in: A, B) depend(out: M2)
  OptimizedStrassenMultiply_par (M2, A, B, ...);
#pragma omp task untied depend(in: S1, S5) depend(out: M5)
  OptimizedStrassenMultiply_par (M5, S1, S5, ...);
#pragma omp task untied depend(in: S2, S6) depend(out: T1sMULT)
  OptimizedStrassenMultiply_par (T1sMULT, S2, S6, ...);
#pragma omp task untied depend(in: S3, S7) depend(out: C22) \
              node_bind (C22[0])
  OptimizedStrassenMultiply_par (C22, S3, S7, ...);
#pragma omp task untied depend(in: A12, B21) depend(out: C) \
              node_bind (C[0])
  OptimizedStrassenMultiply_par (C, A12, B21, ...);
#pragma omp task untied depend(in: S4, B22) depend(out: C12) \
              node_bind (C12[0])
  OptimizedStrassenMultiply_par (C12, S4, B22, ...);
#pragma omp task untied depend(in: A22, S8) depend(out: C21) \
              node_bind (C21[0])
  OptimizedStrassenMultiply_par (C21, A22, S8, ...);
#pragma omp task depend(inout: C) depend(in: M2) ...
  for (Row = 0; Row < QuadrantSize; Row++)
    for (Column = 0; Column < QuadrantSize; Column += 1)
      C[RowWidthC*Row+Column] += M2[Row*QuadrantSize+Column];
```

5 Performance Evaluation

In this section, we measured the performance of the KASTORS benchmark kernels using GCC and our implementation. Table 1 shows the hardware configuration and the memory performance used for the evaluation. Each CPU has 18 physical cores and 2 NUMA nodes (when the COD mode is enabled). The OpenMP version of the Stream Triad benchmark is used to measure the sustainable memory bandwidth. OMP_PROC_BIND is set to CLOSE so that OpenMP threads use the smallest number of NUMA nodes. We used the same value to evaluate KASTORS. We compiled the original KASTOR kernels using GCC, and the modified kernels shown in Sect. 4 using our implementation.

5.1 Result of Jacobi Kernel

Figure 4 shows the performance speedup of the Jacobi kernel against the serial version. The matrix size is 16384×16384 and the block size is 1024. The original FOR, TASK, and TASK DEP version (*task init* and original in Fig. 4) initializes the grid point values in parallel execution of independent tasks so that the memory pages are distributed among NUMA nodes in a random manner. On the other hand, the modified TASK and TASK DEP version showed in Sect. 4 (*node_bind* in Fig. 4) initializes the grid points using loop work sharing in a parallel region. As a result, the memory pages are evenly distributed among nodes.

Table 1. Evalustion environment

Item	Name/Value	
CPU	Intel (R) Xeon (R) CPU E5-2699 v3, 2 sockets	
	18 cores with HT, 2.30 GHz, COD enabled	
Memory	DDR4 128 GB	
Stream performance	1 thread: 14.49	
(Triad, GB/s)	9 threads (1 node): 21.82	18 threads (2 nodes): 43.36
	27 threads (3 nodes): 65.01	36 threads (4 nodes): 86.49
Memory	DDR4 128 GB	
OS	Red Hat Enterprise Linux Server release 7.1	
	Linux Kernel: 3.10.0-229.7.2.el7.x86_64	
Compiler	GNU Compiler gcc version 5.3.0	

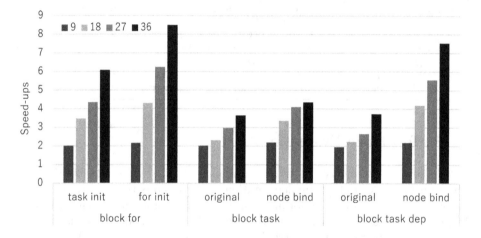

Fig. 4. Parallel performance of Jacobi

The performance of the FOR version shows that the initialization scheme can change the performance. Compared with *for init*, the FOR version initialized using the parallel for construct, *task init* achieves the lower performance than *for init* because the memory pages are allocated randomly among NUMA nodes. *for init* achieves the best performance because the access pattern of the initialization and the computation is perfectly matched.

The modified TASK and TASK DEP version achieve better performance than the original versions for the same reason of *for init*. It reduces remote page access by matching the data allocation pattern and the task scheduling pattern. The reason why the TASK version show the lower scalability than the TASK DEP version is that there is a global synchronization (taskwait construct) between the update phase and the computation phase. The GCC OpenMP runtime eagerly uses the master thread to execute the child tasks to handle the taskwait construct. The same thing happens in our implementation so that the specified task allocation scheme is ignored in the global synchronization.

5.2   Result of SparseLU Kernel

Figure 5 shows the performance speedup of the SparseLU kernel against the serial version. The matrix size is 128 and the submatrix size is 64. The original TASK version allocates submatrices in each task so that the memory pages are distributed in a random manner. The original TASK DEP version allocates submatrices on the master thread before task creation in order to specify task dependency using the submatrix indices. In both cases, remote page access occurs when accessing the output submatrix since the GCC OpenMP runtime does not consider data locality in task scheduling.

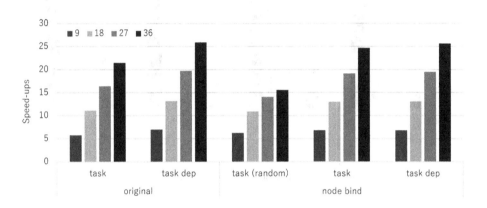

Fig. 5. Parallel performance of SparseLU

node bind in Fig. 5 shows the performance of the modified TASK and TASK DEP version shown in Sect. 4. *task (random)* uses node_bind clauses and submatrices are allocated in the same manner with the original TASK version. *task (random)* achieves lower performance than the original version because of the irregular allocation pattern. All submatrices are allocated in the first iteration of the LU decomposition (when *kk* is 0 in Listing 1.4) and reused in the subsequent iterations. *task (random)* uses the irregular allocation pattern to allocate tasks in every iteration. It causes load imbalance between NUMA nodes.

The modified TASK version solves the problem. It distributes submatrices evenly among nodes using NUMA APIs. The block-cyclic manner used in Fig. 2 guarantees that each NUMA node has the balanced workload in every iteration. As a result, the modified version achieves better performance than the original version. The result shows that the performance of the node_bind clause is sensitive to data distribution.

5.3 Result of Strassen Kernel

Figure 6 shows the performance speedup of the Strassen kernel against the serial version. The modified TASK and TASK DEP version distributes the output matrix C among nodes. The output matrix and temporary arrays allocated in the parent task are used in the child tasks in recursive function calls. Our implementation schedules child tasks to the same node used to the parent task. The explicit data distribution and the task scheduling scheme increase the performance of the TASK DEP version by 7 %.

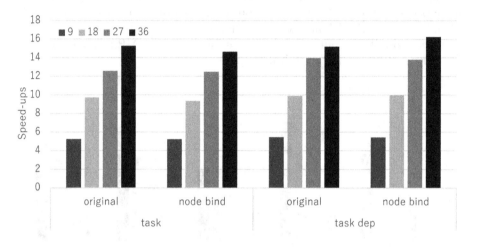

Fig. 6. Parallel performance of Strassen

While the output matrix is localized, the input matrices should be copied from remote NUMA nodes due to the data dependency coming from the Strassen algorithm. For the further improvement, we are testing some techniques to reduce the remote page access, such as duplicating input data among nodes.

6 Conclusion

In this paper, we proposed the node_bind clause for the OpenMP task construct specifying the NUMA node id that the task should be scheduled. The extension can be combined with explicit data distribution to reduce remote page access, as shown in Sect. 4. Although it requires additional programming effort, the results of the performance evaluation using the KASTOR benchmark showed that NUMA-aware task allocation improved the parallel performance. The Jacobi kernel using our approach shows 3.6 times better performance than GCC when using 36 threads on a 36-core, 4-NUMA node machine. Techniques for distributing data and reducing communication have been studied extensively in cluster computing. We found that those techniques can be also helpful for the NUMA architecture. Currently, we are designing an OpenMP extension to describe data distribution instead of using Linux OS system calls and NUMA APIs.

References

1. Barcelona OpenMP Task Suite (BOTS). https://pm.bsc.es/projects/bots/
2. Drebes, A., Heydemann, K., Drach, N., Pop, A., Cohen, A.: Topology-aware and dependence-aware scheduling and memory allocation for task-parallel languages. ACM Trans. Archit. Code Optim. **11**(3), 30:1–30:25 (2014). http://doi.acm.org/10.1145/2641764
3. Duran, A., Teruel, X., Ferrer, R., Martorell, X., Ayguade, E.: Barcelona OpenMP tasks suite: a set of benchmarks targeting the exploitation of task parallelism in OpenMP. In: Proceedings of the 2009 International Conference on Parallel Processing, ICPP 2009, pp. 124–131. IEEE Computer Society, Washington, DC (2009). doi:10.1109/ICPP.2009.64
4. KASTORS Benchmark. https://gforge.inria.fr/projects/kastors/
5. Muddukrishna, A., Jonsson, P.A., Vlassov, V., Brorsson, M.: Locality-aware task scheduling and data distribution on NUMA systems. In: Rendell, A.P., Chapman, B.M., Müller, M.S. (eds.) IWOMP 2013. LNCS, vol. 8122, pp. 156–170. Springer, Heidelberg (2013). doi:10.1007/978-3-642-40698-0_12
6. Olivier, S.L., Porterfield, A.K., Wheeler, K.B., Spiegel, M., Prins, J.F.: OpenMP task scheduling strategies for multicore NUMA systems. Int. J. High Perform. Comput. Appl. **26**(2), 110–124 (2012). doi:10.1177/1094342011434065
7. Olivier, S.L., de Supinski, B.R., Schulz, M., Prins, J.F.: Characterizing and mitigating work time inflation in task parallel programs. In: Proceedings ofthe International Conference on High Performance Computing, Networking, Storage and Analysis, SC 2012, pp. 65:1–65:12. IEEE Computer Society Press, Los Alamitos (2012). http://dl.acm.org/citation.cfm?id=2388996.2389085
8. Tahan, O.: Towards efficient OpenMP strategies for non-uniform architectures. CoRR abs/1411.7131 (2014). http://arxiv.org/abs/1411.7131
9. Vikranth, B., Wankar, R., Rao, C.R.: Topology aware task stealing for on-chip NUMA multi-core processors. Procedia Comput. Sci. **18**, 379–388 (2013). 2013 International Conference on Computational Science. http://www.sciencedirect.com/science/article/pii/S187705091300344X
10. Virouleau, P., Brunet, P., Broquedis, F., Furmento, N., Thibault, S., Aumage, O., Gautier, T.: Evaluation of OpenMP dependent tasks with the KASTORS benchmark suite. In: DeRose, L., de Supinski, B.R., Olivier, S.L., Chapman, B.M., Müller, M.S. (eds.) IWOMP 2014. LNCS, vol. 8766, pp. 16–29. Springer, Heidelberg (2014). doi:10.1007/978-3-319-11454-5_2

Approaches for Task Affinity in OpenMP

Christian Terboven[1]([☒]), Jonas Hahnfeld[1], Xavier Teruel[2], Sergi Mateo[2],
Alejandro Duran[3], Michael Klemm[3], Stephen L. Olivier[4],
and Bronis R. de Supinski[5]

[1] Chair for High Performance Computing, IT Center,
RWTH Aachen University, Aachen, Germany
{terboven,hahnfeld}@itc.rwth-aachen.de
[2] Barcelona Supercomputing Center, Barcelona, Spain
{xavier.teruel,sergi.mateo}@bsc.es
[3] Intel, Santa Clara, USA
{alejandro.duran,michael.klemm}@intel.com
[4] Center for Computing Research, Sandia National Laboratories,
Albuquerque, USA
slolivi@sandia.gov
[5] Lawrence Livermore National Laboratory (LLNL), Livermore, USA
bronis@llnl.gov

Abstract. OpenMP tasking supports parallelization of irregular algorithms. Recent OpenMP specifications extended tasking to increase functionality and to support optimizations, for instance with the `taskloop` construct. However, task scheduling remains opaque, which leads to inconsistent performance on NUMA architectures. We assess design issues for task affinity and explore several approaches to enable it. We evaluate these proposals with implementations in the Nanos++ and LLVM OpenMP runtimes that improve performance up to 40 % and significantly reduce execution time variation.

1 Introduction

The OpenMP[*] API specification first included support for task-based parallelism in version 3.0 [8]. In contrast to OpenMP worksharing constructs, task constructs support parallelization of irregular algorithms, e.g., code with recursion or graph traversals. The flexibility of OpenMP tasks leads to nondeterministic execution including highly dynamic mapping of tasks to threads.

Modern processor architectures do not provide uniform performance since an internal fabric connects multiple processor packages with their local memories to form a single shared memory system. This NUMA (non-uniform memory access) architecture exposes different memory latencies and bandwidth rates, depending on the memory location that is accessed. Two examples are the Intel® Quick Path Interconnect [13] of Intel® Xeon processors and the Bull Coherent Switch [2]. A typical strategy allocates data on its first touch to a physical page

---

© Springer International Publishing Switzerland 2016
N. Maruyama et al. (Eds.): IWOMP 2016, LNCS 9903, pp. 102–115, 2016.
DOI: 10.1007/978-3-319-45550-1_8

in the local memory of the processor that issues the instruction. While OpenMP worksharing constructs can explicitly assign work to individual OpenMP threads, OpenMP tasks do not support this kind of control. Thus, tasking complicates control of page placement and memory locality.

In this paper, we assess issues that arise in extending OpenMP to support task affinity that would address this question. We propose two fundamental approaches to extend existing tasking constructs that provide hints to the OpenMP compiler and runtime that can guide the assignment of tasks to threads in order to improve data placement and memory locality. First, the novel `affinity` clause for the `task` construct suggests a place or thread on which to execute a task. Second, a `taskgroup` extension provides a hint to the runtime system about how to the distribute the tasks of that task group.

The remainder of the paper is organized as follows. Section 2 reviews prior proposals to support task affinity in OpenMP. Section 3 assesses key issues in the design of task affinity support while Sect. 4 presents the proposed syntax and semantics of our two approaches. Section 5 details the prototype implementations of our approaches while we provide a preliminary assessment of their performance in Sect. 6.

2 Related Work

Proposed OpenMP extensions for data, thread, and task affinity by Huang et al. predate offically-adopted OpenMP thread affinity support, but the article only evaluates data and thread, not task, affinity [5]. Terboven et al. found that the status quo of task scheduling – no mechanism to express affinity among tasks or between tasks and threads – leads to inconsistent performance across different OpenMP implementations and between different NUMA architectures [11]. Olivier et al. defined the concept of "work time inflation", additional time spent by threads in a multithreaded computation beyond the time required to perform the same work sequentially [7]. They showed the impact of such work time inflation in OpenMP task parallel programs and proposed OpenMP extensions to specify mappings of tasks to NUMA locality domains, enabling exploitation of first touch placement for tasks. Muddukrishna et al. base task scheduling on available capacity of the last level cache and working sets of the tasks [6]. Our work incorporates the preliminary lessons from many of these prior studies to provide a comprehensive assessment of the issues that arise for task affinity.

Work on task parallelism prior to the OpenMP task model has also examined the issue of task affinity. Acar et al. derive a theoretical bound on cache misses due to differences in the ordering of tasks between sequential and parallel executions [1]. They propose "locality-guided work stealing" that enqueues tasks with affinity to a particular thread into a special "mailbox" that is separate from its main queue. Task scheduling techniques based on system topology particular to other task-based programming models and runtime systems have also been attempted, e.g., for Charm++ [10] and Habanero [4,12]. Cilk's work-first task scheduler exploits task affinity naturally by design for programs in which significant data sharing occurs between parent and child tasks [3]. Such data sharing often, but not always, occurs with recursive algorithms; it frequently does not for general task parallelism. Further, Cilk's design targets temporal locality in private caches, while modern systems have much more complex memory subsystem hierarchies: private and shared caches, multiple memory controllers and generally more complex memory systems. Our work extends OpenMP to assist OpenMP compilers and runtimes in using these increasingly complex memory systems.

3   Design Choices for Task Affinity

Substantially different issues arise with task affinity compared to thread affinity, which OpenMP 4.0 incorporated [9]. We explore several of these issues in this section.

How does task affinity limit task stealing? While OpenMP does not mandate a task scheduling policy, many implementations use task stealing to exploit OpenMP tasking semantics to improve load balance. Prescriptive task affinity extensions would prevent the implementation from exploring the trade-off between load balance and work time inflation. Thus, both of our approaches provide descriptive hints that can guide task scheduling decisions. While our proposals do not mandate task scheduling policies, the user may assume that hints bias task stealing to improve affinity.

How should affinity mechanisms interact with the task scheduling constraints? When a task encounters a task scheduling point it may switch (or not) to begin or resume the execution of a different task. These task switching points are subject to an explicit ruleset described in the OpenMP specification (i.e. the *Task Scheduling Constraints*). Thus, any task affinity scheduler implementation may use the information provided by the affinity clauses to guide task execution but they will always be subject to any constraint explicitly expressed in the OpenMP specification (see *descriptive* vs. *prescriptive* discussion in the previous paragraph).

Should tasks have affinity with threads or data? We could specify which OpenMP thread should execute a given task, which would support the distribution of tasks to threads to which the programmer has already carefully distributed data. Task-to-thread affinity also simplifies an initialization phase that must distribute data appropriately across system resources. Alternatively, we could specify data locations that are used by a given task to enable the task scheduler to execute each task on a resource that is close to its data. Task affinity to a data location may be the right level of abstraction for the programmer as it is independent of the underlying architecture or the data layout. However, the programmer must be able to specify all data important for affinity when the task is created (i.e. this data must be accessible at task creation). While straightforward for simple programs, data access sets of large programs with multiple compilation units are often not apparent where the tasks are created. Since both choices are useful in some cases, our proposals support both.

How should we express task-to-thread affinity? We could specify which thread should execute a task by using OpenMP places or by using OpenMP thread identifiers. Using OpenMP places would restrict the task to be executed by one of the threads bound to the given place(s). While this approach has conceptual appeal, the place list is static and defined through an environment variable before the program starts. Further, the place list heavily depends on the system architecture, which would require the programmer to have that architecture in mind when writing the program and, thus, fail to provide portable semantics. Because of this we decided not to support OpenMP places. Alternatively, while OpenMP thread identifiers may be appropriate if the program distributes data based on them, they also can limit portability and do not capture natural semantics for other data distribution strategies. Thus, our approaches provide this option but also can exploit another mechanism, which specifies higher level policies that capture task-to-thread affinity similarly to OpenMP thread affinity policies (i.e., spread or close). These policies allow the user to specify task-to-thread affinity independently of the exact number of threads or place list.

Which task-to-thread affinity policies should we support? Policies that are similar to those that already exist for thread affinity provide many advantages. First, many users are already familiar with the concepts expressed by those policies. Second, they have proven useful to guide efficient decisions for real applications. It has to be noted that a task affinity policy cannot directly be expressed in the context of the place list. To illustrate this, assume a parallel region with the `proc_bind(master)` clause, which determines all threads to execute within the same place. In this case, the `affinity(spread)` clause on a `taskgroup` construct cannot lead to task affinity outside of this single place, as task are executed by the threads in the current team. We also allow specification of task affinity at different levels of the task hierarchy, similarly thread affinity policies and nested parallelism.

Which memory accesses determine task-to-data affinity? Two types of memory accesses could guide task affinity: allocations or recent task (load/store) accesses. Task affinity could request that a task execute in the same place as the last task that used the same data, which would imply that the place to which task affinity refers changes when task stealing occurs. Alternatively, task affinity could refer to the place on which the data was first touched (allocated), which would fix affinity to the original place. The right choice is application dependent: compute-bound problems with good cache locality benefit from executing where the data was most recently accessed and likely is still resident while the data for memory-bound problems usually does not remain resident except where it was allocated. Thus, we support both patterns.

Should we use the depend clause to express task-to-data affinity? Since tasking constructs already support the `depend` clause to specify a relationship to data locations, we could use it to express task-to-data affinity since the same data location often captures data affinity and synchronization. However, the depend clause tying affinity to synchronization semantics by binding the two concepts would violate the separation of concerns design principle. Therefore, we provide a new clause although we also support a short form that expresses the overlap when appropriate.

On which tasking construct should we express task affinity? Specifying task affinity on the `task` construct would make programs easier to read since the relationship is then visible where it applies. This choice easily supports task-to-data affinity. However, high-level task-to-thread affinity policies affect multiple tasks. Thus, specifying them on the `task` construct would be unclear and could lead to cases in which sibling tasks specify different policies. Thus, we also provide new clauses for thread affinity on the `taskgroup` construct, which clearly marks which tasks are affected by the policy.

It would be also desirable to have affinity support for tasks spawned from the `taskloop` construct. For task-to-thread affinity this is straightforward as spawned tasks are grouped by an implicit `taskgroup`. But to support task-to-data OpenMP currently lacks the language to be able to express the affinity of the different iterations and how that relates to spawned tasks. We therefore have decided to postpone a decision on how to handle task-to-data affinity for the `taskloop` construct.

4   Proposed Syntax and Semantics

As a general concept, this proposal introduces the `affinity` clause for the `task`, `taskgroup` and `taskloop` constructs, as discussed below.

Task: Task affinity could be expressed directly to an OpenMP place or thread, depending on the given specifier, as in the following example:

`#pragma omp task affinity(thread: <thread−identifier>)`

Task affinity could be also expressed by means of the data a task produces, modifies or consumes, indicated by a different specifier:

`#pragma omp task affinity(data: A[i])`

The task shall be executed as close as possible to the location of the specified data reference. Data location can be determined by the assumption of thread affinity (i.e. binding OpenMP threads to cores or sockets) and then grouping tasks that use the same location as close as possible.

A second approach could use system queries to determine where the data is actually allocated[1]. However, this option may be hard to implement: Since every task is executed by a thread, the runtime must first determine the physical location of the variable reference in the system and then perform a mapping into the place list to find the list of threads within that place, which are candidates to execute the task. On current Linux systems this incurs considerable overhead.

---

[1] Future versions of OpenMP may support explicit memory affinity and thereby inhance the definition of a location.

Taskgroup: The affinity to a set of other tasks cannot be expressed directly on a `task` construct, as it stands without the context of the other sibling tasks that may be generated during the execution of the program. In order to define a task distribution policy, the total number of tasks in the context must be known, as it would be with the `taskgroup` construct. Currently the `taskgroup` construct always includes an implied taskwait at the end, but in the following it is assumed that this could be omitted, for example with the introduction of a `nowait` clause.

The following example illustrates the use of the `affinity` clause on a `taskgroup` construct using the `spread` policy, analogous to the corresponding thread affinity policy:

```
#pragma omp taskgroup affinity(spread)
```

Task affinity cannot directly be expressed in the context of the place list, as explained above. To address this, we defined that task affinity `spread` such that the generated tasks shall be spread among the threads in the team, as far and evenly as possible. In the current implementation, the task distribution is determined based on the OpenMP thread ids – another option to implement the task distribution would be to consider the place list as well, which could be evaluated at a later point in time. Similarly, with the `close` policy, the generated tasks shall be executed closely together as far as appropriate in the context of the current thread team. And finally with the `master` policy, the generated tasks shall be executed by the master thread.

As will be discussed below, determining the set of tasks to be used for applying the policy may challenge the implementation, the definition of the policy could be extended with the specification of a number of tasks to be used together:

```
#pragma omp taskgroup affinity(spread:N)
```

In this scenario, the policy will be applied under the assumption that N tasks will be created in the construct. If more tasks are created the distribution will be restarted with task $N + 1$ which may not deliver optimal performance as multiple tasks get scheduled on the same thread.

Taskloop: In its current form, the number of tasks to be generated is known. Consequently, the same task affinity policies discussed in the previous section are also useful in this case.

5 Prototype Implementations

As described above, some options were implemented and evaluated. Expression of task affinity with respect to a place or thread or storage location have been implemented in the Nanos++ runtime, while the task affinity policies on the `taskgroup` and `taskloop` constructs have been implemented in the LLVM runtime.

Nanos++: All changes to the runtime needed for the affinity support were limited to the scheduler submodule. The baseline is the Nanos++ distributed breadth first scheduler. This scheduler has a pair of ready queues per thread: local and private. The only difference in these two set of queues is that local queues allow stealing but private queues do not. Stealing can be enabled in all scheduler policies by means of an environment variable.

Private queues are only used once a tied task has been executed by a thread. At any task switching point, a tied task is queued in the private queue of the executing thread, preventing other threads from stealing the task.

Local queues are used when the task may still be executed by any thread. Usually the encountering task will enqueue newly created tasks in its own local queue. In this manner we ensure certain affinity guidance for multiple creator scenarios (e.g., task creation in loop worksharing constructs or nested tasks created in recursive programs). The only exception to this simple rule is when the runtime encounters a single threaded execution by an implicit task (i.e., inside a single or a master construct). In this case the scheduler policy distributes the work following a round-robin or random pattern (configurable by means of an environment variable) among all the threads of the team. There are cases in which the runtime fails and determines a single creation scheme when actually there are more threads creating tasks simultaneously (e.g., multiple single constructs with the nowait clause).

LLVM: We used the LLVM OpenMP runtime[2] to create a prototype implementation of task affinity policies for the `taskgroup` and `taskloop` constructs, as described in the subsection *Taskgroup* and *Taskloop*. In the LLVM runtime, OpenMP tasking is implemented with a local task queue for each thread. When a thread encounters a `task` construct, it creates a new task and puts it onto its local task queue. If a thread is idle and its local queue is empty, it will steal a task from another thread's queue.

5.1 OpenMP Place/Thread Approach

The extended Nanos++ runtime supports the *thread-id* mapping technique in a very straightforward way. The scheduler policy uses the set of threads local queues but it will target the corresponding queue using the thread identifier provided in the affinity clause.

5.2 Storage Location Approach

The implementation of the data-driven approach may imply different degrees of complexity. In the current discussion we will describe two different Nanos++ implementations when guiding the task affinity using data. In both cases thread local queues are still used in order to group these tasks with a certain affinity among them.

---

[2] http://openmp.llvm.org/.

The first (default) implementation determines the target thread-id using a hash-map function. All tasks providing the same memory address will be enqueued onto the same thread local queue. Our hash-map function relies on the pattern of consecutive memory blocks with the same size and we compute the thread-id by shifting to the right log2(size) the memory address and keeping the modulo number of threads.

The main problem with this approach is that information may not be accurate when stealing occurs. Once a task is enqueued in a thread local queue it should ultimately be executed by that thread. If stealing occurs then the task is actually executed by another thread but the rest of the tasks using the same data will still be scheduled to the formerly assigned thread.

A map can be used to keep track of the actual thread executing a task. The map can be updated when a task is stolen so that related tasks will also be scheduled on the thread that has stolen the task. This map is distributed among threads as mentioned above, so any thread will know in which map a given data can be found.

The latter implementation gets more accurate information for scheduling a task but has the associated cost of keeping track of where the tasks are distributed at different scheduling points: submission, dependence fulfilment and stealing. The evaluation section will give more information about the impact of this specific technique.

5.3   Taskgroup

In order to implement the task affinity policies, we followed the general approach to put each task onto the queue of the corresponding thread, which is determined according to the given policy. To evenly distribute the tasks of a `taskgroup` or `taskloop` construct over the available threads, in our approach it is required to know the total number of tasks to distribute.

Therefore with `affinity(spread)` all recently created tasks are collected in a dedicated list and only distributed among the threads when a `taskwait` is encountered, either explicitly or implicitly. This means that task execution has to be deferred until all tasks are created and ready to be distributed which may negatively impact the performance. With our proposal of `affinity(spread:N)`, the distribution and execution of tasks could start immediately with task creation as the thread to put the task on can be determined a-priori.

Each task maintains a dedicated list of threads to execute its child tasks. This list is partitioned according to the task affinity policy.

When using task affinity in a single producer pattern, and if the team consists of more threads than tasks created in a single recursion step or loop iteration, some threads will not immediately get a task to execute. These threads will try to steal tasks from other threads' task queues, which may disturb affinity. It is not desirable for that to occur too early. To ensure affinity is maintained until all threads are busy, we prevent any thread from stealing until it has at least executed one local task. This ensures that task stealing is still allowed, which is desirable as argued above to perform load balancing, for instance.

5.4 Taskloop

The LLVM OpenMP runtime recently gained support for taskloops, which internally makes use of taskgroups for synchronisation. Consequently we were able to reuse our implementation and extend the support for task affinity on the `taskloop` construct. It accepts the same task affinity policies as described in the semantics and implementation above.

6 Evaluation

Again, task affinity with respect to a place or thread or storage location on the one hand and the task affinity policies on the other hand have been implemented and evaluated differently, with the Nanos++ and LLVM runtimes, respectively (see Table 1 for an overview).

Table 1. Different approaches and their implementations.

Approach	Implementation	Evaluation
Place/Thread	Nanos++ (Subsect. 5.1)	Subsect. 6.1 (Fig. 1)
Storage Location	Nanos++ (Subsect. 5.2)	Subsect. 6.2 (Fig. 1)
Taskgroup Policy	LLVM (Subsect. 5.3)	Subsect. 6.3 (Fig. 2)
Taskloop Policy	LLVM (Subsect. 5.4)	Subsect. 6.4 (Fig. 3)

Measurements with the LLVM and Nanos++ runtimes have been performed on a two-socket Intel Xeon E5-2699 v4 (Broadwell) system, with 44 cores in total. This system exhibits a 2-level NUMA architecture with four memory domains, as the two sockets are each split into two rings and each ring is connected to its local memory controller.

Nanos++ runtime has also been evaluated in the MareNostrum III cluster. This system is based on Intel SandyBridge processors, iDataPlex Compute Racks, a Linux Operating System (based on a SuSe Distribution) and an Infiniband interconnection network. Each node has 2x Intel SandyBridge-EP E5-2670/1600 20M 8-core at 2.6 GHz and 8×4 GB DDR3-1600 DIMMS of memory.

In order to obtain the results presented in this section we used the STREAM synthetic benchmark[3]. The suite is composed by four different kernels described in Table 2 and each execution consists of multiple repetitions of these four kernels.

We evaluated our prototype implementation of task affinity for the `taskgroup` construct with a task parallel merge sort. This program is representative of the class of divide and conquer algorithms. The input size for the merge sort was 2^{33} integer values.

---

[3] Further information about the STREAM benchmark suite available at: http://www.cs.virginia.edu/stream/ref.html.

Table 2. The STREAM benchmark suite: description of kernels.

Name	Kernel	Bytes/Iteration	FLOPS/Iteration
COPY	$a(i) = b(i)$	16	0
SCALE	$a(i) = q*b(i)$	16	1
SUM	$a(i) = b(i) + c(i)$	24	1
TRIAD	$a(i) = b(i) + q*c(i)$	24	2

6.1 Place/Thread

We evaluated our place and thread approach described in Subsect. 5.1 using the aggregated results of the full STREAM suite. Figure 1 shows the performance results of executing this benchmark in SandyBridge and Broadwell respectively. Speedups are computed against the execution time of the very same parallel version without task affinity annotation and using a *per thread* (local queue) round-robin scheduler. The first two bars of each cluster of bars correspond to the thread approach.

SandyBridge results show that we have no penalty/no gain when running on a single socket, but we increase the performance up to 20 % when mapping tasks to threads when both sockets are used.

We have used different numbers of threads configurations when running on the Broadwell system: 11 threads (one ring of a single socket), 22 threads (all the cores of a single socket), 44 threads (all the cores of the two sockets) and 88 threads (enabling hyper-threading). As in the case of SandyBridge there is no penalty/no gain when running on a single NUMA domain but performance increases as we use a thread per core/two sockets (30 % of speed-up) and increases still more when using all threads on the two sockets (up to 44 %).

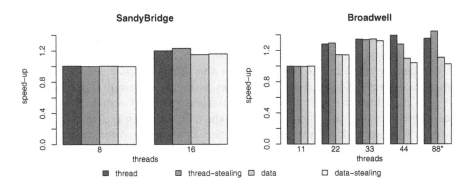

Fig. 1. Thread and storage (data) affinity approaches: STREAM benchmark performance with and without stealing, relative to a round-robin scheduler, on two different architectures using Nanos++.

The Broadwell results also show that stealing induces unpredictable execution behaviour. In some case we observe a performance degradation (e.g., with 44 threads) and in some other cases we the performance improves (e.g., with 88 threads). In this particular comparison (44 vs. 88 threads) the use of hyperthreading may also have an impact on the observed results due the plot also shows how the non-stealing version suffers a slight degradation in the speed-up gain.

6.2   Storage Location

Figure 1 also shows the results for the storage location approach, in the right two bars of each cluster of bars. In all cases we obtain a performance gain (i.e., the speedups are always bigger than 1) with respect to the non-affinity version, but comparing with the thread approach the performance gain is smaller. The gap between 22 and 44 threads in the Broadwell execution is an anomaly. In this specific case the storage affinity approach suffers from a small performance degradation while the thread approach is still able to improve results.

6.3   Taskgroup

The measurements discussed below were done with the Intel C/C++ Compiler in version 17.0 beta, employing our modified LLVM OpenMP runtime. 44 threads (one per physical core) were used, always delivering the best absolute performance.

Figure 2 shows that task affinity resulted in an improvement of approximately 20 % of execution time, and also a significant reduction of the performance variation between trials. Results for three versions of the program are shown. The *default* implementation performs data allocation and initialization in a sequential part, with the result that the whole array is located on only one NUMA domain. In the *first touch* variant, the array has been distributed over the NUMA nodes in chunks of equal size. The *affinity* variant employs the same data distribution together with a `omp taskgroup affinity(spread)` around the task creation points. Note that this currently still includes an implied taskwait synchronization construct at each recursion level, which we envision becoming optional in future versions of the OpenMP specification.

The improvement in execution time for the *affinity* variant stems from the higher percentage of local data accesses, as tasks are distributed according to the data distribution. The reduction in runtime variation occurs because the tasks' distribution to the threads based on the affinity policy is deterministic. In contrast, without task affinity the distribution is determined by stealing which in itself is nondeterministic. When stealing is allowed, data locality and therefore performance differs with every run.

6.4   Taskloop Construct

To evaluate affinity on the rather new `taskloop` construct, we modified the STREAM benchmark to use a single-producer pattern: the `taskloop` construct

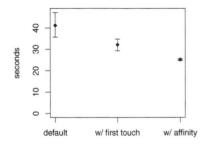

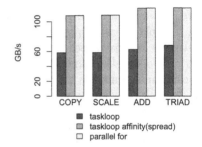

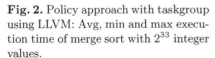

Fig. 2. Policy approach with taskgroup using LLVM: Avg, min and max execution time of merge sort with 2^{33} integer values.

Fig. 3. Policy approach with taskloop using LLVM: STREAM benchmark performance.

is used to parallelize the loops performing the actual operations of the benchmark, and also the data initialization loops. On all instances the number of tasks to be created is set equal to the number of threads (num_tasks(omp_get_num_threads())): thereby the same number of explicit tasks is created as a do worksharing construct would create implicit tasks. As compiler support for this feature was very limited in the Intel compilers, we used a trunk version of the LLVM/Clang compiler. This version required us to use the __builtin_nontemporal_store intrinsic to enable the generation of non temporal stores. This was necessary to achieve maximum memory bandwidth with this code and to allow for a fair comparison. If task affinity is successful, this taskloop implementation should deliver the same memory bandwidth as the do worksharing variant.

Figure 3 compares three variants: the *taskloop* implementation as described with and without *affinity* enabled, and the same benchmark parallelized with the parallel for combined worksharing construct serving as the reference. In the version without affinity, the nondeterminism of the task to thread mapping in the task scheduling – as explained above – limits the achievable memory bandwidth. Enabling the affinity(spread) task affinity policy yields the same bandwidth as using the worksharing construct from the original STREAM benchmark – the ideal outcome.

7   Conclusion

In this paper we have discussed several language extensions to support task affinity in OpenMP. We focus on three different approaches. The first is based on the OpenMP places concept and complements OpenMP thread affinity. The second approach is based on data storage. This approach is more programmer-friendly (assuming programmers understand the data use of the tasks they create) but requires more complexity in the runtime implementation. The third approach is based on distribution policies of a set of tasks (e.g. those generated in taskgroup or taskloop constructs).

We have implemented and evaluated a representative prototype for each approach. The place-based approach is implemented assuming thread to core affinity. The storage approach uses the memory address as a key value to determine and group tasks using the same storage location. The distribution policies approach has been implemented by tracking at each task level the set of valid thread local queues a task can submit work to.

Results show that using this set of affinity guidelines when scheduling OpenMP tasks can help the runtime system to improve the application performance. Having different mechanisms to distribute tasks among threads or group their execution over the same (or a close) physical resource can help programmers to choose the one that fits best with their application. Regular and repetitive patterns of task creation may use thread-based task affinity, irregular patterns of memory usage may benefit from the ease of the storage-based approach, and recursive applications seem to fit with the task set distribution policies.

As future work we plan to further evaluate the different approaches on a wider set of kernels. We also plan to perform more in-depth experiments to better understand the effects of load imbalance and how stealing techniques may impact the performance. Finally, we plan to execute these kernels on additional system architectures to investigate the behavior of our implemented approaches in more complex system architectures (with respect to the NUMA layout). Our evaluations so far show significant benefits for OpenMP task parallel programs using the diverse approaches we investigated.

Acknowledgement. Sandia National Laboratories is a multi-program laboratory managed and operated by Sandia Corporation, a wholly owned subsidiary of Lockheed Martin Corporation, for the U.S. Department of Energys National Nuclear Security Administration under contract DE-AC04-94AL85000.

This work has been developed with the support of the grant SEV-2011-00067 of the Severo Ochoa Program, awarded by the Spanish Government, by the Spanish Ministry of Science and Innovation (TIN2015-65316-P, Computacion de Altas Prestaciones VII) and by the Intel-BSC Exascale Lab collaboration project.

Some of the experiments were performed with computing resources granted by JARA-HPC from RWTH Aachen University under project jara0001. Parts of this work were funded by the German Federal Ministry of Research and Education (BMBF) under grant numbers 01IH13008A(ELP).

Intel and Xeon are trademarks or registered trademarks of Intel Corporation or its subsidiaries in the United States and other countries.

* Other names and brands are the property of their respective owners.

Software and workloads used in performance tests may have been optimized for performance only on Intel microprocessors. Performance tests, such as SYSmark and MobileMark, are measured using specific computer systems, components, software, operations and functions. Any change to any of those factors may cause the results to vary. You should consult other information and performance tests to assist you in fully evaluating your contemplated purchases, including the performance of that product when combined with other products. For more information go to http://www.intel.com/performance.

Intel's compilers may or may not optimize to the same degree for non-Intel microprocessors for optimizations that are not unique to Intel microprocessors. These optimizations include SSE2, SSE3, and SSSE3 instruction sets and other optimizations.

Intel does not guarantee the availability, functionality, or effectiveness of any optimization on microprocessors not manufactured by Intel. Microprocessor-dependent optimizations in this product are intended for use with Intel microprocessors. Certain optimizations not specific to Intel microarchitecture are reserved for Intel microprocessors. Please refer to the applicable product User and Reference Guides for more information regarding the specific instruction sets covered by this notice.

References

1. Acar, U.A., Blelloch, G.E., Blumofe, R.D.: The data locality of work stealing. In: Proceedings of the 12th ACM Symposium on Parallel Algorithms and Architectures, SPAA 2000, pp. 1–12. ACM (2000)
2. Bull Atos Technologies: Bull Coherent Switch. http://support.bull.com/ols/product/platforms/hw-extremcomp/hw-bullx-sup-node. Accessed 25 May 2016
3. Frigo, M., Leiserson, C.E., Randall, K.H.: The implementation of the Cilk-5 multithreaded language. In: Proceedings of the 1998 ACM SIGPLAN Conference on Programming Language Design and Implementation, PLDI 1998, pp. 212–223. ACM (1998)
4. Guo, Y., Zhao, J., Cave, V., Sarkar, V.: SLAW: a scalable locality-aware adaptive work-stealing scheduler for multi-core systems. In: Proceedings of the 15th ACM SIGPLAN Symposium on Principles and Practice of Parallel Programming, PPoPP 2010, pp. 341–342. ACM (2010)
5. Huang, L., Jin, H., Yi, L., Chapman, B.M.: Enabling locality-aware computations in OpenMP. Sci. Program. 18(3–4), 169–181 (2010)
6. Muddukrishna, A., Jonsson, P.A., Brorsson, M.: Locality-aware task scheduling and data distribution for OpenMP programs on NUMA systems and manycore processors. Sci. Program. 2015, 5:1–5:16 (2015)
7. Olivier, S.L., de Supinski, B.R., Schulz, M., Prins, J.F.: Characterizing and mitigating work time inflation in task parallel programs. In: Proceedings of the 24th International Conference on High Performance Computing, Networking, Storage and Analysis, SC 2012, pp. 65:1–65:12. IEEE (2012)
8. OpenMP Architecture Review Board: OpenMP Application Program Interface, Version 3.0. http://www.openmp.org/
9. OpenMP Architecture Review Board: OpenMP Application Program Interface, Version 4.0. http://www.openmp.org/
10. Pilla, L.L., Ribeiro, C.P., Cordeiro, D., Bhatele, A., Navaux, P.O.A., Méhaut, J.F., Kalé, L.V.: Improving parallel system performance with a NUMA-aware load balancer. Technical reort TR-JLPC-11-02, INRIA-Illinois Joint Laboratory on Petascale Computing, Urbana, IL (2011). http://hdl.handle.net/2142/25911
11. Terboven, C., Schmidl, D., Cramer, T., an Mey, D.: Assessing OpenMP tasking implementations on NUMA architectures. In: Chapman, B.M., Massaioli, F., Müller, M.S., Rorro, M. (eds.) IWOMP 2012. LNCS, vol. 7312, pp. 182–195. Springer, Heidelberg (2012)
12. Yan, Y., Zhao, J., Guo, Y., Sarkar, V.: Hierarchical place trees: a portable abstraction for task parallelism and data movement. In: Gao, G.R., Pollock, L.L., Cavazos, J., Li, X. (eds.) LCPC 2009. LNCS, vol. 5898, pp. 172–187. Springer, Heidelberg (2010)
13. Ziakas, D., Baum, A., Maddox, R.A., Safranek, R.J.: Intel QuickPath interconnect architectural features supporting scalable system architectures. In: 2010 18th IEEE Symposium on High Performance Interconnects, pp. 1–6, August 2010

Towards Unifying OpenMP
Under the Task-Parallel Paradigm

Implementation and Performance of the `taskloop` Construct

Artur Podobas[(✉)] and Sven Karlsson

Technical University of Denmark, Kongens Lyngby, Denmark
{`podobas,svea`}`@dtu.dk`

Abstract. OpenMP 4.5 introduced a task-parallel version of the classical thread-parallel for-loop construct: the taskloop construct. With this new construct, programmers are given the opportunity to choose between the two parallel paradigms to parallelize their for loops. However, it is unclear where and when the two approaches should be used when writing efficient parallel applications.

In this paper, we explore the taskloop construct. We study performance differences between traditional thread-parallel for loops and the new **taskloop** directive. We introduce an efficient implementation and compare our implementation to other taskloop implementations using micro- and kernel-benchmarks, as well as an application. We show that our taskloop implementation on average results in a 3.2 % increase in peak performance when compared against corresponding parallel-for loops.

1 Introduction

Task- and thread-parallelism are two different paradigms used to exploit parallel patterns in applications. Thread-parallelism stems from the conceptual abstraction of user-level threads as proxies for physical processors. These threads are made explicitly visible for the user. Task-parallelism is on the other hand fully oblivious of the physical layout of the system and programmers are instead encouraged to focus on exposing parallelism rather than mapping parallelism onto threads. Task-parallelism is argued to be more versatile than thread-level parallelism [3].

Up until version 3.0, OpenMP was a thread-parallel framework. However, with OpenMP 3.0, OpenMP added task-parallelism. Practitioners have since debated what paradigm to use in each case.

With OpenMP 4.5, a new task level construct has been added, the `taskloop` construct. This means that applications that previously used the `omp for` construct can today be re-written using `taskloop` directives. Hence, practically eliminating the need for thread-parallelism. This also means that programmers now need to take a decision which of the two paradigms to use.

© Springer International Publishing Switzerland 2016
N. Maruyama et al. (Eds.): IWOMP 2016, LNCS 9903, pp. 116–129, 2016.
DOI: 10.1007/978-3-319-45550-1_9

We argue that the task-parallel paradigm should be exclusively used. We also argue that a well-implemented `taskloop` can be used instead of the thread-parallel for loops in OpenMP.

The present paper is one step towards verifying our hypotheses. We do so by evaluating how well the recently added `taskloop` construct performs compared to the traditional `for` constructs. We also propose an efficient `taskloop` implementation. We show that using `taskloop`s can on average be 3.2 % faster than corresponding parallel for loops.

In short, our contributions are as follows:

– We reveal implementation details of our `taskloop` implementation, which includes a novel way of load balancing tasks.
– We evaluate the `taskloop` construct using our prototype implementation and the latest GCC implementation. We further compare against parallel-for implementations in GCC and Intel's OpenMP libraries.

For the remaining paper, we will use the term *task-loop* when we refer to the new `omp` `taskloop` directive and use *parallel-for* when we refer to the old `omp` `for` directive.

The paper is structured as followed. Section 2 surveys existing OpenMP `taskloop` implementations and Sect. 3 describes our `taskloop` implementation. Section 4 describes the experimental method with results in Sect. 5. Section 6 position our contributions against similar methods. Finally, we conclude the paper in Sect. 7.

2   Existing OpenMP Task-Loop Implementations

The OpenMP 4.5 `taskloop` decomposes a canonical for-loop into a set of unique tasks, where each task is not bound to any specific processing thread. The task-loop is compliant with the earlier `omp` `for`; the main difference is the lack of schedule- and reduction-clauses in the task-loop. Because both approaches behave in a similar way, programmers can now choose which of the two paradigms to be used in their applications.

Today, the OpenMP `taskloop` construct is supported in two frameworks: OmpSs [8] and GCC version 6.1. Both implementations use a single thread to spawn the entire loop, visually illustrated in Fig. 1:a. GCCs OpenMP implements the decomposition inside the runtime system while OmpSs does so statically through compiler transformations. Unless specified by the programmer, GCCs OpenMP runtime will decompose the iteration space evenly across the number of threads ($num_{task} = num_{threads}$) while OmpSs always requires the programmer to specify the chunk size for each loop.

We have observed three main limitations to OmpSs' and GCCs approaches. First, neither systems recursively decompose tasks, which also means that tasks are not decomposed in parallel. Instead, a single thread bears the responsibility of creating tasks. This leads to increased overheads and a longer critical path.

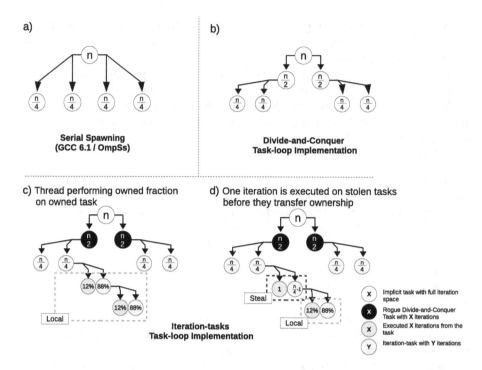

Fig. 1. Different task-loop decomposition strategies. (a) Serial spawn order found in GCC and OmpSs. (b) Divide-and-conquer found in runtime systems such as Cilk+ and Threading Building Blocks. (c)-(d) Proposed iteration tasks

Second, iterations are statically assigned with few opportunities for load balancing.

Third, and this only applies to GCC, a single global local is used when decomposing tasks, which increases the critical path.

3 Improved Task-Loop Implementation and Load Balancing

Based on our observations of the limitations in OmpSs and GCC, we have designed and implemented a scalable task-loop. We have included the implementation into Błysk.

Błysk[1] is our prototype runtime system, primarily developed for research on task-parallel runtime systems. Błysk is API compatible with GCCs OpenMP runtime system. Prior work on Błysk includes research on task dependencies and task-level speculation [6,14].

---

[1] The Błysk prototype implementation can be obtained through https://github.com/podobas/BLYSK.git.

3.1   Implementation

We have focused on the identified problems with GCCs OpenMP and OmpSs'
implementation: overheads, task decomposition and load balancing. As with
GCCs OpenMP, our implementation makes use of the existing tasking infrastructure in Błysk. The infrastructure provides functionality for maintaining and
scheduling tasks. Each thread has a private task-queue, and load balancing is
performed through work-stealing [9]. Accesses to shared data-structures are done
through lock-free operations where possible, which is unlike the global locks used
in GCCs OpenMP.

A task-loop in Błysk is decomposed using a recursive divide-and-conquer
algorithm, illustrated in Fig. 1:b.

The benefits of recursively decomposing work through divide-and-conquer are
many and range from improved cache utilization to a shorter critical path [5,11,13].
This is an improvement over GCCs OpenMP and OmpSs' approach where tasks
are created serially by a single thread.

The divide-and-conquer algorithm will divide the iteration space into finer
and finer tasks, until a cutoff is reached. The cutoff is similar to that of GCCs
OpenMP runtime system. We subdivide the iteration space until we have as
many tasks as we have threads. These leaf tasks of the task graph are called
iteration tasks. We currently subdivide in a binary fashion but for large systems
a higher branching factor is likely more efficient.

3.2   Iteration Tasks

Iteration tasks are the primary way to balance the workload across threads. An
iteration task will have a subset of the iteration space associated with it.

Inspired by existing thread-parallel self-scheduling algorithms, we created a
method for load balancing iteration tasks. The algorithm is visually illustrated
in Fig. 1:c-d.

When a thread creates an iteration task, it will become the owner of that task
and will execute iterations from its iteration space. However, there are situations
where some threads have executed all their iterations while other threads have
iterations left. To handle that, we allow threads to take over, or *steal*, iterations
from other threads.

As an owner, a thread reserves and executes a large fraction of the iteration
task's work, the *owned fraction*, seen in Fig. 1:c. We have heuristically chosen the
owned fraction to be $\frac{1}{8}$ in this paper. The thread will steadily consume fractions
of the owned task, decreasing the work in the task until all work is consumed.
We allow threads to steal work from each other. Any unreserved amount of work
in an iteration task can be stolen, which means that more than one thread can
cooperatively consume iterations. In other words, when a thread tries to reserve
work, another thread might already have stolen it.

When a thread has consumed the work within the task it owns, it will proceed
to steal work from other threads, see Fig. 1:d. A successful steal will not only
steal a single iteration from the task but also migrate the ownership to the thread

that performed the steal. The thread first executes the stolen single iteration. It now owns the iteration task and will continue to reserve and consume iterations reserving an owned fraction in each step.

We have run a number of experiments with different configurations arriving at the aforementioned heuristic. We have explored scheduling and work stealing approaches, including stealing single iterations, not transferring ownership and various owned fractions. We found that an owned fraction of $\frac{1}{8}$ reaches equal performance to more fine-grained strategies but requires fewer steals. We present empirical evidence motivating our decision in Sect. 5.1.

4   Experimental Method

We used a 48 core AMD Opteron 6172-based system for the evaluation. The system consists of four sockets with two AMD Opteron 6172 processors per socket. Each processor contains 6 processing cores. The system runs at 2.1 GHz and have a total of 64 GB of RAM. The operating system running on the system is CentOS 6.5 with Linux kernel 2.6.32.

GCC version 6.1 was used to build all benchmarks as well as the Błysk runtime system. All benchmarks were compiled with aggressive optimizations, -O3. Intels OpenMP compiler version 15.0.3 was used to complement the performance evaluation.

4.1   Benchmarks

We evaluated our implementation as well as the GCC and Intels OpenMP implementations using benchmarks and microbenchmarks. It should be noted that our version of Intels OpenMP implementation does not yet support task-loops and so it is not used for any task-loop experiments.

We have developed two microbenchmarks. The first microbenchmark is a stress-test designed to evaluate the runtime systems' resilience to iteration granularity. The microbenchmark contains a for loop where iterations have a controllable amount of work. The chunk size is set to one to isolate per iteration overheads. We have two versions of the benchmark parallelized using task-loop and parallel-for respectively. We vary the amount of work in each iteration, the granularity, and measure the execution time.

The second microbenchmark tests the resilience to variance in the execution time of iterations. We use measurements from the first benchmark to design a benchmark where the average iteration granularity is large enough so that we see linear scalability with all the runtime systems. However, we also introduce a controlled uniformly random variance to the execution time of iterations. We make several runs with different levels of variance to observe the load balancing abilities of the runtime systems.

We have also used kernels from the SpecOMP benchmark suite [2], the Rodinia benchmark suite [7] and Parsec [4]. Table 1 shows the input data sets for the different benchmarks as well as serial execution time. We have selected

Table 1. Benchmarks, their input data set and serial execution time

Benchmark	Input	Source	Serial time
358.botsalgn	prot.100.aa	SpecOMP 2012	$22,25\,s$
359.botspar	8000×8000	SpecOMP 2012	$88,83\,s$
Backward Propagation	4194304 nodes	Rodinia	$3,87\,s$
HeartWall	test.avi / 50 frames	Rodinia	$107,46\,s$
HotSpot3D	512×8	Rodinia	$4,58\,s$
LavaMD	10 boxes	Rodinia	$65,81\,s$
Leukocyte	testfile.avi / 10 frames	Rodinia	$71,20\,s$
Prime	all primes 0-300,000	Selfmade	$77,84\,s$
BlackScholes	in_10M.txt	Parsec	$281,68\,s$

benchmarks which GCC 6.1 can handle. GCC 6.1 is, as of this writing, the current GCC version which also has some shortcomings.

GCC can currently, for example, not handle the case when a `parallel` or `single` construct is encountered in the same compound statement as a `taskloop` construct.

We compare the performance when using GCCs task-loop implementation as well as our own. In addition, we also measure the performance of benchmarks when using parallel-for.

The main metric for performance chosen is speed-up over the serial implementation, given as: $\frac{t_{serial}}{t_{parallel}}$

The speed-up shows how well the performance of the runtime system and application scales with the number of processors. All benchmarks were executed ten times and we show the mean value.

5   Results

We study performance in two principle ways. First, we study the scalability and load balancing capabilities of different task-loop and parallel-for implementations. Second, we observe the execution time of a set of benchmarks.

We use the two microbenchmarks we developed to study how well task-loop and parallel-for implementations scale and how well they handle load balancing problems.

First, we use our first microbenchmark and vary the number of loop iterations and their execution time. This will show what overheads runtime system incur with different number of iterations and iterations with different execution times. Figure 2 shows results for 2400 and 4800 iterations. The speed-up over a serial loop execution is plotted on the y-axis against the execution time of each iteration.

The best performing implementation is that of the older statically scheduled parallel-for loops, where Intel's OpenMP implementation performs with as low as 24 cycle iteration granularity and GCC's OpenMP implementation requires

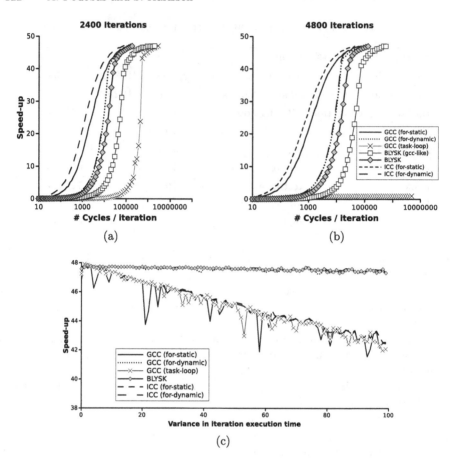

Fig. 2. Evaluation of different scheduling strategies using microbenchmarks with respect to: (a–b) resilience to iteration granularity, and (c) resilience to variance in iteration execution time

400 cycles per iteration. Both Intel's and GCC's parallel-for with a dynamic schedule perform worse than their static counterpart. GCC's task-loop implementation, GCC task-loop in Fig. 2, has the poorest performance, requiring coarser than 150,000 cycles/iteration to start performing well. Our re-implementation of the same algorithm, labeled "BLYSK (gcc-like)", results in better performance and start scaling at nearly 148,000 cycles shorter iterations. The increased performance of the Błysk re-implementation is due to Błysks better tasking infrastructure. For our proposed improved implementation, called Błysk in Fig. 2 and other figures, the Błysk scheduler can reach performance levels comparable to those of Intel's or GCC's dynamic parallel-for. Note how GCC's task-loop implementation refuses to scale in the case of 4800 iterations. Here GCCs runtime system actually refuses to spawn parallel tasks. GCC will not create any tasks if the aggregated number of spawned tasks is higher than

64 times the number of executing threads. That is the case in this situation and so the task-loop is executed serially.

We now use the second microbenchmark. We use a granularity of 1 million cycles per iteration to allow all runtime systems to scale to 48 threads. Figure 2:c shows the results of the second microbenchmark, where we see the speed-up plotted against the variance in per iteration execution time. Here the static parallel-for scheduler is showing its weakness. As we increase the variance, the load balancing properties of the static schedule decreases, yielding lower and lower performance. Because the algorithm of parallel-for static and GCC's OpenMP task-loop are similar, they both suffer from the same weakness to increased variance.

Intel's and GCC's parallel-for with dynamic schedule and our implementation of `taskloop` continue to scale to 48 threads, unaffected by the variance in iteration granularity.

5.1 Scheduling Heuristics

We now argue for our chosen scheduling heuristic, where we set the owned fraction to 12 % ($\frac{1}{8}$).

Figure 3 shows results of the second microbenchmark when executed under different scheduling heuristics with three different metrics in mind: performance, stealing activity and unbroken iterations. Executing long, unbroken iterations is important as it often honors the user's effort to write loops with good spatial and temporal cache locality [1]. A large amount of steals can lead to resource contention.

The evaluated heuristics range from a single iteration up-to consuming half the remaining iterations of a task.

Figure 3:a shows the performance when varying the amount of iterations consumed from tasks. Performance vary with the owned fraction, with diminishing returns as the owned fraction is reduced. For high performance, we need to use an owned fraction no larger than 12 %!

The number of steals that are occurring using the different heuristics is shown in Fig. 3:b. A steal is recorded every time a thread has to take iterations from a task it does not own. We see that consuming a smaller owned fraction leads to increased stealing activity. For example, using a single iteration leads to the highest stealing activity while using an owned fraction of 50 % results in the least amount of steals. This is intuitive as consuming a larger owned fraction leaves fewer iterations for potential load balancing purposes. The 12 % heuristic we have chosen steals on average 25 % less than the 6 % heuristic and 40 % less than the single iteration case.

Figure 3:c shows the average length of unbroken iterations for the three heuristics that yield the best performance. Our heuristic executes the longest continuous chain of iterations.

To summarize, our results shows that stealing 12 % of the iterations of a task in a controlled benchmark offers good performance with the fewest number of steals and the longest unbroken iteration chain.

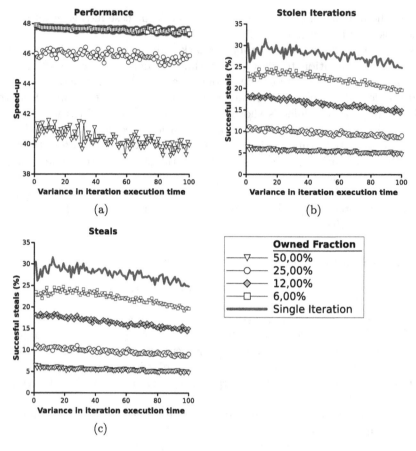

Fig. 3. Evaluation of different scheduling heuristics with respect to (a) performance, (b) number of steals and (c) average unbroken iteration length

5.2   Benchmark Performance

Figure 4 shows the performance of the various benchmarks. Here the speed-up is plotted against the number of threads allocated to the application.

For most benchmarks, the performance of the parallel-for version is comparable with our task-loop implementation. Some benchmarks, such as `rodinia.Backprop`, `rodinia.Hotspot` and `rodinia.Heartwall` scale poorly. This is mainly due to the lack of enough parallelism to occupy the 48 cores in the system. Others, such as `rodinia.lavaMD`, show an increase in performance for our proposed task-loop version when compared against GCC's parallel-for version. `rodinia.Leokocyte` and `parsec.BlackScholes` are both fairly coarse-grained applications that scale well for all runtime systems irrespective of the chosen paradigm.

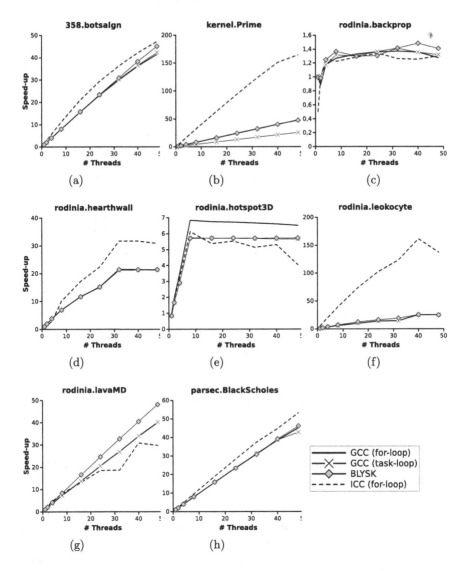

Fig. 4. Speed-up of benchmarks using task-loop and parallel-for OpenMP constructs

The 358.botsalign benchmark shows a small performance difference between our and GCCs OpenMP implementations, to our advantage. The performance increase is mainly due to the hybrid nature of the application. Unlike other benchmarks, 358.botsalign exploits both task- and thread-parallelism. The performance improvements of our task-loop come from the faster tasking infrastructure compared to GCCs OpenMP. However, note that GCCs implementation of task-loop slightly outperforms the GCC parallel-for version on 358.botsalign, indicating that mixing the two paradigms is unfavorable.

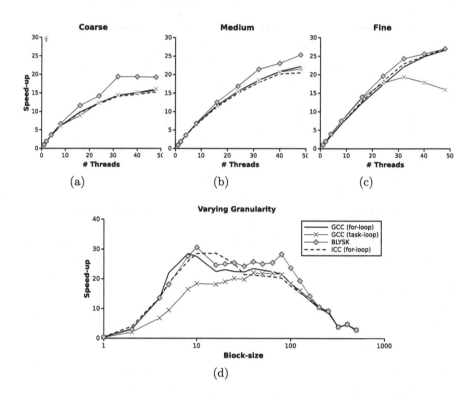

Fig. 5. Performance of the sparse LU benchmark when varying the task granularity.

Overall, our implementation of the task-loop outperforms the GCC task-loop implementation in all cases. This is attribute to both lower overheads and better load balancing.

The case of overheads is more clearly shown in Fig. 5:a–c. The figure shows 359.botspar which implements a sparse LU factorization based on either the parallel-for or task-loop implementation. Here we see the performance obtained when the entire matrix is split into block-sizes of varying granularity. The various granularities represent the amount of parallelism available in the application to solve the LU decomposition.

Our task-loop implementation outperforms the other runtime systems consistently. For the coarse-grained case, the main reason is the poor decomposition done by the other runtime systems, which can be fixed by manually tuning grain-sizes. Notice how GCCs task-loop implementation fails to scale in the fine-grained case. This decrease in performance is due to the overhead increase associated with tasking. We also see that the overall performance increase as we decrease the granularity, which leads to increased parallelism and thus better performance.

Figure 5:d shows the speed-up as a function of the amount of parallelism, when varied from decomposing the matrix into 1×1 sized blocks all the way up to 500×500 sized blocks. Note how the highest performance is reached by our task-loop implementation at a block-size of 8×8. The valley between the two peak points is mainly due to the uneven balance of parallelism that these block-sizes yield. While the parallelism increases, it does not increase enough to actually reduce the critical path of the application. The amount of application-level parallelism cannot be evenly distributed across the threads, which leads to some threads being idle.

We have included the performance of Intel's OpenMP implementation primary as a source of reference. However, it is more complicated to scrutinize the performance because the compilation infrastructure is different between Intels compiler and GCC. For example, the `kernel.Prime` benchmark performance is in part due to the vectorization capabilities of the Intel compiler. On the other hand, Intels runtime system degrades in performance on benchmarks such as `rodinia.Hotspot3D` and `rodinia.lavaMD`. We have not attempted to isolate the performance losses in Intel's OpenMP runtime system.

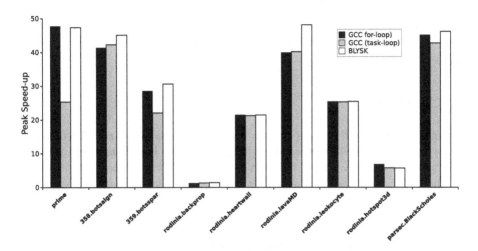

Fig. 6. The peak speed-up observed running with the different implementations for all the benchmarks using GCC's compilation framework

Figure 6 shows a summary of the peak performance that was obtained for each of benchmarks under the different implementations. The average reduction in performance when migrating from GCCs parallel-for to GCCs task-loops amount to a decrease of 9.6 % in performance. The average difference in performance between GCCs parallel-for and our improved task-loop is on the other hand an *increase* of 3.2 % in peak performance.

6   Related Work

Task based scheduling of for loops exists in several well-known task-based frameworks, such as Cilk++/Intel Cilk+ [12] and Intel Threading Build Blocks [10].

These frameworks decompose the iteration space using divide-and-conquer algorithms, most commonly using a binary division such similar to the one used in our implementation of task-loop. However, unlike our implementation, which introduces a new type of tasking primitive, the iteration tasks, said frameworks spawn a large number of tasks. Our approach is to spawn no more tasks than the number of threads and still achieves good load balancing properties.

Our task-loop approach is more closely related to that of classical thread-parallel iteration scheduling policies, though we adapt it to the task-parallel paradigm. More precisely, we position our work closely to the Chunk or Guided Chunk Self-Schedulers, GSS [15]. The main differences between our method and GSS is the parallelization paradigm and that our approach use the concept of ownership to help balance iteration. In GSS the stolen iteration are fixed. Other similar work is the Trapzeoid Self-Scheduler [16] which is similar to GSS but with a linear rather than nonlinear decreasing iteration distribution. Our proposed algorithm is of the nonlinear kind.

Another direction is to use several different scheduling algorithms combined. These are called N-level schedulers where different schedulers are used on various invocations of the same for loop [18] or on subsets of the iteration space [17]. However, N-level schedulers require profiling which has been shown to be costly in the task-parallel paradigm.

7   Conclusions

Our main purpose for this paper is to evaluate the `taskloop` construct. To do so, we have introduced an efficient implementation for load balancing task-loop iterations. We have evaluated this and existing `taskloop` implementations and can show that using `taskloop` can on average be 3.2 % faster than corresponding parallel for loops.

We used established kernel- and application-benchmarks to evaluate performance and conclude that the performance of a task-loop implementation could rival that of a traditional thread-parallel for loop.

Based on our results, we argue that the task-parallel paradigm in OpenMP is now poised to displace the thread-parallel paradigm.

Acknowledgments. We acknowledge the reviewers for their suggestions in making this paper better. The research leading to these results has received funding from the ARTEMIS Joint Undertaking under grant agreement number 332913 for project COPCAMS.

References

1. Acar, U.A., Blelloch, G.E., Blumofe, R.D.: The data locality of work stealing. In: Proceedings of the Annual ACM Symposium on Parallel Algorithms and Architectures, pp. 1–12. ACM (2000)

2. Aslot, V., Domeika, M., Eigenmann, R., Gaertner, G., Jones, W.B., Parady, B.: SPEComp: a new benchmark suite for measuring parallel computer performance. In: Eigenmann, R., Voss, M.J. (eds.) WOMPAT 2001. LNCS, vol. 2104, pp. 1–10. Springer, Heidelberg (2001)
3. Ayguadé, E., Copty, N., Duran, A., Hoeflinger, J., Lin, Y., Massaioli, F., Teruel, X., Unnikrishnan, P., Zhang, G.: The design of OpenMP tasks. IEEE Trans. Parallel Distrib. Syst. **20**(3), 404–418 (2009)
4. Bienia, C., Li, K.: PARSEC 2.0: a new benchmark suite for chip-multiprocessors. In: Proceedings of the Annual Workshop on Modeling, Benchmarking and Simulation, vol. 2011 (2009)
5. Bohme, D., Wolf, F., Supinski, D., Bronis, R., Schulz, M., Geimer, M.: Scalable critical-path based performance analysis. In: Proceedings of Parallel & Distributed Processing Symposium, pp. 1330–1340. IEEE (2012)
6. Bonnichsen, L., Podobas, A.: Using transactional memory to avoid blocking in OpenMP synchronization directives. In: Terboven, C., et al. (eds.) IWOMP 2015. LNCS, vol. 9342, pp. 149–161. Springer, Heidelberg (2015). doi:10.1007/978-3-319-24595-9_11
7. Che, S., Boyer, M., Meng, J., Tarjan, D., Sheaffer, J.W., Lee, S.-H., Skadron, K.: Rodinia: a benchmark suite for heterogeneous computing. In: Proceedings of IEEE International Symposium on Workload Characterization, pp. 44–54. IEEE (2009)
8. Duran, A., Ayguadé, E., Badia, R.M., Labarta, J., Martinell, L., Martorell, X., Planas, J.: OmpSs: a proposal for programming heterogeneous multi-core architectures. Parallel Process. Lett. **21**(02), 173–193 (2011)
9. Goldstein, S.C., Schauser, K.E., Culler, D.E.: Lazy threads: implementing a fast parallel call. J. Parallel Distrib. Comput. **37**(1), 5–20 (1996)
10. González, C.H., Fraguela, B.B.: A generic algorithm template for divide-and-conquer in multicore systems. In: Proceedings of IEEE International Conference on High Performance Computing and Communications, pp. 79–88. IEEE (2010)
11. Kumar, P.: Cache oblivious algorithms. In: Petreschi, R., Persiano, G., Silvestri, R. (eds.) CIAC 2003. LNCS, vol. 2653, pp. 193–212. Springer, Heidelberg (2003)
12. Leiserson, C.E.: The Cilk++ concurrency platform. J. Supercomput. **51**(3), 244–257 (2010)
13. Mohr, E., Kranz, D.A., Halstead Jr., R.H.: Lazy task creation: a technique for increasing the granularity of parallel programs. IEEE Trans. Parallel Distrib. Syst. **2**(3), 264–280 (1991)
14. Podobas, A., Brorsson, M., Vlassov, V.: TurboBŁYSK: scheduling for improved data-driven task performance with fast dependency resolution. In: DeRose, L., Supinski, B.R., Olivier, S.L., Chapman, B.M., Müller, M.S. (eds.) IWOMP 2014. LNCS, vol. 8766, pp. 45–57. Springer, Heidelberg (2014)
15. Polychronopoulos, C.D., Kuck, D.J.: Guided self-scheduling: a practical scheduling scheme for parallel supercomputers. IEEE Trans. Comput. **100**(12), 1425–1439 (1987)
16. Tzen, H.T., Ni, L.M.: Trapezoid self-scheduling: a practical scheduling scheme for parallel compilers. IEEE Trans. Parallel Distrib. Syst. **4**(1), 87–98 (1993)
17. Zhang, Y., Burcea, M., Cheng, V., Ho, R., Voss, M.: An adaptive OpenMP loop scheduler for hyperthreaded SMPs. In: Proceedings of International Conference on Parallel and Distributed Computing (and Communications) Systems, pp. 256–263 (2004)
18. Zhang, Y., Voss, M., Rogers, E.S.: Runtime empirical selection of loop schedulers on hyperthreaded smps. In: Proceedings of International Parallel and Distributed Processing Symposium, p. 44b. IEEE (2005)

A Case for Extending Task Dependencies

Tom Scogland[(✉)] and Bronis de Supinski

Lawrence Livermore National Laboratory, Livermore, CA 94550, USA
{scogland1,bronis}@llnl.gov

Abstract. Tasks offer a natural mechanism to express asynchronous operations in OpenMP as well as to express parallel patterns with dynamic sizes and shapes. Since the release of OpenMP 4 task dependencies have made an already flexible tool practical in many more situations. Even so, while tasks can be made asynchronous with respect to the encountering thread, there are no mechanisms to tie an OpenMP task into a truly asynchronous operation outside of OpenMP without blocking an OpenMP thread. Additionally, producer/consumer parallel patterns, or more generally pipeline parallel patterns, suffer from the lack of a convenient and efficient point-to-point synchronization and data passing mechanism. This paper presents a set of extensions, leveraging the task and dependency mechanisms, that can help users and implementers tie tasks into other asynchronous systems and more naturally express pipeline parallelism while decreasing the overhead of passing data between otherwise small tasks by as much as 80 %.

Keywords: Tasks · Producer/consumer · Interoperability

1 Introduction

The addition of tasks to OpenMP marked a fundamental shift in the programming paradigms available to OpenMP users. Programs are no longer tied to statically sized and shaped parallel algorithms, but support recursive or dynamic structures as well. The addition of task dependencies in OpenMP 4.0, and more recently the addition of the `taskloop` construct, have continued to build on this support for dynamic parallelism. Despite these advances, some patterns remain elusive. This paper presents proposed extensions to OpenMP to target two such patterns: efficient interoperability with other asynchronous models, frameworks or hardware; and efficiently expressing fine-grained producer/consumer relationships.

Much as OpenMP has incorporated progressively more dynamic parallelism through the last several versions, many programming models and frameworks have been building in support for asynchronous operations. Some of the more

---

The rights of this work are transferred to the extent transferable according to title 17 U.S.C. 105.

This work was performed under the auspices of the U.S. Department of Energy by Lawrence Livermore National Laboratory under Contract DE-AC52-07NA27344. (LLNL-CONF-694789).

N. Maruyama et al. (Eds.): IWOMP 2016, LNCS 9903, pp. 130–140, 2016.
DOI: 10.1007/978-3-319-45550-1_10

commonly used of the programming models include CUDA [1] and OpenCL [2], both of which rely on asynchronous data motion and kernel execution for efficiency. At the same time libraries and frameworks such as MPI [7], libuv, or even Linux native asyncio expose programmers to ever more options for asynchronous communication independent of their programming model. All of these can be incorporated into the OpenMP task graph by wrapping a call to them in a task, to be sure, but there is a downside to this approach. The call must block, or be caused to block, within that task for dependencies to resolve correctly in OpenMP. As a result, all of these potentially asynchronous options either must not be integrated into the task graph, or must consume an OpenMP thread for their entire duration, forcing them to effectively be synchronous. We propose an extension to the task and dependency system to support unstructured tasks, tasks encompassing a dynamic region, to incorporate these models and frameworks more efficiently and cleanly with the OpenMP model.

Producer/consumer models have been poster-children for OpenMP tasking, especially since the advent of dependencies. Tasks are, in general, a natural way to express producer/consumer and more general pipeline models, and OpenMP tasks are no exception in this respect. Unfortunately however, OpenMP lacks an efficient point-to-point data passing mechanism to support very fine-grained producer/consumer parallelism. The built-in way to pass an element from a producer to a consumer is for the producer to create a task, which is a relatively expensive operation that must be amortized. We propose adding a new type of dependency, queue dependencies, that carry typed concurrent queues to reduce the necessity to create additional tasks while providing an efficient point-to-point data transfer mechanism for OpenMP.

Our contributions are as follows:

- A design for unstructured tasks, allowing general interoperability between the OpenMP task graph and external asynchronous models
- An extension to task dependencies to carry data channels, enhancing support for fine-grained producer/consumer codes
- An evaluation of our queue-based producer/consumer dependencies.

The rest of this paper is laid out as follows. First we present the base global dependency extension on which the others are built in Sect. 2. Our design for task interoperability with unstructured task regions follows in Sect. 3. Next we discuss and evaluate our design for queue dependencies in Sect. 4, followed by related work in Sect. 5.

2   Global Dependencies

Our extensions revolve around improving point to point synchronization between tasks and integration of external synchronization mechanisms into the OpenMP task graph. Both of these goals benefit from one base extension, the ability to define a global, or at least cross-task, dependency or synchronization directed synchronization mechanism. Depending on the shape this takes, different extensions become possible as either API routines or directives. This section discusses the global dependency mechanism itself, as well as two extensions that either make use of it or exploit the added potential for point-to-point synchronization in a system that incorporates the concept. Specifically we propose extensions for writing advanced interoperability interfaces that can help integrate other asynchronous runtimes or mechanisms with the OpenMP task graph and integrating producer consumer relationships either through dependency directives, or through an analogous queue API.

For the purpose of this paper, we assume the existence of an extra attribute, `global`, on the `depend` clause that can be specified before the dependency direction. For example, `depend(global, inout: a)` would introduce an input dependency on all tasks, regardless of their parent task or sibling relationship, that have an output dependency on `a`. Likewise it specifies an output dependency that applies to all tasks created by all threads that specify an input dependency on `a` thereafter. This kind of dependency can be thought of much like an `omp single` directive for structured parallel regions, in that it ensures that only that one task, of all tasks that have dependencies on a given list item, can be running at a time. One example use would be to block work on a given data element, or set of same, to synchronize or otherwise communicate with other processes in a distributed memory setting. The nature of a global dependence is that its ordering with respect to specific tasks encountered in other threads is not guaranteed without external synchronization, but it can provide a useful serialization point.

3   Unstructured Tasks

Especially with the uptake of heterogeneous architectures and computational coprocessors, asynchronous operations are becoming more and more common in high performance computing. OpenMP provides an interface to asynchronously offloading work with the target directives, and memory motion if necessary, with the device data constructs. If there is an operation that isn't directly provided by OpenMP however, integrating it without wasting a thread is less than straightforward for even the most advanced users.

As an example, a user writing an asynchronous version of `omp_target_memcpy` with an underlying asynchronous call provided by their system might write the code in Fig. 1. The resulting implementation is asynchronous with respect to the encountering task and the encountering thread. Even so, if they take the simple option, it requires a CPU thread to remain blocked in the `async_wait()` call in order to ensure the memcpy is done before the task dependence is satisfied. To avoid blocking the thread the entire time, the user may add polling using `taskyield` to re-invoke the task scheduler. While this certainly works, it introduces additional invocations of the task scheduler and of a polling interface to function, where an asynchronous response mechanism may already be available and may further be more efficient or may be the only mechanism available. To address cases like this, where an already asynchronous event should be integrated into the task dependency graph, we propose to introduce *unstructured tasks*.

```
1    void naive_async_memcpy(void *dst, void *src,
2                            size_t size, void **dep) {
3        // Wait for all OpenMP tasks that have out depends on *dep
4        #pragma omp task depend(inout: *dep)
5        {
6            // start asynchronous memcpy
7            async_memcpy(dst, src, size);
8            // wait for the memcpy to complete
9            async_wait();
10           // OR
11           while(!async_poll_done()) {
12               #pragma omp taskyield
13           }
14       }
15   }
```

Fig. 1. A naive attempt at an asynchronous `memcpy`

Figure 2 shows the constructs of the extension we propose for this use case. Much like the device data constructs, specifically **target enter data** and **target exit data**, the **taskenter** and **taskexit** directives form an unstructured region. Rather than an unstructured data environment however, these form an unstructured task region to allow manipulation of dependency satisfaction based on external factors. The **taskenter** directive takes an identifier clause, which is used to fill a passed variable with the identifier later used to satisfy the task dependency, and optionally accepts an associated block and a **depend** clause. A **taskenter** without a depend clause is allowed, but is treated as though it begins with a **taskwait** construct. If no block is provided, the encountering thread blocks on a task scheduling point until all input dependencies are satisfied. Otherwise, if a block is provided, it is treated as a deferrable task that will be executed when dependencies are resolved, allowing the encountering thread to continue immediately.

The main difference between **taskenter** and a regular OpenMP task is that output dependencies *are not satisfied* at the end of the **taskenter** construct. In order to satisfy the output dependencies on an unstructured task, a **taskexit** directive with a matching **identifier** clause must be used. If the dependency is a standard, local, dependency then the **taskexit** must be encountered by the task that encountered the **taskenter** construct. For a global dependency, any thread executing on the same device is allowed to encounter the **taskexit**.

The example in Fig. 3 illustrates the usage of an unstructured task to improve integration with a native asynchronous memcpy. This version uses a **taskenter** directive to create a global input and output dependency on the value passed in by the user, and since it has an associated block and no **if** clause, the task is deferred. While the encountering thread continues, the task waits for input dependencies to be satisfied. Once they are, the external asynchronous memcpy is invoked, and a callback registered with the external library to satisfy the

```
1   // Begin an unstructured task region:
2   #pragma omp taskenter identifier(list-item) \
3                     [depend([global,] \
4                             [in|out|inout[:]] \
5                             <list-items>) ...] \
6                     [untied] \
7                     [if(<condition>)]
8   // {} Optional block to be run as a task when in dependencies
9   //    are satisfied
10  // End an unstructured task region, satisfy out dependencies
11  #pragma omp taskexit identifier(list-item)
```

Fig. 2. Unstructured tasks

```
1   struct dep_ident {void ** dep; void * ident;};
2   void extended_async_memcpy(void *dst, void *src,
3                       size_t size, void **dep) {
4       struct dep_ident *i = malloc(sizeof(struct dep_ident));
5       i->dep = dep;
6       // Wait for all OpenMP tasks that have out depends on *dep
7       #pragma omp taskenter identifier(i->ident) \
8                       untied \
9                       depend(global, inout: *dep)
10      {
11          async_memcpy(dst, src, size);
12          async_callback_on_complete(clear_dependency, i);
13      }// Note: *dep out is not satisfied here
14  }

15  void clear_memcpy_dependency (void *dep) {
16      struct dep_ident *i = dep;
17      // Satisfy the currently outstanding out dependency on *dep
18      // note: since this is a global dependency, any thread may clear the
19      //       dependency
20      #pragma omp taskexit identifier(i->ident)
21  }
```

Fig. 3. Produce and consume as dependence types

OpenMP dependence on *dep once the copy is complete. Using the extension, the external memcpy now offers nearly the same level of task integration that unstructured device data constructs do through the nowait clause, but through a wholly user-controllable mechanism.

It is worth noting that this interface would be meant for advanced users only, primarily for those writing runtime systems, optimized native libraries supporting OpenMP or integrations with other systems. In giving the user control over an unstructured dependency region, it is possible for a user to create a deadlock by never completing an unstructured task in the same way it is possible for them to cause a deadlock by never unlocking a lock that threads are waiting on. That said, the potential advantages of being able to integrate more tightly with the dependency mechanisms of system libraries, or even communication libraries such as MPI, are substantial.

4   Queue Dependencies

OpenMP tasks are frequently taught with certain specific dynamic workloads in mind. The most common of these appear to be parallelizing recursive algorithms and parallel processing of dynamically sized containers like linked lists. Right behind these in lists of use-cases however is to model a parallel producer and consumer. While this use-case appears in many lists, actual code for a task-based producer consumer is rarely included in examples, preferring to fall back on `critical` sections to create ad-hoc queues to implement the pattern. The resulting code requires external dependencies, or manual implementation of data transfers, neither of which is necessary for a version using tasks. As an example, see Figs. 4 and 5. Both figures implement the same pattern, but the critical section version requires a queue to store intermediate work, and takes nearly twice as many lines of code as the task version. Admittedly, the critical section version offers a known first-in first-out order, which the task version does not, but not all producer consume problems require such an ordering.

```
1   serial_queue_t sq = INIT_SERIAL_QUEUE;
2   int done = 0;
3   #pragma omp parallel
4   while (!done) {
5       int product = 0;
6       if (omp_get_thread_num () == 0) {
7           done = produce(&product);
8           if (done) {
9               #pragma omp flush
10              break;
11          }
12          #pragma omp critical(product_queue)
13          enqueue(&sq, product);
14      }
15      #pragma omp critical(product_queue)
16      int status = dequeue(&sq, &product);
17      if (status == QUEUE_EMPTY) continue;
18      consume(product);
19  }
```

Fig. 4. A simple single producer multiple consumer with critical sections

```
1   #pragma omp parallel
2   #pragma omp serial
3   while (1) {
4       int product = 0;
5       int done = produce (&product);
6       if (done) break;
7       #pragma omp task firstprivate(product)
8       consume (product);
9   }
```

Fig. 5. A simple single producer multiple consumer with tasks

While there are clear upsides to the task version, unfortunately there is also a hidden downside. The task version incurs more overhead, for which we will provide specific numbers below. What both of these have in common is that they share the work of consumption across available threads by passing produced data through an intermediate data structure. In Fig. 4 the structure is an is explicit queue. The task version in Fig. 5 uses an implicit structure, the task queue inside the OpenMP runtime itself, to accomplish the same ends. Each task storing its required data element to be consumed when a thread is available. In order to improve the usability of this idiom in OpenMP, we propose to incorporate a new dependency type that also serves to pass data between tasks, allowing them to be reused rather than rebuilt.

The core of the extension is to add the new dependency types **produce** and **consume**, along with corresponding directives **omp produce** and **omp consume**. When a **produce** or **consume** dependency is encountered, a multi-producer multi-consumer queue is logically created and associated with the address of the list-item passed to the **depend** clause. If one already exists in the current thread, it is found and reused, or if the dependency uses the **global** attribute it would be found in any thread in the contention group. The queue thus created would persist until either all producer tasks using it have completed and it is empty or until the parallel region ends, whichever comes first. Within the region of a producer task the **omp produce(<arg>[[, <full>], <complete>])** directive may be used to add items to the queue. The first argument to the directive is copied into the queue as they would be by a **firstprivate** clause. If the queue is full and the **<full>** variable is omitted, the operation blocks on a task scheduling point until room is available. If the **<full>** argument is specified, then the operation is non-blocking, and sets that argument a boolean representing whether the **<arg>** was successfully placed into the queue or not. If the **<full>** parameter is true, the application is responsible for caring for the argument value until it can be passed. Finally, when all producer tasks for a given queue are complete, the queue becomes closed, allowing consumers to detect that there will be no more values to consume by specifying something to be set for the closed argument.

```
1   int done = 0;
2   #pragma omp parallel
3   while (!done) {
4       int product = 0, more = 0;
5       #pragma omp master
6       #pragma omp task depend(global, produce: product)
7       while (1) {
8           done = produce (&product);
9           if (done) {
10              #pragma omp flush
11              break;
12          }
13          more = 1;
14          #pragma omp produce(product)
15      }
16      #pragma omp task depend(global, consume: product)
17      while(1) {
18          #pragma omp consume(product, more)
19          if (!more)
20              break;
21          consume (product);
22      }
23  }
```

Fig. 6. A simple single producer multiple consumer with queue dependencies

On the opposite side, a task with a `consume` dependence becomes a consumer task, and uses the same mechanism to locate the queue it is to read from. Within the region, the `omp consume(<arg>[[, <more>], <complete>])` directive can be used to retrieve a value from the queue into `<arg>`, a boolean representing whether the value retrieved is new or the queue was empty in `<more>` and `<closed>` which denotes whether the queue has been closed. If a consumer is encountered without a matching producer having been encountered, the consumer will act as though the producer exists and is both empty and closed.

Using these constructs, we can produce the example presented in Fig. 6. This example uses producer and consumer tasks to create a pipeline that can continue as long as the queue has room in a parallel context, and yet retains a correct serial elision when OpenMP is not used. This example shows the master encountering a producing task while all the other threads, and subsequently the master itself, encounter consuming tasks. All of these become logically connected by the same multi-producer multi-consumer queue because the dependency specification on each is global. The producer blocks when the queue is full, but due to the task scheduling point therein it can be re-scheduled to continue in the original loop and help process consuming tasks until the queue runs dry. Threads may spin through the outer loop, but because the lifetime of the queue is tied to the enclosing parallel region, it is only created and destroyed once in this construct.

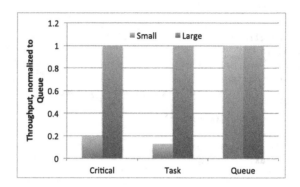

Fig. 7. Producer/consumer microbenchmark normalized element throughput

The main downside to this construction is the relative verbosity and complexity, it is in fact longer than using a third-party queue with critical sections, but it holds an advantage in potential throughput. The main complication is maintaining serial elision correctness while using directives for the data passing and synchronization mechanism. This could likely be alleviated by shifting to an API-based approach somewhat, or certainly by providing a progress guarantee between tasks even when run with one thread, but those options are outside the scope of this paper.

Figure 7 shows results for a simple producer/consumer microbenchmark implemented with each of these three mechanisms. Each run uses a single producer, the master thread, and eight consumers (one of which is also the producer), one per thread on the 8-core Intel i7 CPU, 500,000 elements are produced, retrieved and consumption is a simple sum for the small case or a loop over 5,000 elements in the large case. The underlying queue implementation for the concurrent queue is a blocking multi-producer multi-consumer queue equivalent to that proposed by Scogland et al. [10]. These results show that for producer/consumer problems with relatively small work, or a requirement for high throughput, the queue extensions can be highly beneficial. For medium or larger, long running, tasks the overhead is dwarfed by the task execution time.

5   Related Work

Integrating task systems with one another has been a popular topic of research in recent years. OmpSs [4,6], a precursor to many of OpenMP's tasking features, incorporates both CUDA and OpenCL asynchronous communications into its runtime, and provides the results to the user at the beginning of their tasks. The runtime backing the StarPU [3] task system performs similar background management of data as well. This approach differs from the one we propose for OpenMP in that we want to give users control over the machinery that allows OpenMP to coexist with another asynchronous model peacefully. The automated asynchronous data movement these models use is a good candidate for optimizations of the device data constructs, and possibly other areas, but does not address quite the same problem.

The concept of using channels, or queues, between independent tasks or threads of control to provide synchronization and communication is certainly not a new one. Discussions of a method like it go at least as far back as discussions of communicating or cooperating sequential processes and coroutines by Dijkstra [5] and Hoare [8] who discuss communication between coroutines via a variety of mechanisms as fundamental to programming. In more recent times the use of blocking channels in combination with lightweight tasks has been popularized by the Go [9] language, which incorporates both a coroutine analog and synchronous typed channels as basic language types. The main distinctions between our extension and channels as used by Go are that Go's channels support serial execution only with guaranteed progress despite blocking on channels, where our extension is designed to always result in a valid serial elision that does not require task swapping to be correct. A progress guarantee of this type might be a useful future extension, but it is beyond the scope of this paper.

6   Conclusions

We have presented three extensions to OpenMP's tasking model. First, at the base, is allowing a `global` modifier to make a task dependency apply across a contention group, rather than just to sibling tasks. Leveraging that, we present unstructured tasks, which give users and runtime implementers a way to more closely and efficiently integrate their asynchronous mechanisms with OpenMP's task graph. Finally we presented an extension for producer/consumer dependencies, allowing OpenMP runtimes to provide a queue-like data-passing and synchronization abstraction for producer/consumer models. We show that using the queue mechanism allows a user to generate far fewer tasks, and pay less overhead per iteration of each of the producer and consumer. For very small consumer workloads, we found an improvement of as much as 80 % and no performance decrease for larger tasks. In the future we would like to investigate these mechanisms in terms of larger applications, and explore the possibility of gracefully handling an unstructured task left unsatisfied as well as investigating the possibility of a formal progress model for OpenMP tasking.

References

1. CUDA   programming   guide   (2007).   http://docs.nvidia.com/cuda/cuda-c-programming-guide/
2. The OpenCL Specification, November 2012. https://www.khronos.org/registry/cl/specs/opencl-1.2.pdf
3. Augonnet, C., Thibault, S., Namyst, R., Wacrenier, P.-A.: STARPU: a unified platform for task scheduling on heterogeneous multicore architectures. In: Sips, H., Epema, D., Lin, H.-X. (eds.) Euro-Par 2009. LNCS, vol. 5704, pp. 863–874. Springer, Heidelberg (2009). http://www.springerlink.com/index/h013578235633mw3.pdf

4. Bueno, J., Planas, J., Duran, A., Badia, R.M., Martorell, X., Ayguadé, E., Labarta, J.: Productive programming of GPU clusters with OmpSs. In: International Parallel and Distributed Processing Symposium, pp. 557–568 (2012). http://ieeexplore.ieee.org/xpl/articleDetails.jsp?tp=&arnumber=6267858 &contentType=Conference+Publications&matchBoolean%3Dtrue %26rowsPerPage%3D30%26searchField%3DSearch_All%26queryText%3D%28 %22Productive+Programming+of+GPU+Clusters+with+OmpSs%22%29

5. Dijkstra, E.W.: Cooperating sequential processes. In: Hansen, P.B. (ed.) The Origin of Concurrent Programming, pp. 65–138. Springer, New York (1968)

6. Duran, A., Ayguadé, E., Badia, R.M., Labarta, J., Martinell, L., Martorell, X., Planas, J.: OmpSs: a proposal for programming heterogeneous multi-core architectures. Parallel Process. Lett. **21**(2), 173–193 (2011). http://www.worldscinet.com/abstract?id=pii:S0129626411000151

7. Forum, M.P.I.: MPI: a message-passing interface standard. Technical report (1994). http://citeseer.ist.psu.edu/article/forum94mpi.html

8. Hoare, C.A.R.: Communicating sequential processes. Commun. ACM **21**(8), 666–677 (1978). http://portal.acm.org/citation.cfm?doid=359576.359585

9. Pike, R.: The go programming language. Talk given at Google's Tech Talks (2009)

10. Scogland, T.R.W., Feng, W.: Design and evaluation of scalable concurrent queues for many-core architectures. In: ACM/SPEC International Conference on Performance Engineering (ICPE), February 2015

OpenMP as a High-Level Specification Language for Parallelism

And its use in Evaluating Parallel Programming Systems

Max Grossman[✉], Jun Shirako, and Vivek Sarkar

Department of Computer Science, Rice University, Houston, USA
{max.grossman,shirako,vsarkar}@rice.edu

Abstract. While OpenMP is the de facto standard of shared memory parallel programming models, a number of alternative programming models and runtime systems have arisen in recent years. Fairly evaluating these programming systems can be challenging and can require significant manual effort on the part of researchers. However, it is important to facilitate these comparisons as a way of advancing both the available OpenMP runtimes and the research being done with these novel programming systems.

In this paper we present the OpenMP-to-X framework, an open source tool for mapping OpenMP constructs and APIs to other parallel programming systems. We apply OpenMP-to-X to the HClib parallel programming library, and use it to enable a fair and objective comparison of performance and programmability among HClib, GNU OpenMP, and Intel OpenMP. We use this investigation to expose performance bottlenecks in both the Intel OpenMP and HClib runtimes, to motivate improvements to the HClib programming model and runtime, and to propose potential extensions to the OpenMP standard. Our performance analysis shows that, across a wide range of benchmarks, HClib demonstrates significantly less volatility in its performance with a median standard deviation of 1.03 % in execution times and outperforms the two OpenMP implementations on 15 out of 24 benchmarks.

1 Motivation

The OpenMP specification offers a high-level way of expressing shared-memory parallelism. The level of abstraction offered by OpenMP provides a number of benefits, and has contributed significantly to OpenMP's success in three ways. First, OpenMP offers users a high-level programming model to work in, by default only requiring that they express the parallelism in their application and not the low-level details of how to exploit the parallelism on a given hardware platform. Second, OpenMP's abstractions offer runtime builders flexibility in the optimizations and techniques they can use to produce a well-performing OpenMP implementation. Third, OpenMP's abstractions map well across hardware platforms and generations, offering both backwards compatibility and the promise of portability to future platforms.

© Springer International Publishing Switzerland 2016
N. Maruyama et al. (Eds.): IWOMP 2016, LNCS 9903, pp. 141–155, 2016.
DOI: 10.1007/978-3-319-45550-1_11

However, there are an increasing number of alternative shared memory parallel programming systems, including HClib [10], Cilk [4], TBB [16], C++ language extensions for parallelism [13], Kokkos [8], Raja [12], X10 [6], and more. None of these models has experienced the widespread acceptance of OpenMP, but facilitating comparisons among them and OpenMP helps move the entire parallel programming models community forward.

To encourage and improve the rigor of these comparisons, this paper looks at OpenMP as a high-level specification of parallelism, a format that is universally understood and applicable and can be mapped to other programming models and runtimes through source-to-source transformations. In this way we can validate both the performance and programmability of these novel parallel programming systems. If a novel parallel programming model is sufficiently flexible to support a reasonable subset of the latest OpenMP standard, we can assume it has the potential for broad applicability. We can also say that if a novel parallel runtime is sufficiently well-performing to match the performance of the various OpenMP runtimes, we can assume that it has the potential to handle real world applications. Otherwise, this comparison can help to identify performance bottlenecks in current runtime efforts.

While these comparisons can clearly motivate improvements to the novel parallel programming system being evaluated, they can also benefit the development of the OpenMP standard. For example, recently the OpenMP standard underwent a massive expansion in the programming constructs and hardware platforms supported, e.g. task-parallel programming and accelerator programming. However, these constructs were not new and unique in their introduction to OpenMP: all were based on existing implementations in existing programming models.

When proposing, defining, and building these new OpenMP features it is important to be able to provide an early prototype of the extension, and then verify that production implementations of accepted extensions are well implemented. The OpenMP-to-X framework solves both of these problems for new OpenMP features by facilitating their construction on top of, and direct comparison to, existing programming systems.

This work contributes the OpenMP-to-X framework for implementing the OpenMP standard on top of other parallel programming models. We see two primary contributions of this work:

1. Using OpenMP as a high level specification of parallelism enables a more direct and fair performance and programmability comparison among programming models, both OpenMP vs. X and X vs. Y.
2. By enabling the OpenMP standard on top of other parallel programming models, we facilitate the extension of OpenMP with experimental abstractions on top of a pre-existing implementation.

In particular, we target the HClib [10] parallel programming library and compare its performance and feature set against the GNU and Intel OpenMP implementations.

The rest of this paper is structured as follows. In Sect. 2 we provide background on the HClib parallel programming library that we experiment with in this work. In Sect. 3 we describe the design and implementation of our OpenMP-to-X framework. In Sect. 4 we use this framework to directly compare HClib and various OpenMP implementations. In Sect. 5 we discuss the qualitative benefits and potential applications of our OpenMP-to-X framework. We conclude this paper in Sect. 6.

2   HClib

HClib is a C/C++ library for programming multi-core and heterogeneous systems. It uses a task-based programming model, and supports constructs such as parallel-for, finish-async, promises, and atomic variables.

HClib sits on top of a lightweight work-stealing runtime that load balances user-created tasks across persistent worker threads. Locality is a first-class citizen in the HClib runtime and programming model.

The HClib runtime scheduler is built around the concept of *places*. A single place represents a single hardware component, e.g. an L1 cache, a GPU's memory, the DRAM attached to a socket. Locales are bi-directionally connected to each other so as to emulate the structure of the underlying hardware. For example, a user might configure an L1 place to be connected to an L2 place, rather than being connected directly to system memory because this would more accurately represent the hardware component connectivity.

When making load balancing decisions at runtime, the HClib scheduler uses this graph of places to encourage locality-aware scheduling decisions. These places are also exposed through the programming model so that users can choose to explicitly pin task execution to a particular set of places, or allow more flexibility in their scheduling, thereby improving load balancing opportunities.

HClib tasks consist of an executable body and a closure (lambda) capturing any context from the task's creation point. HClib tasks can block on certain operations, in which case HClib uses runtime-managed stacks to switch the task off of its worker thread, allowing that worker thread to pick up more useful work to complete. The blocked task is automatically made eligible to execute again once its dependencies have been satisfied.

HClib shares many constructs with OpenMP, such as parallel-for, asynchronous task creation, and accelerator offload. However, each programming model also includes constructs that are unique to it; for example, HClib's futures do not require an underlying sequential ordering in the way that OpenMP's task dependencies do. Hence, there are sufficient similarities between HClib and OpenMP that a fair and one-to-one performance comparison can be made at the programming model level, but also enough difference in both their programming constructs and runtime implementation to make that comparison interesting.

3 Methods

In this section, we describe our OpenMP-to-X source-to-source compilation framework, provide more details on the HClib APIs that this framework currently targets, and describe the mapping from OpenMP APIs to HClib APIs. OpenMP-to-X source code and tests are available open source at https://github.com/agrippa/omp-to-x.

3.1 OpenMP-to-X Compile-Time Mechanics

OpenMP-to-X is constructed on top of Clang LibTooling [1], a framework for traversing and transforming the AST of a C/C++ program.

OpenMP-to-X iterates over each function in the source program. Inside each function, OpenMP-to-X constructs a representation of the nesting of OpenMP pragmas. At the same time, OpenMP-to-X also tracks visible variables at each OpenMP pragma to enable later closure creation if necessary.

Once the full OpenMP pragma tree is constructed, OpenMP-to-X traverses it from the leaves to the root and applies a pragma-specific transformation at each node. At the completion of this postorder traversal of the OpenMP pragma tree, the current function will have been entirely converted from OpenMP to a different parallel programming model.

3.2 The HClib APIs Targeted by OpenMP-to-X

In this work, we use the HClib parallel programming library as a case study of the OpenMP-to-X framework. Most of this work was performed using HClib's C APIs. However, below we discuss the equivalent C++ APIs as they are more concise.

The **async** API creates a single-threaded task running asynchronously with respect to the task which created it:

```
hclib :: async ([=] {  ...  });
```

HClib asynchronous tasks can be chained through the use of futures and promises. For example, to ensure some work B() is not performed until some other work A() has completed one could use the **async_future** and **async_await** APIs:

```
hclib :: future_t *fut = async_future ([] { A(); });
async_await ([] { B(); }, fut );
```

Promise and future objects can also be explicitly created, satisfied, and waited on by the programmer.

Another way to synchronize on tasks is to use **start_finish** and **end_finish**, whose semantics are the same as those of the **finish** statement in X10, Habanero-Java [5], and Habanero-C [7]. **end_finish** waits for all tasks spawned after the preceding **start_finish** to complete:

```
hclib :: start_finish ();
hclib :: async ([] {
   hclib :: async ([] { B(); });
   A();
});
hclib :: end_finish ();
// A and B must have completed here.
```

For convenience, HClib also supports a parallel for construct called `forasync`. There is no implicit finish at the end of `forasync` like there is for an `omp parallel for` region. The execution of an `forasync` parallel region can also be dependent on a future, and the completion of all iterations can satisfy a promise.

```
hclib :: finish ([] {
   hclib :: forasync1D (niters , [] (int iter) {
      std :: cout << "Hello_from_iter" << iter << std :: endl;
   });
});
```

`forasync` can be combined with HClib places to launch parallel for loops on accelerators, e.g.:

```
hclib :: place_t *gpu_place = hclib :: closest_place_of_type (GPU);
hclib :: finish ([] {
   hclib :: forasync1D_at (gpu_place , niters , [] (int iter) {
      ...
   });
});
```

Related to accelerators, HClib also supports place-aware memory allocation and copies, e.g.:

```
hclib :: place_t *gpu_place = hclib :: get_closest_place_of_type (GPU);
void *d_ptr = hclib :: allocate_at (nbytes , gpu_place );
hclib :: finish ([] {
   hclib :: async_copy (gpu_place , d_ptr , cpu_place , h_ptr , nbytes );
});
```

3.3   Mapping OpenMP to HClib

Currently, OpenMP-to-X supports the transformation of the OpenMP constructs listed in Table 1. Where relevant, the `private`, `firstprivate`, and `shared` data sharing clauses are also supported. The selection of which constructs and clauses to support was empirically motivated by the constructs used in our benchmarks.

Note that `single` and `master` are not supported in the general case, only as single-threaded task-launching regions. Additionally, the SPMD `parallel` region is not supported by our framework. However, in the benchmarks evaluated in this work these parallel constructs were not used. Our use of OpenMP was partly motivated by its widespread use, and the fact that supporting OpenMP applications on top of another programming model was a strong indicator for the generality of that programming model. However, if in practice particular OpenMP constructs are not widely used (e.g. SPMD `parallel`, `threadprivate`), we do not consider it important that they be used to evaluate other programming models.

Table 1. A summary of the OpenMP constructs supported by OpenMP-to-X.

Construct	Clauses	Mapping
critical		pthread mutexes
atomic		Atomic builtins
task	depend, if	async
taskwait		start-finish/end-finish
single		
master		async-at
parallel for	reduction	for-async

Supporting task and taskwait. OpenMP's task construct has a natural mapping to the async HClib API discussed in Sect. 3.2. To ensure strict adherence to the OpenMP specification, the OpenMP-to-X framework explicitly constructs a closure for each async launched. In this closure, a private variable simply has a field declared for it. A firstprivate variable has a field declared for it which is initialized from the launching context. A shared variable has a field declared for it that is initialized with the address of the shared variable in the launching context.

An OpenMP task is translated to an async call with the same body. The body of the task must be transformed to unpack private and firstprivate variables from the closure. Additionally, every reference to a shared variable in the task body is translated to be a dereference of the corresponding pointer field in the closure.

HClib has no direct equivalent to OpenMP's taskwait construct as there is no implicit tracking of child tasks. Instead, we wrap the body of each async in a start_finish and end_finish pair. When a taskwait must be handled, a call to end_finish is emitted to ensure all preceding tasks created by the current task have completed. Then, a call to start_finish is emitted to open a new task scope. Note that this finish scope does not affect the parallel execution of the async it is inside of, it only allows the creating async to block on previously created tasks.

OpenMP-to-X also supports the depend clause on task constructs. While both depend and HClib promise/future objects are ways of expressing dependencies between tasks, there are subtle differences that make it challenging to efficiently implement depend on top of promises and futures. depend uses memory address ranges to specify input and output dependencies, and relies on a sequential creation of dependent tasks to ensure tasks are ordered properly (i.e. a task must be created after all of the tasks it is dependent on). On the other hand, promises and futures are more explicit ways of expressing dependency and must be handled by the programmer, but do not rely on any creation ordering.

To support depend on top of promises and futures, OpenMP-to-X stores a mapping from any memory address range designated as an output range of a created OpenMP task to the future object that dependent tasks should be registered on. This design is concerning, as for programs that make heavy use of **depend** this map could grow to be a space and time bottleneck. Indeed, if we ignore small opportunities for compile-time dependency resolution among tasks, it is hard to see how **depend** could be implemented in any OpenMP runtime without an analogous lookup structure. While OpenMP's design of **depend** does offer an intuitive interface to programmers, it seems it also introduces more overheads than user-managed future and promise objects might.

Supporting `single` and `master`. As stated earlier, OpenMP-to-X does not currently support the `single` and `master` contructs in the general case, but only in their use as single-threaded regions inside a wrapping parallel region for the creation of OpenMP tasks, e.g.:

```
#pragma omp parallel
#pragma omp single
{
}
```

`single` is trivial to handle in this case, as it is equivalent to removing both OpenMP pragmas. For `master`, we use HClib locality abstractions and the `async_at` API to force the execution of a `master` region on the main thread of the program.

Supporting `parallel for`. While OpenMP-to-X does not support SPMD `parallel` regions, it does support the translation of the combined `parallel for` construct to the `forasync_future` API. For example, the following code:

```
#pragma omp parallel for
for (int i = 0; i < N; i++) { ... }
```

translates in to:

```
hclib::future_t *fut = hclib::forasync_future (...);
fut->wait ();
```

Similar code generation could be used to support the new `taskloop` pragma, as the semantics of a `parallel for` are similar in the most common scenario (e.g., without thread-private data). In the case of thread-private OpenMP data, OpenMP-to-X would detect a currently unsupported OpenMP command and exit with an error message.

With the above transformations, a reasonable subset of all OpenMP programs can be automatically and directly converted to use the HClib APIs. This conversion enables a more fair and direct performance comparison between existing OpenMP runtimes and research parallel runtimes (covered in Sect. 4) and enables prototyping of novel OpenMP constructs and clauses (discussed in Sect. 5).

4   Experimental Evaluation

In this section, we compare the performance of the HClib, Intel OpenMP, and GNU OpenMP runtimes on a range of benchmarks from the Rodinia, BOTS, and Kastors benchmark suites. All HClib benchmark implementations were automatically generated using the OpenMP-to-X framework. The automatic nature of the OpenMP-to-X framework enables a more fair and comprehensive performance comparison than would be possible manually.

These experiments were performed on a dedicated 12-core 2.80GHz Intel X5660 CPU node in the Rice DAVINCI cluster with 48GB of system RAM. The GNU compiler toolchain v4.8.5 and Intel compiler toolchain v15.0.2 were used. The version of HClib this work used can be found at https://github.com/habanero-rice/hclib/tree/resource_workers. All experiments were repeated ten times, and the `taskset` tool was used to pin threads to cores for both the HClib and OpenMP experiments. The ith software thread is bound to the ith logical core, and all experiments were run with 12 software threads.

When possible, we compare both "small" and "large" datasets for each benchmark. For a complete list of benchmarks and configurations, please refer to https://github.com/habanero-rice/hclib/blob/resource_workers/test/performance-regression/cpu-only/datasets.sh.

4.1 Variance of each Runtime

The first metric to consider is how much variance exists across ten runs of the same benchmark for a given runtime. The percent standard deviation of each benchmark and dataset is plotted in Fig. 1. We measured a median percent standard deviation of 10.59 %, 3.44 %, and 1.03 % for IOMP, GOMP, and HClib, respectively.

The main trend of importance is the lower variance offered by the HClib runtime. Our first thought on seeing these results was that some OpenMP initialization code was being measured, and that it was causing high overheads

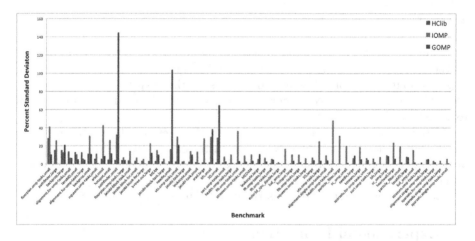

Fig. 1. The percent standard deviation of each benchmark and dataset on all runtimes, sorted from most to least variance on HClib. Higher values indicate more variance from run to run.

and high variance. However, even when we investigate the two benchmark configurations with the highest variance on the IOMP runtime (srad,small and floorplan.omp-tasks,small) and manually modify them to ensure any OpenMP initialization must have occured prior to the timed code region, we continue to see high variance.

Additionally, these two high-variance benchmarks have significantly different patterns of parallelism: srad consists of an outer sequential loop wrapped around two inner parallel-for regions, and floorplan uses the task and taskwait constructs. This suggests that this volatility is not a localized problem, but rather one that might be exposed by many applications. Admittedly, these are both short-running benchmarks so a small amount of volatility can appear as a large percentage. However, the fact that this volatility is not reflected in the HClib results suggests that it is not an intrinsic characteristic of these benchmarks.

Further analysis of these two benchmark configurations using HPCToolkit [2] reveals that HClib does a better job of utilizing worker threads. For example, in the srad,small benchmark configuration 45.5 % of IOMP execution time is spent under two IOMP internal functions: __kmp_fork_barrier and __kmp_join_barrier. In contrast, HClib spends 24.9 % of time in runtime internal functions related to load balancing. These high runtime overheads and thread idleness might contribute to the observed volatility in IOMP and GOMP execution times.

4.2   Overall Performance

We also consider the overall performance achieved by HClib, IOMP, and GOMP for benchmarks where a percent standard deviation below 10 % was observed. Focusing only on benchmarks that achieve reasonably consistent performance on all runtimes allows us more confidence in any conclusions drawn. Figure 2 plots the median speedup for all consistent benchmarks, normalized to GOMP performance.

For 15 out of a total 24 consistent benchmarks, HClib outperforms IOMP and GOMP. For 6, IOMP is the highest performer, and for 3 we see the best performance from GOMP. While the mean speedup for HClib relative to GOMP is slightly lower than IOMP at 2.45x and 2.59x respectively, HClib demonstrates more consistent results by having a median speedup of 1.34x compared to IOMP's median of 1.02x.

To better understand the cause of the performance difference between the two highest performing runtimes, HClib and IOMP, we also investigated various hardware counters. The main trends we observed for both runtimes was that higher performance was strongly correlated with (1) fewer last-level cache misses, and (2) fewer instructions executed. This indicates the importance of locality, and the importance of keeping overheads to a minimum. For example, on the Kastors jacobi-block-task benchmark with the large dataset, IOMP's 70 % performance improvement over HClib was correlated with a 4.5x reduction in last-level cache misses. On the BOTS sparselu benchmark, HClib demonstrated a 5.50x and 3.04x speedup on the small and large datasets, respectively.

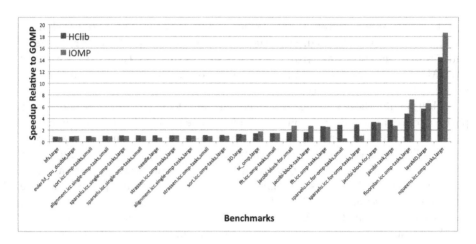

Fig. 2. The speedup of each benchmark and dataset that demonstrated a percent standard deviation below 10 % on all runtimes, normalized to the GOMP results and sorted from lowest to highest speedup on the HClib runtime. Higher values are better.

This was correlated with a 2.94x and 4.25x reduction in instructions executed. These hardware counter results continue to support the observations from Sect. 4.1: HClib's work-stealing runtime implementation keeps useful computation on the worker threads, rather than internal runtime logic.

We also used built-in HClib metrics to analyze these benchmarks. We observe that for many of the benchmarks where HClib experienced the highest speedup there is a single worker thread producing most of the tasks in the application, with the others all stealing from it. This insight combined with the more consistent results shown in Sect. 4.1 and the HPCToolkit investigation above indicates that HClib's work-stealing scheduler may be more aggressive about load balancing while exhibiting lower overhead than IOMP's or GOMP's task schedulers.

It is important to point out that one of the common shortcomings of source-to-source code generation is that naive techniques can often break compiler optimizations by making application source code more difficult to analyze (e.g., by taking the address of variables that would normally be stored in registers). While it is difficult to isolate the performance side effects OpenMP-to-X's transformations would have, the side effects of the optimization-limiting transformations (e.g., taking addresses of shared variables, passing function pointers, adding volatile qualifiers) are fundamentally required for correctly implementing OpenMP semantics, regardless of programming model. For example, while taking the address of a shared OpenMP variable as part of OpenMP-to-X's transformations might force the compiler to allocate stack space for it, that space must have been allocated in the OpenMP version of the program as well in order for multiple threads to access it. Therefore, we believe the optimization-limiting side effects of OpenMP-to-X transformations would be similar to the loss of optimization necessary to support OpenMP semantics and would not significantly affect these performance results.

5 Discussion

In our experience, OpenMP-to-X has proven to be a powerful tool for runtime comparisons. It can motivate changes and offer insights in to both the current state of the OpenMP standard and runtimes, as well as current research runtimes.

5.1 Insights Gained into HClib

The comparative analysis enabled by the OpenMP-to-X framework and performed as part of this work identified several bottlenecks in the HClib runtime. In particular, memory allocations for finish-scope management, runtime-managed stacks, and future/promise object management were identified as limiting the scalability of the HClib runtime, and addressed. These results validate the OpenMP-to-X framework as a tool for motivating improvements to parallel research runtimes.

This work also motivated the addition of atomic variables as a first-class citizen of HClib, as a result of the heavy usage of omp atomic in many of the benchmarks used in this work. The use of atomic compiler intrinsics as the target for omp atomic in the OpenMP-to-X framework was observed as a performance bottleneck for some generated HClib codes. While HClib atomic variables were not used in the performance analysis in Sect. 4, they are an example of how comparisons enabled by the OpenMP-to-X framework can motivate improvements to the programming model of a research runtime.

As part of these experiments, we identified several features of OpenMP that are desirable for performance or programmability but which have no analogue in HClib. For example, static scheduling of parallel for loops is not something currently supported in HClib, but would reduce runtime overheads further. Tied task continuations could benefit locality in fork-join style programs. The master construct is useful when interacting with third-party libraries which have restrictions on the calling thread. One interesting note about these constructs is that while they are distinct entities in OpenMP, they could also be unified if OpenMP had the concept of locality built in to its programming model (as HClib does with hierarchical places). A statically scheduled parallel for loop is simply one which places the constituent tasks of that parallel for at specific cores for execution, precluding any dynamic load balancing. A tied task is simply a task whose continuation is launched at the same core as was originally executing it. A master region is a code block launched at the core on which the master thread resides. This suggests that a well-defined locality model in the OpenMP standard would allow for a unification of many constructs that are disjoint today.

One challenge in this work was supporting the `task depend` clause on HClib. While HClib supports dependent tasks, it does so through programmer-managed promise and future objects. In OpenMP, dependencies are programmer-managed, but there are no explicitly managed dependency objects. While we find both models easy to work with, we found the underlying sequential semantics requirements of the OpenMP approach somewhat restricting, and have concerns over the ability to scale this approach to many tasks since large numbers of tasks will require large numbers of lookups on an ever-growing table of tasks and their output relations.

Perhaps the largest difference between OpenMP and the HClib runtime is that the OpenMP approach is able to take advantage of compile-time optimizations and code transformations, while HClib is purely a library. While in theory the hybrid compiler-runtime approach should have performance benefits, these results show that a purely library-based approach can also produce consistent and well-performing parallel programs.

5.2   Motivating Extensions to OpenMP

As part of this work, we also reflected on the current OpenMP standard and what features of HClib could lead to potential OpenMP extensions in the future.

As part of our experimental evaluation, we found metrics exposed by the HClib runtime to be useful when reasoning about the behavior of parallel programs. However, without matching metrics from the OpenMP runtimes it is difficult to make strong conclusions. The proposed OpenMP Tools API [9] seems to be a synergistic project with the OpenMP-to-X framework which could help provide this missing functionality.

One of the largest differences between HClib and the current OpenMP specification is the inclusion of locality constructs in the programming model. HClib's hierarchical place trees allow programmers to indicate both where tasks may run and where memory should be allocated. In future systems with deeper memory hierarchies, this locality support within the programming model itself may be crucial for productive parallel programming. However, the quantitative benefits of these constructs were not evaluated as part of this work.

5.3   Other Targets for OpenMP-to-X

While HClib was selected as the target of this work because of the authors' familiarity with it, many other shared-memory programming models could benefit from evaluation using OpenMP-to-X.

Work-in-progress is using OpenMP-to-X to target CUDA as a backend. CUDA's constrained, data-parallel programming model and discrete address spaces present unique challenges to supporting it under OpenMP-to-X. It has necessitated significant extensions to OpenMP-to-X, mirroring the developer effort normally required to convert an OpenMP program to an equivalent CUDA version. Despite this, the scope of the OpenMP specification that can be supported on CUDA is far more limited than for HClib. This work has already demonstrated successful automatic conversion of OpenMP `parallel for` loops to CUDA using OpenMP-to-X, similar to past works [3,14,15].

One strong candidate for evaluation would be the Kokkos programming model [8]. While Kokkos has received attention as a fundamental execution layer for the Trilinos project [11], it has also received criticism in its applicability as a general-purpose programming model as a result of its restricted programming model. However, the Kokkos runtime's focus on performance and low overheads would also make for an interesting comparison on the subset of the OpenMP specification it can support.

Both the Intel Thread Building Blocks [16] and Cilk [4] programming models would be good case studies as well, as they are arguably the next most commonly used shared-memory parallel programming models after OpenMP.

We note that HClib, Kokkos, TBB, and Cilk are all syntactically C/C++ programming models. Due to its construction on top of the Clang compiler frontend, targeting C/C++ programming models with OpenMP-to-X is a requirement of the current implementation. While it would be possible to extend this framework to support targeting significantly different programming models or languages, this remains future work.

Targeting other programming models that are not syntactically similar to C/C++ would include all of the usual challenges that come with converting one programming language to another. Programming languages with a C/C++ compatibility layer (e.g. Java) would reduce these challenges.

Targeting parallel programming models that are syntactically C/C++ but diverge significantly from OpenMP in their abstractions (e.g., graph programming models) may also be possible. However, OpenMP-to-X's relevance as a tool for performance or programmability comparison would be lessened. In general, programming models with non-overlapping APIs arise from different motivations, and so the comparison of them might be meaningless.

6   Conclusions and Future Work

In this work, we used the OpenMP-to-X source-to-source code generation framework to enable a variety of experiments. We compared various parallel runtimes, using OpenMP as an intermediate representation for parallelism. We performed feature comparisons by studying how OpenMP operations could be mapped to other parallel programming models, and used that information to motivate extensions to both OpenMP and other parallel programming models. Through these studies, we have improved on the flexibility and performance of the HClib runtime and demonstrated overheads in the Intel and GNU OpenMP runtimes that merit further investigation.

While many past studies have compared OpenMP to other parallel programming models and runtimes, this is the first attempt we are aware of to standarize that process by using the same input OpenMP programs to evaluate different runtimes. By building a framework for consistent and automated generation of parallel programs from OpenMP programs, we enable more comprehensive and fair performance comparisons between parallel programming models in the future, as well as a path to rapid prototyping of novel OpenMP functionality.

Acknowledgments. This work was supported in part by the Data Analysis and Visualization Cyberinfrastructure funded by NSF under grant OCI-0959097 and Rice University.

The authors would also like to acknowledge the contributions of Vivek Kumar, Nick Vrvilo, and Vincent Cave to the HClib project.

References

1. Clang libtooling. http://clang.llvm.org/docs/LibTooling.html
2. Adhianto, L.: Hpctoolkit: tools for performance analysis of optimized parallel programs. Concur. Comput. Pract. Exp. **22**, 685–701 (2010)
3. Baskaran, M.M., Ramanujam, J., Sadayappan, P.: Automatic C-to-CUDA code generation for affine programs. In: Gupta, R. (ed.) CC 2010. LNCS, vol. 6011, pp. 244–263. Springer, Heidelberg (2010)
4. Blumofe, R.D., Joerg, C.F., Kuszmaul, B.C., Leiserson, C.E., Randall, K.H., Zhou, Y.: Cilk: an efficient multithreaded runtime system. J. Parallel Distrib. Comput. **37**(1), 55–69 (1996)
5. Cavé, V., Zhao, J., Shirako, J., Sarkar, V.: Habanero-Java: the new adventures of old X10. In: Proceedings of the 9th International Conference on Principles and Practice of Programming in Java, pp. 51–61. ACM (2011)
6. Charles, P., Grothoff, C., Saraswat, V., Donawa, C., Kielstra, A., Ebcioglu, K., Von Praun, C., Sarkar, V.: X10: an object-oriented approach to non-uniform cluster computing. ACM Sigplan Not. **40**(10), 519–538 (2005)
7. Chatterjee, S., Tasirlar, S., Budimlic, Z., Cave, V., Chabbi, M., Grossman, M., Sarkar, V., Yan, Y.: Integrating asynchronous task parallelism with MPI. In: 2013 IEEE 27th International Symposium on Parallel & Distributed Processing (IPDPS), pp. 712–725. IEEE (2013)
8. Edwards, H.C., Trott, C.R., Sunderland, D.: Kokkos: enabling manycore performance portability through polymorphic memory access patterns. J. Parallel Distrib. Comput. **74**(12), 3202–3216 (2014)
9. Eichenberger, A., Mellor-Crummey, J., Schulz, M., Copty, N., DelSignore, J., Dietrich, R., Liu, X., Loh, E., Lorenz, D.: OMPT and OMPD: Openmp tools application programming interfaces for performance analysis and debugging. In: International Workshop on OpenMP (IWOMp 2013) (2013)
10. Habanero Research Group: Hclib: a library implementation of the habanero-c language (2013). http://hc.rice.edu
11. Heroux, M.A., Bartlett, R.A., Howle, V.E., Hoekstra, R.J., Hu, J.J., Kolda, T.G., Lehoucq, R.B., Long, K.R., Pawlowski, R.P., Phipps, E.T., et al.: An overview of the trilinos project. ACM Trans. Math. Softw. (TOMS) **31**(3), 397–423 (2005)
12. Hornung, R., Keasler, J.: The raja portability layer: overview and status (2014)

13. International Organization for Standardization. The C++ Programming Language Standard (2014). https://isocpp.org/std/the-standard
14. Lee, S., Min, S.-J., Eigenmann, R.: OpenMP to GPGPU: a compiler framework for automatic translation and optimization. ACM Sigplan Not. **44**(4), 101–110 (2009)
15. Ohshima, S., Hirasawa, S., Honda, H.: OMPCUDA : OpenMP execution framework for CUDA based on Omni OpenMP compiler. In: Sato, M., Hanawa, T., Müller, M.S., Chapman, B.M., Supinski, B.R. (eds.) IWOMP 2010. LNCS, vol. 6132, pp. 161–173. Springer, Heidelberg (2010)
16. Reinders, J.: Intel Threading Building Blocks: Outfitting C++ for Multi-core Processor Parallelism. O'Reilly Media Inc., Sebastopol (2007)

Scaling FMM with Data-Driven OpenMP Tasks on Multicore Architectures

Abdelhalim Amer[1]([✉]), Satoshi Matsuoka[2], Miquel Pericàs[3],
Naoya Maruyama[4], Kenjiro Taura[5], Rio Yokota[2], and Pavan Balaji[1]

[1] Argonne National Laboratory, Lemont, IL 60439, USA
aamer@anl.gov
[2] Tokyo Institute of Technology, Tokyo 152-8550, Japan
[3] Chalmers University of Technology, 412 96 Gothenburg, Sweden
[4] RIKEN Advanced Institute of Computational Science, Hyogo 650-0047, Japan
[5] University of Tokyo, Tokyo 113-0033, Japan

Abstract. Poor scalability on parallel architectures can be attributed to several factors, among which *idle times*, *data movement*, and *runtime overhead* are predominant. Conventional parallel loops and nested parallelism have proved successful for regular computational patterns. For more complex and irregular cases, however, these methods often perform poorly because they consider only a subset of these costs. Although data-driven methods are gaining popularity for efficiently utilizing computational cores, their data movement and runtime costs can be prohibitive for highly dynamic and irregular algorithms, such as fast multipole methods (FMMs). Furthermore, loop tiling, a technique that promotes data locality and has been successful for regular parallel methods, has received little attention in the context of dynamic and irregular parallelism.

We present a method to exploit loop tiling in data-driven parallel methods. Here, we specify a methodology to spawn work units characterized by a high data locality potential. Work units operate on tiled computational patterns and serve as building blocks in an OpenMP task-based data-driven execution. In particular, by the adjusting work unit granularity, idle times and runtime overheads are also taken into account. We apply this method to a popular FMM implementation and show that, with careful tuning, the new method outperforms existing parallel-loop and user-level thread-based implementations by up to fourfold on 48 cores.

1 Introduction

The technology trend of increasing core densities and deepening memory hierarchies in high-end processor packages is exacerbating the difficulty of harnessing their computational power. Higher core counts imply that applications have to expose more concurrent work in order to feed the computational units. Moreover, the performance of the memory subsystem is not keeping up with the core density. Consequently, pressure on the memory subsystem (e.g., caches, interconnects) and the distances that remote data has to traverse are increasing, adding to the existing CPU-memory performance gap.

© Springer International Publishing Switzerland 2016
N. Maruyama et al. (Eds.): IWOMP 2016, LNCS 9903, pp. 156–170, 2016.
DOI: 10.1007/978-3-319-45550-1_12

A parallel execution can be formulated as a dynamic scheduling optimization problem. The goal is to minimize the makespan of a schedule of work units (*tasks, loop chunks*) on a set of computational cores. Unfortunately, finding an optimal schedule has proved to be an NP-complete problem even in the simple case of static scheduling, two processors, and one or two time units for task weights [11]. In practice, the model that dictates parallel execution (e.g., bulk-synchronous, data-driven) affects the resulting schedule and does not guarantee optimality.

The effectiveness of the resulting schedule is often quantified in terms of *parallel efficiency* relative to a sequential execution. Recent literature has shown that loss in parallel efficiency can be attributed to three primary factors: *idle times, data movement,* and *runtime overhead*[1] [7,9]. In order to mitigate these costs, parallel algorithms must expose sufficient parallelism (i.e., *parallel slackness*) and reduce data movement while keeping the runtime overhead low. Conventional parallel loops and nested parallelism have proved successful for regular computational patterns. For more complex and irregular cases, however, such methods often perform poorly because they take into account only a subset of these factors. For instance, bulk-synchronous approaches, exemplified by parallel loops, can suffer from underutilization of resources because of insufficient parallel slackness within or across computational steps. Data-driven methods can maximize resource utilization but often suffer from poor data locality (e.g., cache thrashing) and costly task management.

The difficulty of reducing data-movement costs in data-driven methods is often caused by high degrees of parallel slackness and poor data-locality incentives. Higher parallel slackness implies that the complexity of a proper work-unit-to-core mapping by the underlying runtime increases as well. Combined with poor data locality incentives, runtimes often operate with greedy heuristics (e.g. work-first and work-stealing policies) and thus execute work units in a data-locality-oblivious manner. Consequently, the resulting mapping can exhibit little data reuse and often causes substantial cache thrashing. Although some incentives have been proposed, such as hierarchical place trees [12], they remedy only part of the issue (e.g., reduction in remote memory accesses) and do not provide sufficient data reuse. On the other hand, loop tiling, a technique that promotes data locality and has been successful for regular parallelism, has seen little application in the context of data-driven and asynchronous tasking. In particular, it is arduous for these methods to exploit loop tiling within or across work units because of their fine-grained nature.

In this work, we investigate using OpenMP for a highly irregular fast multipole method (FMM) implementation. We choose FMM for its rich set of heterogeneous computational kernels and its complex dependencies that stress parallel efficiency. Furthermore, FMM input parameters allow us to control computation and synchronization requirements to help generalize our results. We propose a methodology to generate work units inherently suitable for data locality and amenable for granularity tuning to control the degree of parallel slackness and management overhead, thus taking into account all the primary factors that

---

[1] The time spent managing work units (e.g., creation, destruction, and scheduling).

influence parallel efficiency. Specifically, work units operate on input-output data in tiled computational patterns inspired by cache-blocking techniques. Since tile sizes correlate with task granularity, they are exposed as tuning parameters. This method was applied in the context of an OpenMP task-based data-driven implementation that relies on the task construct to expose parallelism and the depend clause to express data dependence.

Results after applying this method to the kernel-independent FMM (KIFMM) of Ying et al. [13] showed substantial scalability improvements over existing parallel loop and user-level thread-based implementations, where up to fourfold improvements have been observed on 48 cores. Furthermore, we show that the tuned parameter values can be portable for several other input problems except when the parallel slackness is severely hindered, such as with small problem sizes and large tasks. We also show the limits of our data-locality optimization on a heavy cache-coherent non-uniform memory access (ccNUMA) machine. These results indicate that tiling to improve temporal and spacial data locality needs to be combined with NUMA awareness in order to further reduce data movement costs.

2   Related Work

Although scheduling work on parallel machines has long been studied, its NP-completeness and the rapid growth in scale and complexity of the parallel computing landscape make it an important and open research topic. We discuss here recent work and the perspectives from which the researchers tackle the problem of parallel efficiency loss.

Tasirlar and Sarkar introduced the implementation of data-driven tasks as an extension to the *async-finish* model to allow arbitrary runtime task graphs execution [10]. The authors focused mostly on the syntax and semantics of the model, however, with little attention paid to data locality. Yan et al. abstracted the memory hierarchy using a hierarchical place trees (HPT) model [12]. However, HPT is not flexible enough to express arbitrary dependencies between tasks and hence may result in a lack in parallel slackness. Furthermore, their data locality incentive through the concept of *places* is weak, does not exploit spatial locality, and does not tackle cache-thrashing issues. Olivier et al. explored the concept of *locality domains*, similar to *places*, by extending OpenMP with runtime routines that allow users to implement locality-aware divide-and-conquer algorithms [7]. This approach, however, shares the same data-locality issues as do *places*. In addition, the study focused on loop parallelism and divide-and-conquer task-parallel algorithms that are prone to parallel slackness issues.

Data-driven methods have been used (e.g., [5,8]) to tackle the irregular nature of FMM. The FMM implementations used by these works did not exhibit data-locality issues, however, and work focused mostly on parallel slackness. In prior work we also characterized FMM implementations that exhibited opposing trade-offs: a bulk-synchronous that suffered mostly from idle times and a fine-grained data-driven implementation that was losing more on data locality [2].

Here, we strive for a better balance between the different trade-offs by exploiting tiling in a data-driven execution. A preliminary description of this method was introduced in the doctoral dissertation of the lead author [1]. Here, we provide a more in-depth description, analysis, and evaluation of the method.

3   About the FMM Case Study

The fast multipole method is a technique developed to accelerate solving N-body problems. The challenge is to evaluate pairwise interactions between N bodies. A direct computation results in an $O(N^2)$ complexity, which makes it expensive for large problem sizes. FMM was proposed as a fast solution that uses a rapidly convergent method and has a $O(N)$ complexity [4].

In this work we use the kernel-independent FMM variant developed by Ying et al., which relies only on kernel evaluations and extends FMMs to a wider range of engineering and scientific problems [13]. KIFMM operates on three-dimensional domains containing the target simulation bodies. The domain is hierarchically decomposed into smaller boxes, or cells, with each box containing a maximum of q bodies, where q is an input parameter and the hierarchy of boxes forms an octree. Computation of the effect of bodies in a source box on other bodies in a target box depends on the proximity between the two boxes. For close boxes, direct computation is employed; for far boxes, a multistep far-field approximation is used instead. In KIFMM, proximity between boxes is represented by a set of interaction lists computed following Greengard notation [4]: U, V, X and, W. KIFMM implements the force evaluation through the following steps: U-list, Upward, V-list, W-list, X-list, and Downward. We distinguish two independent flows of computation: the near field *direct evaluation*, which is represented by the U-list computation, and the *far-field approximation*, which starts from the Upward step, proceeds with the V-list, W-list, and X-list computations, and finishes with the Downward step.

The performance of KIFMM is highly dependent on the balance between its kernels. The reason is the heterogeneity between them in terms of arithmetic intensity, data accesses, and synchronization.[2] This balance depends on the density and pattern of the body distribution and the maximum number of bodies allowed in each cells, q. Large values of q result in small trees and converge KIFMM toward a direct $O(N^2)$ complexity, which is expensive even on modern hardware. Smaller values lead to larger trees, where most of the computation is performed by the far-field approximation, a step dominated by the memory-intensive V-list kernel and heavy synchronizations. This balance property allows us to simulate application runs in different regimes and thus to generalize our findings. Consequently, the primary challenge here is to ensure scalable performance in all regimes. In the following, we present the existing thread-level parallelization strategies that will serve as baselines.

---

[2] For example, U-list kernels are compute intensive; V-list ones are memory intensive and incur sparse memory accesses.

```
void* V-list-step () {
    #pragma omp parallel for schedule(OMP_SCHED)
    for(trg=0; trg < trgNodeMax; trg++)    //Traverse all target nodes
        for(src in  Vlist(trg))            //Accumulate the contribution of all
            compute_V(trg,src);            //source nodes into the target
}
```

Fig. 1. OpenMP parallel loop of the V-list step. The OMP_SCHED macro controls the scheduling policy and takes the values static or dynamic (chunk_size defaults to 1).

Bulk-Synchronous with OpenMP: This is a highly optimized implementation for multicore architectures [3]. All steps rely on OpenMP work-sharing constructs to parallelize the work on the target nodes of the octree. In particular, the Upward and Downward steps ensure parent-children dependencies through OpenMP barriers. To better expose the trade-off between parallel slackness and data-locality, we explored two opposing scheduling policies to implement all phases: (1) a static approach that divides the target node list equally among the threads without taking into account the workload variation and (2) a dynamic approach that distributes dynamically the workload. Figure 1 shows how this is applied to the V-list step, where OMP_SCHED controls the scheduling policy.

Fine-Grained Data-Driven with Lightweight Threads: In this implementation, tasks operate at the tree node granularity and are spawned as lightweight threads using the MassiveThreads library [6]. That is, the flow of execution goes from source to the target boxes, where the far-field and direct evaluation computations are merged into a single flow by starting the Upward step and the direct evaluation at the same time. Here, fine-grained synchronization is required in order to respect data dependencies. Tasks are created only when their dependencies are satisfied; dependency tracking is achieved through fork-join control flows and atomic counters. Figure 2 gives an example of how a V-list task is executed for a source cell (src) after being called by an Up task (see [2] for more details about this implementation). Our analysis showed that the way the tasks are spawned in this data-driven implementation generates subtree working sets that have a positive data locality impact on the Upward and Downward steps, but it does not help with the communication-intensive V-list computation. Despite exposing massive parallel slackness, this implementation scales poorly for data-locality-sensitive scenarios.

```
void* V (src) {
    for(trg in Vlist(src)) {               //Compute the contribution of src
        compute_V(trg,src);                //to all dependent target cells
        trg.down_counter++;                //Atomic increment of the sync counter
        if(trg.down_counter = in_depend(trg)) //all dependencies satisfied ?
            create_task(Down, trg); }      //Create Down computation task
}
```

Fig. 2. V-list computation in a fine-grained data-driven implementation. The create_task function is a generic wrapper around lightweight thread creation.

4   Tasking Through Temporal and Spatial Blocking

The difficulty of reconciling the factors affecting parallel efficiency lies in their orthogonal effect. Reducing idle times requires high degrees of parallel slackness and dynamic scheduling. The primary goal of dynamic scheduling is to balance work across computational units and is often data locality agnostic. This results in poor scheduling decisions that cause more cache thrashing from heterogeneous working sets than would a more homogeneous static scheduling approach. Furthermore, work unit management costs is higher at fine-grained levels. The previously described dynamic bulk-synchronous and fine-grained data-driven approaches suffer from this problem because they operate[3] without appropriate data locality incentives. In this section, we present a method that retains the advantages of dynamic scheduling while taking into account data locality and work unit granularity in order to lower data movement and work unit management costs. This method was primarily designed for data-driven implementations, but was also applied to parallel loops for later comparison.

In KIFMM, steps operate on objects that are arrays of basic elements. Each element is a data structure that encapsulates information required by a subset of the computational steps at the *tree node granularity*. The access pattern of each computational step can be modeled as a sparse matrix whose dimension depends on the number of objects manipulated. In the bulk-synchronous case, basic elements are written individually (dynamic scheduling) or in blocks (static scheduling), but reading is sparse and depends on the interaction lists. The lightweight-threads implementation has a similar pattern but is source centric; reads are individual, and writes are sparse. The sparsity of the memory access pattern is a major issue especially for the memory-intensive V-list step.

To improve the data locality of such sparse memory accesses, we present a partitioning scheme where tasks operate on every object in blocks of basic elements (both reads and writes). The resulting partitioning is a multidimensional tiling that clusters computational patterns that operate on contiguous data and exhibit high temporal and spatial locality. This is similar to existing cache-blocking techniques found in linear algebra optimizations. In KIFMM, however, we target the high levels of the memory hierarchy (e.g., last-level cache) because operations on tree nodes operate on larger data. For instance, an operation between two tree nodes can be composed of matrix multiplications or FFT transformations. These computations are carried out by external libraries and are often well optimized for lower-level caches. Figure 3a shows a quad-tree for a two dimensional domain where partitions are aligned to tree levels in order to avoid complex dependencies. The resulting partitions serve as the tile size for one data object. Considering a computation step that operates on two data objects, the resulting tiling is two dimensional. Figure 3b illustrates how the data is partitioned for the V-list step. In the following We use the same tile size for the tasks of all steps to simplify dependency tracking and tuning. Exploring different tile sizes for the various steps is left as a future work. We present below how the tiling method is applied for both to parallel loops and to data-driven tasks.

---

[3] Loop chunks or lightweight threads operate at the level of a single octree node.

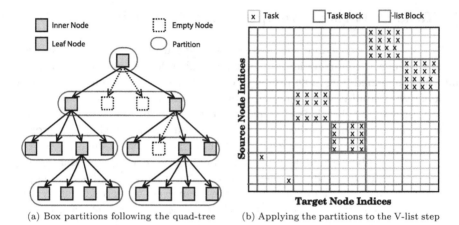

(a) Box partitions following the quad-tree   (b) Applying the partitions to the V-list step

Fig. 3. Partitioning example for a two dimensional domain (resulting in a quad-tree): (a) partition ranges within tree level boundaries to reduce unnecessary dependencies; (b) example of V-list interaction pattern between source and target boxes. The same partitioning scheme in (a) is applied to achieve two-dimensional tiles. A secondary tiling level is applied within work units for V-list.

```
void* V-list-step (){
    #pragma omp parallel for schedule(dynamic)
    for(i=0; i < trgNodeMax; i+=BS)          //Traverse all target blocks
        for(j=0; j < srcNodeMax; j+=BS)      //Traverse all source blocks
            for(trg=i; trg < BS; trg++)      //Traverse the targets in the block
                for(src=j; src < BS; src++)  //Traverse the sources in the block
                    if(src in  Vlist(trg))   //Accumulate the contribution of all
                        compute_V(trg,src);  //source nodes into the target
}
```

Fig. 4. Example of a bulk-synchronous tiled V-list computation with dynamic scheduling. BS denotes the block size.

Tiled Bulk-Synchronous: We applied the previous tiling method to the bulk-synchronous method. Figure 4 illustrates how the V-list phase is implemented with OpenMP work-sharing constructs and a blocking factor (BS). Our implementation breaks the outer loop manually, but the same result could have been achieved by using the OpenMP chunk parameter.

Tiled Data-Driven with OpenMP: Task-dependency tracking was introduced in OpenMP 4.0 through the depend clause of the task construct. This clause takes as arguments the input-output storage locations, which can be scalar variables or arrays sections. In KIFMM, specifying individual array elements as dependencies is impractical because of the task management overhead. Passing the sparse storage locations directly (e.g., as a linked list) is not possible because the depend clause accepts only scalar variables and array sections. Thus, we express those dependencies conservatively by using array sections. This approach

```
#define DATA_OUT  eff_val[beg_eval:trg_stride]
#define DATA_IN   eff_den[beg_eden:src_stride]
void* V-list-step (){
  for(i=0; i < trgNodeMax; i+=BS) {     //Traverse all target blocks
    int trg_stride = eff_trg_size*BS, beg_eval = trg_stride*i;
    for(j=0; j < srcNodeMax; j+=BS) {  //Traverse all source blocks
      int src_stride = eff_src_size*BS, beg_eden = src_stride*j;
      #pragma omp parallel task depend(out: DATA_OUT) depend(in: DATA_IN)
      for(n=i; n < i+BS; n+=VBS)             //Traverse the target V-list blocks
        for(m=j; m < j+BS; m+=VBS)           //Traverse the source V-list blocks
          for(trg=n; trg < n+VBS; trg++)     //Traverse targets in a V-list block
            for(src=m; src < m+VBS; src++)   //Traverse sources in a V-list block
              if(src in  Vlist(trg))         //Accumulate the contribution of all
                compute_V(trg,src);    }} //source nodes into the target
}
```

Fig. 5. V-list computation in the tiled data-driven implementation using OpenMP tasks. Here, **eff_val** and **eff_den** are the input and output vectors, respectively. BS and **VBS** are the maximum task and V-list tile sizes, respectively.

expresses more dependencies than necessary but incurs less dependency tracking overhead with large array sections. We then apply the tiling method by mapping tiles or blocks to array sections. In addition, we expose another blocking factor for the V-list step because communication-intensive kernels often perform worse in a data-driven execution as a result of cache thrashing from sharing cache with tasks that operate on different data[4]. Figure 3b illustrates how the data is partitioned in KIFMM with particular attention to the V-list blocks. Figure 5 shows how we implemented the V-list phase. We observe that this method is relatively simple to implement with OpenMP. The resulting manual tiling, however, makes the code less readable. We believe directive extensions to OpenMP to express tiled algorithms would be beneficial. For instance, the **taskloop** construct could be extended with tiling clauses. The rest of the stages are implemented similarly to allow a full data-driven execution.

Tuning Method: One of the limits of tuning methods is the rapid growth of the design space with the number of parameters and the ranges of discrete values they can take. To reduce this complexity, we operate in several steps, starting from tuning single-threaded performance, then moving to tuning the parallel data-driven implementation. Previously, with KIFMM, single-threaded performance was manually tuned [3]. We only tune q in single-threaded since it affects performance significantly across input problems and hardware specifications. The most important step here is to explore the design space of the task granularity and the V-list block size.

5   Characterization and Evaluation

We describe here a characterization study to identify the bottleneck sources of each implementation. We then present a performance scalability evaluation.

---

[4] Tiling with parallel loops achieves good data locality without this secondary tiling factor as will be shown in Sect. 5.1.

Table 1. Target machine specifications

	Sandy Bridge	Magny-Cours
Processor	Xeon E5-2670	Opteron 6172
CPU Frequency (Ghz)	2.6	2.1
# Sockets	2	4
# NUMA-Nodes	2	8
#Cores/NUMA-Nodes	8	6
L3 Cache size (MB)	20	6-1
Compiler	ICC 15.0.0	GCC 4.9.2

Experimental Setup: We follow the same input problems as in [3]. That is, we simulate the evaluation of a single step where the bodies are spread following two distributions: a randomly uniform and an elliptical distribution. For the interaction that governs the physics, we use the Laplace kernel. We consider only double-precision computation because of its higher pressure on the memory subsystem, which we consider more insightful. For the target architectures we select representatives of ccNUMA multicore architectures, with a two-socket Intel Sandy Bridge and 8 four-socket NUMA nodes on an AMD Magny-Cours; detailed specifications are given in Table 1.

Tuning Results: Tuning results for a uniform and an elliptical distribution on both target platforms are shown in Fig. 6 for the bulk-synchronous approach and in Fig. 7 for the data-driven approach. We observe that performance is highly variable depending on the task granularity and the V-list block size. In addition, we notice that the optimal parameters depend on the type of the input distribution and across hardware architectures. The portability of the tuned parameters

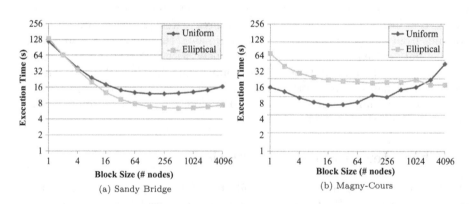

(a) Sandy Bridge

(b) Magny-Cours

Fig. 6. Tuning the tiled bulk-synchronous implementation with 2^{22} bodies and $q = 128$ at full concurrency on each machine.

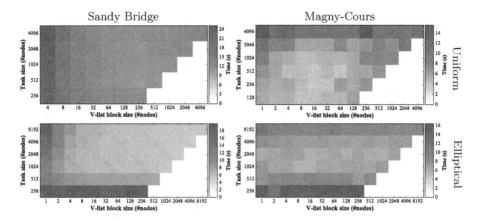

Fig. 7. Tuning the tiled data-driven implementation with 2^{22} bodies and $q = 128$ at fully concurrency on each machine.

with respect to the problem size and the parameter q is discussed further in a subsequent section. An important observation is the time explosion for small tasks when using an elliptical distribution. That inflation is due mostly to runtime overheads. Unfortunately, we do not have a quantitative measure of the runtime overhead, although we believe that this overhead is negligible for large enough tasks and that idle times and data movement dominate.

5.1 Characterizing Data Locality and Idleness

Here we analyze all implementations under the same conditions and correlate the performance differences with idle times and data locality.

Data Locality Characterization: Assuming work units are atomic, that is, not susceptible to preemption,[5] we show in Fig. 8a the cumulative execution time of all instances of two kernels that are atomic and contribute to most of the KIFMM work time. The *Direct* kernel is compute intensive and called by all the higher-level kernels except V-list. This latter phase relies heavily on the memory-intensive *Pointwise* kernel. Compared with a sequential execution, kernel times with the parallel methods increase slightly for the compute-intensive kernel but can increase significantly for the communication-intensive kernel for some methods. Since the work units are atomic, runtime scheduling overheads and idle times should not affect these results. Thus, data movement is the primary factor that influences the variation of kernel times across the parallelization methods.

---

[5] An atomic work unit executes to completion without interruption after being scheduled. In the context of parallel runtimes, such unit should not perform synchronization and scheduling operations, such as yielding execution.

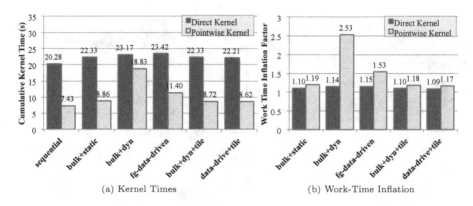

(a) Kernel Times   (b) Work-Time Inflation

Fig. 8. Data locality with an elliptical distribution, 2^{22} bodies, and $q = 128$ on Sandy Bridge.

To better capture the inflation when running such atomic work units in parallel, we rely on the *work time inflation* metric, which measures the factor of the parallel execution time over a sequential execution for a given work unit [7,9]. We measured the work time inflation for the aforementioned kernels on the Sandy Bridge machine and show the results in Fig. 8b. We notice that all methods have little inflation except the *Pointwise* kernel, which shows significant inflation in the case of the dynamic bulk-synchronous and the fine-grained data-driven implementations (2.53x and 1.53x inflation, respectively). Furthermore, we observe that the inflation was reduced substantially by the tiled implementations, incurring less than 1.20x inflation.

Idleness Characterization: To characterize idleness, we manually instrumented the implementations to record the number of tasks running in parallel per interval of time. This metric indicates idle threads if the number of running tasks is less than the number of threads. The metric involves a sampling approach using the POSIX timer interface. Figure 9 shows the results with sample intervals of 5 ms that ensure a low tracing overhead. We confirm that the data-driven approach exhibits the fewest idle threads among all approaches and that it offers a major advantage over the bulk-synchronous approach even after tuning the block sizes.

5.2 Performance Evaluation

The goals of this section are threefold: (1) evaluate all implementations in terms of scalability; (2) discuss the portability of the tuning parameters; and (3) correlate scalability and time to solution.

Scalability Evaluation: Figure 10 shows scalability results with an input problem of 2^{22} bodies. We observe that the Sandy Bridge results reflect the previous

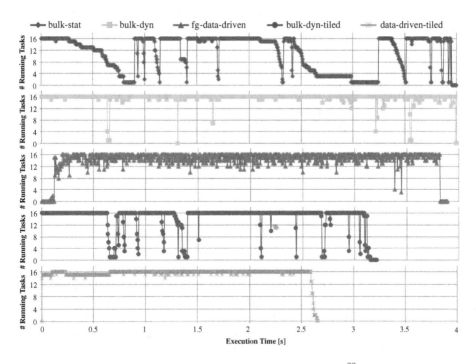

Fig. 9. Profiling idle time with an elliptical distribution and 2^{22} bodies and $q = 128$ on Sandy Bridge.

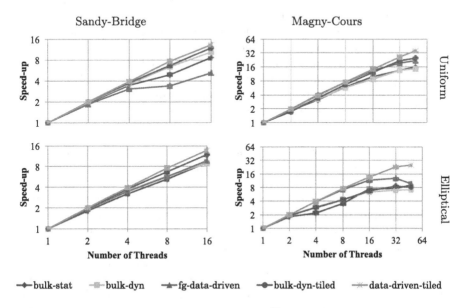

Fig. 10. Scalability evaluation with 2^{22} bodies and $q = 128$.

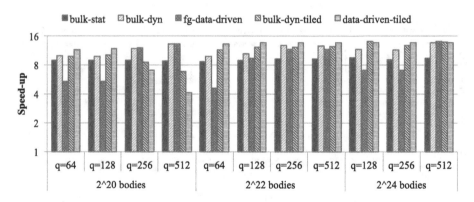

Fig. 11. Portability of the tuning parameters with an elliptical distribution on Sandy Bridge with respect to the input problem size and q.

characterization, where the tiled data-driven implementation is the most scalable, followed by the tiled bulk-synchronous method, because it suffers little work time inflation and idleness. This method also performs the best on Magny-Cours, although the parallel efficiency at full concurrency is not perfect. The reason is the data movement costs since the platform is a heavy ccNUMA machine and our data locality optimizations are not NUMA aware.

Tuning Values Portability: Here we fix the task block and V-list block sizes after tuning them for 2^{22} bodies in a uniform distribution and $q = 128$ on Sandy Bridge. We then vary the input problem while monitoring the speedup (Fig. 11). We observe that the tiled implementations perform the best in most cases except for small problem sizes and large values of q. In this latter case, the resulting octree is small; and since our decomposition is performed at the tree node level, tasks are too coarse grained, and thus parallel slackness is severely hindered. Furthermore, large values of q imply a compute-intensive regime that does not benefit from our data locality optimizations.

Scalability vs. Efficiency: Figure 11 also shows that the fine-grained dynamic implementations (bulk-synchronous and fine-grained data-driven) perform similar to or outperform the tiled implementations in compute-intensive regimes (i.e., large q). A misleading decision by application developers is to aim at generating a large number of compute-intensive tasks and schedule them dynamically; the belief is that by having few memory-intensive tasks, the dynamic execution should be able to scale almost linearly. Scalability, however, does not necessarily mean optimal time to solution. Figure 12 shows the execution time necessary for one KIFMM iteration to solve a large problem. We note that using large values of q translates into worse performance, although Fig. 11 exhibits almost linear scalability with all dynamic executions. The issue here is that a large ratio of compute-intensive tasks moves the complexity of the whole application

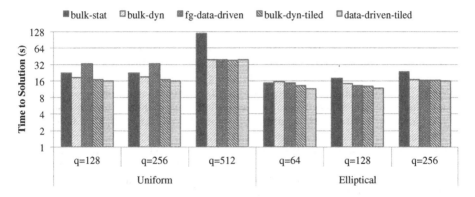

Fig. 12. Time to solution at full scale (16 cores) for an elliptical distribution with respect to the implementation method and the values of q for a large problem size (2^{24} bodies).

toward $O(N^2)$, which is heavy and slow even on modern hardware. As a result, managing data locality in the presence of memory-intensive tasks can be more efficient. In addition, other applications might not have such balance between heterogeneous kernels and might have a more homogeneous communication-intensive nature and thus will require careful data locality optimizations.

6   Conclusion and Future Work

We presented in this paper a methodology to express parallelism while taking into account data locality through tiling computation patterns when using work-sharing and task constructs. The resulting tiled bulk-synchronous and data-driven implementations showed substantial improvement, with the data-driven method being the most scalable. In addition, the tuning parameters proved to be fairly portable except when parallel slackness was severely reduced.

From a programming model perspective, the tiled implementations required more extensive changes. One of the desirable feature that was missing was the ability to write tiled algorithms readily. From a performance perspective, we showed that optimizing for data locality not only requires spatial and temporal locality but also necessitates NUMA awareness in order to reduce expensive remote data-movement. We plan to investigate methods of combining tiling abstractions with NUMA awareness, by using OpenMP places for instance.

Acknowledgment. This material is based upon work supported by the U.S. Department of Energy, Office of Science, under Contract DE-AC02-06CH11357, and by JST, CREST (Research Areas: Advanced Core Technologies for Big Data Integration; Development of System Software Technologies for post-Peta Scale High Performance Computing).

References

1. Amer, A.: Parallelism, data movement, and synchronization in threading models on massively parallel systems. Technical report, Tokyo Institute of Technology, Department of Mathematical and Computing Sciences (2015)
2. Amer, A., Maruyama, N., Pericàs, M., Taura, K., Yokota, R., Matsuoka, S.: Fork-join and data-driven execution models on multi-core architectures: case study of the FMM. In: Kunkel, J.M., Ludwig, T., Meuer, H.W. (eds.) ISC 2013. LNCS, vol. 7905, pp. 255–266. Springer, Heidelberg (2013)
3. Chandramowlishwaran, A., Williams, S., Oliker, L., Lashuk, I., Biros, G., Vuduc, R.: Optimizing and tuning the fast multipole method for state-of-the-art multi-core architectures. In: 2010 IEEE International Symposium on Parallel Distributed Processing (IPDPS), pp. 1–12 (2010)
4. Greengard, L.: The Rapid Evaluation of Potential Fields in Particle Systems, vol. 52. MIT Press, Cambridge (1988)
5. Ltaief, H., Yokota, R.: Data-driven execution of fast multipole methods (2012)
6. Nakashima, J., Taura, K.: Massivethreads: a thread library for high productivity languages. In: Agha, G., Igarashi, A., Kobayashi, N., Masuhara, H., Matsuoka, S., Shibayama, E., Taura, K. (eds.) Concurrent Objects and Beyond. LNCS, vol. 8665, pp. 222–238. Springer, Heidelberg (2014)
7. Olivier, S.L., De Supinski, B.R., Schulz, M., Prins, J.F.: Characterizing and mitigating work time inflation in task parallel programs. In: Proceedings of the 2012 ACM/IEEE Conference on Supercomputing, pp. 1–12. IEEE (2012)
8. Pericas, M., Amer, A., Fukuda, K., Maruyama, N., Yokota, R., Matsuoka, S.: Towards a dataflow FMM using the OmpSs programming model. In: 136th IPSJ Conference on High Performance Computing (2012)
9. Pericàs, M., Amer, A., Taura, K., Matsuoka, S.: Analysis of data reuse in task-parallel runtimes. In: Jarvis, S.A., Wright, S.A., Hammond, S.D. (eds.) PMBS 2013. LNCS, vol. 8551, pp. 73–87. Springer, Heidelberg (2014)
10. Tasirlar, S., Sarkar, V.: Data-driven tasks and their implementation. In: 2011 International Conference on Parallel Processing (ICPP), pp. 652–661 (2011)
11. Ullman, J.D.: NP-complete scheduling problems. J. Comput. Syst. Sci. 10(3), 384–393 (1975)
12. Yan, Y., Zhao, J., Guo, Y., Sarkar, V.: Hierarchical place trees: a portable abstraction for task parallelism and data movement. In: Gao, G.R., Pollock, L.L., Cavazos, J., Li, X. (eds.) LCPC 2009. LNCS, vol. 5898, pp. 172–187. Springer, Heidelberg (2010)
13. Ying, L., Biros, G., Zorin, D., Langston, H.: A new parallel kernel-independent fast multipole method. In: ACM/IEEE Conference on Supercomputing, p. 14 (2003)

Extensions

Reducing the Functionality Gap Between Auto-Vectorization and Explicit Vectorization

Compress/Expand and Histogram

Hideki Saito[✉], Serge Preis, Nikolay Panchenko, and Xinmin Tian

Software and Solutions Group, Intel Corporation, Santa Clara, USA
{hideki.saito, serguei.v.preis, nikolay.panchenko,
xinmin.tian}@intel.com

Abstract. Explicit vectorization of C/C++ and FORTRAN application programs are pioneered by Intel® Cilk™ Plus and then inherited and enhanced by OpenMP 4.0 and 4.5 standardization. There is a known functionality gap, where some auto-vectorizable code does not have adequate syntax support for explicit vector programming. In this paper, we propose and discuss a few syntax extensions to reduce the gap for compress/expand and histogram idioms, which are commonly seen in high performance computing.

Keywords: Compress · Expand · Histogram · OpenMP · omp ordered simd

1 Introduction

Explicit vectorization of C/C++ and FORTRAN application programs are pioneered by Intel® Cilk™ Plus [1–3] and then inherited and enhanced by OpenMP 4.0 and 4.5 standardization [4, 5]. As we started the initial definition work of explicit vector syntax, we have been aware of the functionality gap, where some auto-vectorizable code does not have adequate syntax support for explicit vector programming. However, we still continued to define the initial specification and implement it, because it already covered a significant portion of the programmer needs. The gap, which mainly comes from overcoming backward cross iteration dependencies beyond well-understood reductions and linear inductions, cannot be filled overnight. Careful considerations in the syntax and the semantics are needed to make extentions easy to understand and friendly to use by the programmers. In this paper, we propose and discuss a few syntax extensions to reduce the gap for compress/expand and histogram idioms, both of which are auto-vectorizable through Intel® C/C++ and FORTRAN compilers version 16.0. Figure 1 shows a compress idiom and Intel® AVX512 assembly code auto-vectorized for the Intel® Xeon™ Phi processor codenamed KnightsLanding. Popcnt instruction helps in the vector execution of conditional count=count+1. Vcompressps instruction helps vectorizing the store to B[count]. We would like to come up with a syntax extension usable with #pragma omp simd in order to enable such an optimization instead of simply relying on the compiler to prove that application of such an optimization to omp ordered simd construct is legal.

© Springer International Publishing Switzerland 2016
N. Maruyama et al. (Eds.): IWOMP 2016, LNCS 9903, pp. 173–186, 2016.
DOI: 10.1007/978-3-319-45550-1_13

| // compress
int count = 0;
for(i=0;i<N;i++){
  if (A[i]>0) {
    B[count] = A[i];
    count = count+1;
  }
} | ..B1.14:
  vmovups   (%rdi,%r11,4), %zmm2
  vcmpps $6, %zmm0, %zmm2, %k1
  kmovw   %k1, %edx
  testl   %edx, %edx
  je ..B1.16
..B1.15:
  popcnt   %edx, %edx
  movl $65535, %r10d
  vcompressps %zmm2, %zmm1{%k1}
  movslq   %ebx, %rbx
  shlx   %edx, %r10d, %r12d
  notl   %r12d
  kmovw   %r12d, %k1
  vmovups   %zmm1, (%rsi,%rbx,4){%k1}
  addl   %edx, %ebx
..B1.16:
  addq $16, %r11
  cmpq   %r9, %r11
  jb ..B1.14 |

Fig. 1. Compress example and AVX512 assembly code for Intel(R) Xeon Phi Processor

2   Compress and Expand

Figure 2 shows simple loops with compress/expand code patterns, in C and FOR-TRAN. In this example, the compress code extracts all the positive elements from the array A[] and stores them in a compressed manner in the array B[]. The expand example, on the other hand, performs the opposite of compress by replacing positive elements of the array A[] with contents of the compressed array B[]. Concepts of compress and expand are not new. They have been operators in the APL language for more than 50 years [6] and these APL operators came from the mathematical operations on the arrays. Data compression/decompression are common in High Performance Computing and many other areas, to save memory/disk usage and to improve locality. Figure 3 illustrates how the elements of the array A[] are compressed into and

| // compress
int count = 0;
for(i=0;i<N;i++){
  if (A[i]>0) {
    B[count] = A[i];
    count = count+1;
  }
} | ! COMPRESS
ICOUNT = 0
DO I=1,N
  IF (A(I) .GT. 0) THEN
    B(ICOUNT) = A(I)
    ICOUNT = ICOUNT+1
  ENDIF
ENDDO |
| // expand
int count = 0;
for(i=0;i<N;i++){
  if (A[i]>0) {
    A[i] = B[count];
    count = count+1;
  }
} | ! EXPAND
ICOUNT = 0
DO I=1,N
  IF (A(I) .GT. 0) THEN
    A(I) = B(ICOUNT)
    ICOUNT = ICOUNT+1
  ENDIF
ENDDO |

Fig. 2. Simple compress/expand examples in C/C++ and FORTRAN

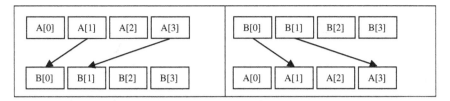

Fig. 3. Compress (left) and Expand (right) operations

expanded from the array B[], for four consecutive iterations (i = 0..3), when the condition A[i] > 0 evaluates to [F, T, F, T].

These operations can be implemented in a number of different ways depending on the available instruction sets and their performance characteristics. Intel® AVX-512 provides direct support with v[p]compress and v[p]expand instructions. Other architectures have various ways to implement this functionality. Some prefer a "preceding true count" that can be used to construct an index vector such as [0, 0, 1, 1] from [F, T, F, T]. Masked gather/scatter would then be able to use the index vector [*, 0, *, 1] with the mask value of [F, T, F, T]. On others, a masked unit stride load/store combined with shuffles is used. As a last resort, the code region of interest or the entire loop can also be serialized.

Figure 4 highlights the difficulty in applying explicit vectorization on compress/expand codes by showing the data dependence graph, assuming that arrays A[] and B[] are independent. Figure 4 (left) has a backward flow dependence from the update of count to the use in the B[count], and the cyclic flow/anti dependence on the update of count. OpenMP 4.5 provides the following five mechanisms to deal with cross-iteration dependencies within a SIMD construct:

- Forward dependencies can be resolved without special handling. With a statement reordering (and appropriate massaging of the array index), we can change the backward flow dependence on count in B[count] to a forward flow dependence on count in B[count-1] (See Fig. 4 (right)).
- The PRIVATE clause is not applicable since the usage of the variable count (ICOUNT in FORTRAN example) is not independent from one iteration of the loop to next iteration.
- The REDUCTION clause with + operator is not applicable since there is a non-reduction use of the variable count in indexing the array B[]. Without such a use, programmers would employ a REDUCTION clause. If we blindly apply "For each list item, a private copy is created in each implicit task or SIMD lane, and is initialized with the initializer value of the reduction-indentifier" (Sect. 2.15.3.6 of [5]), B[0] would be assigned twice, once at i = 1 and then at i = 3, instead of B[0] and B[1] being assigned, respectively.
- The LINEAR clause is not applicable since updates to the variable count are conditional.
- The ORDERED SIMD construct (technically speaking, it is the ORDERED construct with a SIMD clause) can be used, by enclosing two mutually dependent statements

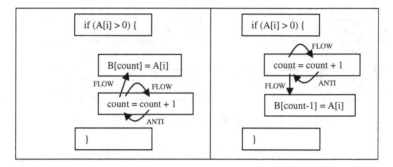

Fig. 4. Data dependence graph for the compress example

(Fig. 4 (left)) or by enclosing the statement updating count (Fig. 4 (right)). Current semantics of the construct is serialize the enclosed code block.

Even with the massaged code in Fig. 4 (right), we still have the unresolved cyclic dependency. Is there a way to teach the explicit-vectorizer about the knowledge auto-vectorizer can derive from the source code? Update of count is strikingly similar to a linear update, including the loop-invariant step value. If the update happens in every iteration of the loop, count is linear. Therefore, it should be possible to borrow the LINEAR syntax, but tell the compiler that it is conditionally updated.

2.1 Loop-Level Syntax

Figure 5 is the loop-level clause syntax version. There are other spelling ideas, such as monotonic instead of conditional_linear. Compress/expand memory accesses have invariant bases with unit-step conditional_linear indices.

Section 2.15.3.7 of the OpenMP 4.5 specification [5] describes the linear clause as follows:

> When a linear clause is specified on a construct, the value of the new list item on each iteration of the associated loop(s) corresponds to the value of the original list item before entering the construct plus the logical number of the iteration times linear-step. The value corresponding to the sequentially last iteration of the associated loop(s) is assigned to the original list item.

```
int count = 0;
#pragma omp simd conditional_linear(count:1)
for(i=0;i<N;i++){
  if (A[i]>0) {
    count = count+1;
    B[count-1] = A[i];
  }
}
```

Fig. 5. Loop-level syntax for compress/expand

The `conditional_linear` clause in Fig. 5 would need to modify the above to

> When a *conditional_linear* (or *monotonic*) clause is specified on a *simd* construct, the value of the new list item on each iteration of the associated loop(s) corresponds to the value of the original list item before entering the construct plus the number of the iterations *for which the conditional update happens prior to the current iteration* times linear-step. The value corresponding to the sequentially last iteration of the associated loop(s) is assigned to the original list item.

As such, it is important to find out under which conditions the conditional update of the list item happens. Instead of forcing the compiler to scan the loop body, a block-level syntax can be used to assist in finding such conditional updates.

2.2   Block-Level Syntax

One of the ways to make this happen is to add a qualifier to `ordered` construct with `simd` clause, instead of using a loop-level syntax. Figure 6 is the block-level syntax version (using `monotonic` spelling). This representation has two advantages over the loop level syntax; (1) If the compiler does not know how to process the `monotonic` qualifier, it can be simply ignored and the code is still functionally correct via an `ordered simd`. (2) The condition for the update is clearly identifiable in the source level context, and it can be evaluated at the source location of the `ordered simd`. Some suggested that `monotonic` as a new clause is better, as in `ordered monotonic()`, instead of `ordered simd monotonic()`. Others suggested `monotonic` as a new construct, instead of attaching it to `ordered` construct.

Using the block-level syntax, the description of the qualifier would then need to be revised as

> When a *conditional_linear* (or *monotonic*) qualifier is specified on an *ordered* construct with *simd* clause, the value of the new list item on each iteration, of the associated loop(s), corresponds to the value of the original list item before entering the *associated loop* plus the number of the iterations for which the conditional update happens prior to the current iteration times linear-step. The value corresponding to the sequentially last iteration of the associated loop(s) is assigned to the original list item.

New Construct versus New Qualifier to ORDERED SIMD. We would like to enable (or promote) more optimal code generation through the introduction of the *conditional*

```
int count = 0;
#pragma omp simd
for(i=0;i<N;i++){
   if (A[i]>0) {
#pragma omp ordered simd monotonic(count:1)
      {
         count = count+1;
      }
      B[count-1] = A[i];
   }
}
```

Fig. 6. Block-level syntax for compress/expand

linear (or *monotonic*) concept in the explicit vector loop. Such an optimization would be easier to accomplish if a new construct is proposed, rather than the alternative of inheriting the properties of an existing construct. However, initial informal feedback from a few active OpenMP community members indicates a preference for adding a qualifier to the existing `ordered` construct with `simd` clause. citing similarities to `ordered depend` in the threading context. Then, the question arises whether the qualifier(s) attached to `ordered simd` should resolve all cross-iteration dependences within the construct or should they just resolve the ones explicitly specified by the qualifier(s). We propose to interpret in the former sense. In other words, when an `ordered simd` is qualified with one or more qualifiers, there should be no other cross-iteration dependencies to resolve within that construct. This is analogous to `ordered depend` in specifying "what order to enforce". Some people suggested the `strict` and `relaxed` qualifiers to `ordered simd` and requiring the `relaxed` qualifier for interpreting "what order to enforce" assertions.

2.3 Semantics Discussion

Suppose the block-level syntax is formalized as follows:

#pragma omp ordered simd monotonic(*list:step*) *new-line*
structured block of code

The following two semantics of block-level syntax behave equally inside the block:

- When a vector iteration reaches the *structured block of code*, it evaluates *step*. This must yield an integral or pointer value. The simd execution *mask* under which the *structured block of code* is executed is also computed. Private copies of each monotonic *list item* are created for the *structured block of code* and initialized to *item, item+step, item+2*step*, … for each executing (i.e., mask==T) simd element (from lower iteration index to higher). At the end of the *structured block of code* execution, a uniform copy of *item* is updated as *item+popcount(mask)*step* and private copies of *list items* become undefined.
- When a vector iteration reaches the *structured block of code*, it evaluates *step*. This must yield an integral or pointer value. The simd execution *mask* under which the *structured block of code* is executed is also computed. Private copies of each monotonic *list item* are created for the *structured block of code* and initialized to *item, item+step, item+2*step*, … for each executing (i.e., mask==T) simd element (from lower iteration index to higher). At the end of the vector iteration, a uniform copy of *item* is updated as *item+popcount(mask)*step* and private copies of *list items* become undefined.

The latter, however, allows forward dependencies on the list item, outside of the associated `ordered simd` construct and thus appears more powerful. For example, in Fig. 6, usage of `count` in `B[count-1]` has undefined behavior if the former semantics is employed. The use of the list item prior to the associated `ordered simd` construct creates a backward dependence and therefore such usage should be disallowed. Likewise, if the same list item appears in more than one `ordered simd` construct, this usage creates a backward dependence and should be disallowed.

On the other hand, we should allow backward dependences within the associated `ordered simd` construct. The implementation support is rather mechanical. Figure 7 illustrates this use case. Assume that `cond(i)` evaluates to [F,T,T,F,T,F,F,T] for i = 0..7. `Vcount` is the private copy of the list item, and is created and initialized in each entry to the statement block. Multiple updates of the list item, within the same `ordered simd` construct, should be allowed and the translation is equally mechanical. Just like the `linear` clause, the step value should reflect the aggregated step amount from the multiple updates.

Figure 8 illustrates a case where the update to the list item is under a different execution mask from the `ordered simd` construct. This prevents mechanical translation of the code and thus should be considered a programmer error (misuse of the qualifier).

Lastly, we should disallow the use of `conditional_linear` clause when an `ordered simd` construct is inside an inner loop of the `simd` construct. Making it unconditional does not yield linear values.

```
count = 0;
inc = 1;
#pragma omp simd
for(i=0; i<N; i++){
  if (cond(i)) {
#pragma omp ordered simd monotonic(count:inc)
    {
      A[count] = B[i];   // compress
      count+=inc;
      B[i] = C[count];      // expand
    }
  }
}
// For each entry to ordered simd monotonic...
Vmask= ...                     // [F,T,T,F,T,F,F,T]
Vt1 = #TRUEs_to_left(Vmask)  // [0,0,1,2,2,3,3,3]
Vt1 = Vt1 *bcast(inc)        // [0,0,1,2,2,3,3,3]
Vcount = bcast(count)+Vt1    // [0,0,1,2,2,3,3,3]

// A[count] = B[i]
Vt2 = maskload(B[i],Vmask)       // loads from B[1],B[2],B[4],B[7]
maskscatter(A[Vcount],Vmask,Vt2) // stores to A[0..3]

// count+=inc
Vcount = maskadd(Vcount, bcast(inc), Vmask) // [0,1,2,2,3,3,3,4]
count += popcount(Vmask)*inc

// B[i] = C[count]
Vt3 = maskgather(C[Vcount],Vmask)// loads from C[1,2,3,4]
Maskstore(B[i],Vmask,Vt3)        // stores to B[1],-B[2],B[4],B[7]
```

Fig. 7. Backward dependence within the ordered simd construct

```
int count = 0;
#pragma omp simd
for(i=0;i<N;i++){
  if (A[i]>0) {
#pragma omp ordered simd monotonic(count:1)
    {
        if (A[i]<10) {
          count = count+1;
        }
    }
    B[count-1] = A[i];
  }
}
```

Fig. 8. Update of list item under different mask from the construct

2.4   Combination with omp declare simd

Conditional_linear has uses cases in omp declare simd (or SIMD-enabled) functions also. A list item can be passed as a parameter, and/or a conditional_- linear update can appear inside a SIMD-enabled function.

Figure 9 contains three calls to the SIMD-enabled function foo(). Assuming that we employ the semantics of "monotonic handling resolves all cross-iteration dependencies in the construct", compiler is allowed to utilize the vectorized variants of foo(). At the call site #1, the execution condition of the call is identical to the conditional linear update. Therefore, the value sequence can be recreated within the caller by using the starting value, the increment value, and the mask value. As such, the compiler can utilize the variant with a monotonic parameter specifier. That'll allow X [cnt] assignment to be translated into compressed store in such a variant. Both call site #2 and #3, on the other hands, the execution conditions of the calls do not match the conditional linear update condition. Therefore, the cnt parameter would be considered to have a vector of integers without identifiable patterns, the variant without a

```
#pragma   omp   declare   simd   uniform(X),   monoton-
ic(cnt:1)
#pragma omp declare simd uniform(X)
void foo(int cnt, int *X, int val){
  X[cnt] = val;
};
int count = 0;
#pragma omp simd
for(i=0;i<N;i++){
  if (A[i]>0) {
#pragma omp ordered simd monotonic(count:1)
    {
        count = count+1;
        foo(count-1, B, A[i]);        // Call site #1
        if (A[i] < 10) {
          foo(count-1, C, A[i]);      // Call site #2
        }
    }
  }
  foo(count-1, D, A[i]);             // Call site #3
}
```

Fig. 9. Conditional_linear list item as a parameter to a SIMD-enabled function call

```
int x;
#pragma omp declare simd uniform(y),
                        linear(z), uniform(A,B,C,D)
void foo(int &y, int z, int w, int val,
         int *A, int *B, int *C, int *D){
#pragma omp ordered simd monotonic(x:1)   // okay
  {
    x = x + 1;
    A[x] = val;
  }
#pragma omp ordered simd monotonic(y:1)   // okay
  {
    y = y + 1;
    B[y] = val;
  }
#pragma omp ordered simd monotonic(z:1)   // error
  {
    z = z + 1;
    C[z] = val;
  }
#pragma omp ordered simd monotonic(w:1)   // error
  {
    w = w + 1;
    D[x] = val;
  }
};
```

Fig. 10. omp ordered simd monotonic inside SIMD-enabled function

monotonic specifier would be chosen, and the X[cnt] assignment in such a variant would not be a good match for compressed store.

When ordered simd monotonic is used inside a SIMD-enabled function, each original list item must be explicitly uniform (i.e., a uniform parameter) or implicitly uniform (i.e., a global variable). Monotonicity is applied separately for each invocation of the SIMD-enabled function. In Fig. 10, variables x and y can be used as monotonic list items since they are uniform, but not z and w. Ordered simd monotonic should not be allowed inside a loop within a SIMD-enabled function.

Figure 11 illustrates the side effect of enabling vector variant function call from ordered simd monotonic. Assume that A[i] is always positive, if vector function invocation is not allowed, B[0:3] and C[0:3] would be {0, 2, 4, 6} and {1, 3, 5, 7}, respectively. If vector variant invocation is allowed, B[0:3] and C[0:3] would become {0, 1, 2, 3} and {4, 5, 6, 7}, respectively. This undesirable consequence may be a good reason to disallow vector variant function call inside any extensions of ordered simd construct. Alternatively, we can document the anomaly well and the programmers can make an informed decision, possibly with an aid of a warning from the compilers.

2.5   Unit Test Performance

Figure 12 (left) shows the normalized speedup of compress, against ordered simd, for a unit test on an Intel® Xeon™ Phi processor, where the loop body is

```
if (A[i]) {B[j ++]] = C[i];}
```

```
int x;
#pragma omp declare simd linear(p)
void foo(int *p){
#pragma omp ordered simd
   {
      *p = x;
      x = x + 1;
   }
};
...
x = 0;
for (i=0;i<N;i++){
   if (A[i]>0){
#pragma omp ordered simd mononotnic(cnt)
      {
         cnt = cnt + 1;
         foo(&B[i]); // { 0,2,4,6 } or { 0,1,2,3 }?
         foo(&C[i]); // { 1,3,5,7 } or { 4,5,6,7 }?
      }
   }
}
```

Fig. 11. Side effect of allowing SIMD-enabled function call inside `ordered simd monotonic`

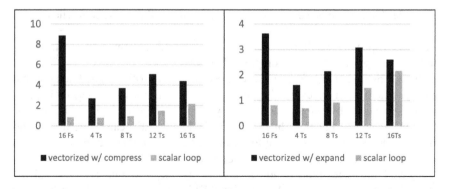

Fig. 12. Normalized speedup of compress/expand relative to `ordered simd`

and the trip count is 1,000,000,000. Data type for A is 32bit integer, and B and C are 32bit floating point. X-axis is the number of times A[i] is non-zero within a 16-way vector (or the number of times condition evaluates to True or False). At the leftmost, A[i] is always zero (16 Falses). At the rightmost, A[i] is always non-zero. Difference between scalar loop and `ordered simd` is most likely coming from the unrolling difference (`ordered simd` is effectively 16-way unrolled) impacting branch predictor behavior and the overhead of extracting individual mask value (A[i]) from a vector. As one would expect, vector code performance, in absolute terms, is relatively flat between 4-, 8-, 12-, or 16-values since it execute the same code. Figure 12 (right) shows the normalized speedup of expand, similar to the compress test case mention above. The bar height (speedup factor) is different from compress, but the graph shape is interestingly similar.

3   Histogram

Figure 13 shows simple histogram patterns in C and FORTRAN. Depending on the contents of the index array B[] (or variable inx) and the target architecture, it can be implemented in the following ways (and within possible explicit vector syntax):

```
// histogram                ! HISTOGRAM
for(i=0;i<N;i++){           DO I=1,N
    int inx = B[i];            INX = B(I)
    A[inx]=A[inx]+C[i];        A(INX)=A(INX)+C(I)
}                           ENDDO
```

Fig. 13. Simple histogram examples

- Gather-update-scatter implementation if inx values are unique. (Simply apply SIMD construct)
- Scalar reduction implementation if all values of inx are the same. (Use SIMD construct and reduce to scalar variable)
- Array reduction implementation if inx may have overlapping values and the size of A[] is small enough that the overhead of last value accumulation can be amortized. (Use SIMD construct and reduction over array A[]).
- Serial implementation. (Use SIMD construct and enclose the statement inside ORDERED SIMD)
- Partial gather-update-scatter implementation and repeat for overlapping inx values.

The last approach is currently lacking an explicit vector syntax support. Figure 14 illustrates overlapping index versus non-overlapping index cases. The code pattern is commonly seen in high performance computing, and typically, the compiler knows nothing about the index values. Therefore, the compiler has to conservatively assume that the index values may overlap unless the programmer explicitly says "no implicit dependence".

3.1   Loop-Level Syntax

Figure 15 shows two loop-level syntax examples, with and without the qualifier expression. Other keyword suggestions include: conflict, overlap, unique, nonunique, histogram, and ordered_duplicates. The example on the left (without the qualifier expression) relies on the compiler's analysis to determine if the value of inx is subject to an overlapping value check. This syntax is possible for some input programs, but it is not ideal for explicit vector syntax, which aims to eliminate reliance on compiler analysis. Furthermore, both cases rely on the compiler's analysis to determine where in the loop body we should perform an overlapping value check, and which section of code is subject to repeat execution if a conflict (i.e., one or

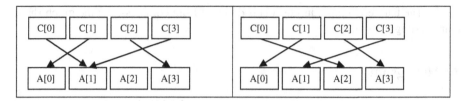

Fig. 14. Histogram case (left) and gather-update-scatter case (right)

```
// histogram
#pragma omp simd conflict_check
  for(i=0;i<N;i++){
    int inx = B[i];
    A[inx]=A[inx]+C[i];
  }
```
```
// histogram
#pragma omp simd conflict_check(inx)
  for(i=0;i<N;i++){
    int inx = B[i];
    A[inx]=A[inx]+C[i];
  }
```

Fig. 15. Loop-level syntax for conflict check, with (right) and without (left) qualifier expression

overlapping values) is found. Even with the qualifier expression, the same expression may evaluate to different values at different parts of the loop body.

3.2   Block-Level Syntax

Figure 16 is a block-level syntax with qualifier expression attached to the `ordered simd`. The new construct versus new qualifier argument is also applicable here. This representation has three advantages over the loop-level syntax; (1) If the compiler does not know how to process the `conflict_check` qualifier, it can simply ignore this qualifier, but the `ordered simd` still ensures correct execution, (2) The repeat region for overlapping values are clearly specified in the source code, and (3) The overlapping value check can be performed at the source location of the associated `ordered simd` construct. Semantics of this block-level syntax can be described as the following:

> When an iteration reaches *stmt*, it evaluates *inx* as an r-value, which must yield an integral or pointer value. The implementation must ensure that if two iterations of the enclosing SIMD loop compute the same *inx* value, the iteration with the lower logical iteration number must complete execution of *stmt* before the other iteration starts execution of *stmt*.

In Fig. 16, suppose `B[i]` is [11,45,11,34,11,45,23,43] for i = 0..7. Partial orders required by the conflict_check() assertion are the following:

- `A[11] +=C[0]` → `A[11] +=C[2]` → `A[11] +=C[4]`
- `A[45] +=C[1]` → `A[45] +=C[5]`

Total ordering is not implied. However, implementation defined deterministic total ordering may be desired for ease of debugging. It is the programmer's responsibility to check whether the partial ordering is sufficient for any possible aliasing between `A[]` and `C[]` (because of the qualifier attached to `ordered simd`).

```
// histogram
  #pragma omp simd
  for(i=0;i<N;i++){
    int inx = B[i];
    #pragma omp ordered simd conflict_check(inx)
    {
       A[inx]=A[inx]+C[i];
    }
  }
```

Fig. 16. Block-level syntax for conflict check

```
// histogram
  #pragma omp simd
  for(i=0;i<N;i++){
    int inx = B[i];
    #pragma omp ordered simd conflict_check(inx)
    {
       A[inx]=A[inx]+C[i];
    }
    D[inx] = D[inx]+C[i];
  }
```

Fig. 17. Scope of conflict check

3.3   Block-Level Syntax Scoping

Figure 17 shows what happens when the programmer encloses one conflicting code inside the block-level syntax, but forgets to enclose another similar one. In our proposed semantics, conflict check should be limited to the update to A[] and not applicable to the update of D[]. A smart compiler may be able to issue a warning.

3.4   Unit Test Performance

Figure 18 shows the normalized speedup, against ordered simd, for a unit test on an Intel® Xeon™ Phi processor, where the loop body is A[B[i]] = C[i] and the trip count is 1,000,000,000. Data type for A and C are 32bit floating point, and B is 32bit integer. X-axis is the number of extra repeats due to conflict. At the leftmost, all indices are unique and thus no repeats. At the rightmost, all indices in a 16-way vector are the same and therefore requires 15 times to repeat (in addition to the first time). The data indicates that ordered simd is an high overhead construct and thus the ability to vectorize it using an additional guidance like conflict_check is critical to avoid negatively impacting the loop-level vector speedup. High-performance implementation of vpconflictd instruction on this processor makes it easier for the compilers to deploy.

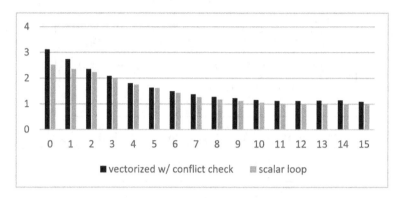

Fig. 18. Normalized speedup of conflict relative to `ordered simd`

4 Conclusion

Vectorization technology continues to evolve in both hardware and software, and we expect to find more ways to break cross-iteration dependencies in creative fashions. Ultimately, this will widen the gaps between auto-vectorization and explicit-vectorization, especially when the syntax and semantics are not straightforward to define. As a community, we should continue to push the envelope of explicit vectorization support in order to minimize and, hopefully, eliminate such gaps, and to fully realize the advancement of SIMD hardware/software development. In this paper, we proposed two qualifers for OpenMP `ordered simd` construct in order to deal with compress/expand and histogram code patterns, and discussed semantic interpretations of the proposed qualifiers. We are currently prototyping them in our pre-production C/C++ and FORTRAN compilers and expect to bring a formal proposal to the OpenMP ARB with the goal of reaching standardization in OpenMP 5.0.

References

1. Intel Corporation. "Intel® Parallel Composer 2011 Users Guide", October 2010
2. Tian, X., Saito, H., Girkar, M., Preis, S., Kozhukhov, S., Cherkasov, A., Nelson, C., Panchenko, N., Geva, R.: Compiling C/C ++ SIMD extensions for function and loop vectorization on multicore SIMD processors. In: Proceedings of the 2012 IPDPS Workshops & Ph.D. Forum (2012)
3. Klemm, M., Duran, A., Tian, X., Saito, H., Caballero, D., Martorell, X.: Extending OpenMP* with vector constructs for modern multicore SIMD architectures. In: Chapman, B.M., Massaioli, F., Müller, M.S., Rorro, M. (eds.) IWOMP 2012. LNCS, vol. 7312, pp. 59–72. Springer, Heidelberg (2012)
4. OpenMP ARB. "OpenMP 4.0 Specifications", July 2013
5. OpenMP ARB. "OpenMP 4.5 Specifications", November 2015
6. Iverson, K.E.: A Programming Language. Wiley, New York (1962)

A Proposal to OpenMP for Addressing the CPU Oversubscription Challenge

Yonghong Yan[1,5]([✉]), Jeff R. Hammond[2,5], Chunhua Liao[3],
and Alexandre E. Eichenberger[4,5]

[1] Department of Computer Science and Engineering,
Oakland University, Rochester, USA
`yan@oakland.edu`
[2] Parallel Computing Lab, Intel Corp., Santa Clara, USA
`jeff_hammond@acm.org`
[3] Center for Applied Scientific Computing,
Lawrence Livermore National Laboratory, Livermore, USA
`liao6@llnl.gov`
[4] Thomas J. Watson Research Center, IBM, Yorktown Heights, USA
`alexe@us.ibm.com`
[5] OpenMP Interoperability Language Subcommittee, Houston, USA

Abstract. OpenMP has become a successful programming model for developing multi-threaded applications. However, there are still some challenges in terms of OpenMP's interoperability within itself and with other parallel programming APIs. In this paper, we explore typical use cases that expose OpenMP's interoperability challenges and report our proposed solutions for addressing the resource oversubscription issue as the efforts by the OpenMP Interoperability language subcommittee. The solutions include OpenMP runtime routines for changing the wait policies, which include ACTIVE(SPIN_BUSY or SPIN_PAUSE), PASSIVE (SPIN_YIELD or SUSPEND), of idling threads for improved resource management, and routines for supporting contributing OpenMP threads to other thread libraries or tasks. Our initial implementations are being done by extending two OpenMP runtime libraries, Intel OpenMP (IOMP) and GNU OpenMP (GOMP). The evaluation results demonstrate the effectiveness of the proposed approach to address the CPU oversubscription challenge and detailed analysis provide heuristics for selecting an optimal wait policy according to the oversubscription ratios.

1 Introduction

OpenMP® is the most popular programming model for multi-threading in HPC, although it is far from the only one. Other portable threading models that may be used in HPC include POSIX threads, Intel® Threading Building Blocks (TBB) [13], ISO C11 and C++ threads, Cilkplus™ and OpenCL™, to name a few. In addition to the explicit use of threads in HPC applications, threads may be used implicitly in language concurrent features such as ISO C++11 std::async and std::future, ISO Fortran 2008 DO CONCURRENT and coarray images.

© Springer International Publishing Switzerland 2016
N. Maruyama et al. (Eds.): IWOMP 2016, LNCS 9903, pp. 187–202, 2016.
DOI: 10.1007/978-3-319-45550-1_14

Both compute and communication libraries may use threads; compute libraries that implement BLAS, LAPACK or FFT functions currently use at least four different threading models internally and communication libraries such as MPI may spawn threads to implement asynchronous progress.

Large-scale parallel applications are typically developed using multiple parallel programming APIs aforementioned, e.g. the hybrid MPI+OpenMP, and using one or multiple pre-built parallel scientific libraries such as Intel Math Kernel Library (MKL) [15]. Each of these APIs often has its own runtime system to handle scheduling of work units and management of computational and data movement tasks. One of the challenges for using multiple models in one application is the interoperability and interaction of their threading runtimes, for example the issues of naming conflicts and resource oversubscription.

This paper reports our proposal to OpenMP for combating the resource oversubscription challenge as efforts from the OpenMP Interoperability language subcommittee. The work makes three contributions: (1) a study of interoperability challenge in OpenMP and other parallel APIs and the limitation of the current standard to address this challenge; (2) proposed extensions to OpenMP to improve the thread management to enhance OpenMP's interoperability with other threading models; (3) evaluation and performance study that demonstrate the effectiveness of the proposed solution and guidelines for selecting thread wait policies according to the oversubscription ratios. We think the similar challenge exists in other threading based libraries and language implementations, and believe the solutions we provided will work for them too.

The rest of the paper is organized as follows: Sect. 2 discusses the interoperability use cases, challenges and motivations. Section 3 describes the proposed solutions for OpenMP. Section 4 presents our implementation and evaluation. Finally, Sect. 5 discusses related work and Sect. 6 contains our conclusions.

2   Use Cases and Challenges of Interoperability

In this section, we describe three use cases of interoperating OpenMP with other parallel systems and discuss the interoperability challenge of OpenMP.

2.1   Three Use Cases

In cases where OpenMP is coexisting with at least one other threading model, we can identify at least three classes of scenarios in which to consider interoperability: Phased, Concurrent and Nested. These are illustrated in Fig. 1. Threaded applications that call threaded libraries from a sequential region are a good example of the Phased motif. The thread(s) inside of e.g. an MPI library used by an OpenMP application matches with the Concurrent motif. Nested can be either OpenMP threads calling application or library functions that use another threading model, or the other way around. Of course, in all cases, the coexistence may not be as regular as the picture describes, but these simple cases are sufficient to reveal the challenges of interoperating multiple threading models.

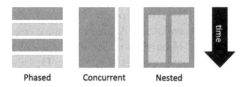

Fig. 1. Pictorial description of Phased, Concurrent and Nested motifs where two threading models must interoperate.

Interacting with User Threads. A typical example of the Phased class is the use of user threads in a program. A user thread is the thread that is explicitly created by user, for examples PThreads or Windows Native threads created using POSIX or Win32 APIs, or C++11 threads. A user thread could become an OpenMP initial thread that creates OpenMP parallel regions, or nested inside a parallel region when an OpenMP thread spawns a user thread, or the mix of both.

Interoperability with Inter-node Model, E.g. MPI. Hybrid parallel programming in the form of internode+intranode, e.g. MPI+X model are widely used for HPC, which is the typical example for the Concurrent class. This hybrid approach reflects the two-level hierarchy of hardware parallelism in current HPC systems, in which network connects many highly parallel nodes. Interoperability between inter- and intra-node APIs such as MPI+OpenMP has long been a productivity and composability goal within the HPC community. We however still have not agreed on a standard solution from either of the two communities.

Interacting with Parallel Libraries and Language Concurrency Features. A common case of the Nested class is an application that uses multiple parallel libraries at the same time, which could be developed using OpenMP, TBB, Cilkplus, C++11, and other parallel libraries. For example, a Cholesky Factorization [1] uses OpenMP tasking and BLAS operations provided by Intel MKL parallel math library. The runtime will then need to coordinate the two parallel runtimes if the two do not integrate. It is also possible that multiple OpenMP runtime instances from either the same or different libraries coexist, which may incur even more challenges than the coexistence of different runtime instances, e.g. the naming conflict.

2.2 Issues with No or Poor Interoperability

In the use cases for intra-node interoperability, the coexistence of multiple user threads and other runtime instances adds additional level(s) in the overall "threading" hierarchy of a program. These additional levels increase the complexity of a program for users and complicate the reasoning of parallel and synchronization behaviors of parallel tasks. More critically, it introduces at least two performance issues since most OpenMP implementations ignore their existence in the decision making for runtime scheduling and resource management.

CPU Oversubscription. Oversubscription happens when resources are claimed and held than what are available. A program may request more OpenMP threads than the total amount of hardware threads available when entering a parallel region, which causes excessive competition among OpenMP threads for hardware cores and increases runtime overhead. When program execution enters into sequential stage after exiting a parallel region, those native threads that support the OpenMP threads in the parallel region may still alive in the background consuming CPU cycles. This will make those hardware cores unavailable to others.

The two scenarios we mentioned above are the two kinds of oversubscription we should try to avoid: **(1) Active oversubscription**: Claiming or requesting more threads than what are available by the system. **(2) Passive oversubscription**: Thread resources are not released after parallel execution. It is important to note that holding hardware threads after parallel execution may not always hurt the performance overall, e.g. it may improve the start-up performance of the upcoming parallel region.

Conflicting Thread Affinity. Memory is another kind of resource that should be coordinately allocated and managed among multiple parallel runtimes. When the OpenMP runtime binds threads data to certain memory places (cache or NUMA region) that are already occupied by the affinity requests of another runtime, thread affinity conflict happens. Such memory overlaps cause excessive cache or memory spills or relocation of data to farther places, resulting increased memory access latency because of false sharing or poor locality of thread and its data. The affinity conflicts can happen even the total number of threads requested does not exceed the number of hardware threads available.

2.3   Limitation of Interoperability Support in the Standard

The current OpenMP standard (4.5) provides limited support for users to influence the runtime for better managing hardware resources and OpenMP threads to minimize the performance impact of oversubscription. First, the OMP_DYNAMIC environment variable, and the omp_set_dynamic routine, indicate the OpenMP runtime to adjust the number of threads to use for executing parallel regions in order to optimize the use of system resources. This approach address only the active oversubscription issue and it heavily depends on how the runtime supports this feature.

Second, the ACTIVE setting for the OMP_WAIT_POLICY variable dictates the waiting thread in sequential region to be actively waiting, which may consume CPU cycles. The PASSIVE setting allows those threads to yield CPUs for others to use, which addresses the passive oversubscription issue. The standard however only allows one time setting when the program starts, thus preventing the dynamic adjustment of thread waiting behavior during the execution.

Thirdly, the OMP_THREAD_LIMIT environment give users an option to set the maximum number of OpenMP threads when the program starts, addressing oversubscription issues in certain degree. It however does not provide an interface to adjust the upper bound of the threads for an OpenMP program during program execution, limiting its actually usage in real applications.

OpenMP's interoperability is also limited by the global scope of its environment variables. For example, users cannot set different wait policies for multiple concurrent parallel regions in nested parallel cases.

As the combinations of different parallel programming APIs in one application at different system levels are becoming more practical solution than creating a single unified and comprehensive model, it becomes urgent for OpenMP to enhance its interoperability support. The proposal in this paper provides solutions to the CPU oversubscription issue and a comprehensive solution will provide an extensible set of interfaces for addressing other interoperability issues.

3 Extensions to Address the Oversubscription Challenge

A typical OpenMP runtime maintains an internal thread pool to keep track of the native threads created by the runtime, even during the sequential execution of the program. In the OpenMP's fork-join execution model, a native thread in the thread pool is summoned to participate in an OpenMP team for computation upon the fork of a parallel region. The native thread returns back to the thread pool when the parallel region is finished at the join barrier. While in the thread pool, a native thread blocks in a fork barrier. OpenMP runtime may also maintain internal hot teams that keep threads actively waiting for the upcoming parallel regions. So an OpenMP program could consume cycles of multiple CPU cores even if it is in sequential execution stages.

Often an OpenMP program explicitly creates native threads, e.g. PThreads, and each native thread has its own OpenMP parallel regions. In such a hybrid threading model (using user-level native threads and OpenMP threads), a runtime maintains internal descendant hierarchies for the native threads created by users and those by the OpenMP runtime. Borrowing the term from Intel OpenMP runtime, we refer to the native threads created by users as root threads. Based on the most recent OpenMP standard, a root thread forms a contention group and we thus consider all the descendant threads are members of the group.

The oversubscription challenge is then concerned with how to coordinate the CPU resource sharing between two or more contention groups, and between multiple runtime instances, which could be of the same or different runtime libraries. Our solutions for addressing it provide users APIs for dynamically setting the wait policy of the blocking threads to minimize the consumption of CPU cycles.

3.1 Definition of the ACTIVE and PASSIVE Wait Policies

Our proposal defines more specifically the ACTIVE and PASSIVE policies and also extends each to include multiple sub-policies that dictate more specifically the exact behavior of the waiting thread. When a thread is waiting in an ACTIVE state, it should not initiate calls to relinquish the CPU, though technically the

Table 1. Wait policies

Wait policy		Description	Pseudo code
ACTIVE	SPIN_BUSY	Busy wait in user level	while (!finished()) ;
	SPIN_PAUSE	Busy wait while pausing CPU	while (!finished()) cpu_pause();
PASSIVE	SPIN_YIELD	Busy wait with yield	while (!finished()) sched_yield();
	SUSPEND	Thread sleeps. Others wake it up.	mutex_wait(); mutex_wake();
	TERMINATE	Thread terminates	pthread_exit();

OS kernel or hardware may switch it out of the core it occupies. When in a PASSIVE state, a thread initiates yielding or suspension operation to give up the CPU core. The extensions of each of the policies are summarized in Table 1 and detailed description are as follows.

ACTIVE SPIN_BUSY: The blocking thread waits in a loop purely in user space. It consumes CPU cycles and memory bandwidth while iteratively checking the condition for being released. This policy allows the fastest response time when a thread is released from the barrier.

ACTIVE SPIN_PAUSE: The blocking thread waits using a loop and also pauses the CPU core in each loop iteration. The pause operation introduces a slight delay in the loop, reducing the amount of instructions fed into the CPU pipeline as well as the energy consumption. This policy also allows for very fast response time but consumes less amount of CPU cycles and memory bandwidth than the SPIN_BUSY policy.

PASSIVE SPIN_YIELD: The blocking thread waits using a loop and relinquishes the CPU in each iteration by a kernel system call (e.g. *sched_yield*). CPU yielding causes the thread to be moved to the end of the kernel scheduling queue for its static priority. A thread in this stage can only be released to the OpenMP runtime by the kernel. A kernel context switch is involved in each loop iteration, thus having higher overhead than the two ACTIVE policies. This policy provides average response time, but allows the kernel to schedule other tasks to the same CPU core while the thread yields.

PASSIVE SUSPEND: The thread is suspended when waiting in the barrier call. A suspended thread can only be resumed by other threads, being timed out, or upon some hardware state change[1]. A suspended thread, also known as sleeping, does not consume CPU cycles. However the operations of suspending or resuming a thread are costly. Thus this approach has the longest response time

---

[1] On Intel platforms, this can be implemented using *monitor-mwait*. Blue Gene/Q supported a "wake-up unit" for fast thread resumption. Other processors may have similar features.

and the kernel can completely allocate other tasks to the CPU core previously used by the suspended thread.

PASSIVE TERMINATE: The thread will be terminated instead of waiting in the runtime. Though not technically accurate as a "waiting" policy, it is categorized as the PASSIVE policy because of the same effect of it as the PASSIVE SUSPEND policy. By introducing this policy, we give users an option to return completely the CPU cores to the system, though the future request of thread requires recreating the thread. The termination and recreation of a thread cost more than suspending and resuming a thread.

3.2 Proposed Runtime Routines

Our extensions to OpenMP are runtime routines that can expose certain functionalities of the runtime system for users to proactively adjust the behavior of the waiting threads. They also include routines for the runtime to contribute OpenMP threads for another parallel runtime, without the need to create a parallel region. The specifications are included in the follow list.

```
typedef enum omp_wait_policy {
    OMP_SPIN_BUSY_WAIT = 1,   /* 0x1 */
    OMP_SPIN_PAUSE_WAIT = 2,  /* 0x10 */
    OMP_SPIN_YIELD_WAIT = 4,  /* 0x100 */
    OMP_SUSPEND_WAIT = 8,     /* 0x1000 */
    OMP_TERMINATE = 16,       /* 0x10000 */

    OMP_ACTIVE_WAIT = OMP_SPIN_PAUSE_WAIT,
    OMP_PASSIVE_WAIT = OMP_SUSPEND_WAIT;
} omp_wait_policy_t;

int omp_get_num_threads_runtime(omp_wait_policy_t state);

void omp_set_wait_policy(omp_wait_policy_t wait_policy);
int omp_get_wait_policy(void);

int omp_quiesce(omp_wait_policy_t state);

typedef void * omp_thread_t;
int omp_thread_create (omp_thread_t * th, int place,
    void *(*start_routine)(void *), void *arg, void * new_stack);
void omp_thread_exit(void *value_ptr);
int omp_thread_join(omp_thread_t thread, void **value_ptr);
```

The omp_wait_policy_t enum defines the valid thread wait policies that can be passed to the related runtime routines. The value for OMP_ACTIVE_WAIT and OMP_PASSIVE_WAIT could be defined in the standard. It is also possible that the standard does not define the five specific policies, and let the implementations specify the meaning of ACTIVE or PASSIVE policies. The use of the binary position bit (0x1, 0x10, etc.) as values allows for setting multiple wait policies for a thread such that the thread can automatically change its waiting behavior according to the needs of the application.

3.3   The Omp_get_num_threads_runtime **Runtime Routine**

This routine returns the number of runtime threads that are under the specified policy. The binding thread set of the function is the team threads when being called inside a parallel region, and all the threads in the current contention group when being called in the sequential region. The information provided by calls to this routines can be used by users to make resource management decisions when oversubscription become an issue in a program.

3.4   The Omp_set_wait_policy **and** omp_get_wait_policy **Runtime Routines**

The omp_set_wait_policy runtime setter routine sets the wait policy of binding thread(s). When being called inside a parallel region, the routine sets the wait policy of the calling thread. When being called in a sequential region, the routine sets the wait policy for all the threads of the binding contention group. The omp_get_wait_policy routine returns the wait policy of the binding thread if it is being called inside a parallel region. If being called in a sequential region, this getter routine returns the wait policy of the contention group if the policy is set before by the setter. If no wait policy has been set for the contention group by the setter, the getter routine returns the wait policies of all the threads as a combined integer. For example, the return value of 0x1011 indicates that OMP_SUSPEND_WAIT, OMP_SPIN_PAUSE_WAIT and OMP_SPIN_BUSY_WAIT policies have been set for the threads of the contention group. The difference of the binding thread set according to where the setter is called (a parallel region or sequential region) allows users to set different policies of the selected threads in a contention group. For example, the omp_set_wait_policy(OMP_PASSIVE_WAIT) call in the sequential region followed by the omp_set_wait_policy(OMP_ACTIVE_WAIT) call inside a parallel region enables those threads that are not part of the parallel region to be PASSIVE waiting while other threads to be ACTIVE waiting. The setter call makes changes of the wait policy to individual threads, thus overriding the default setting by the wait-policy-var ICV and OMP_WAIT_POLICY variable.

The omp_set_wait_policy routine can be used for addressing both active and passive oversubscription depending on the location of the call to this routine. Similar routines have been provided in compilers from IBM, Cray and Oracle [3,8,10]. There are also different variants of this features depending how much details users can configure the wait policy. For example, Oracle OpenMP runtime allows users to set policies for specific execution point, e.g., at OpenMP barrier or after a parallel region.

3.5   The Omp_quiesce **Runtime Routine**

The omp_quiesce routine quiesces all OpenMP threads of the runtime according to sthe pecified threading behavior by the argument, which could be either

OMP_SUSPEND_WAIT or OMP_TERMINATE. Thus quiescence involves termination of threads or otherwise inactivating them. The binding thread set includes all the threads of the runtime instance. The routine returns zero if quiescence has been achieved, otherwise it returns a non-zero error code.

3.6   The Omp_thread_create/exit/join **Runtime Routines**

The omp_thread_create/exit/join APIs are introduced for users to create OpenMP threads similarly as the way of creating PThreads. Those threads however are tracked by the OpenMP runtime, though they do not belong to any thread team. The place parameter is used for specifying the place where the thread should be created from. By using those APIs, an OpenMP thread can be created as regular thread without creating an OpenMP parallel region. Those threads can be used to form another parallel runtime for other programming models.

4   Implementation and Evaluation

The implementation is performed in the latest Intel OpenMP runtime (IOMP) and GNU Compiler Runtime (GOMP).

For IOMP, the implementation of omp_set_wait_policy leverages the available implementation of suspending and resuming a thread (using pthread condition variables and mutex) used for the barrier. Setting OMP_SUSPEND_WAIT policy is implemented by setting thread-specific variables. For setting the ACTIVE policies or the OMP_SPIN_YIELD policy, the implementation needs resuming those suspended threads. We validate the correctness of our implementation by checking the kernel state (in /proc/ RAM file system on Linux) of each thread of a program when being executed. The omp_quiesce implementation leverages the support for omp_set_wait_policy except that it should change the behavior of all the threads when it is called with OMP_SUSPENDED_WAIT argument. The implementation of omp_quiesce(OMP_TERMINATE) is a wrapper of the __kmp_internal_end_fini internal API which shuts down the runtime system [9].

The implementation of omp_thread_create/exit/join needs to work around the need of a team when creating a thread, and the requirement of a fork barrier and join barrier when assigning any work to a thread in the runtime. An internal team object is created when creating a thread using the omp_thread_create function. The implementation first checks the thread pool to find a waiting thread. If there is no thread in the pool, it creates a native thread (PThread in Unix/Linux) launched into the runtime loop. The thread will be released for performing user specified routine by the fork barrier. But it will skip the join barrier since it does not form a team with any other thread.

For GOMP, the implementation is very similar to IOMP. Both IOMP and GOMP use timeout mechanism (blocktime in IOMP and spin count in GOMP) to control how long a thread waits actively before waiting passively. The implementations set the timeout value to either 0 or the max integer for PASSIVE waiting or ACTIVE waiting, respectively. For the wait policies, Table 1 shows implementation pseudo code snippets applicable to both of the two runtime systems, though for GOMP, the cpu_pause function is called cpu_relax(). The GOMP implementation of omp_quiesce(OMP_TERMINATE) is a wrapper of gomp_free_thread which frees a thread pool and releases its threads.

4.1   Evaluation

The evaluation was performed on a machine using two Intel® Xeon® E5-2699v3 (Haswell) processors with total 36 cores supporting 72 threads. We use the latest LLVM compiler version 3.8.0 for evaluating IOMP implementation. Test programs were designed to evaluate the overhead of these functions.

We first developed microbenchmarks for evaluating parallel start-up cost after applying different wait polices or quiescing the runtime system, as well as the cost for the omp_set_wait_policy and omp_quiesce routines. Figure 2 shows the results of the evaluation. The use of each of the two ACTIVE policies and the PASSIVE SPIN_YIELD policy introduces very minimum overhead to the parallel region start-up. When PASSIVE SUSPEND policy is applied, we observed significant increase of overhead of creating parallel regions, which can be explained by the cost to suspend and resume the runtime threads when the policy is in effect. The use of omp_quiesce with TERMINATE policy, which completely shutdowns the runtime, dramatically increases the overhead, close to 1000x, of starting a new parallel region. In this scenario, the cost of initializing the whole runtime is counted toward parallel start-up overhead. Second, for the overhead of the two routines, omp_set_wait_policy incurs very minimum overhead. The omp_quiesce(OMP_TERMINATE) routine however incurs high overhead since it needs to terminate the runtime threads as well as destroy all the resources allocated for the runtime (e.g. mutex, condition variables and memory, etc.).

Overhead (us)	Policies	Number of OpenMP Threads								
		1	2	4	8	16	32	36	48	64
Additional overhead for OpenMP parallel startup when applying wait policy	ACTIVE	0	0	0	0	3	4	4	4	6
	PASSIVE(SPIN_YIELD)	0	0	0	0	2	4	5	3	5
	PASSITVE(SUSPEND)	0	15	23	39	44	66	69	74	94
	QUIESCE(TERMINATE)	4383	4493	4530	6414	16498	35303	36890	60160	89746
Overhead for set_wait_policy/quiesce overhead	ACTIVE	0	1	1	0	0	1	1	6	6
	PASSIVE(SPIN_YIELD)	0	1	0	0	1	0	2	6	4
	PASSITVE(SUSPEND)	0	0	0	0	0	0	3	6	5
	QUIESCE(TERMINATE)	34	143	159	219	397	711	886	751	1173

Fig. 2. Overheads for OpenMP parallel start-up and for omp_set_wait_policy and omp_quiesce implementation

Our next evaluation was designed to measure the execution time of hybrid PThread/OpenMP programs when different wait policies are applied. We developed a program in which multiple PThreads are created, each of which executes the function shown in the following list.

```
    int user_thread_id = (int) ptr;
    for (int i=0; i<NUM_ITERATIONS; i++) {
        busy_waiting(user_thread_id*3000);
#pragma omp parallel num_threads(num_ompthreads)
        {
            busy_waiting(3000); /* act as computation */
        }
        omp_set_wait_policy(policy);
    }
}
```

Each PThread first spin-waits for a specific period of time, and then enters into a parallel region in which it mimics computation by performing busy-waiting for 3000 us. The time periods of the two busy waiting (one is in sequential and the other is in parallel) are carefully designed for all PThreads so only one PThread enters into its parallel region a time. By this design, if the parallel region of each PThread has N number of threads, which is less than or equal to the total number of threads in the system (72 in our test system), there are total N number of threads that compute at any point of the program execution regardless of the number of PThreads we create. When there are enough cores or *hardware threads* to support all threads (including the PThreads and OpenMP threads), which means no oversubscription, minimum scheduling overhead and context switch are incurred, thus achieving optimal performance. If the total number of threads are greater than the total number of *hardware threads* in the system, the runtime system and OS kernel need to schedule those threads among the *hardware threads*, which stress-tests the effectiveness of different wait policies. In this test case, we define two crosspoints as the number of total threads in the program. The first crosspoint (#1) is when oversubscription over the total number of cores (36 cores) happens and the second one (#2) is when oversubscription over the total number of *hardware threads* (72) happens.

The evaluation results using 2, 4, and 8 PThreads, each of which creates parallel region ranging from 2 to 72 threads, are shown in Figs. 3, 4 and 5. The two crosspoints for each configuration are marked in the figures and the policy that delivers the best performance is highlighted in green and the worst performance in red. The results clearly show the significant impact of using different wait policies. For all the three configurations, before the crosspoint #2 from which oversubscription just starts to occur, the two ACTIVE wait polices (SPIN_BUSY and SPIN_PAUSE), deliver the best performance and the PASSIVE SUSPEND delivers the worst (max 2x time slower). The PASSIVE SPIN_YIELD delivers slightly worse performance than the two ACTIVE policies, but still much better than the PASSIVE SUSPEND policy. It can be explained that minimum overhead from OS kernel scheduling and context switches are incurred for the ACTIVE policies since the program does not oversubscribe the hardware threads. The results also show that there are not much changes of the performance by those policies when crossing the crosspoint #1.

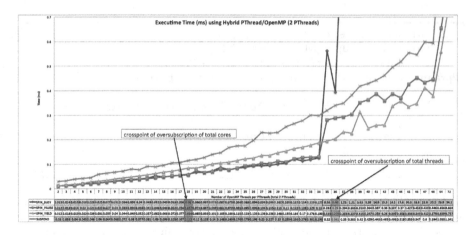

Fig. 3. Performance (ms) for hybrid PThreads/OpenMP execution (2 PThreads)

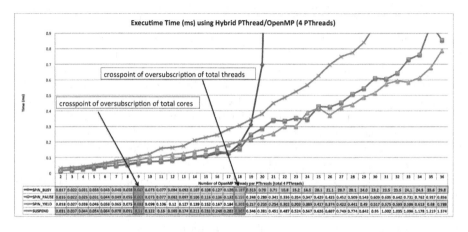

Fig. 4. Performance (ms) for hybrid PThreads/OpenMP execution (4 PThreads)

After passing the crosspoint #2, the results clearly show that using the ACTIVE SPIN_BUSY policy dramatically increases the execution time (5x to 10x). This policy does not help address oversubscription because of the large amount of overhead from OS kernel scheduling and context switches incurred when the threads are competing for hardware cores. The mild increase of the execution time when using either ACTIVE SPIN_PAUSE or PASSIVE SPIN_YIELD policy clearly shows the effect of the two policies to address the oversubscription issue. The PASSIVE SPIN_YIELD also performs better than ACTIVE SPIN_PAUSE policy. We also observed that the two policies consistently outperform the PASSIVE SUS-PEND policy (20 % to 40 %) for the configuration using 2 and 4 PThreads. The 8-PThread configuration shows that the PASSIVE SUSPEND policy outperforms the other policies from 39 OpenMP threads/PThread on wards for as much as 35 %.

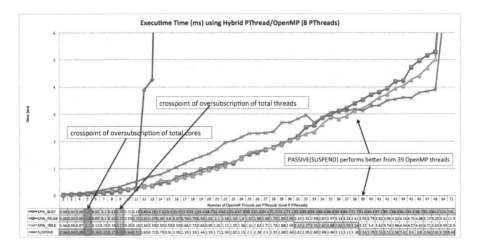

Fig. 5. Performance (ms) for hybrid PThreads/OpenMP execution (8 PThreads)

This indicates that for a program that heavily oversubscribes hardware resources, the PASSIVE SUSPEND policy is the best option among the four.

4.2   Performance with Regards to the Oversubscription Ratio

To further study the effects of the four policies, we introduce the term "oversubscription ratio" as the ratio of total number of threads requested by a program to the total number of hardware threads. In Fig. 6, we consolidate the results from the previous three figures and plot them with regards to the oversubscription ratio. The left figure shows that when the ratio is less than 1.0 (no oversubscription), the ACTIVE SPIN_BUSY and SPIN_PAUSE deliver similar performance between each other and better performance over other policies. When the ratio is between 1.0 to 4.0 (mild oversubscription), the ACTIVE SPIN_PAUSE and PASSIVE SPIN_YIELD policies perform similar and consistently better than others, but being gradually caught up by the PASSIVE SUSPEND policy as the ratio

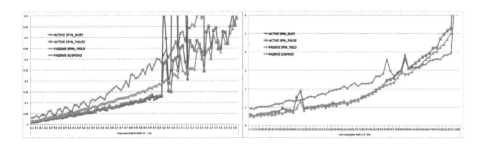

Fig. 6. Performance (ms) of using different wait policy with regards to the oversubscription ratio

increases. The ACTIVE SPIN_BUSY performs very poorly right after the ratio passes 1.0. When the ratio is above 4.0 (heavy oversubscription), the PASSIVE SUSPEND policy performs the best.

In summary, the evaluation demonstrates the effectiveness of using wait policies for combating the performance impacts of oversubscription. Heuristics for selecting the right policy could be drawn from this single but representative experiment as follows: the ACTIVE SPIN_BUSY or SPIN_PAUSE policy should be used when there is no oversubscription. For mild oversubscription (ratio less than 4), both ACTIVE SPIN_PAUSE and PASSIVE SPIN_YIELD are good options. For heavily oversubscribed system (ratio greater than 4), the PASSIVE SUSPEND policy should be considered to coordinate resources between parallel runtime.

5   Related Work

Previous studies address interoperability and composability of parallel programming models and libraries from different aspect and for different programming models. Tian et al. [14] explored interoperability between OpenMP threads and system threads in the Intel OpenMP compiler. For ease of use for programmers, they decided not to share thread identifiers between system threads and their OpenMP parent and not to share threadprivate variables among system threads. Callisto [6] and Lithe [11] address the interoperability challenge through the design of a low-level software layer for common resource management underneath multiple parallel runtime systems. In order to compose multiple simultaneously executing parallel applications, Hugo et al. [7] extends the starPU runtime system to allow confined execution environments (called scheduling contexts) which can be used to partition computing resources. A hypervisor is used to automatically expand or shrink contexts based on runtime resource utilization feedback.

The MPC (Multi-Processor Computing) framework [12] is a unified parallel runtime designed for clusters of large NUMA nodes. Through process virtualization and thread-based MPI implementation, MPC enables efficient mixing of MPI, OpenMP, and PThreads. The MPI endpoints [4] proposal to the MPI standard relaxes the one-to-one relationship between processes and ranks. It allows registering a thread in an MPI process as a MPI communicator rank that is able to independently participate in message passing operations. There are also efforts of integrating MPI calls as tasks in a intra-node workstealing runtime [2].

To enable interoperability among distributed HPC programming models, Epperly et al. [5] proposed a mixed-language environment supporting arbitrary combination of software written in PGAS languages (Co-Array Fortran, UPC, and Titanium) and HPCS languages (Chapel, X10, and Fortress). They designed the Scientific Interface Definition Language (SIDL) and Babel Intermediate Object Representation (IOR) as a language-independent object-oriented programming model and type system to allow software components to share complicated data structures across various languages.

6 Conclusions and Future Work

In this paper, we have studied use cases of using OpenMP with other parallel programming models in order to expose its interoperability challenges. In particular, we focused on the CPU oversubscription challenge and proposed a set of new runtime routines of OpenMP to change thread wait policies and contribute OpenMP threads to other thread libraries. Initial implementation has been done using two OpenMP runtime libraries with demonstrated effectiveness to address resource oversubscription and detailed analysis for selecting optimal wait policies.

For future work, we will conduct in-depth evaluation using representative benchmarks to demonstrate the benefits of our extensions. We will investigate the thread affinity conflict issue and address other interoperability challenges.

Acknowledgments. We thank members from the OpenMP Interoperability language subcommittee and the language committee in general for providing insightful comments of the design. We are also grateful to Terry Wilmarth and Brian Bliss from Intel for providing information that help our implementation. This material is based upon work supported by the National Science Foundation under Grant No. SHF-1409946 and SHF-1551182. This work performed under the auspices of the U.S. Department of Energy by Lawrence Livermore National Laboratory under Contract DE-AC52-07NA27344.

References

1. INTERTWinE: Programming Model INTERoperability ToWards Exascale. http://www.intertwine-project.eu
2. Chatterjee, S., Tasirlar, S., Budimlic, Z., Cavé, V., Chabbi, M., Grossman, M., Sarkar, V., Yan, Y.: Integrating asynchronous task parallelism with MPI. In: 2013 IEEE 27th International Symposium on Parallel Distributed Processing (IPDPS), pp. 712–725, May 2013
3. Cray. Cray C/C++ Reference Manual. http://docs.cray.com/cgi-bin/craydoc.cgi?mode=View;id=S-2179-82;right=/books/S-2179-82/html-S-2179-82//z1050591602oswald.html%23section-6yjyhx7c-esti
4. Dinan, J., Balaji, P., Goodell, D., Miller, D., Snir, M., Thakur, R.: Enabling MPI interoperability through flexible communication endpoints. In: Proceedings of the 20th European MPI Users' Group Meeting, EuroMPI 2013, pp. 13–18. ACM, New York, NY, USA (2013)
5. Epperly, T., Prantl, A., Chamberlain, B.: Composite parallelism: Creating interoperability between PGAS languages, HPCS languages and message passing libraries. Technical report LLNL-AR-499171 (2011)
6. Harris, T., Maas, M., Marathe, V.J.: Callisto: Co-scheduling parallel runtime systems. In: Proceedings of the Ninth European Conference on Computer Systems, EuroSys 2014, p. 24:1–24:14. ACM, New York, NY, USA (2014)
7. Hugo, A., Guermouche, A., Wacrenier, P.-A., Namyst, R.: Composing multiple StarPU applications over heterogeneous machines: a supervised approach. Int. J. High Perform. Comput. Appl. **28**(3), 285–300 (2014)
8. IBM Knowledge Center. XLSMPOPTS Runtime options: IBM XL C/C++ for Linux 12.1.0. http://docs.oracle.com/cd/E24457_01/html/E21996/aewcb.html#gentextid-475

9. Intel. User and Reference Guide for the Intel®C++ Compiler 15.0. https://software.intel.com/en-us/compiler_15.0_ug_c

10. ORACLE. Oracle Solaris Studio 12.3: OpenMP API User's Guide. http://docs.oracle.com/cd/E24457_01/html/E21996/aewcb.html#gentextid-475

11. Pan, H., Hindman, B., Asanović, K.: Lithe: enabling efficient composition of parallel libraries. In: Proceedings of the First USENIX Conference on Hot Topics in Parallelism, HotPar 2009, pp. 11–11. Berkeley, CA, USA (2009)

12. Pérache, M., Jourdren, H., Namyst, R.: MPC: a unified parallel runtime for clusters of NUMA machines. In: Luque, E., Margalef, T., Benítez, D. (eds.) Euro-Par 2008. LNCS, vol. 5168, pp. 78–88. Springer, Heidelberg (2008)

13. Pheatt, C.: Intel®threading building blocks. J. Comput. Sci. Coll. **23**(4), 298–298 (2008)

14. Tian, X., Girkar, M., Shah, S., Armstrong, D., Ernesto, S., Petersen, P.: Compiler and runtime support for running OpenMP programs on pentium-and itanium-architectures. In: 2003 Proceedings of International Parallel and Distributed Processing Symposium, p. 9. IEEE (2003)

15. Wang, E., Zhang, Q., Shen, B., Zhang, G., Xiaowei, L., Qing, W., Wang, Y.: Intel math kernel library. In: Wang, E., Zhang, Q., Shen, B., Zhang, G., Xiaowei, L., Qing, W., Wang, Y. (eds.) High-Performance Computing on the Intel®Xeon Phi^{TM}, pp. 167–188. Springer, Heidelberg (2014)

Tools

Testing Infrastructure for OpenMP Debugging Interface Implementations

Joachim Protze[1,2], Dong H. Ahn[3], Ignacio Laguna[3(✉)], Martin Schulz[3], and Matthias S. Müller[1,2]

[1] RWTH Aachen University, 52056 Aachen, Germany
{protze,mueller}@itc.rwth-aachen.de
[2] JARA–High-Performance Computing, 52062 Aachen, Germany
[3] Lawrence Livermore National Laboratory, Livermore, CA 94550, USA
{ahn1,lagunaperalt1,schulzm}@llnl.gov

Abstract. With complex codes moving to systems of greater on-node parallelism using OpenMP, debugging these codes is becoming increasingly challenging. While debuggers can significantly aid programmers, OpenMP support within existing debuggers is either largely ineffective or unsustainable. The OpenMP tools working group is working to specify a debugging interface for the OpenMP standard to be implemented by every OpenMP runtime implementation. To increase the acceptance of this interface by runtime implementers and to ensure the quality of these interface implementations, availability of a common testing infrastructure compatible with any runtime implementation is critical. In this paper, we present a promising software architecture for such a testing infrastructure.

1 Introduction

Debugging OpenMP applications at the level conceived by programmers is critical to effectively resolving bugs. However, no formal support has been defined and adopted within the OpenMP standard to allow debuggers to build full knowledge about the high-level constructs and objects of OpenMP. As a result, debuggers currently rely on OpenMP runtime implementation-specific mechanisms, an unsustainable model, or simply make no attempt to provide OpenMP-aware debugging.

The OpenMP tools working group is actively working on the specification of a OpenMP debugging interface (OMPD) [2,6]. The goal is to provide a debugger with a general, runtime implementation-independent interface to extract the internal state of the OpenMP runtime. Figure 1 shows the usage of the OpenMP debugging library. The debugger first loads the OMPD library into its address space, and then queries this library to obtain OpenMP's current state information. Upon receiving these queries, this OMPD library in turn uses the debugger-provided callbacks to resolve symbols and read runtime memory to fetch the state information from the OpenMP runtime library that resides in the process address space of the target application. Note that the way the OMPD

The rights of this work are transferred to the extent transferable according to title 17 U.S.C. 105.

N. Maruyama et al. (Eds.): IWOMP 2016, LNCS 9903, pp. 205–216, 2016.
DOI: 10.1007/978-3-319-45550-1_15

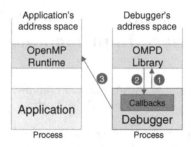

Fig. 1. Overview of the tool flow of OMPD: (1) the debugger requests information about OpenMP (e.g., the state of an OpenMP thread, parallel region, task, etc.) via an OMPD query API function call; (2) the OMPD library calls back the debugger to request information of the OpenMP runtime (e.g., the value of a symbol in the runtime); (3) the debugger fetches this information from the runtime.

library interprets the information that returns from debugger callbacks is opaque to the debugger (i.e., it is completely up to the OMPD library how to interpret this information); similarly, how the debugger fetches the requested information is opaque to the OMPD library. This way, neither the debugger nor the OMPD library have to rely on the implementation details of each other. This approach has successfully been used for many years in other debugging libraries including libthread_db [11] for POSIX Threads and the message queue debugging interface for MPI [5].

An OMPD library needs to access the internals of its corresponding OpenMP runtime implementation. Therefore, it is likely to be implemented by runtime implementers themselves, who may not have much experience with implementing such a third-party debug interface. To increase the acceptance of this interface by these runtime implementers and to facilitate high-quality implementations, the OpenMP community has an urgent need to make available a common testing infrastructure that is compatible with any runtime implementation. Using this infrastructure, all of the stakeholders of this interface–OpenMP runtime implementers, debugger implementers and users–can easily verify whether an OMPD implementation complies with the specification.

In this paper, we propose a software architecture for OMPD testing infrastructure. The OMPD library involves two interfaces, exposing a query interface while using a debugger callback interface. To test the query interface, our architecture exploits the very nature of the OMPD interface: OMPD makes state information—that is natively available to a first-party tool (i.e., agents that reside in the process address space of the OpenMP program)— also available to a third-party tool (e.g., a debugger running in its own process). Therefore, we use state values gathered using a first-party tool as the baseline to determine the correctness of an OMPD library: the values obtained from an OMPD query must match with those obtained from our first-party agent.

Further, coordinating all of the distributed components that participate in testing—the target application, first-party tool agent, debugger, and

OMPD—requires great care. We will discuss an effective coordination scheme which can lead to a good testing coverage over all kinds of OpenMP constructs and objects while minimizing redundant coverage. Finally, the OMPD interface can only be tested with a debugger callback implementation available. To make our testing infrastructure self-contained, we also need a commonly available OMPD callback interface implementation. We discuss how we adapted Dyninst [9] as our common OMPD callback interface implementation.

2 Architecture

The concept of our proposed testing infrastructure assumes that the debugging library is designed to provide a debugger with information directly accessible by a first-party tool from the OpenMP runtime. This is true for the OMPD: all information provided by OMPD inquiry functions can also be gathered by a first-party tool using inquiry functions of the OMPT, a performance tools interface for OpenMP, or OpenMP execution environment routines. To compare the information collected from two different sources, our testing infrastructure implements and employs both a first-party runtime tool and a debugger. Our approach can generally be applicable for testing other debugging libraries. We will detail our discussion on general applicability in Sect. 6.

2.1 Debugging Interface

A debugging library is typically loaded by the debugger into the debugger's process address space. Having the debugging library loaded into the debugger memory allows it to inspect the target program even when the application process is in a bad state or to analyse core files after a crash. In both scenarios, the debugger cannot query the runtime directly for information. The debugging library helps the debugger to assemble the internal state about the target runtime library.

A debugging interface typically consists of two components. First, the debugging interface defines a set of inquiry functions. These functions are a runtime implementation-independent way to provide the debugger with information about the internal runtime state. This is the main interface to be tested by our testing infrastructure.

Second, a debugging interface often also defines a set of callback functions to be provided by the debugger. They typically include functions for symbol lookups and target process memory access. The debugging library will use these callbacks to collect information from the target runtime library. The task of the debugging library is then to know the right symbols in the runtime, interpret this information, and finally provide the answer to the inquiry. The debugging library does not implement the callback functions; it is the debugger's responsibility to provide them. Therefore, we will not test the callback implementation. However, to test the debugging library, the testing infrastructure must provide the callback functions. Providing the callbacks means to be able to resolve symbol names (i.e. variable names) to virtual memory addresses in the target and to read values from these addresses. Fully featured debuggers use low-level libraries and services such as `libdwarf` [1] and `ptrace` for this purpose, but implementing our callbacks from these primitives and making them robust would be time consuming.

Many HPC tools like VampirTrace [12], Open |SpeedShop [3], TAU [10], or STAT [4] already rely on Dyninst [9] to implement basic debugging functionalities in a portable way. In particular, Dyninst provides SymtabAPI to resolve symbols to addresses as well as ProcControlAPI to control the target process and threads. A Dyninst-based implementation of our OMPD callbacks will be useful for a wide range of tools that already use Dyninst. Thus, we decided to implement our callbacks as a standalone library. More details on this library can be found in Sect. 4.

2.2   OpenMP Debugging Interface

The OpenMP Debugging Interface (OMPD) has concepts that are somewhat different from other debugging interfaces. The OMPD introduces the concept of *address-space context* and *thread context*. The address-space context refers to the address space of a process or a target device. This is still quite similar to the concept of `ps_prochandle` and `td_thragent` as used in `libthread_db`. The thread context refers to thread-local data within an address space context (process or target device). It is important to find a common language of debugger and debugging library about devices and threads.

Further, the OMPD introduces a handle for each type of OpenMP scopes:

- `thread_handle`
- `parallel_handle`
- `task_handle`

Additionally, the OMPD introduces an `address_space_handle` for initialization of an OpenMP process. Starting with the `address_space_handle`, a debugger can derive `thread_handle`s and fetch information about the threads. From a `thread_handle` the debugger can derive handles for the currently active parallel region as well as currently active task region. More handles are accessible via the ancestor regions until the initial task or the implicit parallel region is reached. All OMPD inquiry functions take one of these scope handles, which is used to determine the scope of the query. This differs from the OMPT inquiry functions and the OpenMP execution environment routines.

2.3   OpenMP Runtime Functions

The OpenMP runtime provides two sets of functions of interest for our testing library. These are the OpenMP execution environment routines as specified in the OpenMP standard and OMPT inquiry functions as specified in the OpenMP tools interface. For these functions, the scope is given implicitly because these functions get invoked in the thread context of the running application.

The OpenMP standard specifies a *binding* for all of the runtime library routines. An execution environment routine is typically bound to the encountering thread and the innermost enclosing parallel region, or the generating task. So the implicitly given scope of an OMPT inquiry function is the currently active parallel region or task region on the local thread. To address the scope of a parent region, some OpenMP execution environment routines accept an argument that specifies the nesting level. The initial parallel region has nesting level 0, the value returned by `omp_get_level()` points to the currently active parallel region.

Like the OpenMP runtime functions, OMPT inquiry functions also rely on the implicitly given scope, but the notion of parents is slightly different. The integer argument for the level provides an anchestor level, that means the currently active region is specified by `ancestor_level=0`, the value increases with each parent level.

3   Implementation

This section details the design decisions specific to the OMPD. While we will compare the properties between OMPT and OMPD, which are specific to OpenMP, the mechanisms to trigger our testing checks can easily be adapted for testing other debugging libraries.

While we were implementing the callbacks for OMPD, we found that none of the existing libraries provide a mechanisms by which our tester can look up thread local storage (TLS) symbols from within the same address space of the target program. Thus, we decided to split the testing infrastructure in two parts. A first-party driver library is responsible for collecting all of the available values from the runtime. A third-party testing application sets breakpoints on trigger

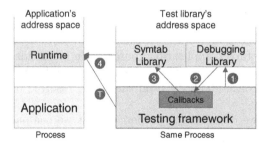

Fig. 2. Overview of the testing flow: (T) the test library requests information directly from the targeted runtime using runtime functions; (1) the test library requests the same runtime state information using a function call provided by the debugging library; (2) the debugging library calls back the test library to request debugging information from within the runtime (e.g., the value of a symbol in the runtime); (3) the test library uses a library like `libdwarf` ("symtab library") to look up symbols and values in the targeted runtime library; (4) the symtab library fetches this information from the runtime. Finally, the test library compares results of (T) and (1).

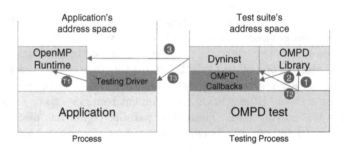

Fig. 3. Overview of the testing flow of OMPD: (T1) the testing driver requests information about OpenMP (e.g., the state of an OpenMP thread, parallel region, task, etc.) via an OMP or OMPT API function call; the information is stored locally in the driver; (T2) the test suite reads the stored information (T3) using Dyninst; (1) the test suite requests the same information about OpenMP via an OMPD API function call; (2) the OMPD library uses the callbacks implemented in the OMPD-callbacks library (see Sect. 4) which is based on Dyninst to request information of the OpenMP runtime (e.g., the value of a symbol in the runtime); (3) the Dyninst library fetches this information from the runtime. Finally, the test suite compares results of (T2) and (1).

functions and compares the information collected by the first-party driver with the values gathered using the OMPD library. This modified design is shown in Fig. 3. For debugging libraries that do not need to look up TLS variables, a single library implementation as depicted in Fig. 2 might provide an easier setup.

To control the testing target from the very beginning, our testing infrastructure starts the target program under its control. This is the same as what a debugger would do. Dyninst provides a function to start a new process and immediately stop and attach to this process.

3.1   Comparing Properties

As discussed, we collect the values provided by the OMPD and the first-party mechanisms in the target application context. We store this information in a global thread-private structure. This has an advantage in that we only need to resolve the address once and copy from that same resolved address every time we start checks.

In this section we describe the properties that we compare for the various OpenMP scopes.

Process. OpenMP offers two functions that provide information about the process settings. We compare the return value of `omp_get_num_procs` with the value provided by `ompd_get_num_procs` and the return value of `omp_get_thread_limit` with the value provided by `ompd_get_thread_limit`. These values should be constant during the entire execution of a process.

Threads. The OMPD specification has only one function to get the properties on threads, which this is the third party equivalent to an OMPT inquiry function. We compare `ompt_get_state` with the information provided by `ompd_get_state`.

Parallel Teams. We compare `omp_get_level` and `omp_get_active_level` with the information provided by `ompd_get_level` and `ompd_get_active_level` respectively. The value provided by `omp_get_level` gives the nesting level of parallel regions. OpenMP has two functions regarding the size of a team. The OpenMP function `omp_get_num_threads` returns the team size of the currently active parallel region, and `omp_get_team_size` takes an integer argument to specify the nesting level of the parallel region. `level=0` labels the initial parallel region. We compare the values of `ompd_get_num_threads` for the current and all of the ancestor parallel regions with `omp_get_team_size` except for the the topmost parallel region. For the topmost region, we simply use `omp_get_num_threads`.

Tasks. Both the OMPD and OpenMP runtime provide lookup functions for an array of ICVs and we also compare one another accordingly. Other than that, the OMPD and OMPT provide the functions `ompd_get_task_frame` `ompt_get_task_frame` respectively to lookup runtime frame information for each level of tasks. `ompt_get_task_frame` takes the ancestor level as an argument, and `ancestor_level=0` labels the currently running parallel region. We compare the values of both functions for all ancestor levels.

3.2   Triggers for Checks

In this section, we describe the mechanisms we use to start various sets of checks during the execution of a targeted application. The first-party driver library collects the data and then calls an empty function to allow the testing library to set a breakpoint and compare all of the collected data with the values gathered using the OMPD.

OMPT Events. We register the driver library with all of the events provided by the OMPT. Most of the functions provide a list of arguments. Where applicable, we compare these arguments against the values from the OMPD. We signal the actually updated values in the structure by invalidating all entries initially. Therefore, only updated values will be compared with the OMPD values. As an example we discuss this based on the current specification of the OMPT event for the begining of a parallel region:

```
void ompt_event_parallel_begin (
  ompt_task_data_t        parent_task_data,
  const ompt_frame_t    *parent_frame,
  ompt_parallel_data_t *parallel_data,
```

```
uint32_t              requested_team_size,
uint32_t              actual_team_size,
ompt_invoker_t        invoker,
const void            *codeptr_ra
);
```

We can compare the argument parent_frame with the frame information of the parent task. Further, we can compare the actual_team_size with the team size of the current parallel region using ompd_get_num_threads. We store this information in a structure that we put into the parallel_data argument. Also, we get the information provided by the parent_task_data argument and use this information for comparison.

The drawback of using the OMPT events to trigger the tests is that calling OpenMP runtime execution functions within an event handler is unsafe. Thus, we can only test against values provided by the event arguments or OMPT inquiry functions.

Ompd_test. We introduce the function ompd_test to explicitly trigger the full set of checks. This function collects all available information from the runtime using all the OMPT inquiry functions and OpenMP runtime execution functions. We place this function into the testing targets so that the right contexts are checked with the goal of covering all kinds of potential states in the OpenMP runtime library.

4   OMPD Callback Library for Dyninst

When looking at the implementation and usage of the OMPD callback library based on Dyninst, it is important to understand the difference of a *first party tool* and a *third party tool*. A first party tool is located in the same address space as the targeted application. A third party tool runs in another process than the targeted application. Debugger typically work as third party tool, while some profiling or runtime correctness checking tools run first party. A third party tool is typically able to connect to multiple processes. Many libraries that support debugging are targeted for the usage by third party tools; as an example this is the case for libthread_db. But also data access is completely different for a first or third party tool.

Dyninst is designed to be used in first and third party tools, with the goal to provide a very similar interface for both use cases if applicable. For example the difference when using the Stackwalker API is an additional argument for a process handle in the constructor for third party access.

Providing addresses to thread local variables is a requirement when implementing the OMPD callback interface. Unfortunately, Dyninst does not support resolving TLS variables for first party access, but only for third party access. This means, that the OMPD callback implementation based on Dyninst only supports third party access.

4.1   Interface of LibOmpdCallback

The interface consists of the two functions `initOMPDCallback` for initialization and `closeOMPDCallback` for finalization, and a callback `signal_ready_t` to signal back for the case, the target process was not ready initially. The initialization function takes an argument specifying the target process and returns the address handle for this process. The third argument callback is used for the case the target process was not ready to initialize OMPD:

```
ompd_rc_t initOMPDCallback(
    Dyninst::ProcControlAPI::Process::const_ptr& proc,
    ompd_address_space_handle_t** addrhandle,
    signal_ready_t callback);
```

This function looks up the ompd library in the OpenMP runtime using the hints provided in the symbol `ompd_dll_locations`. If OMPD is ready, this function calls the OMPD initialization functions `ompd_initialize` and `ompd_initialize_process` for getting the address space handle. The function also sets up the OMPD callback functions and context handle. A tool using this library will not come in touch with the context handle management.

If `ompd_dll_locations` is `NULL`, the runtime is not initialized yet, and thus not ready to initialize OMPD. In this case the function registers a breakpoint on `ompd_dll_locations_valid()` and initialize the `addrhandle` calling the OMPD initialization function when the breakpoint is reached. In this case the `callback` will be used to signal to the calling library that OMPD was initialized for this process.

The finalization function has the prototype:

```
ompd_rc_t closeOMPDCallback(
    ompd_address_space_handle_t* addrhandle);
```

This function calls `ompd_release_address_space_handle` for cleaning up the address space in OMPD and is also cleans up the data about this process in the library.

The callback is defined as following:

```
typedef void (*signal_ready_t) (
    Dyninst::ProcControlAPI::Process::const_ptr& proc,
    ompd_address_space_handle_t* addrhandle,
)
```

4.2   Using the LibOmpdCallback for Stackwalker

Due to the discussed limitations, OMPD can only be used to implement the third party Stackwalker for OpenMP. The constructor of the OpenMP aware Stackwalker calls the init function of *libOmpdCallback*, that initializes the address space handle. If this fails because the init is too early, the Stackwalker waits for the call to the callback function, before the OMPD functions are used. In the meantime OMPD inquiry functions are not used to improve stack traces. Since OMPD is initialized with the first OpenMP specific action, there should be no OpenMP specific stacktrace needed until OMPD is initialized and ready.

To use the Stackwalker for first party tools, we use OMPT to enhance the stack trace information. Got that we do not need the callbacks, but run into the issue that we explicitly need to look up the OMPT functions. This means that no other OMPT tool can use the OMPT interface at the same time.

5   Issues Detected in the OMPD Library Implementation

We applied the test suite on the OMPD library [8] for the LLVM/Intel OpenMP runtime and identified some issues of the OMPD implementation that were hidden before. We identified three classes of issues.

For the issues in the first class, the OMPD library used the wrong type size to read the values from runtime memory. Source for this type if mistake might be simple copy and paste of data access code. With awareness for this potential issue, it is quite simple to fix the problem.

For the issues in the second class, the OMPD library accessed the wrong member elements to answer an inquiry function. Again, the problem might be copy and paste of code or a misunderstanding of internal runtime data structures.

For the last class of issues, the OMPD library assumed that the runtime would use a direct mapping for an enum like `omp_sched_t`. Thus, OMPD would just read the value from the runtime memory and use the value for `ompd_get_schedule`. But the runtime internally differs between more values for the schedule. For the implementation of `ompd_get_schedule` this means, that more logic is necessary, to provide the right value.

All classes of identified issues are not really hard to fix, but are hard to identify without a proper testing environment.

6   Applicability for Other Debugging Interfaces

The main concept of the proposed testing infrastructure is to use first party API functions as base line for testing the debugging API.

This concept can be used to check an MPI debugging interface for the opaque MPI handles. The MPI standard [7] has a bunch of opaque handles for communicators, groups, data types, or files to name just a few. During debugging these handles are not generally understood by a debugger. A debugging interface could help the debugger to display more expressive information. For a first party tool, the necessary information is presented by the MPI interface or the MPI_T interface. A debugging library for MPI handles could be perfectly tested by a infrastructure as proposed in this paper.

Further, we think that a future programming paradigm for large HPC systems will only gain acceptance if proper debugging support is available. To provide sufficient information, the debugger needs to understand the internal model of the programming paradigm. So each parallel paradigm should provide a decent debugging interface. This can be checked with a testing infrastructure as we suggested it in this paper.

7   Conclusions

In this paper, we describe the design of a testing infrastructure for an OpenMP debugging library. The testing infrastructure is independent of the OpenMP runtime implementation and loads the matching OMPD library as described in the OMPD specification. We propose to use values queried directly from the runtime as baseline for testing the OMPD inquiry function implementation. We present the mappings of individual values from OpenMP functions to the matching OMPD function calls. Further, we present a standalone library that implements the OMPD callback interface based in Dyninst which can be reused by other tools building on Dyninst to query information from OMPD. We applied the test suite on the OMPD library [8] for the LLVM/Intel OpenMP runtime and identified some issues of the OMPD implementation that were hidden before. Having such a test suite available during development of the OMPD library could make the implementation work way easier.

Acknowledgments. The authors would like to thank Lai Wei for the initial OMPD Stackwalker implementation for Dyninst. The authors would also like to thank Matthew LeGendre and Greg Lee for their insights and hints to interact with Dyninst.

Part of this work was performed under the auspices of the U.S. Department of Energy by Lawrence Livermore National Laboratory under Contract DE-AC52-07NA27344. (LLNL-CONF-692845).

References

1. David A's DWARF Page, May 2016. https://www.prevanders.net/dwarf.html
2. OMPD specification in github, May 2016. https://github.com/OpenMPToolsInterface/OMPD-Technical-Report
3. OpenSpeedShop, May 2016. https://openspeedshop.org/
4. Ahn, D.H., Brim, M.J., de Supinski, B.R., Gamblin, T. Lee, G.L., LeGendre, M.P., Miller, B.P., Moody, A., Schulz, M.: Efficient and scalable retrieval techniques for global file properties. In: 27th IEEE International Symposium on Parallel and Distributed Processing, IPDpPS, Cambridge, MA, USA, 20–24 May 2013, pp. 369–380 (2013)
5. Cownie, J., Gropp, W.D.: A standard interface for debugger access to message queue information in MPI. In: Margalef, T., Dongarra, J., Luque, E. (eds.) PVM/MPI 1999. LNCS, vol. 1697, pp. 51–58. Springer, Heidelberg (1999)
6. Alexandre Eichenberger et al. OMPT and OMPD: OpenMP Tools Application Programming Interfaces for Performance Analysis and Debugging. Technical report, OpenMP.org, May 2013 (2016). http://openmp.org/mp-documents/ompt-tr.pdf
7. MPI Forum. MPI: A Message-Passing Interface Standard. Version 3.1, 4 June 2015, May 2016. http://www.mpi-forum.org

8. Protze, J., Laguna, I., Ahn, D.H., Signore, J.D., Burton, A., Schulz, M., Müller, M.S.: Lessons learned from implementing OMPD: a debugging interface for openMP. In: OpenMP: Heterogenous Execution and Data Movements- Proceedings of the 11th International Workshop on OpenMP, IWOMP 2015, Aachen, Germany, 1–2 October 2015, pp. 89–101 (2015)

9. Ravipati, G., Bernat, A.R., Rosenblum, N., Miller, B.P., Hollingsworth, J.K.: Toward the deconstruction of dyninst. Technical report, Computer Sciences Department, University of Wisconsin, Madison (2007). ftp://ftp.cs.wisc.edu/paradyn/papers/Ravipati07SymtabAPI.pdf

10. Shende, S.S., Malony, A.D.: The TAU parallel performance system. Int. J. High Perform. Comput. Appl. **20**(2), 287–311 (2006)

11. Inc. Sun Microsystems. man pages section 3: Threads and realtime library functions. User documentation, May 2002 (2016). https://docs.oracle.com/cd/E19683-01/816-0216/816-0216.pdf

12. ZIH. VampirTrace (May 2016). https://tu-dresden.de/zih/vampirtrace/

The Secrets of the Accelerators Unveiled: Tracing Heterogeneous Executions Through OMPT

Germán Llort[1,2]([✉]), Antonio Filgueras[1,2], Daniel Jiménez-González[1,2],
Harald Servat[3], Xavier Teruel[1,2], Estanislao Mercadal[1,2], Carlos Álvarez[1,2],
Judit Giménez[1,2], Xavier Martorell[1,2], Eduard Ayguadé[1,2],
and Jesús Labarta[1,2]

[1] Department of Computer Sciences,
Barcelona Supercomputing Center, Barcelona, Spain
german.llort@bsc.es
[2] Department of Computer Architecture,
Polytechnic University of Catalonia-BarcelonaTech, Barcelona, Spain
[3] Intel Corporation Iberia, Torre Picasso, 25th Floor,
Plaza Pablo Ruiz Picasso, 1, 28020 Madrid, Spain

Abstract. Heterogeneous systems are an important trend in the future of supercomputers, yet they can be hard to program and developers still lack powerful tools to gain understanding about how well their accelerated codes perform and how to improve them.

Having different types of hardware accelerators available, each with their own specific low-level APIs to program them, there is not yet a clear consensus on a standard way to retrieve information about the accelerator's performance. To improve this scenario, OMPT is a novel performance monitoring interface that is being considered for integration into the OpenMP standard. OMPT allows analysis tools to monitor the execution of parallel OpenMP applications by providing detailed information about the activity of the runtime through a standard API. For accelerated devices, OMPT also facilitates the exchange of performance information between the runtime and the analysis tool. We implement part of the OMPT specification that refers to the use of accelerators both in the Nanos++ parallel runtime system and the Extrae tracing framework, obtaining detailed performance information about the execution of the tasks issued to the accelerated devices to later conduct insightful analysis.

Our work extends previous efforts in the field to expose detailed information from the OpenMP and OmpSs runtimes, regarding the activity and performance of task-based parallel applications. In this paper, we focus on the evaluation of FPGA devices studying the performance of two common kernels in scientific algorithms: matrix multiplication and Cholesky decomposition. Furthermore, this development is seamlessly applicable for the analysis of GPGPU accelerators and Intel® Xeon Phi™ co-processors operating under the OmpSs programming model.

© Springer International Publishing Switzerland 2016
N. Maruyama et al. (Eds.): IWOMP 2016, LNCS 9903, pp. 217–236, 2016.
DOI: 10.1007/978-3-319-45550-1_16

1   Introduction

Heterogeneous systems are an important trend in the future of supercomputers. Since their introduction, the rate at which accelerators are being integrated into HPC platforms has surged. Nowadays, more than 100 heterogeneous systems on the TOP500 list of the world's most powerful supercomputers [7] are based on accelerators. This rapid uptake is mainly due to the quick and successful response of programmers to adapt their previously serial codes to take benefit from the extra computational power, achieving in turn significant throughput increases for a modest effort investment.

However, the change of programming paradigm in using accelerators also presents challenges. On the one hand, hardware accelerators are difficult to program. Even with modern programming interfaces like CUDA [6] and OpenCL [12], the programmer often requires domain-specific knowledge of the algorithm's parallelism and specialized knowledge of the target architecture. To ease this task several parallel programming models, noteworthy among which are OpenMP [10] and OmpSs [9], offer a very convenient solution to offload the work to the accelerators, just by adding simple annotations in the code.

OpenMP is a widely known shared memory parallel programming model that allows implementing parallel applications by using a set of compiler directives. The OpenMP runtime deals with the parallel thread execution (including fork, execution and join of the slave threads) and offers incremental parallel development to the user by adding the compiler directives gradually. Since version 3.0, OpenMP allows to express irregular parallelism through the new OpenMP Tasking constructs. A task is a unit of parallel work used to express unstructured parallelism that will be executed by one of the threads at a time, while different parts of a task may be executed by different threads. Likewise, OmpSs is a parallel programming model based on the OpenMP standard that extends the OpenMP Tasking constructs to support new features to allow data-flow execution of tasks directed by dependence clauses, and to accelerate tasks in devices other than a General Purpose Processor (GPP): GPU, FPGA, Intel® Xeon Phi™, etc.

A challenge in using accelerator devices concerns the evaluation and optimization of their performance. Hardware accelerators are fairly new and yet not well known computing resources, very architecture dependent, and they introduce many heterogeneous characteristics with respect to their host CPU: different hardware, clock frequencies, memory access latency, and overall, different performance behavior. In order to use these new devices efficiently, it is crucial to gain understanding on how they behave, how they impact the application's performance, and more importantly, how well they integrate and cooperate with the host system to achieve the maximum possible performance.

To date, there is not yet a clear consensus between vendors and users on a uniform way to collect and query performance information about the accelerators behavior. To fill this gap, the OpenMP Tools Application Programming Interface for Performance Analysis (OMPT) [14] is a new proposed standard monitoring interface considered for integration into OpenMP. The general objective of OMPT is to enable performance analysis tools to monitor the execution of the applications and to retrieve performance information about the runtime activity. The specification also defines an interface for target accelerators that copes with the typical difficulties associated to these devices of operating asynchronously with respect to their host.

In this paper we present an extension to the OmpSs programming model that implements the OMPT standard performance monitoring interface, to enable analysis tools to collect performance metrics both for the hosts and the accelerators during the execution. The proposed framework improves the performance analysis life-cycle by providing an integrated mechanism to gather accelerated application's performance data. Furthermore, we demonstrate the utility of exposing this information by analyzing two common kernels in scientific algorithms: matrix multiplication and Cholesky decomposition. Due to the increasing interest on FPGA accelerators (some vendors have recently announced integrated CPU plus FPGA solutions), we focus on the evaluation of these accelerators, but this development is being seamlessly extended for the analysis of General Purpose GPU (GPGPU) accelerators and Intel® Xeon Phi^{TM} co-processors.

The rest of this paper is organized as follows: Sect. 2 presents a summary of the tools involved in this work. Section 3 describes our design and implementation choices. Sections 4 and 5 report a detailed performance analysis of two common accelerated algorithms. We discuss related work in the literature in Sect. 6. Finally, we draw some conclusions and present future directions in Sect. 7.

2   Background

The OmpSs programming model [9] extended OpenMP [10] with new directives to support asynchronous parallelism and heterogeneity (devices like GPGPUs [24], FPGAs [15], Intel® Xeon Phi^{TM} [19], etc.). It can also be seen as an extension to other accelerator-based APIs like CUDA [6] or OpenCL [12]. The OmpSs environment is built on top of the Mercurium compiler [4] and the Nanos++ runtime system [5], which can optionally load dynamic plug-ins to support application instrumentation. In the current implementation, the instrumentation system is built on top of Extrae [3].

Extrae is the open-source tracing framework of the BSC tool-suite [1]. This package provides instrumentation and sampling mechanisms to collect performance measurements from the most common parallel programming models automatically; like from MPI, OpenMP, POSIX threads, CUDA, OpenCL, and also OmpSs, and combinations of these paradigms. The information captured by Extrae typically includes the activity of the parallel runtime (e.g. message exchanges in MPI and parallel loops in OpenMP), as well as performance counters (through the PAPI [11] interface), and call-stack information to correlate the measurements with the actual source code.

The result of an instrumented run with Extrae is a Paraver trace, a sequence of time-stamped events that reflects the actual execution of the parallel application. Paraver is the visualization tool of the BSC tool-suite, which enables to conduct a global qualitative analysis of the main performance issues in the execution by visual inspection, and then focus on the detailed quantitative analysis of the detected bottlenecks. The performance information is mapped into the application resources that were assigned in the execution up to three levels (namely: application, process and thread). The information comprised in the trace includes events, states and communications. Events are punctual information that occurs in an object (i.e. a thread or process) of the application. Typical events include entry and exit points of user routines, invocations to the parallel runtime, and measurements of a variety of metrics, among others. States reflect the activity of an object for a period of time (e.g. scheduling or transferring data). Lastly, communications represent relations between two objects (e.g. sender/receiver or task data dependencies).

Today, it is still difficult to produce tools that support performance analysis of OpenMP programs without tightly integrating them with a particular runtime implementation. Likewise, it is even more difficult to support the analysis of hardware-accelerated devices, as their runtime interfaces require very low-level, architecture-bound programming. OMPT [14] was defined to address this issue. OMPT is a novel API for first-party performance tools, that extends the OpenMP standard to allow building performance tools that will support any standard-compliant parallel runtime implementation. This API enables the runtime implementers to expose the system's internal activity and performance metrics to the tools, in a standard and uniform way, both for the host and accelerated devices.

In the following Section we describe the integration of the aforementioned technologies, adapting the Nanos++ runtime system and the Extrae tracing system to comply with the OMPT standard, enabling the analysis of OpenMP, OmpSs and accelerated applications with the BSC tool-suite.

3   Implementation

In this section we discuss the extensions developed for the Nanos++ runtime library and the Extrae instrumentation package to comply with the OMPT standard performance monitoring interface.

To support the OMPT interface for tools, the runtime basically has to maintain information about the state of the execution, and provide a set of callbacks to notify a tool of various runtime events during the run, such as thread begin/end, parallel region begin/end, and task region begin/end, among others. Meanwhile the tool must implement these callbacks to retrieve the information emitted by the runtime, and process and store it as required.

Regarding accelerators, OMPT proposes two mechanisms to pass information to the tool. On the one hand, the Native Record Types interface (see Sect. 6.2 of the OMPT API [14]) enables to invoke native control functions directly on the accelerator, binding the implementation to the architecture. On the other hand, the OMPT Record Types are a set of standard events that express the activity of the accelerator. These events are a generic abstraction of the activity of the device that unifies different types of hardware accelerators. We have opted to rely on the use of OMPT Record Types, so the tool is always agnostic of the underlying devices, with the consequent advantages of reducing software dependencies.

The sections below describe the modifications applied both to the Nanos++ runtime as well as to the Extrae instrumentation library. The extensions in Nanos++ include the addition of new query services to instrument the FPGA device, a reshaping phase of this information into Nanos++ internal events and the extension of the OMPT plugin: first to capture and handle these new device events, and then completing the callback interface established with the tool. On the tool side, the extensions in Extrae include support for the tracing buffer management during the program's execution, as well as considerations about the data representation for analysis.

3.1   Runtime Support for OMPT

Nanos++ is a library designed to serve as runtime support for parallel environments. It is mainly used to support OpenMP-like programming models by providing services to exploit task parallelism synchronized by means of data-dependencies. Tasks are run by user-level threads when their data-dependencies are satisfied. The runtime also provides support for maintaining coherence across different address spaces (such as GPUs, cluster nodes or FPGAs).

One of the principles of design of the Nanos++ Runtime Library is modularity. Figure 1 shows a simplified schema of the Nanos++ modules involved in the management of the accelerated devices and the instrumentation mechanisms, and how these modules interact. For each supported hardware device, Nanos++ provides a specific plug-in that implements all the necessary logic to execute a task in the target architecture.

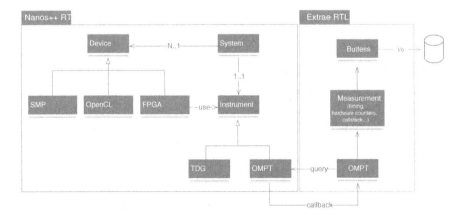

Fig. 1. Nanos++ Runtime Library partial class diagram: device components and instrumentation.

The execution of a task on a device that works with a different memory address space, such as the case of FPGAs, involves several steps. In this case, the device plug-in is responsible for the allocation and copy of input data to the device memory, issue the task for execution, and deallocate and copy results back to the host.

The instrumentation support for the executed tasks is also provided by plug-ins as TDG and OMPT. TDG is an example of monitoring tool that provides a graphical representation of the program's tasks dependencies. In this work, we added the new instrumentation plug-in to support OMPT, that will be used by the FPGA device to provide performance information regarding the execution of the tasks on the accelerator.

The device plug-in notifies about the activity of the hardware using a set of internal events representing the state of the accelerator (i.e. copying data and running a task) to the OMPT plug-in. In turn, the OMPT plug-in stores these events in separate memory buffers for each active device. This requires to develop mechanisms to manage the creation of event buffers, as well as query services (e.g. register a new device, number of devices, device identifier, target identifier) to associate the devices with their corresponding buffers.

The device plug-in is also responsible for retrieving the time-stamps in which the hardware produces the events, and provides this information to the OMPT plug-in. The FPGA hardware timings may not be based on a real-time clock, but on internal clock cycles counters. For this reason, the device plug-in needs to provide a mechanism to query and translate the hardware timings into unified time-stamps, according to the OMPT standard.

All the events stored in the OMPT plug-in from the devices are assembled into OMPT Record Types, a set of standard events designed to exchange data between the runtime and the tool. When the buffers are full, or on demand by the tool, the runtime will provide the event information to the performance tool through several callbacks set during the initialization phase. Then, the tool will parse the information through a set of iterator routines for the OMPT Record Types that the instrumentation plug-in provides. This process is explained in detail in Sect. 3.2.

3.2   Instrumentation Support for OMPT

The Extrae instrumentation framework has been accordingly extended to implement the OMPT standard in order to monitor the activity of the parallel runtime, enabling to capture performance information about the work offloaded to hardware accelerators. The information collected will help the analyst to understand which application's tasks are executed on which device, as well as their duration.

Integrating the OMPT interface on the tool side involves two main design aspects: The first one concerns the data storage and management. Most accelerators do not have a local memory to allocate instrumentation buffers in which to store the tracing events, neither access to the I/O subsystem to store them. To circumvent this limitation, our solution relies on hosting the tracing buffers for the accelerators on the host processor's main memory. The tool is then responsible for

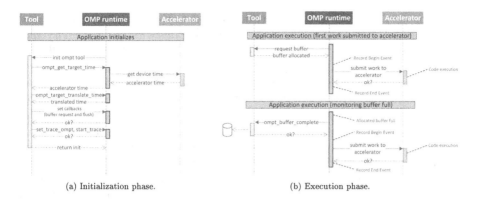

(a) Initialization phase.   (b) Execution phase.

Fig. 2. Simplified call sequence between the monitoring tool, runtime and accelerator device.

allocating the memory for the events that the runtime will produce and storing the data to disk, while the emission of the events is delegated to the runtime.

The second issue refers to the data representation for the analysis. It is important that the tool presents a clear view of which task ran on which accelerator. There are two main representations: First, assign one timeline for each host H and one timeline for each accelerator A (for a total of $H+A$ timelines). Second, show one timeline of each accelerator for each host (resulting in $H \times A$ timelines). Thereby, each accelerator timeline only contains the activities that originate on the according host. We chose the latter because it allows to visualize more clearly the interactions between host and accelerator. Furthermore, we split each accelerator timeline into its main logical components (kernel computation, input and output memory transfers) to highlight the chain of execution and the tasks' data dependencies.

From the implementation standpoint[1], a simplified call sequence interaction between the tracing tool, the runtime and the application through the OMPT API is shown in Fig. 2. In the initialization phase (see Fig. 2a) the tool needs to correct the time latency between the clocks on the host and the target accelerator (using `ompt_target_get_time` and `ompt_target_translate_time`), and also assign synthetic thread identifiers that will be used for representation purposes for the different logical components of each accelerator for each host, as explained above.

---

[1] At the moment of writing this document, the OMPT specification has gone through a major simplification. Due to the large number of changes in the latest version of the OMPT specification, our implementation is based on a hybrid version based on an earlier specification plus the latest target specification. As a result, the implementation we propose is a prototype and cannot be considered definitive but more an approach that shows how performance tools can take advantage of the OMPT specification for capturing accelerator activity.

Then, the tool needs to provide two callbacks to the runtime for the tracing buffer management during the program's execution: one will handle memory allocation requests, and the other will process a buffer of events when it is full. The first callback allocates a buffer for a target accelerator within the host address space, which will be returned to the runtime on demand to have it filled with the monitored tracing events (see Fig. 2b). The second callback receives a full buffer from the runtime that contains the traced events of a target accelerator, and the tool is the one responsible for storing the data into disk. As mentioned earlier, the runtime records the traced events into OMPT Record Types, which the tool can parse with provided iterators (`ompt_target_buffer_get_record_ompt`, etc.) to serialize the data into the final trace. In particular, the events that we are currently monitoring are `ompt_event_task_begin`, `ompt_event_task_switch` and `ompt_event_task_end`, which enables us to keep track of the tasks offloaded to the accelerators and their duration.

More precisely, the `ompt_event_task_begin` event notifies about the current active task in the accelerator, and provides information about the task identifier and the outlined function. The event `ompt_event_task_switch` notifies when a task is *scheduled in* and *out* of the device, which can be used to mark in the trace the real execution life span of the task in the accelerator. In order to record the actual time-stamps of these events, it is necessary to synchronize the target device's clock with the host's, applying the previously calculated time corrections. In turn, the `ompt_event_task_end` event indicates the finalization of the given task, but some runtimes may omit this event and only emit a last `ompt_event_task_switch` marking the task as *scheduled out*.

Lastly, the tool notifies the runtime to start monitoring the host and the accelerators activity (`ompt_target_set_trace_ompt` and `ompt_target_start_trace`). Once the execution finishes, the tool still needs to store the remaining events in the tracing buffers that may have not been flushed yet. To this end, the tool calls to `ompt_target_stop_trace` for each accelerator device, which implicitly requests the runtime to flush the associated allocated buffer for the given accelerator through the corresponding callback provided by the tool.

4   Experimental Setup

Results on Sect. 5 have been obtained on a Zynq SoC 702 board. This platform integrates a SMP dual core ARM Cortex A9 processor running at 666 MHz plus a programmable logic (FPGA) region based on Xilinx's Artix 7 FPGA [8]. The OmpSs ecosystem for FPGA/SMP heterogeneous execution used to obtain these results is based on the Mercurium compiler 1.99.9, the Nanos++ runtime 0.10a, and Extrae tracing framework 3.3.0. In order to generate the FPGA bitstream that implements the accelerator/s logic for the OmpSs task/s with target device `fpga`, Vivado and Vivado HLS, Xilinx's proprietary tools, both version 2015.4, have been used. In the case of floating-point applications, Vivado HLS synthesizes code compliant with the IEEE-754 standard. All the applications and libraries have been cross-compiled using arm-linux-gnueabihf-gcc 4.8.4 (Ubuntu/Linaro 4.8.4-2ubuntu1 14.04.1).

```
#pragma omp target device(fpga)
#pragma omp task in([BS*BS]A,[BS*BS]B) inout([BS*BS]C)
void MxM(REAL *A, REAL *B, REAL *C)
{
  for (int i = 0; i < BS; i++)
    for (int k = 0; k < BS; k++) {
      REAL tmp = A[i*BS+k];
      for (int j = 0; j < BS; j++)
        C[i*BS+j] += tmp * B[k*BS+j];
    }
}

void matmul(REAL **AA, REAL **BB, REAL **CC, int NB)
{
  for (int k = 0; k < NB; k++)
    for(int i = 0; i < NB; i++)
      for (int j = 0; j < NB; j++)
        MxM(AA[i*NB+k], BB[k*NB+j], CC[i*NB+j]);
}
```

Fig. 3. Matrix multiplication annotated with OmpSs directives. `matmul` is the blocking matrix multiplication function, and `MxM` performs the matrix multiplication of a block.

```
#pragma omp target device(fpga)
#pragma omp task in([BS*BS]A) inout([BS*BS]C)
void dsyrk(double *A, double *C, int BS);

#pragma omp task inout([BS*BS]A)
void dpotrf(double *A, int t, int BS );

#pragma omp task in([BS*BS]A) inout([BS*BS]B)
void dtrsm(double *A, double *B, int t, int BS);

#pragma omp target device(fpga)
#pragma omp task in([BS*BS]A, [BS*BS]B) inout([BS*BS]C)
void dgemm(double *A,double *B,double *C,int t,int BS);

void chol_ll(double **AA, int t, int NB, int BS)
{
  for (int k = 0; k < NB; k++ ) {
    for (int j=0; j<k; j++)
      dsyrk(AA[j*NB+k], AA[k*NB+k], BS);

    dpotrf(AA[k*NB+k], t, BS );

    for (int i = k+1; i < NB; i++)
      for (int j=0; j<k; j++)
        dgemm(AA[j*NB+i],AA[j*NB+k], AA[k*NB+i],t,BS);

    for (int i = k+1; i < NB; i++)
      dtrsm(AA[k*NB+k], AA[k*NB+i], t, BS );
  }
}
```

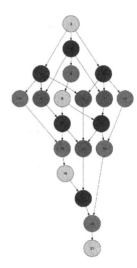

(a) Code annotated with OmpSs directives. Each function call will be a task instance (**dgemm**, **dsyrk**: target device (**fpga**); **dtrsm**, **dpotrf**: no target device is defined, which is (**smp**) by default.

(b) Task dependency graph for number of blocks equal to 4. Light green, red, blue, dark green nodes correspond to tasks **dpotrf**, **dsyrk**, **dgemm**, **dtrsm**, respectively.

Fig. 4. Cholesky decomposition (Color figure online)

We show trace execution results for two tiled applications: matrix multiply and Cholesky decomposition, using the following **fpga** task granularities for the tiles (blocks): 64×64-block and 32×32 single-precision floating point matrix multiply, and 64×64-block double-precision floating point Cholesky decomposition.

Matrix multiply (Fig. 3) is a well known and common scientific computation kernel that provides a reasonably simple scenario to illustrate how our framework is able to display the activity of the accelerated system.

Cholesky decomposition (Fig. 4a) is a more complex scientific computation kernel due to the task data dependencies, as it can be seen in Fig. 4b. In this case, two out of four of the kernels are annotated to be able to run in the FPGA (using the directive `target device (fpga)`). The other two have not been considered to be mapped to the FPGA by the programmer. This approach has been selected with the purpose of showing the potential of the proposed tracing although is not the configuration that achieves the best performance [20].

5 Results

In this section, we present results for several execution scenarios varying the number and type of accelerators, with the objective of showing the significant insight that trace-based performance analysis of the accelerators activity provides to the user.

5.1 Matrix Multiplication

Tiled matrix multiplication is analyzed varying the number of accelerators, the level of optimization of those hardware accelerators, and the number of MxM instances in the code (unroll degree). The problem size is a 256×256 matrix, divided into smaller blocks of 64×64 tiles, which are automatically offloaded to the accelerators programmed in the FPGA by the Nanos++ runtime of OmpSs. In addition, we present some results for 32×32 tiled matrix multiplication, that show some special characteristics due to the fine-grain granularity of the tasks.

Figure 5a shows an execution trace of the application when using one single `fpga` accelerator device. Rows represent the different computational and communication components of the system. From top to bottom: the master thread (Master), the kernel computations (FPGA acc MxM.1), and the DMA memory transfer copies from main memory to the accelerator (DMA_in MxM.1) and from the accelerator to main memory (DMA_out MxM.1). We can observe that (1) all tasks are offloaded to the `fpga` accelerator device since there is not any task execution in the Master thread (this corresponds to the MxM target device specification), and (2) there are two MxM different tasks. In particular, the accelerator device is only one (FPGA acc MxM.1) but two different colors appear because two different MxM instances in the OmpSs program are called (the innermost loop of `matmul` function in Fig. 3 has been unrolled by two).

Figure 5b shows a detailed view of the computation of 6 tiles (3 for each multiplication task), where the reader can clearly see that they execute alternately. We can observe a clear dependency chain between computations and memory transfers. First, the data has to be copied from the main memory to the accelerator, which is shown in the DMA_in row. As soon as the data has been copied, the computation of the task can start, displayed in the FPGA acc.

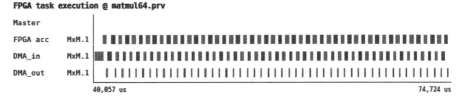

(a) Partial trace view showing the data transfer, accelerator, and master thread.

(b) Zoom in of the the data transfer and accelerator execution

Fig. 5. MxM execution trace using one MxM hardware accelerator and two MxM task instances.

Table 1. Average time per computation and transfer for a 64×64 MxM

	Task #1 (red)	Task #2 (blue)
FPGA acc MxM.1	334.81 us	337.53 us
DMA_in MxM.1	260.43 us	246.53 us
DMA_out MxM.1	82.82 us	82.76 us

Table 2. Average time per computation and transfer for a 32×32 MxM

	Task #1 (red)	Task #2 (blue)
FPGA acc MxM.1	46.51 us	44.51 us
DMA_in MxM.1	229.02 us	256.37 us
DMA_out MxM.1	80.49 us	82.33 us

Once the computation of the kernel has finished, the data is copied back to the main memory, as shown in the DMA_out. We can observe that the next iteration does not start until the previous one has finished copying the data back to the host. Looking at the depicted execution pattern, we can also infer a potential improvement for the runtime, that could consider overlapping the input/output memory transfers and hardware computation between iterations since the DMA channels are independent.

Table 1 shows the average execution time of each of the stages of the task execution in an accelerator: input DMA transfer (DMA_in), acceleration execution (FPGA acc) and output DMA transfer (DMA_out). These measurements

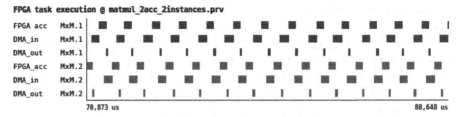

(a) Execution using two accelerators and two MxM task instances.

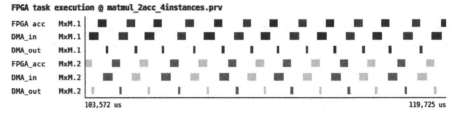

(b) Execution using two accelerators and four MxM task instances.

Fig. 6. MxM execution trace using two MxM hardware accelerator and two/four MxM task instances.

Table 3. Time % overlap between DMA transfers and FPGA accelerator computation in matrix multiply

	DMA_in MxM.1	DMA_out MxM.1	FPGA acc MxM.1
DMA_in MxM.2	0 %	21.4 %	17.0 %
DMA_out MxM.2	20.1 %	0 %	0 %
FPGA_acc MxM.2	11.2 %	0 %	0 %

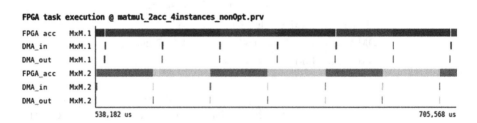

Fig. 7. Execution of 4 tasks using 2 time consuming accelerators and 4 task instances.

have been obtained using the Paraver profiling feature and validate that the MxM computation latency matches the High Level Synthesis tool estimation, and the DMA transfer times are very similar to the expected times.

On the one hand, the input/output DMA transfer time ratio is close to 3, and corresponds to the three input matrices and one output matrix needed by the hardware accelerator. However, this ratio may change for other task granularities. For instance, we have analyzed the trace execution for 32×32 block size (see Table 2) and the input/output ratio is $2 - 2.24\times$, which is less than the expected. In general, the DMA transfer performance may vary due to two main reasons: (1) the different DMA input/output bandwidth [20] and (2) the different waiting time for the corresponding DMA submit (i.e. the runtime programming the DMA), that can be significant for fine-grain task granularites. Note that a DMA transfer is not started until the corresponding submit is done. For instance, the task granularity in the 64×64 case is large enough to allow the runtime perform the DMA submit before the execution of the MxM task concludes. Therefore, the DMA_out transfer can start immediately after the hardware computation, and so the listed time accounts for actual transfer time. On the contrary, in the finer-granularity case of 32×32 MxM, with 8× less computation latency, the hardware computation is completed so fast that the runtime does not arrive on time to issue the DMA submit beforehand. Therefore, the DMA_out transfer time of the 32×32 case also includes the waiting time for the DMA submit to arrive. All the above explains why the 32×32 MxM DMA_out transfer time is higher than expected and similar to the 64×64 case.

On the other hand, the hardware computation and the input DMA transfer times are similar for the 64×64 MxM, but they may vary depending on the task granularity, the computation complexity and the hardware optimizations applied, which may be more or less aggressive depending on the FPGA resources availability. Thus, the execution time for two different approaches of the same 64×64 hardware accelerator may vary from $0.17ms$ to $26.34ms$, having the same input and output memory transfer times. For an optimized version of a 32×32 tiled matrix multiplication, the input DMA transfer/FPGA acc execution time ratio goes up to 5 (Table 2), being the hardware computation time significantly lower than the data transfer times.

Figure 6a and b show detailed views of the execution of the same problem using two accelerators and two and four matrix multiplication (MxM) instances respectively. In these cases each MxM instance may be assigned to any of the two accelerator devices. It can be seen that tasks overlap in time, increasing the occupation of resources and the parallelism. Table 3 shows the execution time percentage of overlapping DMA memory transfers and hardware computations between the two accelerators. As the reader can see, there are overlaps between input and output DMA transfers, and between input DMA transfers and hardware computations. However, both input and output DMA channels are never active simultaneously due to the runtime's task scheduling pattern. Likewise, the hardware computations from both accelerators neither overlap due to their small execution times. For slower or more time consuming accelerators, the hardware computations can overlap in time, as we can observe in Fig. 7. This view presents a detailed zoom of the execution trace of a matrix multiplication using two accelerators and four MxM instances, where the MxM tile is computed by a non-optimized accelerator. In this case, the execution overlap between FPGA accelerators is above 90 %.

Therefore, tracing the accelerator activity provides insight about DMA memory transfers and hardware computation overlap and their real latency information, which is not provided by any High Level Synthesis tool to the best of our knowledge. This analysis can help to improve the runtime memory management and scheduling policy.

5.2 Cholesky Decomposition

In the case of the tiled Cholesky decomposition we have evaluated one of the possible smp/fpga target device assignments of the application's task kernels.

In order to simplify the example, the problem size is fixed (256×256), the task granularity is fixed (64×64 blocks), and the combination of software/hardware partition analyzed is: one hardware accelerator for each dgemm and dsyrk tasks, and dpotrf and dtrsm tasks running in the SMP. Figure 8 shows the trace execution of the Cholesky application using this software/hardware partition. The begin/end of the smp tasks (in Master), the DMA transfers, and the fpga tasks, are marked with green flags to help distinguish consecutive instances of the smp tasks. This trace shows how the proposed OMPT-based tracing combines the accelerator and SMP partial traces into one single trace that helps to gain overall understanding of the whole application. While dpotrf and dtrsm tasks run in the Master thread (first row, light and dark green colors respectively), dgemm and dsyrk tasks (blue and red color respectively) are offloaded to the accelerator devices. We can observe that the task execution order matches the task data dependency graph in Fig. 4b, where the tasks are represented by the same colors.

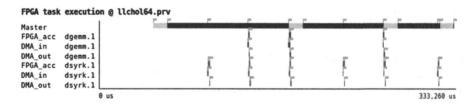

Fig. 8. Cholesky execution using 2 fpga accelerators for dgemm &dsyrk. dpotrf &dtrsm run in SMP. (Colour figure online)

Figure 8 also provides significant insight on the task acceleration in the FPGA. For instance, the first dsyrk task presents an unexpected input/output data transfer duration that is significantly higher than the rest of dsyrk tasks (see Fig. 9). Figure 9a shows the very first DMA memory transfer (DMA_in) in the application, which costs twice as much as any other DMA_in transfer of the same kernel (see Fig. 9b). This likely results from the DMA driver initialization during the very first fpga task acceleration.

Furthermore, Fig. 8 shows that the dtrsm tasks (dark green phases in Master preceding the accelerated kernels) are in the critical execution path of the current

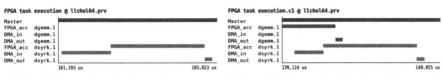

(a) First DMA transfer of the input of `dsyrk` task.   (b) Second DMA transfer of the input of `dsyrk` task.

Fig. 9. Comparison of two different runtime configurations for hardware acceleration.

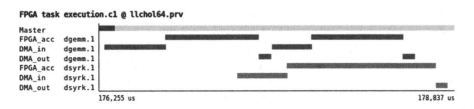

Fig. 10. Execution overlap of `dgemm` and `dsyrk` tasks. dpotrf and `dtrsm` tasks run in SMP.

Table 4. Time % overlap between DMA transfers and FPGA accelerator computation in Cholesky

	DMA_in dgemm.1	DMA_out dgemm.1	FPGA acc dgemm.1
DMA_in dsyrk.1	2.79 %	3.63 %	19.51 %
DMA_out dsyrk.1	0 %	0 %	0 %
FPGA_acc dsyrk.1	2.27 %	3.78 %	12.06 %

application implementation. The `dtrsm` tasks have a relatively low performance compared to the FPGA acceleration, and only few `dgemm` and `dsyrk` instances can be ready to be executed after a `dtrsm` task execution. In addition, the `dgemm` and `dsyrk` tasks are executed much faster, leaving the hardware accelerators idle for a long time (e.g. the `dtrsm` task latency). With this information, the programmer may decide to accelerate the `dtrsm` tasks in hardware. Another possible solution is to execute the slow SMP tasks (`dpotrf` and `dtrsm`) in more than one core of the SMP so that two or more `dtrsm` tasks can be executed in parallel. However, this would incur in over-subscription with the current environment: the Zynq system (with two Cortex-A9 SMP) and the current implementation of OmpSs, that uses one internal thread to submit the hardware computations.

Either way, once the programmer solves this application design issue, the `dgemm` and `dsyrk` tasks may turn to be in the critical execution path. The execution pattern of `dgemm` and `dsyrk` tasks is always the same for each iteration of the algorithm (see Fig. 4a): all the `dgemm` tasks are executed first, and then the `dsyrk` task execution follows, although there are no task dependencies between them. This behavior is attributed to the runtime scheduling policy, which results in a low degree of overlapping between these two kernels, as only the last `dgemm` task is able to overlap execution with the `dsyrk` task of the same iteration, as shown in Fig. 10. Table 4 highlights this behavior, showing that the hardware computations of both kernels can not concur more than 12 % of the execution time. Therefore, improving the application design issue that was initially observed, will likely uncover this second issue regarding the runtime scheduling policy.

A possible solution to reduce the potential scheduling policy impact is to enable one internal runtime thread per accelerator device, so that each internal runtime thread will take care of one type of accelerator. This solution would decouple the execution order of ready tasks in their corresponding hardware accelerators. However, this approach of using one internal runtime thread per accelerator is not the ideal solution because that may entail over-subscription in systems with a small number of cores. Therefore, other solutions should be explored to parallelize task offloading using a single internal runtime thread. The current runtime implementation has only one internal runtime thread for all the hardware accelerators.

6   Related Work

Previous work has aimed at capturing detailed information about the runtime system internal activity. Fürlinger et al. proposed a performance profiling system for OpenMP 3.0 [16]. They used OPARI2 [22] to instrument OpenMP applications that use OpenMP tasking constructs. In their work, they provide a summary of the time spent on each task, the function executed as such, in addition to imbalance, overhead and synchronization time. Servat et al. [25] proposed a similar technique to collect information about the execution of OpenMP-based tasks on top of the OmpSs runtime. But instead of collecting summary profiles, their approach relies on instrumentation-based measurements that enable to provide rich details about the execution, displayed in a trace timeline representation with new task-centric displays.

Our work derives from the definition of OMPT, an effort to define a standard OpenMP API for tools to collect performance measurements. In turn, OMPT is based on two prior efforts: the POMP API [23] and the Sun/Oracle Collector API [18,21]. The POMP API provides support for instrumentation-based measurement. The main drawback of this approach is that its overhead can be high because an operation, e.g. an iteration of an OpenMP worksharing loop, may take less time than tool callbacks monitoring its execution. In contrast, the Sun/Oracle Collector API provides support for asynchronous sampling-based measurement. This approach reduces the overhead, but does not provide enough instrumentation hooks to provide full tool support for statically-linked executables. OMPT was designed upon ideas from these two previous approaches, and provides support for asynchronous sampling, callbacks suitable for instrumentation-based monitoring of runtime events, and interfaces to correlate performance symptoms and causes. Furthermore, it also provides a standard interface for the tools to retrieve performance measurements both from the host and the hardware accelerator devices. The first extension of OMPT to include support for accelerators was proposed in [13]. Similarly, OMPD [14] has been proposed as a standard interface for debugger introspection of OpenMP programs, and recent studies aim at extending OMPD to fetch information from the OpenMP target regions offloaded to a hardware device [17].

The more specialized parallel computing platforms CUDA and OpenCL also provide mechanisms to retrieve information about the activity of the accelerators. The CUDA API [6] supports two different approaches to monitor the execution of GPU-accelerated applications. First, the CUPTI [2] extension allows a monitoring tool to use callbacks to capture the application activity at different levels, including driver and runtime. CUDA also provides the capability to inject events into the device that are processed by the device itself among all the other programmed commands. When the accelerator processes these events, it assigns them a timestamp that the monitoring tool can collect to determine the elapsed time between injected events and keep track of the activity. The OpenCL API [12] also provides a way for monitoring applications to capture the state of the accelerators. This mechanism is supported by a special parameter passed to the OpenCL calls that delegate work to the accelerator (i.e. launching kernels, memory transfers). Whenever this parameter is set, the monitoring tool can capture the timestamps of the different stages that the activity has progressed through (e.g. from submission on the host side to completion).

In the case of the FPGA, the profiling mechanisms are usually part of the debugging/developing phase of the hardware/software co-design; necessary to reduce the development and verification of new hardware. However, those mechanisms are not thought for parallel tracing purposes, being usually integrated on the vendor development tools like Altera Quartus® and Xilinx Vivado (now integrated the SDSoc) and focused on sequential execution. In this work a non-intrusive hardware instrumentation has been used in order to provide deferred trace information of the FPGA internal execution to the instrumentation tool. Indeed, the mechanism allows tracing of several accelerators at the same time so that parallel execution analysis can be done in a heterogeneous parallel application. This hardware support together with the OMPT support for device tracing is novel to the best of our knowledge.

7   Conclusions

In this paper we have described the integration of the OpenMP Tools Application Programming Interface for Performance Analysis (OMPT) into a parallel runtime system that supports task offloading to accelerated devices, and into an instrumentation framework. The synergy of these tools enables to generate highly detailed information about the program execution, including performance data regarding the activity of the accelerated devices and the runtime internal state.

Focusing on the analysis of FPGA-enabled applications, we have presented execution trace displays showing the runtime task offloading, the kernel computations and the DMA memory transfers between the host processor and the FPGA target devices. With this representation we can easily follow the lifetime of a certain task through a timeline and see how it switches from one device to another. Furthermore, we can easily visualize tasks execution and their data dependencies. All in all, the trace representation provides useful insight that enables the identification of performance issues that could not be detected before. On one hand, tracing analysis may help to improve the runtime programming model. For instance, our experiments expose that a different scheduling policy may increase the application performance when using hardware accelerators of different types and improve the automatic memory management between SMP and devices. Also, it may be considered to accelerate other tasks in the same device to reduce the memory transfers between the SMP and the devices or just to reduce the critical execution path. On the other hand, the computation/communication analysis can help to determine a better task/data decomposition, reducing the visible communication overhead. In the current implementation, an aggressive fine-grain task granularity can lead to a low application performance due to a high communication/computation ratio. An alternative solution to solve the previous issues is using more than one single internal runtime thread to submit the hardware accelerations, in order to decouple the execution order of ready tasks. However, that may entail over-subscription in systems with a small number of cores like the Zynq 702 board.

OMPT has enabled a standard cooperation between the runtime and the tool to exchange performance information. Moreover, supporting the standard brings the major advantage of providing seamless software interoperability, enabling to easily switch to another compliant runtime or performance tool. Even though the definition of the standard is still under development, the current specification is already general enough to support different types of accelerators transparently, enabling tools to abstract from the underlying hardware and easily retrieve relevant performance data from the runtime. In this direction, we are working on extending the runtime support for both GPGPU and Intel® Xeon Phi™ co-processors to conduct further performance analysis studies.

We are also working on extending the instrumentation support to include manual events in the accelerated code to mark phases of the algorithm, logical states and other punctual information. The instrumentation part could also take advantage of the OMPT task-dependency events to track task dependencies not only on tasks that run in the host but also on the accelerators, giving a broader picture of the whole execution. Furthermore, unveiling the secrets of the device executions opens an interesting door to include detailed power efficiency information in the trace analysis.

Acknowledgments. This work was partially supported by the European Union H2020 program through the AXIOM project (grant ICT-01-2014 GA 645496) and the Mont-Blanc 2 project, by the *Ministerio de Economía y Competitividad*, under contracts *Computación de Altas Prestaciones VII* (TIN2015-65316-P); *Departament d'Innovació, Universitats i Empresa de la Generalitat de Catalunya*, under projects *MPEXPAR: Models de Programaciói Entorns d'Execució Paral·lels* (2014-SGR-1051) and 2009-SGR-980; the BSC-CNS *Severo Ochoa* program (SEV-2011-00067); the Intel-BSC Exascale Laboratory project; and the OMPT Working Group.

References

1. BSC Tools. http://www.bsc.es/computer-sciences/performance-tools
2. CUDA Profiling Tools Interface. http://docs.nvidia.com/cuda/cupti
3. Extrae instrumentation package. http://www.bsc.es/paraver
4. Mercurium C/C++ source-to-source compiler. http://pm.bsc.es/projects/mcxx
5. Nanos++ RTL. http://pm.bsc.es/projects/nanox
6. NVIDIA CUDA Compute Unified Device Architecture Programming Guide. http://docs.nvidia.com
7. Top 500 supercomputing sites. http://www.top500.org
8. Zynq-7000 All Programmable SoC Overview. http://www.xilinx.com/support/documentation/data_sheets/ds190-Zynq-7000-Overview.pdf
9. Ayguade, E., Badia, R.M., Cabrera, D., Duran, A., Gonzalez, M., Igual, F., Jimenez, D., Labarta, J., Martorell, X., Mayo, R., Perez, J.M., Quintana-Ortí, E.S.: A proposal to extend the OpenMP tasking model for heterogeneous architectures. In: Müller, M.S., de Supinski, B.R., Chapman, B.M. (eds.) IWOMP 2009. LNCS, vol. 5568, pp. 154–167. Springer, Heidelberg (2009)
10. OpenMP Architecture Review Board. OpenMP Application Program Interface v 3.0, May 2008
11. Browne, S., Dongarra, J., Garner, N., Ho, G., Mucci, P.: A portable programming interface for performance evaluation on modern processors. Int. J. High Perform. Comput. Appl. **14**, 189–204 (2000)
12. Munshi, A., et al. (eds.) Khronos OpenCL Working Group. The OpenCL specification (2009). https://www.khronos.org/registry/cl/specs/opencl-2.0.pdf
13. Cramer, T., Dietrich, R., Terboven, C., Müller, M.S., Nagel, W.E.: Performance analysis for target devices with the openmp tools interface. In: IEEE International Parallel and Distributed Processing Symposium Workshop, IPDpPS, Hyderabad, India, 25–29 May 2015, pp. 215–224 (2015)
14. Eichenberger, A.E., Mellor-Crummey, J., Schulz, M., Wong, M., Copty, N., Dietrich, R., Liu, X., Loh, E., Lorenz, D.: OMPT: an OpenMP tools application programming interface for performance analysis. In: Rendell, A.P., Chapman, B.M., Müller, M.S. (eds.) IWOMP 2013. LNCS, vol. 8122, pp. 171–185. Springer, Heidelberg (2013)
15. Filgueras, A., Gil, E., Jimenez-Gonzalez, D., Alvarez, C., Martorell, X., Langer, J., Noguera, J., Vissers, K.: Ompss@zynq all-programmable SoC ecosystem. In: Proceedings of the ACM/SIGDA International Symposium on Field-programmable Gate Arrays, FPGA 2014, pp. 137–146, New York, NY, USA. ACM (2014)
16. Fürlinger, K., Skinner, D.: Performance profiling for OpenMP tasks. In: Müller, M.S., de Supinski, B.R., Chapman, B.M. (eds.) IWOMP 2009. LNCS, vol. 5568, pp. 132–139. Springer, Heidelberg (2009)
17. Hindborg, A., Laguna, I., Karlsson, S., Ahn, D.H.: A Standard Debug Interface for OpenMP Target Regions
18. Itzkowitz, M., Mazurov, O., Copty, N., Lin, Y.: An OpenMP Runtime API for Profiling. Sun Microsystems, Inc., OpenMP ARB White Paper. http://www.compunity.org/futures/omp-api.html
19. Jeffers, J., Reinders, J.: Intel Xeon Phi Coprocessor High Performance Programming, 1st edn. Morgan Kaufmann Publishers Inc., San Francisco (2013)
20. Jiménez-González, D., Álvarez, C., Filgueras, A., Martorell, X., Langer, J., Noguera, J., Vissers, K.A.: Coarse-grain performance estimator for heterogeneous parallel computing architectures like zynq all-programmable SoC (2015). CoRR, abs/1508.06830

21. Jost, G., Mazurov, O., an Mey, D.: Adding new dimensions to performance analysis through user-defined objects. In: Mueller, M.S., Chapman, B.M., de Supinski, B.R., Malony, A.D., Voss, M. (eds.) IWOMP 2005 and IWOMP 2006. LNCS, vol. 4315, pp. 255–266. Springer, Heidelberg (2008)
22. Lorenz, D., Mohr, B., Rössel, C., Schmidl, D., Wolf, F.: How to reconcile event-based performance analysis with tasking in OpenMP. In: Sato, M., Hanawa, T., Müller, M.S., Chapman, B.M., de Supinski, B.R. (eds.) IWOMP 2010. LNCS, vol. 6132, pp. 109–121. Springer, Heidelberg (2010)
23. Mohr, B., Malony, A., Hoppe, H.-C., Schlimbach, F., Haab, G., Shah, S.: A performance monitoring interface for OpenMP. In: Proceedings of the 4th European Workshop on OpenMP (EWOMP 2002), Rom, Italien, 2002. Record converted from VDB: 12 November 2012, September 2002
24. Owens, J.D., Luebke, D., Govindaraju, N., Harris, M., Krüger, J., Lefohn, A.E., Purcell, T.J.: A survey of general-purpose computation on graphics hardware. In: Computer Graphics Forum, vol. 26, pp. 80–113. Wiley Online Library (2007)
25. Servat, H., Teruel, X., Llort, G., Duran, A., Giménez, J., Martorell, X., Ayguadé, E., Labarta, J.: On the Instrumentation of OpenMP and OmpSs tasking constructs. In: Caragiannis, I., et al. (eds.) Euro-Par Workshops 2012. LNCS, vol. 7640, pp. 414–428. Springer, Heidelberg (2013)

Language-Centric Performance Analysis of OpenMP Programs with Aftermath

Andi Drebes[1(✉)], Jean-Baptiste Bréjon[3], Antoniu Pop[1], Karine Heydemann[2], and Albert Cohen[3,4]

[1] School of Computer Science, The University of Manchester, Manchester, UK
andi.drebes@manchester.ac.uk
[2] Sorbonne Universités, UPMC Paris 06, CNRS, UMR 7606, LIP6, Paris, France
[3] Inria, Paris, France
[4] École Normale Supérieure, Paris, France

Abstract. We present a new set of tools for the language-centric performance analysis and debugging of OpenMP programs that allows programmers to relate dynamic information from parallel execution to OpenMP constructs. Users can visualize execution traces, examine aggregate metrics on parallel loops and tasks, such as load imbalance or synchronization overhead, and obtain detailed information on specific events, such as the partitioning of a loop's iteration space, its distribution to workers according to the scheduling policy and fine-grain synchronization. Our work is based on the Aftermath performance analysis tool and a ready-to-use, instrumented version of the LLVM/CLANG OpenMP run-time with negligible overhead for tracing. By analyzing the performance of the *MG* application of the NPB suite, we show that language-centric performance analysis in general and our tools in particular can help improve the performance of large-scale OpenMP applications significantly.

Keywords: OpenMP · Performance analysis · Tracing

1 Introduction

Optimizing OpenMP programs to exploit modern hardware efficiently is a challenging task. Performance depends on many aspects, such as the amount parallelism exposed by a program, the interaction of the run-time system and the operating system, the locality of memory accesses, and optimizations for sequential performance by the compiler. To identify and eliminate performance bottlenecks, it is crucial for the programmer to understand each of the components involved in the execution as well as their interactions. Such interactions between the parallel program, the hardware and system software is generally out of reach of static analysis. Hence, it is customary to capture *dynamic events* into a trace file at execution time and to perform post-mortem analyses of the trace with appropriate tools [1,15,16]. Many existing tools enable the analysis of performance metrics, such as function call profiles, hardware performance counter data and memory

© Springer International Publishing Switzerland 2016
N. Maruyama et al. (Eds.): IWOMP 2016, LNCS 9903, pp. 237–250, 2016.
DOI: 10.1007/978-3-319-45550-1_17

allocation. However, only few tools are able to relate performance data to the OpenMP programming and execution model, e.g., to quantify the time spent in barriers, to attribute idle time to parallel regions, or to analyze the load imbalance in parallel loops—information that is essential for choosing the appropriate partitioning schemes for work and data, OpenMP constructs, synchronization and architecture-specific optimizations. Due to the diversity and complexity of the interplay between hardware, run-time programming constructs, and application behavior, it is crucial to rely on both quantitative metrics and detailed information on specific events related to the programming and execution model.

We present a method to analyze the performance of OpenMP applications that suits the needs of synergistic language and hardware analyses, as stated above. Our solution consists of a graphical user interface for performance analysis and visualization, an instrumented OpenMP run-time for trace generation, and a portable library for the generation of trace files. We designed our solution as an extension to Aftermath [8], a tool for trace-based performance analysis, supporting interactive exploration, visualization, filtering and quantitative analysis of programs with dependent tasks. In addition to our extension of the graphical user interface with OpenMP specific tools, we provide Aftermath-OpenMP, an instrumented OpenMP run-time for trace generation and libaftermath-trace, a library that allows programmers to generate trace files that can be analyzed using Aftermath. In contrast to existing tools, we do not only provide a visual representation, aggregate metrics and statistics, but also detailed information for parallel loops, including information on the partitioning of the iteration space among workers. All components are available under free software licenses.

We illustrate the capabilities of our solution by analyzing the performance of *MG* from the NAS Parallel Benchmarks (NPB), executing on a platform with 192 cores and 24 NUMA nodes. We show how this information can be used to determine the cause of bottlenecks and to improve the code, resulting in a speedup of more than 35×. Finally, we demonstrate that the tracing overhead is negligible and thus allows for the collection of precise data for performance analysis.

The paper is organized as follows. Section 2 introduces the components of our solution. In Sect. 3, we characterize and analyze NPB's *MG* application, then locate and fix two major performance bottlenecks. The overhead induced by trace generation is analyzed in Sect. 4. Section 5 presents related work on performance analysis, in particular for OpenMP, and we conclude in Sect. 6.

2   Aftermath: Trace Generation and Analysis

The trace-based analysis of parallel programs requires a component that records dynamic events at execution time into a trace file and a tool for post-mortem analysis of generated traces. As a result, our performance analysis approach needs two separate components: a trace generator called Aftermath-OpenMP— an instrumented OpenMP run-time, and a graphical user interface for trace analysis. We present both components in this section.

2.1   Trace Generation

The Aftermath-OpenMP run-time is based upon LLVM's run-time [3], itself
derived from the Intel OpenMP run-time [2]. Our contribution to the runtime consists in adding a lightweight profiling layer to gather information about
dynamic events (e.g., execution of parallel loops, barrier synchronization, task
creation and execution) through instrumentation of run-time functions. This
layer also interfaces the libaftermath-trace library, providing functionality to
write all recorded events to a trace file. Libaftermath-trace is a library that provides a common infrastructure for generating trace files compatible with Aftermath and is independent of run-time systems and applications.

To precisely define the tracing capabilities of Aftermath-OpenMP, we introduce the following terms in addition to the terminology of the OpenMP specification [7]: *iteration set*, *iteration period*, and *task period*. We illustrate these
terms on the following example with a parallel region composed of two parallel
loops and a task.

```
1   for(int i = 0; i < 2; i++) {
2     #pragma omp parallel
3     {
4       #pragma omp for schedule(static, 10)
5       for(int j = 0; j < 100; j++)
6         foo();
7
8       #pragma omp for schedule(dynamic, 10)
9       for(int k = 0; k < 100; k++)
10        bar();
11
12      #pragma omp task
13        baz();
14    }
15  }
```

As the parallel region is located in the body of a loop, each parallel loop
will be executed twice. Each execution of a parallel loop is referred to as a *loop*
and each execution of a task as a *task*. These terms are usually associated with
constructs in the source code, yet overloading these terms allows for a simple
terminology for dynamic analysis and remains unambiguous within the respective context. We use the terms *loop construct* and *task construct* to distinguish
constructs and instances when necessary.

Assume that five workers are involved in the execution of the parallel region in
the example. The schedule and the chunk size specified for the first loop imply
that the first worker executes loop iterations 0 to 9 and 50 to 59, the second
worker executes iterations 10 to 19 and 60 to 69, and so on. For a loop with a
static schedule, the generated code usually contains only one call to the run-time
at the beginning and at the end of the execution of the loop. This means that
an instrumented run-time usually cannot distinguish the execution intervals for
a worker's chunks. For example, it cannot determine when the first worker has
finished executing the chunk [0; 9] and starts executing the chunk [50; 59]. We
refer to the entire, not necessarily contiguous portion of the iteration space of
a loop instance associated to a worker as an *iteration set*. Depending on the

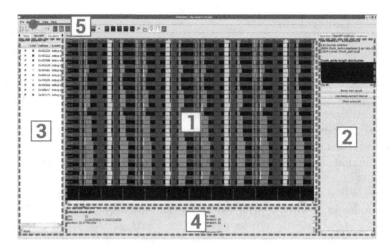

Fig. 1. Main window: timeline (1), filters (2), statistics (3), selected task/event information (4), derived metrics menu (5).

schedule, the increment and the chunk size, a worker can have multiple iteration sets, and its iteration sets might comprise one or multiple chunks, each of which might be composed of multiple iterations. Nested parallel regions and barriers can lead to preempting and resuming an iteration set. We refer to a contiguous interval of execution of an iteration set as an *iteration period*. Similar to the loop terminology, we define a *task* as the execution of a task and a *task period* as a contiguous interval of the execution of a task instance.

The Aftermath-OpenMP run-time is capable of tracing each loop and each task executed at least once. For each invocation of a parallel loop or task, the run-time traces loops and tasks, respectively. For loops with a static schedule, for each worker involved in its execution the run-time traces a single iteration set with all information about the set of chunks associated to the worker. For loops with a dynamic or guided schedule, an iteration set is traced each time a worker requests an additional portion of the iteration space. Iteration periods and task periods are recorded according to preemption through events related to barrier synchronization and recursive invocations of parallel loops.

2.2 A Graphical Interface for Trace Analysis

We call Aftermath a *language-centric* visualization and analysis tool, as its graphical user interface exposes hardware and runtime library events at the level of the programming model. The main window is composed of five parts, shown in Fig. 1: the *timeline* (1), a panel for *statistics* (2), an interface to configure *filters* (3), a *detailed text view* (4) and a *menu bar* (5) providing access to dialogs.

The information displayed on the timeline depends on the activated timeline mode. In the default *state mode*, the timeline shows which run-time states each core has traversed over time (e.g., execution of a single/master construct, waiting on a barrier, execution of a critical region). In *loop construct mode*, Aftermath assigns a different color to each parallel loop construct in the application's source code. This allows the user to obtain a rapid visual overview of which loops have been executed by which processors, when these were executed and how much time their execution has taken. Similarly, in *loop mode, iteration set mode, iteration period mode, task construct mode*, and *task mode*, Aftermath assigns a different color to each loop instance, iteration set, iteration period, task construct and task instance, respectively. The timeline can be overlaid with additional information, e.g., graphs showing the evolution of performance counters recorded for the different cores. In order to explore performance data interactively, the timeline can be zoomed and shifted arbitrarily without noticeable delays, even for large trace files. Intervals without activity (i.e., for which no run-time state was recorded or during which no parallel loop has been executed) are transparent, such that the background of the timeline with an alternating pattern of gray (even cores) and black (odd cores) becomes visible.

The filter interface allows the user to limit the information on the timeline and the statistics panel to specific loop constructs, loop instances, iteration sets, iteration periods, task constructs, task instances, task periods and performance counters. The panel also provides an interface that allows the user to modify the default assignment of colors. All updates are immediately taken into account by the timeline and the statistics panel. The statistics shown in the statistics panel are based on the interval on the timeline selected by the user. For example, the panel shows the duration of the selected interval, how much time has been spent in the different run-time states and a histogram for the distribution of the duration of iteration periods. The text view displays detailed information about a specific item selected from the time line. For a state, it shows its type and duration and for an iteration period, it displays its associated iteration set, loop instance and loop construct, including the number of iterations. The menu bar at the top allows the user to select dialogs to create advanced metrics (e.g., combine two performance counters) or to export data to files (e.g., the contents of the timeline).

On the implementation side, Aftermath is based on libaftermath-core, the interface to load and analyze trace files in Aftermath's native trace format, GTK [20] for standard graphical user interface components, and the CAIRO graphics library [19] for rendering. More information about the algorithms involved for scalable rendering and language-centric visualization can be found in [8].

3 Use Case: Optimization of MG

In this section, we show how the user interface presented in the previous section can be used to identify and locate performance bottlenecks in the *MG* application from the NAS Parallel Benchmarks [5], computing the solution of the

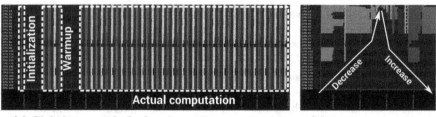

(a) Global view with the benchmark's main phases   (b) Between iterations

Fig. 2. Execution phases of *MG*

three-dimensional scalar Poisson equation using a V-cycle multigrid method. In the experiments, we have used the implementation in the C programming language of NPB-2.3 by the Omni Compiler Project [4]. The test system is an SGI UV2000, composed of 24 Intel Xeon E5-4640 CPUs running at 2.4 GHz with a total of 192 cores and 756 GiB RAM (Hyperthreading disabled). The system runs SUSE Linux Enterprise Server 11 SP3 with kernel 3.0.101-0.46-default. Unless mentioned otherwise, we have set the number of OpenMP workers to 192 with a fixed, round-robin assignment of workers to cores. For a reasonable execution time of several seconds, we have chosen the C input class with $512 \times 512 \times 512$ elements. The benchmark was compiled with LLVM/CLANG, version 3.8.0, and NPB's default compiler flags for optimization.

We first characterize the benchmark's execution phases, then we analyze the execution of parallel loops using Aftermath's timeline, detailed text view and statistics panel in order to locate bottlenecks for performance.

3.1   Identifying Execution Phases

Figure 2a shows Aftermath's timeline in OpenMP loop mode, as presented in Sect. 2.2. This visual representation indicates three different phases of activity during which the workers execute parallel loops, indicated by the colored sections surrounded by dotted rectangles in the figure. These phases are separated by intervals without loop execution, during which the timeline's background is visible. In the first phase, the benchmark allocates a set of global, multi-dimensional matrices and initializes them in parallel. In the subsequent warm-up phase, a single iteration of the algorithm is performed, resulting in the execution of multiple parallel for loops. The third phase consists of the actual computations of the benchmark. This main phase can be identified on the timeline by the long, repetitive pattern, spanning approximately two thirds of the execution time.

Each iteration of the algorithm in the main phase is characterized by a series of parallel for loops with a decreasing number of iterations, followed by a series of parallel for loops with an increasing number of iterations. This pattern can be spotted by zooming on the timeline between two iterations, as shown in Fig. 2b. In the first half of the figure, the height of the colored section decreases, indicating that fewer cores can take part in the execution of loops. In the second

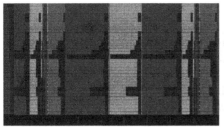   

(a) Interval covering two iterations   (b) Imbalance for a single loop

Fig. 3. Load imbalance between workers in the main computation phase

Fig. 4. Histogram of the duration of iteration sets of the selected loop

half, the colored section becomes taller again, which indicates that an increasing number of cores can be used.

3.2 Identifying Load Imbalance Resulting from NUMA

As the application's source code neither specifies the schedule of parallel loops, nor the size of chunks, the default static schedule and chunk size are applied. That is, the iteration space is divided into approximately equal-sized chunks, which are assigned in a round-robin fashion to the workers. The trip count of 512 iterations of most of the loop instances greatly exceeds the number of cores of the test system, such that most of the time all cores can contribute to the computation. The intervals with low parallelism, shown in Fig. 2b above, only make up a fraction of the execution time. However, a zoom into the main phase on the timeline also reveals a distinct pattern of imbalance on all of the loops, shown in Fig. 3a. To investigate the cause of this imbalance, we arbitrarily pick one of the loops for a detailed analysis.

Figure 3b shows a zoom on one of the loops. The workers with the shortest execution time for this instance are located on cores 88 to 95. As each NUMA node of the machine is composed of eight cores with consecutive core numbers, cores 88 to 95 belong to NUMA node 11. After a click onto one of the associated intervals on the time line, Aftermath provides detailed information about the portion of the iteration space that was executed during this interval. Each of the workers on node 11 executes two iterations of the loop, which takes between 24.15 Mcycles and 29.53 Mcycles. The workers with the longest execution time are located on cores 0 to 15 and 32 to 47 (NUMA nodes 0, 1, 4, and 5). Although these workers only execute one additional iteration in comparison to the worker on cores 88 to 95, their execution time of about 1.4 Gcycles is more than 40 times higher. For other workers, the execution time is between these two extremes. Figure 4 shows the histogram for the duration of iteration sets from the statistics panel for the interval from the beginning of the loop to its end. The distant peaks in this diagram confirm the strong imbalance.

Imbalance is either related to the benchmark itself (e.g., if the amount of work per iteration of a loop varies) or related to unequal access to shared resources due to the topology of the machine (e.g., memory accesses). The parallel loop corresponds to the outermost loop in function *psinv*, with a constant amount of work across iterations, as shown in the listing below.

```
1   static void psinv(double ***r, double ***u, int n1, int n2, int n3,
2                     double c[4], int k)
3   {
4       int i3, i2, i1;
5       double r1[M], r2[M];
6
7       #pragma omp for
8       for (i3 = 1; i3 < n3-1; i3++) {
9           for (i2 = 1; i2 < n2-1; i2++) {
10              for (i1 = 0; i1 < n1; i1++) {
11                  r1[i1] = r[i3][i2-1][i1] + r[i3][i2+1][i1] +
12                           r[i3-1][i2][i1] + r[i3+1][i2][i1];
13                  r2[i1] = r[i3-1][i2-1][i1] + r[i3-1][i2+1][i1] +
14                           r[i3+1][i2-1][i1] + r[i3+1][i2+1][i1];
15              }
16
17              for (i1 = 1; i1 < n1-1; i1++) {
18                  u[i3][i2][i1] = u[i3][i2][i1] +
19                          c[0] * r[i3][i2][i1] +
20                          c[1] * (r[i3][i2][i1-1] + r[i3][i2][i1+1] + r1[i1]) +
21                          c[2] * (r2[i1] + r1[i1-1] + r1[i1+1]);
22              }
23          }
24      }
25  }
```

This supports the hypothesis that the imbalance is related to the topology of the machine. In fact, Fig. 3b also shows that the execution time for workers on the same node is approximately the same. A comparison of the average execution time and the distance[1] of each node to node 11 reveals a correlation between these two metrics. We thus assume that memory accesses are causing the imbalance, with a high fraction of the data placed on the node with the fastest workers, node 11. This suggests a detailed analysis of the memory allocations and initialization of the benchmark.

The initialization routine of *MG* allocates arrays to double precision floating point elements using three and four levels of indirection. The allocation of these hierarchical structures is done stepwise by calling *malloc* from within loopnests:

---

[1] As reported by the **numactl** command line tool of LIBNUMA, invoked with the **--hardware** option.

```
1   u = (double ****)malloc((lt+1)*sizeof(double ***));
2
3   for (l = lt; l >=1; l--) {
4     u[l] = (double ***)malloc(m3[l]*sizeof(double **));
5
6     for (k = 0; k < m3[l]; k++) {
7       u[l][k] = (double **)malloc(m2[l]*sizeof(double *));
8
9       for (j = 0; j < m2[l]; j++)
10        u[l][k][j] = (double *)malloc(m1[l]*sizeof(double));
11    }
12  }
```

The innermost call of *malloc* (Line 10) allocates the space for the actual data. For the input class C, used in the experiments, these allocations have a size that varies between 32 bytes and 4112 bytes. Hence, all of the allocated data regions are smaller than the smallest page size of 4 KiB of the test system, except the largest allocations, which exceed this size by only 16 bytes. Meta data written by the *malloc* function in front of each allocated memory region is likely to be located in the first page of the allocated region. This causes the default first-touch page placement mechanism of the Linux kernel to place the first page of an allocation on the NUMA node associated to the allocating core. Hence, as a side effect of the small allocations of the benchmark, all data pages are placed on a single node. Most of the memory accesses of the main computation phase thus target a single NUMA node, resulting in high memory access latencies due to memory controller contention and remote accesses stressing the machine's interconnect.

To mitigate the early page placement, we have added simple, yet effective custom allocator to the benchmark's source code and replaced the calls to *malloc* in with calls to the new allocator. The revised allocation strategy consists in the allocation of a large, contiguous region of memory on startup and in returning a portion of this region on each invocation of its allocation function. The absence of meta data write accesses delays page placement until the initialization phase of the benchmark. As this initialization is performed in parallel, the first-touch page placement leads to an even distribution across all nodes of the machine, resulting in less contention and thus better performance. With this modification, the execution time is reduced from 48 s to 2.23 s on average for 10 runs.

3.3   Identifying Parallelism Degree Limitations and Imbalance

Figure 5 shows a trace of *MG* after modification of the memory allocation. Although the execution time could be reduced significantly, imbalance between workers is still present. Though, the imbalance pattern has changed, as highlighted by Fig. 5b that provides a zoom into one iteration of the algorithm.

The left side of the figure corresponds to the part of the computation where the number of iterations of the parallel loops is below the number of cores. As the execution time of the main loops has decreased, these phases now represent a larger part of the execution. The loops on the right side of the figure have a high iteration count, exceeding the number of workers. In all of the loops,

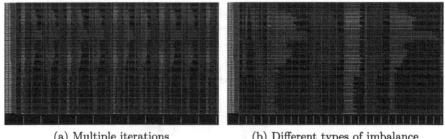

(a) Multiple iterations   (b) Different types of imbalance

Fig. 5. Load imbalance with optimized memory allocation

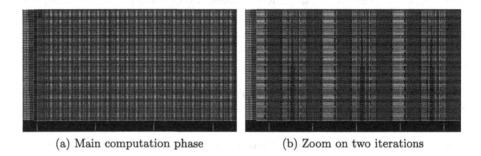

(a) Main computation phase   (b) Zoom on two iterations

Fig. 6. Execution using 128 cores

the first workers at the top of the figure spend significantly more time in the loop than the last workers at the bottom. This is due to a mismatch between the trip counts and the number of cores, making it impossible to partition the iteration space evenly across workers. For the dark green and the beige loop with 512 iterations, the first 128 workers perform three iterations, while the last 64 workers perform only two iterations. Similarly, the first 64 workers executing the gray and light green loops with 256 iterations perform two iterations, while the last 128 workers perform only one iteration. However, for the loops with 256 iterations, the pattern of imbalance is less sharp than for the loops with 512 iterations. This is due to the fact that the memory regions accessed in the additional iterations are placed remotely. Thus, the imbalance pattern resulting from the uneven partitioning is overlaid with an imbalance pattern resulting from the machine topology.

The analysis above implies that an execution with only 128 cores leaves the critical path unchanged with respect to the partitioning of the iteration spaces. Figure 6a shows the main computation phase with this reduced number of cores. The zoom in Fig. 6b shows that both the imbalance from the previously unevenly distributed iteration space and the remote memory accesses have disappeared. The latter effect helped reduce the execution time to 1.35 s, which represents a speedup of more than 35× over the initial execution.

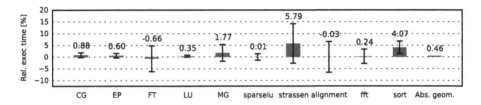

Fig. 7. Relative change of the execution time of tracing wrt. tracing disabled

4   Overhead of Tracing

In this section, we study the overhead induced by the instrumentation of the runtime. In our experiments, we have compared the execution using the unmodified LLVM/CLANG run-time, version 3.8.0 with the execution using our instrumented run-time for a total of 11 applications on the 192-core test system. As the base metric we have used the execution time reported by the benchmarks, i.e., the wall clock execution time, excluding initialization and termination and thus excluding the time needed for disk I/O to write the trace file.

To stress a significant part of the instrumentation code, we have chosen benchmarks from different benchmark suites, covering both benchmarks based on parallel loops and tasks. Loop-based benchmarks are *CG*, *EP*, *FT*, *LU* and *MG* from the C implementation of NPB-2.3 with the C input class, already used in the previous section. For task-based benchmarks, we have chosen *alignment*, *fft*, *floorplan*, *sort*, *sparselu* and *strassen* from the Barcelona OpenMP Task Suite (BOTS, [9]), version 1.1.2. We have used the *omp-tasks* version of the benchmarks where available, otherwise the *for-omp-tasks* version and the largest available inputs.

Some of the benchmarks had to be excluded from the evaluation due to segmentation faults (*BT* of NPB, *nqueens*, *uts* of BOTS), excessive execution time (*SP* of NPB), missing information on the execution time (*IS* of NPB) and unsuccessful verification of the results (*health* of BOTS).

Figure 7 shows the relative change of the execution time in percent when tracing is enabled for a total of 50 executions of each benchmark. These values have been obtained by dividing the execution time of each run with tracing by the average execution time for 50 runs without tracing. Error bars indicate the standard deviation and the values printed above error bars indicate the average change of execution time. The absolute value of the difference is below 6 % for all and below 1 % for the majority of the benchmarks shown in the graph. We have excluded *floorplan* from the plot, as its tracing overhead of 380 % is two orders of magnitude higher than for the other benchmarks. A quick analysis of this benchmark with Aftermath revealed that the huge increase of the execution time is the result of the creation of a large amount of tasks with a very short duration of only a few thousand cycles. However, the geometric mean of the absolute values of the mean differences excluding *floorplan* is below 0.4%, such that the overhead can be considered negligible.

5   Related Work

We compare our approach with the main tools and methodologies for the performance debugging of OpenMP programs. Regarding trace generation, a collaborative API called OMPT is gathering momentum [10]. It is based on the experience of POMP [12] and the Sun/Oracle collector API [13] and is primarily designed for first-party performance tools (i.e., running in address space of the application). OMPT provides limited support for sampling-based performance measurement as well as *blame shifting*, shifting the attribution of costs from symptoms to causes. Depending on the OpenMP implementation, it may be implemented entirely by the compiler, the run-time or both. In its current state, it provides callbacks for thread, parallel region and task begin/end and tracks the state of mutexes, but it does not track loop scheduling, iteration set or iteration period information. This limitation is shared with other tools such as OPARI2 [2], or EXTRAE [3], the library to generate Paraver trace files. Although the latter has wrappers for major OpenMP libraries the semantical information about OpenMP loops is not available. All the later also lack precise information about OpenMP tasks, such as the spawning tree, array sections and dependences.

On the visualization side, VAMPIR [15] is a well-known commercial tool used in high performance computing for almost two decades. It provides a rich user interface for interactive exploration and analysis of huge traces and has an elaborated filter interface. Multiple connected views with different granularity from cluster level to function calls are supported. But unlike Aftermath, the tool is optimized for the analysis of massively parallel applications based on message passing. OpenMP is supported at the granularity of parallel regions only. PARAVER [16] provides powerful independent views on trace data. However, PARAVER focuses on interactive filtering mechanisms for multiple graph types and independent views on trace data. The tool focuses on computation resources rather than loop chunks, task memory access and communication patterns, which are essential to the characterization of performance anomalies of OpenMP programs. On the other hand, Intel's VTUNE [4] provides finer grained, per-parallel-region analysis of load imbalance, potential performance gain, and enables correlations with hardware counters, but it neither models detailed chunk information, nor nested parallelism.

Unlike the former tools, PARAPROF [6] is a retargetable analysis and visualization toolkit, part of TAU [18]. It does not provide ready-to-use solutions for task-based performance analysis. One such solution based on PARAPROF is PERFEXPLORER [11], an interactive data mining application for performance analysis. However, PARAPROF's existing components and those of PERFEXPLORER have little overlap with the specialized ones required for OpenMP loops and tasks applications. As a result, building Aftermath within these frameworks would have been close to the cost of development from scratch.

---

[2] http://www.vi-hps.org/tools/opari2.html.

[3] http://www.bsc.es/computer-sciences/extrae.

[4] https://software.intel.com/en-us/articles/profiling-openmp-applications--with-intel-vtune-amplifier-xe.

Finally, Grain Graphs [14] differentiate for the former, chronogram-based frameworks. Its hierarchical graph representation is aimed at OpenMP programmers with little performance debugging experience, and at improving productivity of performance tuning. It facilitates the localization of performance anomalies on the source code, including load imbalance, limited parallelism degree, and synchronization granularity issues. But it suffers from scalability issues on larger traces and—by design—it does not provide a consistent timeline to correlate specific loop chunk or task events. Complementarities between grain graphs and chronogram-based visualization deserve to be investigated in the future.

6   Conclusion and Future Work

We presented a synergistic language and hardware approach to the performance analysis of OpenMP programs. It is designed and implemented as an extension to the Aftermath trace analyzer and the LLVM/CLANG OpenMP run-time. We contributed an efficient, low-overhead instrumentation of a state-of-the-art OpenMP run-time and a graphical user interface that provides a visual representation of OpenMP constructs, aggregate metrics for statistics, and methods for the detailed inspection of dynamic loop instances, iteration sets, iteration periods, tasks constructs and task instances. We demonstrated that performance analysis at the level of the parallel programming model is essential to characterize and to correct performance bottlenecks on large-scale parallel machines. Application to the *MG* benchmark led to 35× improvement over the baseline OpenMP implementation on a 192-core non-uniform memory access system. We also showed that our solution for trace file generation only causes negligible overhead on the execution time.

We plan to extend the components presented in this paper and the coverage of the programming model. In particular, we will provide support for the tracing of dependent tasks introduced with OpenMP 4, and add tools for the analysis of the task graph, similar to the analyses Aftermath provides for dependent tasks in OPENSTREAM [8,17].

Acknowledgments. Our work was partly supported by the grants EU FET-HPC ExaNoDe H2020-671578, Eurolab-4-HPC H2020-671610, UK EPSRC EP/M004880/1, and France Nano 2017 DEMA. A. Pop is funded by a Royal Academy of Engineering Uni-versity Research Fellowship.

References

1. http://vite.gforge.inria.fr. Accessed May 2016
2. Intel openmp runtime library. https://www.openmprtl.org. Accessed May 2016
3. LLVM OpenMP support. http://openmp.llvm.org. Accessed May 2016
4. Omni compiler project. http://www.hpcs.cs.tsukuba.ac.jp/omni-compiler/download/download-benchmarks.html. Accessed May 2016

5. Bailey, D., Barszcz, E., Barton, J., Browning, D., Carter, R., Dagum, L., Fatoohi, R., Fineberg, S., Frederickson, P., Lasinski, T., Schreiber, R., Simon, H., Venkatakrishnan, V.: The NAS Parallel Benchmarks. Technical report (1994)
6. Bell, R., Malony, A.D., Shende, S.S.: *ParaProf*: a portable, extensible, and scalable tool for parallel performance profile analysis. In: Kosch, H., Böszörményi, L., Hellwagner, H. (eds.) Euro-Par 2003. LNCS, vol. 2790, pp. 17–26. Springer, Heidelberg (2003)
7. OpenMP Architecture Review Board: OpenMP Application Program Interface Version 4.5, November 2015
8. Drebes, A., Pop, A., Heydemann, K., Cohen, A.: Interactive visualization of cross-layer performance anomalies in dynamic task-parallel applications and systems. In: 2016 IEEE International Symposium on Performance Analysis of Systems and Software (ISPASS), April 2016
9. Duran, A., Teruel, X., Ferrer, R., Martorell, X., Ayguade, E.: Barcelona openmp tasks suite: a set of benchmarks targeting the exploitation of task parallelism in openmp. In: Proceedings of the International Conference on Parallel Processing, ICpp 2009, pp. 124–131. IEEE Computer Society, Washington, DC, USA (2009)
10. Eichenberger, A., Mellor-Crummey, J., Schulz, M., Copty, N., Cownie, J., Dietrich, R., Liu, X., Loh, E., Lorenz, D.: OpenMP Technical Report 2 on the OMPT Interface. Technical report (2014)
11. Huck, K.A., Malony, A.D.: Perfexplorer: a performance data mining framework for large-scale parallel computing. In: Proceedings of the ACM/IEEE Conference on Supercomputing, SC 2005, pp. 41–53. IEEE Computer Society, Washington, DC, USA (2005)
12. Itzkowitz, M., Mazurov, O., Copty, N., Lin, Y.: An OpenMP Runtime API for Profiling. http://www.compunity.org/futures/omp-api.html. Accessed May 2016
13. Jost, G., Mazurov, O., an Mey, D.: Adding new dimensions to performance analysis through user-defined objects. In: Mueller, M.S., Chapman, B.M., Supinski, B.R., Malony, A.D., Voss, M. (eds.) IWOMP 2005 and IWOMP 2006. LNCS, vol. 4315, pp. 255–266. Springer, Heidelberg (2008)
14. Muddukrishna, A., Jonsson, P.A., Podobas, A., Brorsson, M.: Grain graphs: openmp performance analysis made easy. In: Proceedings of the 21st ACM SIG-PLAN Symposium on Principles and Practice of Parallel Programming, PPopp 2016, pp. 28:1–28:13. ACM, New York (2016)
15. Müller, M.S., Knüpfer, A., Jurenz, M., Lieber, M.,Brunst, H., Mix, H., Nagel, W.E.: Developing scalable applicationswith Vampir, VampirServer and VampirTrace. In: Proceedings of ParCo 2007. Advances in Parallel Computing, vol. 15, pp. 637–644. IOS Press (2008)
16. Pillet, V., Labarta, J., Cortes, T., Girona, S.: PARAVER: A tool to visualize and analyze parallel code. In: WoTUG-18. Technical report (1995)
17. Pop, A., Cohen, A.: OpenStream: expressiveness and data-flow compilation of OpenMP streaming programs. ACM Trans. Archit. Code Optim. **9**(4), 53:1–53:25 (2013)
18. Shende, S.S., Malony, A.D.: The tau parallel performance system. Int. J. High Perform. Comput. Appl. **20**(2), 287–311 (2006)
19. The Cairo Graphics Team: Cairo graphics. http://www.cairographics.org. Accessed May 2016
20. The GTK+ Team: The GTK+ project. http://www.gtk.org. Accessed May 2016

Accelerator Programming

Pragmatic Performance Portability with OpenMP 4.x

Matt Martineau[1]([✉]), James Price[1], Simon McIntosh-Smith[1],
and Wayne Gaudin[2]

[1] Merchant Venturers Building, University of Bristol, Bristol, UK
m.martineau@bristol.ac.uk
[2] UK Atomic Weapons Establishment, Aldermaston, UK

Abstract. In this paper we investigate the current compiler technologies supporting OpenMP 4.x features targeting a range of devices, in particular, the Cray compiler 8.5.0 targeting an Intel Xeon Broadwell and NVIDIA K20x, IBM's OpenMP 4.5 Clang branch (clang-ykt) targeting an NVIDIA K20x, the Intel compiler 16 targeting an Intel Xeon Phi Knights Landing, and GCC 6.1 targeting an AMD APU. We outline the mechanisms that they use to map the OpenMP model onto their target architectures, and conduct performance testing with a number of representative data parallel kernels. Following this we present a discussion about the current state of play in terms of performance portability and propose some straightforward guidelines for writing performance portable code, derived from our observations. At the time of writing, developers will likely have to rely on the pre-processor for certain kernels to achieve functional portability, but we expect that future homogenisation of required directives between compilers and architectures is feasible.

Keywords: OpenMP 4.x · Performance portability · Parallel programming

1 Introduction

Today's supercomputing facilities are becoming increasingly diverse, with many hosting heterogeneous devices containing increasing levels of parallelism at the core and vector levels. As large HPC centres often need to support monolithic codes, the expense of porting codes for each new architecture is prohibitive, and given the current rate of architectural innovation, this is becoming a significant barrier to scientific progress. In order to exploit the computing resources available today, application developers have had to embrace heterogeneity and begin considering the portability of their codes [5]. The diversity of requirements presented by individual organisations means that it is going to be impossible to create a unified or one-size-fits-all solution to the current performance portability problem, but a pragmatic and forward thinking approach will go someway to protecting future HPC investment.

© Springer International Publishing Switzerland 2016
N. Maruyama et al. (Eds.): IWOMP 2016, LNCS 9903, pp. 253–267, 2016.
DOI: 10.1007/978-3-319-45550-1_18

The OpenMP standard is a popular, mature directive-based model for targeting CPUs and, more recently, heterogeneous devices. Faced with the plethora of parallel programming models currently available, we expect many developers will see OpenMP 4.x as a familiar and attractive option that can balance performance, portability, productivity and maintainability [8]. Of course, there are no guarantees of performance portability offered by the specification and the divergence of existing implementations means that it is currently possible to write code that is non-portable between different implementations even targeting the same architecture.

1.1 Scope

In this paper we aim to develop some best practices for performance portability by considering the different approaches taken by existing compiler vendors. We collect performance results across a range of modern devices, including those seen in large supercomputing clusters, using a suite of optimised kernels, several of which represent the performance critical functions of a range of HPC applications. The compilers that we are discussing contain bugs and lack certain features, for instance neither Clang nor GCC 6.1 provide a reduction implementation. We expect such issues to be fixed in the short to medium term, and so do not discuss these matters in any detail, and work around them wherever possible. The principal focus of this paper is on the specific design decisions made in each implementation, and how they expose long term performance portability concerns. Although we cannot guarantee complete coverage, we expect that our investigation is diverse enough that many of our insights will be applicable to general development with OpenMP 4.x.

2   Background

In July 2013, version 4.0 of the OpenMP specification was released, including a number of new directives that support targeting accelerators using computational offloading. However, up until recently the only commercially supported compiler was provided by Intel for targeting their Xeon Phi Knights Corner architecture. Some experimental compilers were developed in the interim, with the most notable being the Clang OpenMP 4.5 project, which was contributed to by a number of collaborators, including AMD, IBM, Intel, and NVIDIA. In particular, the GPU targeting functionality was developed by IBM, who are actively migrating this functionality into the main trunk of Clang [2]. In September 2015, the Cray Compiling Environment version 8.4 introduced the first official vendor support for OpenMP 4.0 on NVIDIA GPUs, with full support for version 4.0 of the specification. In April 2016, GCC 6.1 introduced support for OpenMP 4.5 offloading to HSA capable GPUs.

Readers who require introduction to the new features in OpenMP 4.x can refer to the existing literature [4,8], and the OpenMP 4.5 specification [11].

3   Implementation-Specific Interpretations

Although the specification is very explicit about how compilers should implement the `teams` and `distribute` directives, there is some flexibility as to how the final scheduling of iterations to threads within a team is conducted. In addition to the opportunities for interpretation exposed within the specification, there are a great many implementation defined aspects of the OpenMP standard. This means that the finer details can be optimised on a per-architecture basis, making it easier for individual compilers to achieve good performance, but allowing for inconsistencies that might harm performance portability.

There is some debate regarding the prescriptive nature of OpenMP 4.x compared to the descriptive capabilities available in OpenACC with the `kernels` directive [6]. We believe that the distinction between the two approaches is actually quite small in practice, perhaps affecting the number of required directives for particular kernels. In those cases where compiler heuristic analysis of loop-level parallelism is possible and more descriptive schemes are applicable, it is not possible to guarantee the reproducibility of the parallelisation. With OpenMP 4.x, the developer certainly has to prescribe the presence of parallelism in a loop nest and direct the compiler to some extent. However, when given the minimal set of directives, the compiler has a suitable level of control over the thread co-ordination and scheduling, and how this maps to the target architecture.

3.1   Thread Co-ordination

It is useful to consider the way that each implementation maps the OpenMP model of leagues of teams of threads that can execute SIMD instructions, onto a target architecture's model, such as the CUDA model of a grid of thread blocks containing threads.

Figure 1 presents a highly simplified perspective of the levels of parallelism exposed by two key target architectures alongside the OpenMP 4.x model. Please note that the CUDA grid does not explicitly include the warps that the threads

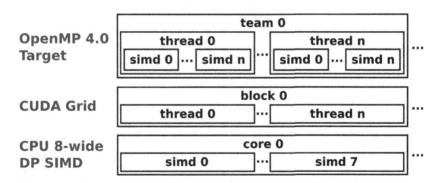

Fig. 1. OpenMP 4.x model alongside simplification of an NVIDIA GPU and Intel CPU.

are blocked into, because CUDA implicitly handles warps and so it is not necessary to prescribe the parallelism at that granularity. There are significant overlaps between the models, but there exist subtle differences in the way that each architectural level must be handled. For instance, the CPU SIMD lanes need to be utilised in a different way to the CUDA threads, requiring the use of vector hardware instructions. In spite of this, the OpenMP model is specified such that the Cray compiler maps the teams onto CUDA thread blocks and then treats them as large vector units.

3.2   Cray Compiler Mapping of OpenMP onto NVIDIA GPUs

Each implementation adopts a different approach to mapping the OpenMP model onto their target architecture, in particular the scheduling of the iteration space across the available resources. For a simple one-dimensional loop prepended with `#pragma omp target teams distribute parallel for simd`, we have made the following observations regarding the way in which the Cray compiler mapped our OpenMP 4.5 code onto an NVIDIA K20x:

- The `teams` directive either initialises $t = $ `num_teams` teams if a value is provided, or $t = 128$ by default. The teams intuitively map to individual CUDA blocks (Fig. 1), with each containing 128 CUDA threads.
- We assume that the number of OpenMP threads directly maps to the number of CUDA threads, but we were not able to prove this hypothesis given that the omp_get_num_threads() API call always returns 0.
- The `distribute` directive partitions the loop into t chunks, and distributes a chunk to the master thread of each team.
- Auto-vectorisation, or vectorisation directed by the `simd` directive, schedules the iterations in each chunk in a round robin schedule across the threads in a team, potentially wrapping such that there are multiple iterations per CUDA thread whilst maintaining coalesced memory accesses.

Code Sample 1.1. Two-dimensional kernel with outer loop parallelism.

```
#pragma omp target teams distribute parallel for
for(int ii = 0; ii < y; ++ii)
{
  #pragma omp simd
  for(int jj = 0; jj < x; ++ii)
  ...
}
```

Although we include it in Code Sample 1.1, note that the Cray compiler implementation does not explicitly require the `parallel for` directive, providing a warning upon compilation that `parallel` regions nested inside `target` regions are limited to a single thread. This warning does not mean that acceleration has failed, but that the compiler does not use the directive to guide parallelisation. In the 2d loop case, as seen in Code Sample 1.1, the number of teams is now determined by the length y of the outer loop, such that $t = l$, and each outer iteration is associated with an independent team. While we could not determine the number of OpenMP threads instantiated, as with the 1d case, we again observed that 128 CUDA threads are created regardless of the number of OpenMP threads. The implication of this is that multiple iterations can be scheduled per CUDA thread, and in the event that fewer than 128 inner iterations are available, some of the warps will be under-utilised. The behaviour seen with two-dimensional case holds for higher dimensional loops, and collapsing can be used to revert higher-dimensional loops to the one-dimensional scheduling process.

3.3 Clang Mapping of OpenMP onto NVIDIA GPUs

Our experimentation has shown that scheduling with the Clang OpenMP 4.5 implementation uses a significantly different mechanism than that used by the Cray compiler. The compiler maps one CUDA block per multiprocessor, so when targeting an NVIDIA K20x that has 14 multiprocessors, the default is to create $t = 14$ teams. By default, each of those blocks will contain 1024 CUDA threads. When a distribute is encountered, the outer iterations are chunked according to the dist_schedule, which evenly splits the iteration space into t chunks by default. Similarly to the Cray compiler, it might be necessary for threads to execute multiple iterations.

Code Sample 1.2. Teams across the outer loop and parallel threads for inner.

```
#pragma omp target teams distribute
for(int ii = 0; ii < y; ++ii)
{
  #pragma omp parallel for schedule(static, 1)
  for(int jj = 0; jj < x; ++ii)
  ...
}
```

Clang considers the **parallel for** directive as instructing the runtime to schedule chunked loop iterations for execution by the threads in a team. This directly follows version 4.0 of the specification, which explicitly states that only when a **parallel for** region is encountered will the other threads within a team begin execution. In version 4.5 of the specification this statement has been removed, and we were not able to find a direct replacement, although the specification states that the **distribute parallel for** composite construct specifies that a loop will be executed by multiple threads of the active teams [11].

As such, to achieve reasonable performance where the outer loop is short, the **parallel for** directive must be placed on a larger inner loop, as in Code Sample 1.2, or the loops must be collapsed. It is important to recognise that the compiler does not automatically schedule iterations in a round robin order, and so when the number of iterations distributed to a team exceeds the number of threads, the directive **schedule(static, 1)** proves essential in order to enable coalescence. Please note that while we would expect kernels targeting the GPU to use a static schedule with a chunk size of 1, this is likely not the best choice when targeting the CPU.

3.4   GCC 6.1 Mapping of OpenMP onto AMD GPUs with HSA

The GCC 6.1 implementation using HSA is currently restricted to a single combined construct `target teams distribute parallel for`. This limitation is strict, and clauses such as `collapse` are not implemented when targeting HSA enabled devices. Although we were not able to use the OpenMP API calls: `omp_get_thread_num()` etc., we analysed the source code in order to ascertain the mapping scheme. Unsurprisingly, this implementation took a different approach to both the Cray compiler and Clang, mapping OpenMP teams as work groups containing 64 work items. The number of work groups, or teams, launched is the size of the iteration space n, divided by the number of threads in a single team t.

3.5   Intel Mapping of OpenMP

Although Intel's offloading capability was primarily targeted towards the Intel Xeon Phi Knights Corner architecture, it is still useful to understand their design decisions from the perspective of performance portability. In spite of the `teams` directive, the Intel compiler only initialises a single team by default, and as such both the `teams` and `distribute` directives can be omitted, although we do not advise this for performance portability. Essentially, the compiler offloads the loops using the CPU approach of threading over the outer loop and vectorising an inner loop, or performing both on the outer loop if one-dimensional or collapsed.

4   Performance Analysis

As many of the implementations are new or experimental and had some deficiencies, it was not possible to collect results across all of the compilers and devices using full applications. Instead we have chosen representative kernels, including several that are performance critical within HPC applications. While we don't explain every kernel in detail, the names serve to describe the basic function, and the source code can be found in our open source repository[1].

The results in Fig. 2 represent the performance data collected for this research in full, and have been sampled across multiple architectures: an NVIDIA K20x GPU, a 44 core Intel Xeon Broadwell CPU, both resident in the Cray XC40 Swan supercomputer, as well as an Intel Xeon Phi Knights Landing (KNL) 7210 and AMD A10-7850K Radeon R7 (Kaveri) APU hosted at the University of Bristol. The CUDA application serves to demonstrate the performance achieved with a naive parallelisation of each kernel on a K20x, collapsing the iteration space

---

[1] https://github.com/UoB-HPC/pragmatic_kernels.

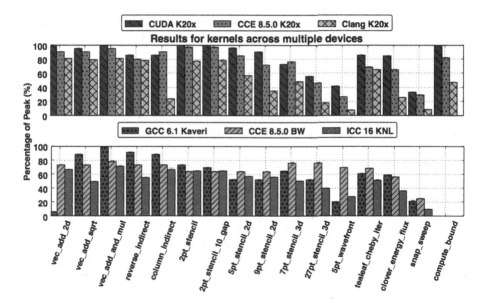

Fig. 2. Kernel performance *(higher is better)*: CCE, Clang, CUDA on K20x (182 GB/s), CCE on 44 Core Broadwell (125 GB/s), ICC on KNL 7210 (439 GB/s), and GCC 6.1 on AMD Kaveri APU (5.4 GB/s).

of all kernels into a one-dimensional grid containing blocks of 128 threads. The Clang results specifically use the `clang-ykt` implementation, which is no longer supported, but represents the most functional open-source Clang implementation that can target GPUs with OpenMP 4.5. GCC 6.1 has a highly constrained interface, providing only a single combined construct, which completely limits the ability to perform optimisation. The results for all kernels, except for `compute_bound`, represent the proportion of peak memory bandwidth.

4.1   Individual Performance

The `vec_add*` kernels serve as a simple baseline for performance, and we expect them to achieve a good proportion of peak. In most cases this proves to be correct, and the results are quite consistent, however the KNL suffers from a noticeable reduction in performance for the `vec_add_sqrt` kernel. As a side note, we observed that the performance on the KNL varied more than expected as the problem size is altered, and achieving peak performance for most of the kernels required the working set to approach the total memory capacity of the device. The Cray compiler is within around 10 % peak bandwidth of the CUDA kernels, while Clang achieves within around 20 % bandwidth, which likely demonstrates the latent overheads present in both implementations. The `vec_add_2d` kernel exposes a performance issue with GCC 6.1, as the nested loops mean that the performance is 20x lower than expected. As the `collapse` statement is not yet supported, loops currently require manual collapsing to achieve reasonable performance. For all other kernels we have manually collapsed the loops to observe some meaningful results.

The *indirect kernels use indirection arrays in their loops, which is a pattern that we have isolated as challenging to accelerate in other applications. The reverse_indirect kernel is an example where the Cray compiler achieved a 3.5x speedup through using the collapse(n) statement. Clang has poor performance for the column_indirect kernel, and this is because the inner loop cannot be collapsed into the iteration space, which limits the available work to the length of the outer loop. The column_indirect kernel is an instance where our OpenMP 4.0 implementation with the Cray compiler has beaten our CUDA implementation, by virtue of the simple scheduling we have performed with all of the CUDA kernels. In our OpenMP 4.x implementations we have only collapsed the loops where the performance was improved, and in this case performance was better if the inner loop was partitioned rather than collapsed into the iteration space. While the results on the Broadwell and using GCC 6.1 are consistent for these kernels, the KNL has slightly worse performance for the reverse_indirect kernel, although we were not yet able to ascertain the cause.

For the stencil operations, the achieved memory bandwidth generally decreases as the size of the stencil increases from 2 up to 27. The Cray compiler stays within 20 % of the peak bandwidth compared to CUDA for all of the kernels, and slightly improves upon the naive CUDA scheduling strategy for the 7pt stencil. The Clang compiler achieves reasonable performance for the small stencils but the 9pt and 27pt stencils drop below 50 % bandwidth compared to CUDA. We did consider that this may be a byproduct of the potential for increased register pressure associated with the larger stencils, but upon checking we discovered that only 48 registers were utilised and the occupancy was above 50 % for both of those kernels, suggesting this is not the issue. The performance of the other implementations was fairly consistent across the kernels.

Our five_point_wavefront kernel represents a unique and challenging parallel data traversal. The Cray compiler attains tolerable performance of around 60 % of the bandwidth compared to CUDA, but Clang achieved under 20 % of CUDA's in spite of all efforts to optimise the kernel. The Broadwell performs well with this kernel, while the KNL results are quite low, but we note that increasing the problem size did improve the performance up until device capacity. Even after manually collapsing the kernel's loop nest, the GCC 6.1 implementation does not perform particularly well with this kernel either.

The application kernels from TeaLeaf, CloverLeaf, and SNAP are important because they provide an indication of the performance that might be seen in a production scientific application. All of the compilers achieve good performance for the tealeaf_cheby_iter kernel on all devices. We note that the TeaLeaf kernel is a case where using the collapse(n) clause indiscriminately leads to poor performance, reducing the kernel's peak bandwidth on a K20x compiled with the Cray compiler from 117 GB/s to 66 GB/s. The loopmark listing file provided by the Cray compiler states 'rediscovery of loop control variables' is introduced, which might be causing an overhead contributing to the reduction in performance, but is likely the sole cause of such a large performance decrease. It is not clear why the performance is not satisfactory, and the only difference between this kernel and others in the suite is the extensive use of ternary conditionals and `fabs`.

We observed that utilisation of peak bandwidth was poor for the `snap_sweep` kernel across all devices, and find similar performance to the 5pt wavefront algorithm, as would be expected given their similarities. On the K20x the Cray compiler is within 10 % of the performance of the CUDA implementation, while the Clang implementation achieves only 24 % of CUDA's peak. All of the other implementations achieve low memory bandwidth, but this is no fault with the implementations as the SNAP kernel is not memory bandwidth bound.

The `compute_bound` kernel executes 128 statements that can be transformed into fused-multiply-add (FMA) instructions, to demonstrate that there is a disparity in the usage of FMAs between the NVIDIA GPU targeting compiler implementations. By inspecting the generated PTX we were able to confirm that the Clang compiler does not transform the statements into FMAs, whereas the Cray compiler does.

4.2   Directives for Performance

Often, the key to achieving good performance was collapsing loops, and placing the `simd` in the appropriate place to enable vectorisation. For the `clang-ykt` version of Clang that we tested, adding `schedule(static, 1)` was also essential, but we have been informed that this will not be a requirement when OpenMP 4.5 functionality is feature complete in the Clang trunk. Kernels like `compute_bound` and `snap_sweep` required the use of `simd`, but the placement of this particular directive was somewhat dependent upon the architecture, and some implementations would suffer a significant performance hit when adding `simd`, as it can change the parallelisation from an optimal scheme.

The OpenMP 4.5 specification stipulates that all scalar variables will default to `firstprivate`, whereas version 4.0 implicitly maps scalar variables at the beginning and end of a kernel. This original behaviour means that there is a small overhead caused by the copying of scalar variables around target invocations. The OpenMP 4.0 workaround is to declare an explicit mapping using `map(to: scalar variables)`. This will make little difference for kernels with lots of work within a single parallel region, but our sweep implementation required many short kernels to be executed across each of the planes. Even though the individual copies took only μs, this happened twice at the end of each plane within the spatial domain, and by mapping the scalar variables as `to` only, we observed a noticeable improvement in runtime. Importantly, for compilers that do not implement the OpenMP 4.5 default data sharing rule, this optimisation is effective and does not hinder performance portability.

In general, we found that achieving performance for all of the devices with all of the compilers was not necessarily trivial. However, even when using preprocessor macros to include compiler-specific directives at the loop level, the benefits compared to managing multiple lower-level codes cannot be overstated. It is clear from the results that we were able to achieve a good level of performance across a range of devices using a single intuitive programming model.

5 Approaching Pragmatic Performance Portability

At the time of writing, it is valid and correct to write OpenMP 4.x code that targets CPU, GPU and KNC using significantly different sets of directives (Code Sample 1.3).

Code Sample 1.3. Different approaches to loop level parallelism.

```
// (a) Example directives for Cray targeting NVIDIA GPUs
#pragma omp target teams distribute simd
for(...)

// (b) Example directives for Clang targeting NVIDIA GPUs
#pragma omp target teams distribute parallel for schedule(static, 1)
for(...)

// (c) Example directives for GCC 6.1 targeting AMD GPUs
#pragma omp target teams distribute parallel for
for(...)

// (d) Example directives for Intel targeting KNC and CPU
#pragma omp target if(offload)
#pragma omp parallel for
for(...)
```

Unfortunately, this divergence in accepted directives means that there is the potential for functional portability issues between the different compilers. All of the options are valid for the Intel compiler, the Cray compiler will also accept (b) and (c), and Clang will accept (c), but will likely perform poorly. GCC is the most constrained, and will only work with the exact construct listed in (c). This is a small but important example of the potential pitfalls that a developer can encounter when developing OpenMP 4.x applications, and it is possible that future implementations from other vendors will make the situation more complicated. Observe that (d) uses the `if` conditional clause to disable the **target** if the CPU is being targeted. This functionality can alleviate some portability issues, allowing the same kernels to be conditionally run on the host or offloaded. Version 4.5 of the OpenMP specification extends the conditional clause to allow the form `if(directive: condition)`, such that both the **target** and **parallel** directives can be conditionally disabled.

It might be possible to extend this conditional functionality to switch on and off the different directives based on the target type, however this suffers from the same issues as using preprocessor conditions, and may end up harming the potential for long term portability. It would be preferable for the developer to be able to express what parallelism exists at the loop-level and then allow the compiler to choose which levels are applicable to the particular target. For instance, on the CPU we might only be concerned with partitioning an outer loop across cores and executing an inner loop with vector instructions. The `parallel` loop construct and `simd` directives are purpose-built to achieve this partitioning, but this is not the only option available with the new directives introduced in version 4.5. The same scheme can be described using the `teams distribute` directives, by limiting each team to a single thread on the CPU, allowing the `simd` directive to describe vectorisation of the inner loop.

We believe that, in order to improve the potential for future functional portability, developers need to aim to provide the most encompassing description of loop-level parallelism possible. Whilst giving as much information as possible is effective, a balance must be struck to avoid inhibiting the ability for the compiler to automatically optimise the scheduling and tuneable widths for each architecture. Essentially, this entails using as many of the *general* directives as possible, as seen in Code Sample 1.1. The natural approach is to use the combined construct `target teams distribute parallel for` to describe the parallelism available at the team and thread level, and the `simd` statement to direct vector level parallelism.

5.1   Homogenising the Directives

Reducing the standard set of directives into an encompassing group was not entirely possible, but we did make progress. In particular we were able to create a set of directives for most kernels using Clang and the Cray compilers. Clang requires `schedule(static, 1)` for performance, but the Cray compiler defaults to this schedule, and so including the directive did not harm performance. A significant obstacle for performance portability was the `simd` directive, as the combined construct `target teams distribute parallel for simd` is not available with GCC 6.1 and negatively affected the performance achieved by Clang.

We did observe that the `collapse(n)` statement is essential for performance in some cases and harmful in others, which made it impossible to merge directives in many cases. Another example where homogenisation was challenging is the `column_indirect` kernel, where the `parallel for` directive had to be added to an inner loop for performance with Clang, but this made the performance unacceptable for Cray. We also noticed that it was essential for performance on the KNL that all methods vectorised successfully, and so this meant using the `simd` statement far more regularly than was necessary with the Broadwell. Overall we have found that there will need to be some progress towards standardisation for future functional inter-compiler portability, and to enable performance portability with homogenised directives.

5.2   Patterns that Can Inhibit Performance Portability

An interesting pattern demonstrated in Code Sample 1.4 uses an indirection on the inner loop that simply contains the value of x in all elements, but inhibited the potential for collapsing. When using Clang, this meant we had to parallelise the inner loop with `parallel for`, and suffered a 3.5x increase in runtime compared to the same kernel without the indirection.

Code Sample 1.4. Indirection use on inner loop.

```
for(int ii = 0; ii < y; ++ii)
{
  for(int jj = 0; jj < indirection[ii]; ++jj)
  {
    ...
  }
}
```

Certain algorithmic patterns appear to contain dependencies that inhibit successful acceleration. The `snap_sweep` kernel is a good example of this, as it uses indirections that are accessed with variables evaluated at runtime, which often resulted in variable success when attempting to parallelise the kernel. We expect that as the implementations are improved in the future, a strict adherence to the developer's independence guarantees are provided. For instance, implementations choosing to map the scheduling of threads across warps within a team as the vectorisation of some inner loop, should always infer that the loop iterations can be executed concurrently as given by the `simd` directive, if it is provided. This will allow the developer to achieve consistent parallelisation without having to restructure the code to support the compiler.

When testing CCE 8.5.0 and Clang, we noticed that our timing code was reporting incorrect results. It transpired that each of the kernels is queued asynchronously as a task, and so our timing between the calls was incorrect. We expected that a directive such as `wait` or `taskwait` would have been well placed to perform the synchronisation that we required, but this was not possible, so we had to rely upon an unnecessary read of a scalar from the device to force synchronisation.

The `collapse` Clause has an important role in the performance portability of OpenMP 4.x applications and, depending on the application, may have a more significant semantic impact than developers would expect. The specification states that the `collapse` statement determines which loops a `distribute` directive will partition, and each loop that is collapsed will have its iteration space combined into a single space. While this is functionally identical to `collapse` relative to a `parallel` region, we have shown in Sect. 3.1 that the design of current implementations means that the `collapse` clause can fundamentally alter the way that thread scheduling occurs for a particular set of loops.

While it may seem tempting to add `collapse(n)` to the stock set of directives included at every loop, we reiterate that on several tests, the Cray compiler suffered a significant performance hit when collapsing loops indiscriminately. In particular, we noticed that a performance penalty will be likely when a loop nest incorporated halo padding, presumably demonstrating the overhead of the more complicated scheduling required once the loop is collapsed. Contrary to this, the clause is essential for increasing the work available to the device. It is imperative that enough work is provided to the device but it isn't necessarily trivial to determine the effect of the `collapse` clause when considering multiple kernels, across multiple devices each with different parallelisation schemes for different devices. As such, we can only suggest that the clause is used judiciously and testing is performed for realistic problem sizes to ensure that it is actually necessary for a particular kernel.

5.3   Concluding Suggestions for Performance Portability

While it is not possible, at the time of writing, to write a single set of directives and achieve functional portability across the range of compilers and devices, we believe that homogenisation will head in a predictable direction. As such, we present some tips that might help future proof codes using OpenMP 4.x:

– *Prefer to include the most extensive combined construct relevant to the loop nest e.g. #pragma omp target teams distribute parallel for simd.* The combined constructs are easier to reason about, and more consistently interpreted between compiler implementations.
– *Always include parallel for, and teams and distribute, even if the compiler does not require them.* Excluding them for compilers that use exclusive mechanisms to map onto the target architecture will inhibit acceleration on other devices, and execution on CPUs.
– *Include the simd directive above the loop you require to be vectorised.* Being explicit about vectorisation improves the chances that all target compilers will succeed in accelerating the code with the intended results.
– *Neither collapse nor schedule should harm functional portability but might inhibit performance portability, so prefer not to include them when possible.* It will be essential to use `collapse(n)` for certain loop nests and compilers, but it should not be included blindly. We expect that future compiler versions targeting devices supporting coalesced memory accesses will default to using `schedule(static, 1)`, and so it might be better for future portability between those devices and the CPU to avoid the clause.
– *Avoid setting num_teams and thread_limit.* Each compiler uses a different scheme for scheduling teams to a device. Making minor adjustments to improve performance with one device might significantly reduce performance on other devices. It would be preferable to only use the clauses where there are performance critical loops that cannot perform with the compiler defaults.

Of course, there will be occasions in applications where these guidelines cannot be followed, and current compilers do not necessarily support the directives and clauses such that future-proof code will execute correctly. For instance, the branched Clang version of OpenMP 4.0 performs poorly with the `simd` directive, and GCC 6.1 targeting HSA does not support any clauses.

6   Related Work

Hart et al. [4] ported the NekBone mini-app to use the Cray compiler's OpenMP 4.0 GPU offloading functionality, detailing the porting process and subsequent optimisation. Bercea et al. [1] analysed the performance of their OpenMP 4.0 port of the CORAL proxy application, and discussed the impact of register spilling. Lin et al. [7] used the ROSE source-to-source compiler to port a number of stencil applications, investigating performance and productivity. In our previous work, we compared the performance of a number of parallel programming models, including OpenMP 4.0, Kokkos, and RAJA [8]. We later discussed the performance of OpenMP 4.0 ports of the TeaLeaf, CloverLeaf, and BUDE mini-apps on NVIDIA GPUs [9]. In some of our earlier performance portability work, we investigated the performance of OpenCL with several structured grid codes, demonstrating a number of techniques that lead to performance portability [10]. Bertolli et al. [3] discuss the coordination of threads within an NVIDIA GPU, and show that their novel approach limits the impact on code generation when integrated into the LLVM compiler infrastructure. They later discussed their approach to integrating OpenMP 4.5 offloading for NVIDIA GPUs into Clang [2].

7   Future Work

While this research has focused purely on data-parallel applications, it will be important to consider the task-parallel capabilities of the specification. It would be useful to track the progress of each of the available compilers, as well as investigating new implementations as they become available. Further to this, the Clang compiler that we used is out of support and as soon as the newest version has been promoted to the trunk it will be important to understand the difference in the parallelisation scheme and performance, if any.

8   Conclusions

Performance portability is not guaranteed by the OpenMP 4.5 specification, and the individual compiler implementations suffer from a number of limitations. The different compiler vendors have interpreted the specification such that it is possible for developers to write codes that are tightly coupled to a single implementation. We have found that good performance can be achieved across a range of HPC devices, using several different implementations. Having tracked the progress made within the last year, there is now strong evidence that performance portability is possible using OpenMP 4.x, and while standardisation and coherence are needed between compiler vendors, the responsibility falls on the developer to prefer portable practices.

Acknowledgements. We would like to thank Cray Inc. for providing access to their XC40 supercomputer Swan, which hosted the Intel Xeon Broadwell, and NVIDIA K20x processors. The Intel Xeon Phi KNL was provided by the Intel Parallel Computing Center at the University of Bristol, and we would like to thank Jim Cownie at Intel for his support. We also want to thank the sponsors of this research, EPSRC and the UK Atomic Weapons Establishment.

References

1. Bercea, G., Bertolli, C., Antao, S., Jacob, A., et al.: Performance analysis of Open-MPon a GPU using a Coral Proxy application. In: Proceedings of the 6th InternationalWorkshop on Performance Modeling, Benchmarking, and Simulation of High Performance Computing Systems, p. 2. ACM (2015)
2. Bertolli, C., Antao, S., Bercea, G.-T., et al.: Integrating GPU support for OpenMP offloading directives into clang. In: Proceedings of the Second Workshop on the LLVM Compiler Infrastructure in HPC, LLVM 2015 (2015)
3. Bertolli, C., Antao, S.F., Eichenberger, A., et al.: Coordinating GPU threads for OpenMP 4.0 in LLVM. In: Proceedings of the LLVM Compiler Infrastructure in HPC, pp. 12–21. IEEE Press (2014)
4. Hart, A.: First experiences porting a parallel application to a hybrid supercomputer with OpenMP 4.0 device constructs. In: Proceedings of the OpenMP: Heterogenous Execution and Data Movements: 11th International Workshop on OpenMP, IWOMP, pp. 73–85 (2015)
5. Kogge, P., Shalf, J.: Exascale computing trends: adjusting to the "New Normal" for computer architecture. Comput. Sci. Eng. **15**(6), 16–26 (2013)
6. Larkin, J.: Performance portability through descriptive parallelism. Presentation at DOE Centers of Execellence Performance Portability Meeting (2016). https://asc.llnl.gov/DOE-COE-Mtg-2016/talks/2-20_Larkin.pdf
7. Lin, P., Liao, C., Quinlan, D., et al.: Experiences of using the OpenMP accelerator model to port DOE stencil applications. In: Proceedings of the OpenMP: Heterogenous Execution and Data Movements: 11th International Workshop on OpenMP, IWOMP 2015, pp. 45–59 (2015)
8. Martineau, M., McIntosh-Smith, S., Boulton, M., Gaudin, W.: An evaluation of emerging many-core parallel programming models. In: Proceedings of the 7th International Workshop on Programming Models and Applications for Multicores and Manycores, PMAM 2016 (2016)
9. Martineau, M., McIntosh-Smith, S., Gaudin, W.: Evaluating OpenMP 4.0's effectiveness as a heterogeneous parallel programming model. In: Proceedings of 21st International Workship on High-Level Parallel Programming Models and Supportive Environments, HIPS 2016 (2016)
10. McIntosh-Smith, S., Boulton, M., Curran, D., Price, J.: On the performance portability of structured grid codes on many-core computer architectures. In: Kunkel, J.M., Ludwig, T., Meuer, H.W. (eds.) ISC 2014. LNCS, vol. 8488, pp. 53–75. Springer, Heidelberg (2014)
11. OpenMP Architecture Review Board. OpenMP Application Program Interface v4.5 (2015)

Multiple Target Task Sharing Support for the OpenMP Accelerator Model

Guray Ozen[1,2]([✉]), Sergi Mateo[1,2], Eduard Ayguadé[1,2], Jesús Labarta[1,2], and James Beyer[3]

[1] Universitat Politècnica de Catalunya (UPC–BarcelonaTECH), Barcelona, Spain
[2] Barcelona Supercomputing Center (BSC-CNS), Barcelona, Spain
{guray.ozen,sergi.mateo,eduard.ayguade,jesus.labarta}@bsc.es
[3] Nvidia Corporation, Santa Clara, USA
jbeyer@nvidia.com

Abstract. The use of GPU accelerators is becoming common in HPC platforms due to the their effective performance and energy efficiency. In addition, new generations of multicore processors are being designed with wider vector units and/or larger hardware thread counts, also contributing to the peak performance of the whole system. Although current directive–based paradigms, such as OpenMP or OpenACC, support both accelerators and multicore-based hosts, they do not provide an effective and efficient way to concurrently use them, usually resulting in accelerated programs in which the potential computational performance of the host is not exploited. In this paper we propose an extension to the OpenMP 4.5 directive-based programming model to support the specification and execution of multiple instances of task regions on different devices (i.e. accelerators in conjunction with the vector and heavily multithreaded capabilities in multicore processors). The compiler is responsible for the generation of device-specific code for each device kind, delegating to the runtime system the dynamic schedule of the tasks to the available devices. The new proposed clause conveys useful insight to guide the scheduler while keeping a clean, abstract and machine independent programmer interface. The potential of the proposal is analyzed in a prototype implementation in the OmpSs compiler and runtime infrastructure. Performance evaluation is done using three kernels (N-Body, tiled matrix multiply and Stream) on different GPU-capable systems based on ARM, Intel x86 and IBM Power8. From the evaluation we observe speed–ups in the 8–20% range compared to versions in which only the GPU is used, reaching 96 % of the additional peak performance thanks to the reduction of data transfers and the benefits introduced by the OmpSs NUMA-aware scheduler.

1 Introduction

The use of accelerators has been gaining popularity in the last years due to their higher peak performance per watt ratio when compared to multicore-based multi-processors. A remarkable increase in the number of systems based

© Springer International Publishing Switzerland 2016
N. Maruyama et al. (Eds.): IWOMP 2016, LNCS 9903, pp. 268–280, 2016.
DOI: 10.1007/978-3-319-45550-1_19

on Nvidia and AMD GPUs and Xeon Phi co-processors can be observed in the Top500 supercomputers list. Besides, with the introduction of new ARM-based heterogeneous architectures, i.e. sockets that incorporate both general-purpose cores and specialized co-processors like GPUs, the potential applicability of these architectures seems evident in all forms of computing.

The programmability wall already risen by multicore architectures is even higher when heterogeneity needs to be considered. Programmers have to deal with different programming models, such as OpenMP [2], CUDA [8] or OpenCL [4], different vector intrinsics and use them with device specific optimization strategies, incurring portability and productivity issues. In addition the programmer may need to manage multiple memory address spaces and maintain their consistent view when necessary.

Existing directive-based programming models [2,9] and their commercial or research implementations [3,5] and variants [6,10] attempt to lower the programmability wall by addressing some of these challenges. Nevertheless, all these proposals do not support offloaded task regions to be concurrently executed by multiple target devices (cores and accelerators) since the annotation of the same code-block for these different targets is not standard. Programmer has to manually transform the code, write multiple versions of these code-blocks and inject code to statically/dynamically offload them to the available devices. Usually this results in small performance benefits that do not compensate the programming effort devoted. This and the explicit management of data sharing over usually low bandwidth interfaces in discrete systems is favouring a programming style in which the bulk of the computation is performed on the accelerators and the general-purpose cores are just used to configure and manage the accelerators, remaining unused most of the time.

This paper contributes with an extension to the OpenMP 4.5 directive-based programming model to support multiple target device code generation and offloading. The proposal is partly inspired in the current device_type clause in OpenACC 2.5, the current capabilities of the OmpSs programming model and the internal discussions in the OpenMP accelerator model committee. The proposal has been included in the MACC [10] compiler, a research compiler for the accelerator model in the OmpSs programming model, and the new features in its runtime system to dynamically schedule tasks to all devices available in the system. In particular we propose new semantics to the already existing device clause, we adopt the conditional if_device construct to specify different thread hierarchies and clauses for different devices[1], and to add a new hint–to–the–runtime resources clause. The complete proposal allows the programmer to annotate offloadable task region for multiple different target devices, considering as devices both host cores as well as accelerators, and gives hints to the runtime system to appropriately schedule multiple instances of the task to the available devices, trying to balance the load assigned to them and taking into account data locality.

---

[1] Currently under discussion in the accelerators subcommittee of the OpenMP Language Committee.

2   Accelerator Support in Directive-Based Approaches

This section briefly describes the heterogeneity support currently provided by the OpenMP 4.5 specification to accelerators programming [2], the OpenACC 2.5 API [9] and the features supported by the MACC compiler for the OmpSs programming model [10].

2.1   Heterogeneity Support in OpenMP Accelerator Model

With the aim of providing a smooth and portable path to program accelerator-based architectures, OpenMP 4.5 provides a programming interface based on a set of directives to offload the execution of code regions onto accelerators, to map loops inside those regions onto the resources available in the device architecture, and to map and move data between address spaces.

The main directive is `target`, which creates the data environment and offload the execution of a code region on an accelerator device. The `device` clause is used in these directives to specify the actual device that will be used to offload the execution of that code region; an integer-expression value sets the device to be used. The specification also brings the `teams` directive to create a thread hierarchy on the target device, with a league of thread teams. In each team the threads other than the master thread do not begin execution until the master thread encounters a `parallel` region. The `distribute` directive specifies how the iterations of one or more loops are distributed across the master threads of all teams that execute the teams region. In addition, OpenMP 4.5 includes the `simd` directive to indicate that a loop can be transformed so that multiple iterations of the loop can be executed concurrently using SIMD instructions.

In the current 4.5 specification there is no sufficient support to tailor the information provided in the `target` directive to different device types. The conditional `if([directive-name-modifier:] scalar-logical-expression)` clause can be used with `target` and in combined/composite constructs that include `target` and `parallel`. In `if(target:scalar-logical-expression)`, when the condition evaluates to false the target region is executed by the host device in the host data environment. In `if(parallel:scalar-logical-expression)`, the evaluation of the condition is used to determine the number of threads to use in the region.

2.2   Heterogeneity Support in OpenACC

OpenACC provides directives that allow programmers to specify code regions to be offloaded to accelerator devices and to control many features of these devices explicitly. The main construct is `kernels`, instructing the compiler to optimize the annotated code region and exploit the available parallelism. OpenACC also offers the `parallel` and `loop` constructs for detailed control of kernel offloading and parallel execution of loops.

For these directives, the current 2.5 specification offers different clauses that the programmer use to specify alternative options for different accelerators using the `device_type` clause. The argument to the clause is a comma-separated list of one or more accelerator architecture name identifiers, or an asterisk. A single directive may have one or several `device_type` clauses. Clauses on a directive with no `device_type` clause apply to all accelerator device types. Clauses that follow a `device_type` clause up to the end of the directive or up to the next `device_type` clause are associated with this `device_type` clause. Clauses associated with a `device_type` clause apply only when compiling for the named accelerator device type. For each directive, only certain clauses may follow a `device_type` clause. For example, for `parallel` the programmer can specify `async`, `wait`, `num_gangs`, `num_workers`, and `vector_length`.

2.3 Heterogeneity Support in OmpSs

The OmpSs task-based programming model offers the programmer a single linear address space on which the data lays. Directionality clauses for the tasks are specified as the mechanism to provide the runtime the information to compute data dependences between tasks and to enforce data consistency on systems with multiple address spaces by managing transfers between different address spaces transparently to the programmer.

In the initial versions, OmpSs relied on the use of CUDA and OpenCL for the specification of tasks to be executed on accelerator devices. The `target` construct was used to simply direct the compilation of the source code to the appropriate backend CUDA or OpenCL compiler and to inject the necessary code for task offloading, including data movement. The `device` clause in the `target` construct is used not to specify the specific device to execute the region but the device type than can execute it, delegating to the runtime system the decision of which device to use in case multiple devices of that type are available. Different versions for the same task, each one tailored to the device kind specified in the `device` clause, can be specified through the `implements` clause.

MACC Compiler. The MACC[2] compiler for the OmpSs programming model supports almost all directives of the OpenMP 4.5 accelerator model with some extensions to enhance code generation capability and minor semantic changes in order to allow their combination with other OmpSs directives.

The `target` construct is always associated to a `task` construct and the need for the OpenMP 4.5 `target data` and `target update` constructs is eliminated reducing programming complexity. The rest of device related OpenMP 4.5 constructs (`teams`, `distribute` and `parallel for`) are thoroughly implemented with the originally specified semantics. MACC adds to OpenMP 4.5 additional data sharing clauses for the `team` construct: `dist_private`, `dist_firstprivate` and `dist_lastprivate`; with the `chunk_size` provided in the `dist_schedule` clause, the compiler is able to make a better use of the memory hierarchy in the device (e.g. global, shared and local memory), allocating portions of arrays in different teams and performs the necessary data movement according to

---

[2] **MACC** is an abbreviation for "Mercurium **ACC**elerator Compiler".

firstprivate and lastprivate semantics. Also, MACC provides nesting of teams constructs and conditional clauses make the use of dynamic parallelism feature of GPU architecture that allows to launch a kernel within a kernel without CPU intervention [11]. It shows it is possible for the compiler to generate code that is then efficiently executed under dynamic runtime scheduling.

3 Proposal and Implementation of Multi Target Approach

In this section we propose an extension to the target directive to provide support for multiple device and conditional compilation. We also comment its implications in the implementation of the compiler and runtime system.

3.1 Target Directive Syntax Extension

In this paper we propose to extend the target construct in three complementary ways: (i) by allowing the a use of the any keyword in the device clause, telling the compiler that the directive applies to more than one device type; (ii) by using new conditional construct if_device to provide different directives for different device types and (iii) with a new resources clause to give hints to the runtime system to appropriately balance the scheduling of tasks to the different devices in the system. Figure 1 shows the proposed syntax extension.

Multiple device targeting example

```
1 #pragma omp target device( any ) distribute parallel for
2   for-loops
```

Multiple device targeting with conditional compilation example

```
1 #pragma omp target device( any )  [clause[ [,] clause] ... ]
2 #pragma omp
3       if_device(archtype, subtype) construct-set resources(percentage-integer) \
4       if_device(archtype, subtype) construct-set resources(percentage-integer)
5   structured-block
```

Fig. 1. Usage of conditional multi targeting support of OpenMP

The upper part in Fig. 1 shows an example of use for the any keyword. When this keyword appears in the device clause, the compiler will have to generate multiple versions for the target region each one tailored to a different kind of device. In other cases, it is possible that the same directive set may not be appropriate for the different devices available. To that end we also propose the if_device construct, allowing the programmer to specify different directive set for different devices. The lower part of Fig. 1 shows the use of this construct. In the construct-set the programmer can specify for the same code block different thread hierarchies and clauses according to the OpenMP 4.5 accelerator model, each one tailored to a device kind. At execution time the runtime system will decide among the different implementations provided the one that is more appropriate for each particular instance of the task to be offloaded.

Finally we also propose the `resources` clause, providing a hint to help the runtime system to decide where to schedule the execution of the next task instance. For each device the programmer specifies a value (or expression) over 100 which indicates the amount of "tokens" consumed every time a task is scheduled on that device; once a task finishes its execution, that number of tokens is restored. If at any time the number of tokens available is not sufficient, the runtime will not be able to schedule the task to that device, choosing a different device that requires less resources if possible.

A more specific example illustrating the use of the proposed extensions is shown in the upper part in Fig. 2; the code corresponds to the main loop of the N-Body simulation kernel that is used later in the evaluation section. In this example, the programmer specifies in line 4 that the target region can be executed in different device types. Device specific directives are specified in lines 5 and 6 for Nvidia accelerators with compute capability 3.5 and for host, respectively. In addition, the programmer specifies the number of tokens consumed/released every time a task is scheduled to execute or finishes its execution on every possible device: 2 token (over 100) when task is offloaded to the Nvidia accelerator or 40 tokens (over 100) when executed in the host. In this case

All-Pairs N-Body Simulation with $\mathcal{O}(n^2)$ Complexity

```
1 //N-Body Computation
2 for (int k = 0; k < n; k+=BS)
3 {
4   #pragma omp target device(any) map(tofrom:vx[k:BS],vy[k:BS],vz[k:BS]) nowait
5   #pragma omp if_device(NVIDIA,cc35) teams distribute parallel for resources(2)
6   #pragma omp if_device(host) parallel for resources(40)
7   for (int i = k; i < k+BS; ++i) {
8     float Fx = 0.0f; float Fy = 0.0f; float Fz = 0.0f;
9
10    #pragma omp simd reduction(+:Fx,Fy,Fz)
11    for (int j = 0; j < n; j++) {
12      float dy = y[j] - y[i];
13      float dz = z[j] - z[i];
14      float dx = x[j] - x[i];
15      float distSqr = dx*dx + dy*dy + dz*dz+CONST;
16      float invDist = 1.0f / sqrtf(distSqr);
17      float invDist3 = invDist * invDist * invDist;
18      Fx += dx * invDist3; Fy += dy * invDist3; Fz += dz * invDist3;
19    }
20    vx[i] += dt*Fx;  vy[i] += dt*Fy;  vz[i] += dt*Fz;
21  }
22 }
```

Transformed NVIDIA-Task Code	*Transformed Host-Task Code*
| ```
1 #pragma omp teams distribute \
2          parallel for resources(2)
3 for (int i ...) {
4   for (int j ...) {
5     ...
6   }
7 }
``` | ```
1 #pragma omp parallel for resources(40)
2 for (int i ...) {
3   #pragma omp simd [ clause ...]
4   for (int j ...) {
5     ...
6   }
7 }
``` |

Fig. 2. N-Body example of MACC IR code transformation

the programmer expresses that no more than 2 tasks should be scheduled to be executed in the host at any time. These combination can be estimated considering separate performance of multiple targets after some initial experiments, or could be auto-tuned by the runtime if `auto` is used instead of an integer number. These two aspects are not considered in this paper and are subject of current research.

3.2   Compiler and Runtime Support to the Proposed Extensions

Figure 3 shows the compilation pipeline in the MACC compiler once the Mercurium Intermediate Representation (IR) has been generated. Different device-specific IR lowering phases can be implemented, each one either transforming the IR (e.g. for the `host` device by inserting the appropriate calls to the OmpSs runtime system) or generating an output file to be compiled by a device-specific native compiler (e.g. CUDA for the `NVIDIA` device). The *multiple device dispatcher* unit is in charge of forwarding a new copy of the IR for each device type in the list of devices in the `device` clause to the appropriate lowering phase. The implementation is extensible as shown with dotted lines and the *nextgen_device* lowering phase. At the end of the compilation pipeline, the compiler driver compiles each output file with appropriate back-end compiler and links object files to generate the final executable file.

Before the execution of the *Host lowering* phase it can be necessary to execute a `host IR reducer` phase when one set of directives are used for all devices. This phase is in charge of adapting the thread hierarchy supported by the OpenMP 4.5 accelerator model (teams and threads) to the flat thread model. This step basically selects the outermost loop affected with a `distribute` or `parallel for` directive and transforms it into a `parallel for` directive. Other directives in the `target` region are ignored for host device, except for `simd` constructs which are then lowered to specific SIMD operations in the host.

The lower part in Fig. 2 shows how the directives are interpreted for each device type in order to adapt the generic thread hierarchy to each specific device: `NVIDIA` on the left and `host` on the right.

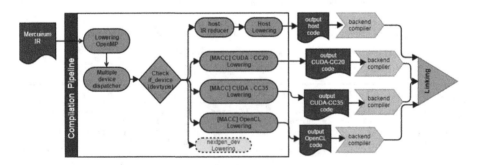

Fig. 3. Overview of device dispatcher and IR lowering units.

3.3   Compiler and Runtime Support for the `resources` Clause

For the `resources` clause, the compiler just parses the two fields for each device kind and pass this information to the runtime system though an internal runtime call. This information is used by the runtime system to account for the total number of resource "tokens" available at any time. When a task is ready for execution, the runtime checks if enough tokens are available for any of the possible target devices; if so, then the runtime subtracts the specified resource tokens for the selected device from the currently available tokens. When the task finishes its execution, the runtime adds the same amount of tokens to the total count. Both operations are done using *atomic* operations.

4   Evaluation

In this section we present the performance evaluation of the multiple targeted task-sharing proposal and its implementation in the MACC compiler and OmpSs runtime system. To that end we use a variety of system configurations and three small kernel applications: N-Body, tiled matrix multiply and the Stream benchmark.

4.1   System Configurations

Table 1 shows the main characteristics of the four systems that have been used for the experimental evaluation of the proposal in this paper. The different system configurations offer different ratios between the performance of the host and the performance of the accelerator devices.

The 1st system is based on an old generation of Nvidia GPUs (Fermi architecture) while the 2nd and 3rd systems are based on a more recent Nvidia GPU (Tesla K40). The first two systems are based on Intel hosts while the 3rd system is based on the emergent IBM Power8 architecture with high memory bandwidth and increased hardware thread counts. Finally the 4th system is based on

Table 1. System configurations

System	Processor	Memory	Nvidia GPU
1	*2 x Intel Xeon(TM) E5649 sockets 6-core/socket at 2.53 GHz*	*24 GB*	*2 x Tesla M2090 (Fermi, 512 cores)*
2	*1 x Intel Core(TM) i7-4820K socket 4-core/socket, 2-hw threads/core at 3.70 GHz*	*64 GB*	*2 x Tesla K40c (Kepler, 2880 cores)*
3	*2 x IBM Power S824L sockets 12-core/socket, 8-hw threads/core at 3.52 GHz*	*1 TB*	*2 x Tesla K40m (Kepler, 2880 cores)*
4	*Nvidia Jetson TK1 SoC 4-core Cortex-A15 up to 2.5 GHz*	*2 GB*	*1 x GK20A (Kepler, 192 cores)*

ARM SoC with a tiny GPU which just includes one Streaming Multiprocessor Architecture (SMX).

All CUDA codes in this paper have been automatically generated by the MACC compiler and compiled with *nvcc* v7.0, except for the 4th system which makes use of v6.0. GCC 4.9 is used to compile host codes on all systems with -O3 optimization level. The `simd` construct in OpenMP 4.5 and auto-vectorization is performed by back-end GCC compiler.

4.2   OmpSs Runtime Configurations and Thread Binding

The OmpSs runtime is used to support the execution of work-sharing and tasking constructs. In addition, the OmpSs runtime manages host/GPU data transfers and concurrent kernel execution and CUDA streams. To that end OmpSs reserves a helper thread in the socket for each GPU device attached to it; the rest of threads are used to execute `host` tasks. The execution of `host` target regions is assigned to sockets in a round-robin way and work-sharing constructs inside an `host` target region are bound to the threads in a single socket.

For the 3rd system based on IBM Power8 processors we have activated the NUMA-aware scheduler feature in the OmpSs runtime. The runtime detects the socket architecture of the system and binds threads properly, distributing tasks according to the memory layout. Besides that, in order to investigate the effect of multithreading inside a core, we adjust the OmpSs thread binding (using an environment variable) to use 1, 2, 4 or 8 threads per core.

4.3   Performance Results

N-Body. This kernel computes the motion of a set of bodies based on the forces between them. For this simulation, an all-pairs algorithm is used with $\mathcal{O}(n^2)$ complexity, as shown in the upper code in Fig. 2. The `resources` values have been set to maximize load balancing between tasks executed on the host processors and the GPU devices.

Figure 4 shows the performance results obtained for the N-Body kernel. The plot on the top-right corner shows the GFLOPs achieved when using the cores in the host for the three first system configurations. The main plot in the same figure shows how much of that performance is actually contributed to the overall performance when using one and two GPUs, observing increases in the 8 %–14 % and 4 %–10 % ranges, respectively. This contributed performance is very close to the ideal performance which could be obtained by just adding the performance of the CPU to the GPU.

Finally, the performance of the N-Body kernel has also been evaluated on the 4th system based on the Jetson TK1. The left plot in the Fig. 5 shows three different results: CPU only, GPU only and combined CPU/GPU. In this case, the performance benefit is up to 20 % due to the relatively close performance of the ARM cores and the small GPU in the SoC.

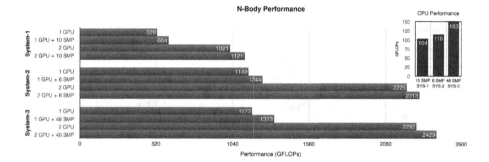

Fig. 4. N-Body simulation performance results.

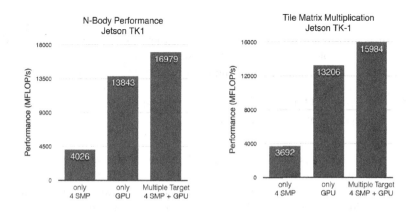

Fig. 5. N-Body and tiled-gemm performance on Jetson TK1.

Tiled Matrix Multiply. The kernel performs a dense matrix multiplication of two square matrices $A \times B = C$. Matrices are divided in blocks and each task is responsible for the computation of one of such blocks of the output matrix C. The matrix size is used 8192×8192 double-precision floating-point elements with 512×512 block size.

The matrix multiply kernel is written using six nested loops: the three innermost ones are annotated with MACC directives for multiple target devices. The MACC compiler transformed them into non-optimized CUDA code (current implementation lacks of many optimization phases that would be necessary to generate an optimized kernel) and highly optimized using expensive optimization features of back-end compiler for the host.

The performance for this kernel has been evaluated on the Nvidia Jetson TK1 (right plot in Fig. 5) and IBM Power8 (Fig. 6) platforms. For the TK1 system we can conclude that the work was shared among the entire SoC elements, with the cores being able to contribute to the performance of the GPU.

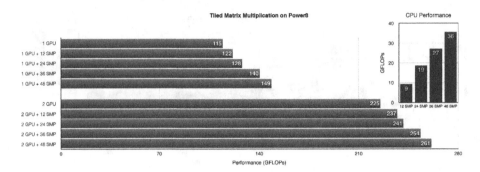

Fig. 6. Matrix multiplication performance results

For the Power8 system, the plot on the top-right corner shows the performance that is obtained when using different numbers different numbers of SMT threads. The main plot in that figure then shows how this performance is contributed to the hybrid system, observing performance increases of 30 % and 16 % when one and two GPUs are used, respectively. Observe that the best result is obtained when two SMT threads per core are activated, since each Power8 core includes two vector unit and load/store unit.

Stream. This code [7] is commonly used to benchmark the memory bandwidth. It consists of four micro-benchmarks accessing three vectors a, b and c and a scalar variable, inside an iterative loop that repeats their execution a number of times. Loop tiling has been applied to the outermost loop in these four operations in order to divide the iterations into multiple tasks and to run them in parallel. Task dependencies are specified between the tasks computing the four different operations.

This benchmark is evaluated using the 2nd and 3rd system. Bot use the same Nvidia GPU (with reported memory bandwidth of 288 GB/s). However, the processors in the 2nd system report a memory bandwidth of 59.7 GB/s while the processors in the 3rd system report average 192 GB/s (with a maximum of 275 GB/s on the individual micro benchmarks [1]). Therefore, comparing these two systems provides a good opportunity to see how the runtime is able to fully exploit the additional bandwidth in the Power8 system.

Figure 7 shows the average bandwidth reported by the Stream benchmark when different numbers of host threads that are called also SMP workers are used, for both systems evaluated. For the Power8 system (right plot), an speed up to 84 % over GPU baseline is achieved when using all the cores in the entire system. For the i7-based system (left plot), the best performance is achieved when only two cores are used, showing the memory bandwidth bottleneck of the socket. When GPU tasks are finished, the runtime steals tasks which were initially assigned to the CPU, forcing the runtime to copy data from host to device.

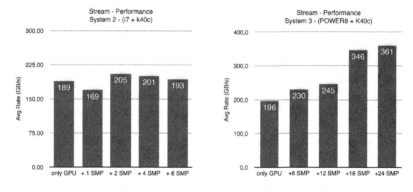

Fig. 7. Stream bandwidth performance avg rate (GB/s)

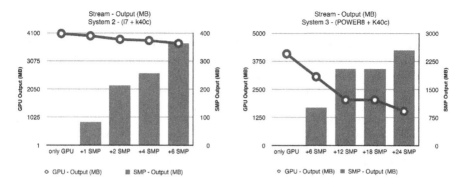

Fig. 8. Output data size of stream benchmark

Finally, Fig. 8 shows the total amount of data that is produced by the different devices. The largest amount of data produced by the CPU is achieved when 24 cores are used on the Power8 system.

5 Conclusions and Future Work

In this paper we have proposed an extension to directive-based programming models to support the possibility of allowing the execution (of multiple instances) of a `target` region on different devices in an heterogenous architecture. We have also analyzed its implementation in the OmpSs compiler and runtime system and evaluated its performance for a variety of system configurations and some kernel applications. The proposed extensions ease the use of multiple accelerators in conjunction with the vector and heavily multithreaded capabilities in multi-core processors without any code modification. The new proposed construct and clause convey useful insight to guide the scheduler while keeping a clean, abstract and machine independent programmer interface. The performance evaluation shows that with the new resources-based scheduler the runtime is able to take benefit of all devices available in the heterogeneous system.

As part of our current work, we plan to extend our implementation to support other architectures, like Xeon Phi and FPGA devices. Then, we will also need to tune our scheduling parameters to fit all of them. We are also investigating the use of nested (dynamic in CUDA terminology) parallelism in target regions [11] and how the proposed extensions in this paper interact with them.

Acknowledgments. This work is partially supported by the IBM/BSC Deep Learning Center Initiative, by the Spanish Government through Programa Severo Ochoa (SEV-2015-0493), by the Spanish Ministry of Science and Technology through TIN2015-65316-P project and by the Generalitat de Catalunya (contract 2014-SGR-1051).

References

1. Adinetz, A.V., Baumeister, P.F., Böttiger, H., Hater, T., Maurer, T., Pleiter, D., Schenck, W., Schifano, S.F.: Performance evaluation of scientific applications on POWER8. In: Jarvis, S.A., Wright, S.A., Hammond, S.D. (eds.) PMBS 2014. LNCS, vol. 8966, pp. 24–45. Springer, Heidelberg (2015)
2. OpenMP ARB. OpenMP application program interface, v. 4.5 (2015)
3. Bertolli, C., Antao, S.F., Eichenberger, A.E., O'Brien, K., Sura, Z., Jacob, A.C., Chen, T., Sallenave, O.: Coordinating GPU threads for OpenMP 4.0 in LLVM. In: Proceedings of the LLVM Compiler Infrastructure in HPC, LLVM-HPC 2014, Piscataway, NJ, USA, pp. 12–21. IEEE Press (2014)
4. Khronos OpenCL Working Group. The OpenCL specification, version 2.0 (2014)
5. The Portland Group. PGI accelerator compilers
6. Lee, S., Vetter, J.S.: OpenARC: Open Accelerator Research Compiler for directive-based, efficient heterogeneous computing. In: The 23rd International Symposium on High-Performance Parallel and Distributed Computing, HPDC 2014, Vancouver, BC, Canada, 23–27 June 2014, pp. 115–120 (2014)
7. McCalpin, J.D.: Stream: sustainable memory bandwidth in high performance computers. Technical report, University of Virginia (2007)
8. NVIDIA. CUDA C programming guide version 7.0. NVIDIA Corporation (2013)
9. OpenACC-Standard.org. OpenACC application programming interface, v. 2.5 (2015)
10. Ozen, G., Ayguadé, E., Labarta, J.: On the roles of the programmer, the compiler and the runtime system when programming accelerators in OpenMP. In: DeRose, L., de Supinski, B.R., Olivier, S.L., Chapman, B.M., Müller, M.S. (eds.) IWOMP 2014. LNCS, vol. 8766, pp. 215–229. Springer, Heidelberg (2014)
11. Ozen, G., Ayguadé, E., Labarta, J.: Exploring dynamic parallelismin OpenMP. In: Proceedings of the Second Workshop on Accelerator Programming using Directives, WACCPD 2015, Austin, Texas, USA, 15 November 2015, pp. 5:1–5:8 (2015)

Early Experiences Porting Three Applications to OpenMP 4.5

Ian Karlin[1](✉), Tom Scogland[1], Arpith C. Jacob[2], Samuel F. Antao[2],
Gheorghe-Teodor Bercea[3], Carlo Bertolli[2], Bronis R. de Supinski[1],
Erik W. Draeger[1], Alexandre E. Eichenberger[2], Jim Glosli[1], Holger Jones[1],
Adam Kunen[1], David Poliakoff[1], and David F. Richards[1]

[1] Lawrence Livermore National Laboratory, Livermore, CA 94550, USA
{karlin1,scogland1,bronis,draeger1,glosli1,jones19,kunen1,
poliakoff1,richards12}@llnl.gov
[2] IBM T.J. Watson Research Center, Yorktown Heights, NY 10598, USA
{acjacob,sfantao,cbertol,alexe}@us.ibm.com
[3] Department of Computing, Imperial College London, London SW7 2AZ, UK
gheorghe-teodor.bercea08@imperial.ac.uk

Abstract. Many application developers need code that runs efficiently on multiple architectures, but cannot afford to maintain architecturally specific codes. With the addition of target directives to support offload accelerators, OpenMP now has the machinery to support performance portable code development. In this paper, we describe application ports of Kripke, Cardioid, and LULESH to OpenMP 4.5 and discuss our successes and failures. Challenges encountered include how OpenMP interacts with C++ including classes with virtual methods and lambda functions. Also, the lack of deep copy support in OpenMP increased code complexity. Finally, GPUs inability to handle virtual function calls required code restructuring. Despite these challenges we demonstrate OpenMP obtains performance within 10 % of hand written CUDA for memory bandwidth bound kernels in LULESH. In addition, we show with a minor change to the OpenMP standard that register usage for OpenMP code can be reduced by up to 10 %.

Keywords: OpenMP 4.5 · Application porting experiences · Performance portability

1 Introduction

Current and planned supercomputer architectures at major centers are built from multiple diverse architectures, including GPU accelerated systems and many-core CPU systems. This diversity presents a challenge for application developers who must balance the performance, portability, maintainability and productivity of their codes. To deal with these challenges many abstraction layers, including RAJA [8], Kokkos [6] and Surge [15] are under development.

The rights of this work are transferred to the extent transferable according to title 17 U.S.C. 105.

© Springer International Publishing Switzerland 2016
N. Maruyama et al. (Eds.): IWOMP 2016, LNCS 9903, pp. 281–292, 2016.
DOI: 10.1007/978-3-319-45550-1_20

The OpenMP 4.5 [1] standard also enables targeting multiple architectures from a single code base. It is also one optional backend for some of the previously mentioned models, such as RAJA. How well various models achieve performance portability as well as how to assess it is a focus of recent research [13]. In these studies OpenMP or the similar OpenACC often produces the best performance for small mini-apps.

Building on the directive based approach this paper looks at the successes and failures of porting three applications Kripke, Cardioid, and LULESH to OpenMP 4.5. For all three applications our target architecture is Nvidia GPUs. We identify various challenges application developers may encounter in moving their code to OpenMP 4.5. In addition, we encounter general code restructuring that is needed to move complex legacy code onto GPUs. The specific applications, and the high level successes and challenges associated with each are:

- A C++03 version of **Kripke** has already been successfully ported to OpenMP 4.5. In this work we port a more performance portable C++11/14 version. We report on the challenges encountered with how OpenMP and C++ abstractions interact. We also, discuss the challenges compiler writers encounter when trying to support two new standards at once.
- **Cardioid** has a larger code base than the two other applications we ported. It was designed using language features and programming paradigms that require it to be significantly refactored to use OpenMP 4.5. Cardioid uses complex classes, virtual functions, and manages its own threads. These design decisions are either incompatible or difficult to work around when using the current OpenMP 4.5 standard. In addition, GPUs do not support various functionality Cardioid relies on, such as virtual methods.
- **LULESH** was successfully ported to OpenMP 4.5 with minor modifications and parts of the code performed almost as well as hand optimized CUDA. However, we discovered various implementation details and default choices that would make portable performance hard to achieve. Working together compiler and application developers have fixed some of these issues already. In addition, we identified and prototyped that adding `firstprivate` support to the standard will further improve performance.

The rest of the paper is organized as follows. First we highlight the successes and challenges of porting each of these applications to OpenMP 4.5. Then we offer suggestions, based on the experiences we document in this paper, of where the OpenMP standard can be improved. Next, we present related work. Finally, we present concluding thoughts and future work on further evaluating the current and future OpenMP standards for cross architecture performance portability.

2   Kripke

Kripke is a discrete ordinance (Sn) deterministic partial transport mini-app [11]. It is being used to explore how the performance of different data layouts, programming models, and parallelization strategies changes as machines vary.

The code version ported uses nested polymorphic lambda functions from C++14 and variadic templates from C++11 to allow compile time generation of various data layouts for selection at runtime and to enable multiple loop orderings to be compiled from a single source [10]. Prior research shows that the best nesting is both problem and architecture dependent, requiring greater than normal code flexibility to achieve high performance.

2.1 Challenges When Using Abstractions

Prior to this work a version of Kripke using only C++03 features was ported to OpenMP 4.5. While the C++03 version supports all the loop ordering variations that the C++14 version supports, it does so by replicating each computational kernel explicitly for each variant. As a result, this version is quite hard to maintain. The trade off occurs because C++03 lacks lambda expressions, to specify kernel bodies, and the variadic templates required to produce a general multi-level loop abstraction. Therefore, it would be preferred to deprecate the C++03 code and move forward with the C++14 version. However, the C++14 version of Kripke needs additional compiler support and better synergy between OpenMP and C++ to perform well.

Abstract wrappers around OpenMP, or related models that extend the C++ standard, such as Cilk+, offer extra challenges. OpenMP is an extension to C and C++, rather than a base language construct. Therefore, there is no well-defined way to apply OpenMP clauses to OpenMP directives through templates or other core C++ mechanisms. As a result, even though OpenMP supports data privatization, reductions, and other useful features, they are not usable through general abstractions. Therefore, developers are forced to implement their own versions rather than use those provided by OpenMP.

Due to its use of both new C++ features and OpenMP features, Kripke presents challenges for compiler writers. The version of Kripke used in these experiments used both nested lambdas and variadic templates containing and contained by OpenMP 4+ target constructs. Reliance on these relatively new and complex C++ features exposed many compiler bugs, particularly in the generation of host and device versions of the lambda bodies. These issues caused us to be unable to produce performance results.

Compiler issues occur not because the C++ features used by Kripke and OpenMP are incompatible, but because they both are new and testing and development of their combination is ongoing. Codes using both new C++ features and OpenMP features at once create challenges for both compiler writers and application developers. This experience caused the Kripke developers to reduce their reliance on new features. The current versions of Kripke now only requires C++11 support because it no longer uses polymorphic lambdas.

For compiler writers using two new standards in combination results in many moving parts that exercise various parts of the compiler in new unexpected combinations. These unexpected interactions require a significant amount of development time to get functioning properly together. In addition, some issues require clarification or updates from the standards bodies themselves. Once functionality is complete, developers will still be left with performance challenges as optimizations take time to implement. Also developers need time to discover best programming practices for extracting performance when using the new standards.

Despite the challenges we encountered when porting our C++14 version of Kripke we believe performance portability is possible using OpenMP. This porting effort was started well in advance of the delivery of the production machine. Therefore, we have enough time to make compiler improvements and work with standards committees to resolve the challenges we encountered. In addition, we have aided this process by refactoring Kripke to not longer require C++14 suport.

3   Cardioid

Cardioid is a high performing simulation code used for human heart simulations [17]. When run on the full Sequoia supercomputer at LLNL it is capable of near real time modeling of the heart and achieves over 60 % of theoretical peak performance. One critical way Cardioid was able to achieve high performance on Sequoia was by manual managing its own threads within a single OpenMP parallel region. In addition, Cardioid uses various C++ features to create a software design that is easier to maintain and develop. These design decisions however interact poorly with the OpenMP 4.5 standard.

3.1   High Performance and C++ Code Challenges

In order to simulate the human heart in near real time Cardioid had to be strong scaled significantly to allow each timestep to occur in 'about 60 microseconds. Therefore, the overhead of synchronizing threads even once per timestep, which is typically one to ten microseconds, would significantly impact performance. To avoid this overhead in the Sequoia version, threads were spawned at the beginning of the simulation and managed manually by the programmers. However, in OpenMP 4.5 teams cannot synchronize within a target region due to limitations of GPUs and other devices that OpenMP needs to support. Therefore, the design options for using OpenMP 4.5 to target GPUs are limited.

The best workaround likely involves using a few very large asynchronous kernels to limit overhead. For the GPU version the host processor can perform other work, such as I/O concurrently. For performance portable single source solutions, time to solution on the CPU will suffer as overheads limit strong scaling. However, more research and porting is needed to determine if the performance tradeoffs of this design are tolerable. If the tradeoffs are not then it is likely that two versions of key kernels will need to be maintained.

Another challenge porting Cardioid is its use of C++ virtual methods. Multiple issues were encountered. First virtual member functions cannot be defined within a `#pragma omp declare target`. This is a restriction imposed by GPU hardware, which is not capable of handling virtual function tables. The second issue is that classes that contain virtual methods cannot be mapped to a device even if only concrete objects are called on the device. In our opinion this is a place where the OpenMP standard is not clear enough on what should be allowed. That standard should require that all classes that contain virtual functions can be mapped to a device as long as only concrete methods are called. As written today the OpenMP standard unnecessarily limits how a developer can define certain classes.

Another challenge with mapping complex classes in Cardioid onto devices is the lack of deep copy operators in OpenMP 4.5. When mapping class members to a device each member must be mapped individually, which is tedious and error prone. In addition, there is no awareness of C++ constructors and destructors or support for serialize/deserialize methods. Support for either of these would make data mapping less tedious and/or error prone. Also, deep copy support where pointers to pointers or class members can be mapped in a single operation would reduce programmer effort and mistakes when mapping data to devices.

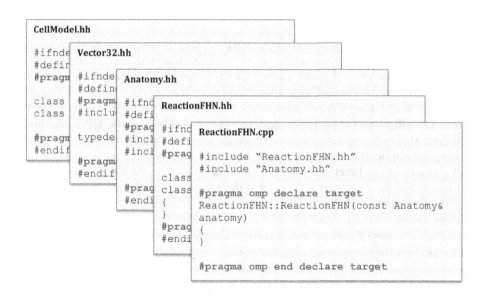

Fig. 1. Example of how function calls result in nested code decoration.

The final challenge encountered in porting Cardioid was its use of header files and inline code. OpenMP 4.5 requires that all code called from within a target region be device code. Satisfying this requirement this often required decorating many levels of header files. An example, taken from the Cardioid port is shown in Fig. 1. While not difficult, this activity is tedious, time consuming, and results in code that is substantially harder to read. While there is no good way to remove the requirement of all code being device code there might be ways to make the programming cleaner.

Cardioid demonstrates some significant challenges legacy codes will encounter when moving to OpenMP 4.5. Significant code refactoring is needed to efficiently use GPUs. However, changes to the OpenMP standard would reduce the amount of refactoring needed. Even with such changes there are hard choices to be made. GPUs and CPUs may require significantly different implementations to meet performance goals and the right balance between performance, portability, and maintainability balance will vary from code to code.

4   LULESH

LULESH is a hydrodynamics proxy application that has been used in many performance and programming model studies [9]. There are optimized versions for both CPUs and GPUs to compare against. Although it is written in C++ it does not make use of newer C++ features, polymorphism, and other features that caused issues during out Kripke and Cardioid ports.

4.1   Porting Challenges

LULESH was successfully ported to OpenMP 4.5 and the version is now available on the web[1]. However, some minor issues were encountered that required code changes. For example, in many cases LULESH checks for negative volumes in the same loop as the volume is calculated and exits if a negative volume is found. Since exit or MPI_Abort is not a supported function on the GPU a flag was set within the offloaded target region and then later checked on the CPU. Within LULESH this only requires touching code in a few places. However, in a large production application it would be a tedious and error prone transformation to find and correct all functions that are not able to run on the GPU. Also, these changes result in a few extra lines of code per change and may have a slight negative performance impact, in particular when strong scaling. However, these changes are unavoidable due to limited coordinated gpu to cpu catastrophic error handling. Reverse offloading would solve the code correctness issue and turn it into a performance issue assuming the compiler correctly identifies the issue.

4.2   Portable Performance Possible with Continued Compiler Work

Initial results showing GPU performance with the IBM compiler were already presented [3]. In this section, we look at performance for the entire code and what changed in the LULESH OpenMP 4.5 port and the compiler to make portable performance possible. We also, show that with a change to the OpenMP standard and continued compiler work we can further improve upon the previous results.

To achieve performance on GPUs a schedule(static, 1) policy is usually best. However, on CPUs schedule(static) is often the best policy. Our initial port required setting the schedule policy for each offload region and using "if clauses" to turn this policy off on CPUs. However, from the lessons we learned through this and other ports the default for GPU kernels is now set

---

[1] https://codesign.llnl.gov/lulesh.php.

to schedule(static, 1). This simplifies user code and makes it more likely that good performance will occur out of the box.

For some codes using #pragma simd would produce the same effect. However, #pragma simd is a stronger statement that will not allow codes with divergence to take advantage of coalesced memory accesses. In addition, using schedule(static) by default requires programmers to mark their code with #pragma simd even when the performance effects are minimal relative to schedule(static, 1) increasing programmer effort. Therefore, schedule(static, 1) is a preferred default with #pragma simd used when possible by the programmer.

One artifact of the current state of the compiler was our splitting pragmas across multiple lines. Once the targeted if directive allows us to turn off single clauses on the same line we can remove this artifact from the code. This change had performance implications as it is easier for the compiler to optimize combined constructs. Combined constructs are one advantage an OpenMP backend to an abstraction layer like RAJA has over passing CUDA kernel headers. The combined constructs are capable of passing more and richer information to the compiler enabling additional optimizations.

Our tests were performed on an OpenPower node with two Power 8 sockets (model PowerNV 8247-42L). The machine also contained two NVIDIA Kepler K40m GPUs. An Ubuntu version 14.04.1 Linux distribution was run on the host processor. All code was compiled with the IBM CLANG research compiler.

Previous work [3] showed that one small kernel produced performance within 10 % of the best CUDA code. When looking across all the LULESH kernels we observed that any kernel where the compiler used less than 64 registers also performed within 10 % of the best CUDA implementation. Using less than 64 registers allows for full occupancy on a GPU and these kernels are often memory bandwidth bound. Therefore, extra instructions or register usage does not impact their performance significantly. For the larger kernels in LULESH register usage was 2-3x that of the comparable CUDA kernels and performance was on average twice as slow. These kernels are a mix of compute and memory bandwidth bound kernels. In all cases when a kernel uses more than 64 registers either register spill increases, resulting in a greater use of cache and memory bandwidth, or occupancy decreases, leading to less latency hiding of slow memory reads. Some of the register usage issues are related to the compiler implementation and we expect them to be reduced with continued development. However, some of the extra register usage is required by the standard.

While the new defaultmap clause in OpenMP 4.5 is needed, it lacks options to change the behavior of aggregates or scalars. The number of registers used would be reduced if aggregates could be made firstprivate[2] by default. A compiler version developed after our initial exploration to test out this theory that allows for firstprivate variables. This version reduces register usage from

---

[2] **firstprivate:** Specifies that each thread should have its own instance of a variable, and that the variable should be initialized with the value of the variable, because it exists before the parallel construct.

176 to 102 for the K16 kernel shown in [3] and result in a 1.19x speedup for the larger 100 problem size. At least 11 of the saved registers are due to the firstprivate clause, which removes the need to use a register per array mapped to the device. However, this is not a perfect experiment as other changes to the runtime and the nvptx backend have happened in the intervening time. However, these results show that with continued work and some help from the standard OpenMP compilers can significantly close the performance gap with CUDA.

While mapping and other clauses to make the code work on the GPU, the number of lines of code changed were small, typically 1–3 lines per loop. In addition, some of this code, or similar code, would be required if OpenMP were to support data motion between multiple levels of the memory hierarchy on self hosted Xeon Phi or other similar devices.

Since the CPU code is unchanged other than the minor changes noted above its performance is not materially impacted. GPU performance was acceptable given the current state of compiler development. We believe with continued compiler and OpenMP standard improvements that overall performance for LULESH will be able to achieve within 25 % of the CUDA version, our goal for performance portability of this application.

Our initial port of LULESH and the improvements made because of it demonstrates the value of compiler writers and application programmers working closely together to evaluate new standards. When developers identify missing functionality or performance bottlenecks compiler writers can implement possible fixes and workarounds. These codesign activities are needed to help drive forward programming practices, compiler implementations, and the OpenMP standard.

5   Suggestions to Address Some Challenges

Our experiences porting Kripke, Cardioid and LULESH to OpenMP 4.5 to target GPUs produced many lessons learned. Throughout this paper we have identified various areas where improvement in the OpenMP standard would help application developers. This section contains our three highest priorities from this work. Other issues, challenges, and concerns that we would like to see addressed, but were not included in this paper are highlighted in a previous technical report [5].

5.1   Clarify OpenMP's Relationship to Key C and C++ Constructs

There are many places where the OpenMP standard is ambiguous that causes pain for developers. Even developers cannot use some constructs in combination with OpenMP, or can only use them in a certain way, having clarity on what can and cannot be done is useful. Clear guidelines are particularly useful when different architectures or runtimes have different capabilities. It would benefit programmers greatly to know the minimum set of functionality they can rely upon when writing code in OpenMP. The experiences we highlight in this paper pointed to a few ambiguities in how OpenMP and the C++ standard interact.

Particularly the handling of dynamic initializers of `declare target` variables and other areas of C++ that are at odds with C are problematic.

One difficulty that crosses both languages is the lack of a documented way to retrieve a function pointer to a device version of a function, or to determine which architecture a function was compiled to target. In fact, the current specification does not define what you get when taking a pointer to a `declare target` function, so it falls under undefined behavior. There are proposals to address this, but none have been approved yet.

5.2 Clarify Virtual Method Support

Due to not all OpenMP devices containing the hardware to support virtual methods the standard likely cannot require support. However, the current restriction is much stronger than disallowing the calling of virtual methods. OpenMP currently does not allow an instance of a class that *has* a virtual method to be mapped onto a device at all. It would simplify porting of existing codes and open up other development options if classes with virtual methods could at least be used for their data and their non-virtual methods. Clearly defining when and where virtual methods can be used within code would allow developers more certainty about the portability of their code.

5.3 Add Deep Copy/Complex Data Structure Support

At present, only relatively simple structures and arrays can be mapped easily to devices. While this is sufficient for some applications, support for mapping complex structures such as arrays of arrays and nested structures, is important as they occur frequently in many applications. This is particularly true for C++ and more modern Fortran variants, where classes and derived types are considered good programming style. More specifically, both a simple mechanism to assist with complex structures and a method for users to define their own transformations would be good. While some users will only want to use the simpler interface, a more general user-defined mechanism will be necessary to support some patterns, for example those where the data should be transformed before use on a device.

6 Related Work

The OpenMP standard for offload accelerators has been evolving for many years. Beyer et al. [4] present one of the initial proposals for a specification. However, it is only recently that compilers have become available that implement the specification that made our study possible. Other initial work by Martineau et al. [14], also shows good performance is possible for three mini-applications using the Cray compiler. Similar to our study with LULESH they see performance close to CUDA for memory bandwidth bound code and performance that is about 2x slower for compute bound code. We build on this work by looking at more complex applications and how C++ constructs interact with OpenMP.

Prior studies of directive based offloading have had to rely on OpenACC compatible compilers to determine the feasibility of using directives to target GPUs. An early study looking at 13 kernels by Lee and Vetter [12] showed promising results for some kernels, but poor performance for others when compared to hand optimized CUDA.

A more recent study by Pickering et al. [16] on a fluid dynamics code showed similar issues with OpenACC as we found with OpenMP. Similar to our experiences with LULESH register allocation in the compiler produced performance degradation. They also looked at manual optimization and showed that by tweaking parameters they could improve performance significantly. In addition, the OpenACC API limited their use of modern Fortran (2003/8) features similar to our struggles using certain C++11/14 features with OpenMP.

Grauer-Gray et al. [7] show another approach using directives along with auto-tuning. Their approach produces runtimes that are as good or better than manually written CUDA and OpenCL code. Similarly, Beckingsale [2] has shown that using RAJA that OpenMP execution policies can be tuned at runtime for CPU systems. In the future we hope to leverage these approaches to close the CUDA to OpenMP performance gap we observed with LULESH.

7   Conclusions and Future Work

Our porting of Kripke, Cardioid, and LULESH to OpenMP 4.5 shows that there is potential for developers to produce performance portable OpenMP code, but much work remains. There are challenges with getting OpenMP to interact well with C++ abstractions due to OpenMP being an extension of C/C++. It has been argued that C++'s threading model, and subsequent adoption of a parallel algorithm library in the STL, may be a sufficient replacement for this. As of now, we have not seen sufficient evidence to believe that the resulting support will be sufficient to provide the control necessary to achieve performance on systems with non-coherent memory domains, and broad support remains a long way off. The current OpenMP programming model requires significant code modifications as well as an ecosystem of device ready libraries. Fully moving large applications that rely on many libraries to this model or onto GPUs in general will be a multi year effort. In some cases, it may require waiting for additional OpenMP features, such as, deep copy and complex data structure support until it is worthwhile to invest in porting certain parts of large applications.

Despite the challenges we faced porting applications our initial experience was promising and informative. We have learned where some of the challenges in using OpenMP are, general porting to GPU roadblocks, and what type of codes are capable of running well today. We realize that because our focus is getting codes running on our future GPU machine that our investigations were GPU centric. While some lessons learned and presented in this paper are general others are not. When LULESH runs well on both the CPU and GPU, and the challenges of using OpenMP and C++ abstractions together should generalize. The challenge of using a single target region in Cardioid likely applies to only the most performance sensitive codes.

As future work we plan to expand our investigations to other hardware platforms and programming models. One area we want to investigate is how to stage data in a performance portable way for both high-bandwidth memory on a Xeon Phi and GPU device memory. For this paper all the codes used were C/C++, but Fortran code is very important to the scientific computing community and it needs to be determined if Fortran and OpenMP 4.5 have any interaction challenges. Finally, as the OpenMP standard continues to evolve and hopefully addresses some of the issues brought up in this paper we plan to evaluate how the changes impact, performance, portability, and programmability.

References

1. Openmp application programming interface, November 2015. http://www.open mp.org/mp-documents/openmp-4.5.pdf
2. Beckingsale, D.: Lightweight models for dynamically tuning data-dependent code, April 2016
3. Bercea, G.T., Bertolli, C., Antao, S.F., Jacob, A.C., Eichenberger, A.E., Chen, T., Sura, Z., Sung, H., Rokos, G., Appelhans, D., et al.: Performance analysis of openmp on a gpu using a coral proxy application. In: Proceedings of the 6th International Workshop on Performance Modeling, Benchmarking, and Simulation of High Performance Computing Systems, p. 2. ACM (2015)
4. Beyer, J.C., Stotzer, E.J., Hart, A., de Supinski, B.R.: OpenMP for accelerators. In: Chapman, B.M., Gropp, W.D., Kumaran, K., Müller, M.S. (eds.) IWOMP 2011. LNCS, vol. 6665, pp. 108–121. Springer, Heidelberg (2011)
5. Draeger, E.W., Karlin, I., Scogland, T., Richards, D., Glosli, J., Jones, H., Poliakoff, D., Kunen, A.: Openmp 4.5 ibm november 2015 hackathon: current status and lessons learned. Technical report LLNL-TR-680824, Lawrence Livermore National Laboratory, January 2016
6. Edwards, H.C., Trott, C.R., Sunderland, D.: Kokkos: enabling manycore performance portability through polymorphic memory access patterns. J. Parallel Distrib. Comput. **74**(12), 3202–3216 (2014)
7. Grauer-Gray, S., Xu, L., Searles, R., Ayalasomayajula, S., Cavazos, J.: Auto-tuning a high-level language targeted to GPU codes. Innov. Parallel Comput. **2012**, 1–10 (2012)
8. Hornung, R., Keasler, J.: The raja portability layer: overview and status. Technical report LLNL-TR-661403, Lawrence Livermore National Laboratory, September 2014
9. Karlin, I., Bhatele, A., Chamberlain, B.L., Cohen, J., Devito, Z., Gokhale, M., Haque, R., Hornung, R., Keasler, J., Laney, D., Luke, E., Lloyd, S., McGraw, J., Neely, R., Richards, D., Schulz, M., Still, C.H., Wang, F., Wong, D.: Lulesh programming model and performance ports overview. Technical report LLNL-TR-608824, December 2012
10. Kunen, A.J.: Tloops - raja-like transformations in kripke, February 2015
11. Kunen, A., Bailey, T., Brown, P.: Kripke-a massively parallel transport mini-app. Technical report LLNL-CONF-675389, Lawrence Livermore National Laboratory, April 2015

12. Lee, S., Vetter, J.S.: Early evaluation of directive-based GPU programming models for productive exascale computing. IEEE Computer Society Press, November 2012
13. Martineau, M., McIntosh-Smith, S., Boulton, M., Gaudin, W.: An evaluation of emerging many-core parallel programming models. In: Proceedings of the 7th International Workshop on Programming Models and Applications for Multicores and Manycores, pp. 1–10. ACM (2016)
14. Martineau, M., McIntosh-Smith, S., Gaudin, W.: Evaluating openmp 4.0's effectiveness as a heterogeneous parallel programming model. In: 2016 IEEE International Parallel and Distributed Processing Symposium Workshop (IPDPSW). IEEE, May 2016
15. Muralidharan, S., Garland, M., Catanzaro, B., Sidelnik, A., Hall, M.: A collection-oriented programming model for performance portability. ACM SIGPLAN Not. **50**, 263–264 (2015). ACM
16. Pickering, B.P., Jackson, C.W., Scogland, T.R., Feng, W.C., Roy, C.J.: Directive-based GPU programming for computational fluid dynamics. Comput. Fluids **114**, 242–253 (2015). http://www.sciencedirect.com/science/article/pii/S004579301500081X
17. Richards, D.F., Glosli, J.N., Draeger, E.W., Mirin, A.A., Chan, B., Fattebert, J., Krauss, W.D., Oppelstrup, T., Butler, C.J., Gunnels, J.A., et al.: Towards real-time simulation of cardiac electrophysiology in a human heart at high resolution. Comput. Meth. Biomech. Biomed. Eng. **16**(7), 802–805 (2013)

Design and Preliminary Evaluation of Omni OpenACC Compiler for Massive MIMD Processor PEZY-SC

Akihiro Tabuchi[1]([✉]), Yasuyuki Kimura[2], Sunao Torii[2], Hideo Matsufuru[3], Tadashi Ishikawa[3], Taisuke Boku[1,4], and Mitsuhisa Sato[1,5]

[1] Graduate School of Systems and Information Engineering,
University of Tsukuba, Tsukuba, Japan
`tabuchi@hpcs.cs.tsukuba.ac.jp`
[2] ExaScaler Inc., Tokyo, Japan
[3] Computing Research Center, High Energy Accelerator Research Organization (KEK), Tsukuba, Japan
[4] Center for Computational Sciences, University of Tsukuba, Tsukuba, Japan
[5] RIKEN Advanced Institute for Computational Science, Kobe, Japan

Abstract. PEZY-SC is a novel massive Multiple Instruction Multiple Data (MIMD) processor used as an accelerator and characterized by high power efficiency. OpenACC is a standard directive-based programming model for accelerators, and programmers can concisely offload data and computation to the accelerators. In this paper, we present the design and preliminary implementation of an OpenACC compiler for a PEZY-SC. Our compiler translates C code with OpenACC directives to the corresponding PZCL code, which is the programming environment for PEZY-SC. The evaluation shows that the performance of the OpenACC version achieves over 98 % at N-body and up to 88 % at NAS Parallel Benchmarks CG than that of the PZCL version. In addition, we examined optimization techniques such as kernel merging and explicit context switching to exploit the PEZY-SC MIMD architecture, which differs from the single instruction multiple data graphics processing units. We found these optimizations useful in improving the performance and will be implemented in the future release.

Keywords: PEZY-SC · OpenACC · Compiler

1 Introduction

Accelerators are widely used in super computers for improving power efficiency because of limitation of power supply. At Green 500 [1], which is a ranking of the 500 most energy-efficient supercomputers, the top 10 systems were equipped with accelerators in November 2015. The top system is the Shoubu Supercomputer at RIKEN and is developed by ExaScaler in Japan. Its accelerator is a PEZY-SC processor, which has 1024 cores and 8192 threads that run in multiple instruction multiple data (MIMD) format. ExaScaler provides PZCL as a

© Springer International Publishing Switzerland 2016
N. Maruyama et al. (Eds.): IWOMP 2016, LNCS 9903, pp. 293–305, 2016.
DOI: 10.1007/978-3-319-45550-1_21

programming environment for PEZY-SC. PZCL is based on OpenCL [2] but its kernel description differs from that of OpenCL. Application development using PZCL is complicated because programmers must describe many codes for offloading data and computations to PEZY-SC. This degrades the application productivity.

In recent years, OpenACC [3] is being widely used for accelerator programming. It is a directive-based programming model for accelerators and allows a programmer to offload codes to accelerators to simplify the porting process for legacy CPU-based applications. Some commercial and research compilers support OpenACC for Graphics Processing Units (GPUs). If PEZY-SC is supported by OpenACC, it will be easier to use because users can rapidly develop applications and reuse the existing OpenACC code. Thus, we designed and preliminarily implemented an OpenACC compiler for PEZY-SC by using the Omni OpenACC compiler [4] originally targeted for NVIDIA GPU. We evaluated the performance of the compiler using the N-Body benchmark and NAS Parallel Benchmarks CG (NPB-CG) [5] and the productivities of PZCL and OpenACC.

The contributions of this paper are summarized as follows:

- We have designed an OpenACC for the massive MIMD many-core processor, PEZY-SC. We determined that OpenACC is useful and provides a good programming model to improve the productivity for programmers of PEZY-SC.
- We propose some optimizations to exploit the PEZY-SC architecture, and show the effectiveness of these optimizations by comparing the performance of the nonoptimized version generated by our current preliminary OpenACC compiler. We examine the implementation of these optimizations by using the compiler and new additional directives.

The remainder of this paper is organized as follows. Section 2 introduces related works and Sect. 3 describes the architecture and programming of PEZY-SC. Section 4 describes the design and detailed implementation of the Omni OpenACC compiler for PEZY-SC. Further, we report the performance and productivity evaluation using two benchmarks in Sect. 5 and discuss on optimization for PEZY-SC and comparison with OpenMP in Sect. 6. Finally, we conclude our study in Sect. 7.

2   Related Work

Several open-sourced OpenACC compilers, such as accULL [6], OpenUH - OpenACC [7], OpenARC [8], and RoseACC [9] have been developed. Moreover, GCC supports OpenACC from version 5.0.1, and the development of future versions are under progress [10]. accULL is the first open-sourced OpenACC compiler, which translates code from OpenACC to CUDA or OpenCL with optimization through the YaCF compiler framework. OpenUH-OpenACC is based on the OpenUH compiler framework and translates OpenACC to CUDA or OpenCL. OpenARC is a compiler framework for accelerators and supports full features in OpenACC 1.0. The compiler is based on the Cetus compiler infrastructure, which

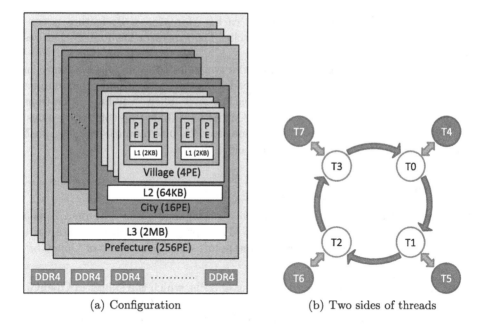

(a) Configuration   (b) Two sides of threads

Fig. 1. PEZY-SC processor

has some code analysis and transformation features. RoseACC is a Rose Compiler based on the OpenACC compiler and translates code to OpenCL. These compilers mainly target GPUs but compilers that translate to OpenCL may be able to target various devices such as CPU, Xeon Phi, and FPGA. However, they are unavailable for PEZY-SC because the description of a kernel in PZCL is specialized for the PEZY-SC architecture and some built-in operations are not supported in OpenCL. We propose the implementation of the Omni OpenACC compiler to translate to PZCL and support PEZY-SC.

3 PEZY-SC

3.1 Architecture

PEZY-SC is a many-core processor developed by PEZY computing. Figure 1(a) shows the structure of the processor. The processor contains 1024 Processing Elements (PEs), which run in MIMD. In each PE, eight threads are executed by using simultaneous multithreading (SMT), that is, 8192 threads run on the processor. The processor is hierarchically constructed with PE, Village, City, and Prefecture in an ascending order. A PE has registers for eight threads, 16 KB local memory, two Arithmetic Logic Units (ALUs), two Floating-Point Units (FPUs), etc. In addition, a Village is constructed with four PEs and a 2 KB L1 cache per two PEs. Further, a City is constructed with four Villages, a Special

Function Unit (SFU), and a 64 KB L2 cache. Moreover, a Prefecture is constructed with 16 cities and a 2 MB L3 cache. The processor has four prefectures or 1024 PEs.

Eight threads in a PE are actually the two sides of 4 threads, as shown in Fig. 1(b). One side of each of the four threads is executed in a round-robin manner every clock cycle, and some synchronizations or explicit switching operations switch the threads to the opposite side. Caches L1–L3 have no coherency. Thus, if a PE reads some values written by another PE, programmers need to flush cached data through a flush operation before the read.

3.2 Programming

PEZY computing provides PZCL, which is a language based on OpenCL as a programming environment for PEYZ-SC. Thus, programmers also need to write the host and device codes; however, some points differ from those of OpenCL.

Host Code. A host code is written using C APIs, which is a subset of OpenCL 1.1. It supports almost all APIs that conventional OpenCL code uses; however, the building and launching of kernels are limited. A conventional OpenCL code usually uses online-compilation, which compiles kernel code at runtime; whereas PZCL only supports offline-compilation, which compiles kernel code at compile time. When launching a kernel, *global_work_size* must be a multiple of 128 because PEZY-SC executes threads by the City and *local_work_size* must be eight because a number of threads in a PE is fixed at eight. Moreover, we can specify at least three dimensions for the shape of a work item in OpenCL, whereas we can specify only one dimension in PZCL. Notably, *global_work_size* should be 8192 or less, otherwise the kernel is launched multiple times.

Device Code. A device code is written in C/C++. Kernels, which are launched from the host, are described as functions same as those in OpenCL. The qualifiers _kernel and __global or __local must be respectively added to the kernel functions and kernel function parameters in OpenCL. Although we must add "pzc_" prefix to the function name and retain the kernel parameters in PZCL, the memory shared among threads in a PE cannot be defined (it corresponds to local memory in OpenCL). In the function body, computation is parallelized using PE and thread IDs, which are obtained through get_pid() and get_tid(), respectively. These correspond to get_group_id(0) and get_local_id(0) in OpenCL. The number of PEs and threads can be obtained using get_maxpid() and get_maxtid(),which correspond to get_num_groups(0) and get_local_size(0) respectively in OpenCL.

PZCL provides some functions for PEZY-SC specific features as follows. The function chgthread() switches the thread to its opposite side explicitly, and sync() synchronizes all threads in a processor. In addition, functions sync_L1(), sync_L2(), and sync_L3() synchronize threads by the Village, City, and Prefecture, respectively. Further, flush() synchronizes all threads in a processor and flushes all cached data. Moreover, flush_L1() synchronizes threads by the Village and flushes L1 cache data, and flush_L2() synchronizes threads by the City and flushes L1 and L2 cache data. We need to optimize kernel functions using these built-in functions for obtaining the best performance. Here, we describe two optimizations used in this study.

Kernel merging. In CUDA or OpenCL, there is no synchronization among thread-blocks (CUDA) or work-groups (OpenCL); thus, we need to divide a kernel code into several kernel functions at global synchronization points. This leads to the increase of kernel launch overhead. However, PZCL provides global synchronization in a processor (sync()); therefore, we do not need to divide the kernel code and the kernel launch overhead can be reduced.

Explicit thread switching. This optimization has two benefits. (1) The improvement of cache utilization. Paired threads tend to access data that are closer because the difference between the thread numbers is four. The explicit switching allows the opposite side to access data before the cache is removed and improves the cache hit ratio. (2) The second benefit is latency hiding of memory access. Switching to the opposite side reduces stall through memory access.

4   Omni OpenACC Compiler

This section describes the design and implementation of the Omni OpenACC compiler for PEZY-SC.

4.1   Design

OpenACC supports C, C++, and Fortran; however, our compiler only supports C. The Omni OpenACC compiler is a source-to-source compiler, and thus translates an OpenACC C code to a host C code and a kernel PZCL code. Thus, the device code for PEZY-SC can be generated by the PZCL compiler. In the host code, the directives are translated to some runtime library calls for maintaining portability. In the kernel code, the offloaded code is translated using functions for simplification and commonization.

4.2   Implementation

To realize the code translation, we used the Omni compiler infrastructure [11], which is a set of programs for a source-to-source compiler with code analysis and transformation. Figure 2 shows the flow for compilation. An OpenACC translator is used to translate an input OpenACC C code to host C and kernel PZCL codes. The host code is compiled using a general C compiler (e.g., GCC and ICC) and linked with the Omni OpenACC runtime library for PZCL. The kernel code is compiled to a kernel binary code using a PZCL compiler, and the binary is loaded at runtime. Note that our preliminary implementation does not currently support the optimizations for PEZY-SC.

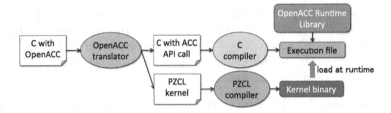

Fig. 2. Compilation flow

```
int a[100], b;
#pragma acc data copy(a) copyout(b)
{
  /* some codes using a and b */
}
```

(a) data construct

```
int a[100], b;
{
  void *DESC_a,*DEV_ADDR_a,*DESC_b,*DEV_ADDR_b;
  unsigned long long _lower[] = {0};
  unsigned long long _length[] = {100};
  _ACC_init_data(&(DESC_a),&(DEV_ADDR_a),a,sizeof(int),1,_lower,_length);
  _ACC_init_data(&(DESC_b),&(DEV_ADDR_b),&(b),sizeof(int),0,NULL,NULL);
  _ACC_copy_data(DESC_a,_ACC_HOST_TO_DEVICE,_ACC_ASYNC_SYNC);
  {
    /* some codes using a and b */
  }
  _ACC_copy_data(DESC_a,_ACC_DEVICE_TO_HOST,_ACC_ASYNC_SYNC);
  _ACC_copy_data(DESC_b,_ACC_DEVICE_TO_HOST,_ACC_ASYNC_SYNC);
  _ACC_finalize_data(DESC_a);
  _ACC_finalize_data(DESC_b);
}
```

(b) translated code

Fig. 3. Code translation of data construct

Translation of Data Construct. A **data** construct declares data on an accelerator in the following region. According to clauses, device memory is allocated and data is transferred from host to device at the beginning, and data is transferred from device to host and device memory is released at the end. The compiler translates these operations to runtime library calls.

Figure 3 illustrates a **data** construct and the translated code. This data construct specifies that an array a and a variable b are allocated on a device at the beginning of the region and freed at the end. The array a in the **copy** clause is transferred at the beginning and end of the region, and the variable b in the **copyout** clause is transferred at the end of the region. The function _ACC_init_data allocates data on the device. If the data is an array, the lower bound and length of each dimension are passed. The variable DEV_ADDR_$name$ is a pointer to the device memory that corresponds to the host memory of $name$. The DESC_$name$ is a pointer to the structure, which has the host address, device address, shape, element size, etc. The function _ACC_copy_data transfers data between the host and device, and the function _ACC_finalize_data frees data on the device.

Translation of Parallel Construct. A `parallel` construct offloads the following region to a device. OpenACC supports three-level parallelism: gang, worker, and vector. However, PZCL provides only the PE and thread. Although our preliminary implementation maps the gang to PE and the vector to thread in PEZY-SC and does not use worker-level parallelism, this correspondence might be changed in the future. The compiler generates a kernel function from the offloading region. Variables, which are accessed in the region, become the function parameters, unless they are specified in the `private` clauses. The function is launched from the host code with device memory objects or values as arguments. Additionally, the number of launch PEs is specified by the `num_gangs` clause. Alternatively, it may be determined by the number of loop iteration in the region.

Figure 4 illustrates a `parallel` construct and the translated code. The function pzc__ACC_kernel_0 is a kernel function. There are 16 PEs from the `num_gangs` clause and the number of threads is fixed at 8. The array _ACC_args contains the kernel arguments and the array _ACC_argsizes contains the sizes of the arguments. Further, the function _ACC_launch launches the kernel function. The first argument _ACC_program is a pointer of structure, which contains kernel objects loaded from a kernel binary file, and the second argument is the kernel number. In the function _ACC_launch, the kernel is launched after the number of total threads is adjusted to multiples of 128 and 8192 or less for PEZY-SC.

Translation of Loop Construct. A `loop` construct specifies parallelization of the following loop in an offloaded region. If parallelisms (gang or vector) are specified, the compiler parallelizes the loop with them; otherwise, the compiler

```
#pragma acc parallel present(a) num_gangs(16)
{
  /* codes in parallel region */
}
```

(a) parallel construct

```
/* host code */
{
  int _ACC_ngangs = 16;
  int _ACC_nworkers = 1;
  int _ACC_veclen = 8;
  int _ACC_conf[] = {_ACC_ngangs, _ACC_nworkers, _ACC_veclen};

  void* _ACC_args[] = {&DEV_ADDR_a};
  size_t _ACC_argsizes[] = {sizeof(void*)};
  _ACC_launch(_ACC_program, 0, _ACC_conf, ACC_ASYNC_SYNC, 1, args, arg_sizes);
}

/* kernel function in device code */
void pzc__ACC_kernel_0(int *a)
{
  /* codes in parallel region */
}
```

(b) translated code

Fig. 4. Code translation of parallel construct

```
/* inside parallel region */
#pragma acc loop vector reduction(+:sum)
for(i = 0; i < N; i++){
  a[i]++;
  sum += a[i];
}
```

(a) loop construct

```
/* inside kernel function */
int _niter_i, _idx, _init, _cond, _step, _red_sum;
_ACC_init_reduction_var(&_red_sum,0);
_ACC_calc_niter(&_niter_i, 0, N, 1);
_ACC_init_thread_iter(&_init,&_cond,&_step,_niter_i);
for(_idx = _init; _idx < _cond; _idx += _step){
  int i;
  _ACC_calc_idx(_idx, &i, 0, N, 1);
  a[i]++;
  _red_sum += a[i];
}
_ACC_reduction_thread(sum,_red_sum, 0);
```

(b) translated code

Fig. 5. Code translation of loop construct

automatically determines parallelisms. The loop iterations are cyclically scheduled for both PE and thread. If `reduction` clauses are present, private variables are prepared before the loop, and their reduced values are stored in reduction variables after the loop.

Figure 5 illustrates a `loop` construct and the translated code. The function _ACC_calc_niter calculates the number of iterations of the loop, and the function _ACC_init_thread_iter obtains the initial, conditional, and step values of the iteration for its thread. In the loop body, the function _ACC_calc_idx obtains the value of the loop variable. For reduction, the function _ACC_init_reduction_var initializes the thread local variable, and then the function _ACC_reduction_thread reduces the value of the variable among threads in the PE.

5   Evaluation

This section presents the evaluation of our compiler's performance and productivity of OpenACC.

5.1   Benchmark

For evaluation, we used the N-body benchmark and NPB-CG. The N-body benchmark simulates the motion of particles that interact and calculates the interactions of all pairs in a simple manner using a single-precision floating-point value. NPB-CG is a benchmark, which evaluates the smallest eigenvalue of a large sparse symmetric positive definite matrix by using the conjugate gradient method. We developed the following versions of the benchmarks.

PZCL (Base). The baseline code written in PZCL. This uses kernel functions separated at global synchronization points.

Table 1. Evaluation environment

	Suiren Blue	HA-PACS/TCA
CPU	Intel Xeon-E5 2618Lv3 2.3 GHz	Intel Xeon-E5 2680v2 2.8 GHz×2
Memory	DDR4 64 GB, 1866 MHz	DDR3 128 GB, 1866 MHz
Accelerator	PEZY-SC×4	Tesla K20X×4
-Peak perf.	SP: 3 TFlops, DP: 1.5 TFlops	SP: 3.95 TFlops, DP: 1.31 TFlops
-Memory	DDR4 16 GB, 1866 MHz	GDDR5 6 GB
-Memory BW	153.6 GB/s	250 GB/s
Compiler	ICC 14.0.2, PZSDK 2.1, Omni OpenACC compiler 0.9.3 for PEZY-SC	PGI 15.10, CUDA 7.5, Omni OpenACC compiler 0.9.3

PZCL (A). PZCL (Base) with optimization A (Kernel merging)
PZCL (A, B). PZCL (Base) with optimizations A and B (Explicit thread switching)
OpenACC. The code written in C with OpenACC

The performance of OpenACC should be equal to that of PZCL (Base) because our compiler does not support the optimizations.

5.2   Performance

We measured the performance using Suiren Blue and HA-PACS/TCA, and the evaluation environments are shown in Table 1.

Figure 6(a) shows the performance of the N-body benchmark on PEZY-SC. The results show flops under an assumption of 38 floating-point operations per interaction [12]. The performance of OpenACC version is 97.8–100.0 % of PZCL versions. The effects of optimizations A and B are slight because the calculation of interactions is dominant.

Figure 6(b) shows the performance of the NPB-CG benchmark on PEZY-SC. "mop/s" implies mega operations per second. The performance of OpenACC version is over 91.9 % of PZCL (base) version. Moreover, the OpenACC version has unnecessary transfers related to reduction kernels. The value of the reduction variable is copied from the host to device despite the initial value being always zero. The optimization A is effective when the matrix size is small, especially because the ratio of kernel launch overhead is large. The optimization B has a good effect when the matrix size is large because the opposite-side threads can utilize cached data before it is removed. The performance of OpenACC version is 61.6–87.5 % of the PZCL (A,B).

Finally, for comparison, we measured the performance of the benchmarks of the OpenACC version on Tesla K20X and compared it with that of the benchmarks on PEZY-SC, as shown in Fig. 7(a) and (b). For K20X, we measured the performance using both PGI and Omni compilers. For the N-body benchmark,

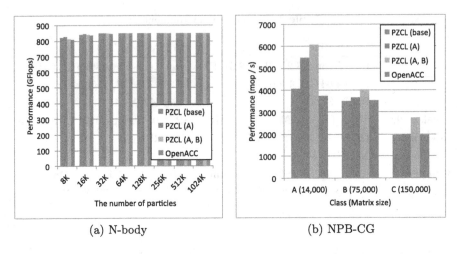

(a) N-body   (b) NPB-CG

Fig. 6. Performance of benchmarks on PEZY-SC

the performance of Omni version is less than half of the performance of the PGI version because particle data is loaded as scalars in the Omni version and as a vector in the PGI version. For the NPB-CG benchmark, the Omni version outperforms the PGI version because the Omni compiler utilizes warp shuffle operation during reduction and the adjustment of the number of thread-blocks is better than in PGI. Even when considering that the OpenACC compiler for PEZY-SC is not optimized, the performance of PEZY-SC is unsatisfactory compared with that of K20X. This may be because PEZY-SC has small number of SFUs, which calculate the reciprocal square root for N-body, and the memory bandwidth is low for NPB-CG.

5.3 Productivity

In PZCL, programmers need to manage memory and kernel execution on the accelerator using many complex API calls same as in OpenCL, and write parallelized kernel functions in the PZCL-specific description. Contrastively, in OpenACC, programmers can directly offload and parallelize parts of serial code by using several simple directives. Moreover, OpenACC is a standard specification; therefore, OpenACC code is available for all accelerators.

We counted the Source Lines Of Code (SLOC) to measure the productivity quantitatively. Table 2 shows the SLOC of N-body and NPB-CG. The SLOC of OpenACC version are 48 % and 45 % of those of the PZCL version for N-Body and NPB-CG respectively, and these are almost the same as their serial codes. Therefore, OpenACC shows better productivity than PZCL.

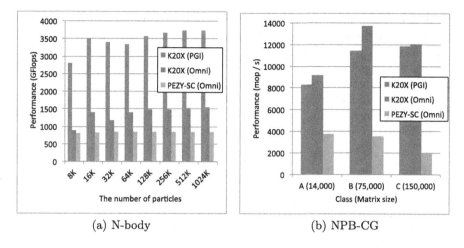

(a) N-body   (b) NPB-CG

Fig. 7. Performance of OpenACC version on K20X and PEZY-SC

Table 2. SLOC of N-Body and NPB CG. The number in parentheses represent the lines of directives.

	N-Body	NPB CG
Serial	109	418
PZCL (A, B)	240	1001
OpenACC	114 (5)	447 (25)

6 Discussion

6.1 Optimization for PEZY-SC

We have not yet implemented the proposed optimizations in our OpenACC compiler. In this subsection, we describe how to apply these optimizations.

The optimization of kernel merging can be implemented in the translation of **kernels** constructs. Similar to a **parallel** construct, a **kernels** construct offloads the following region to a device. While the **parallel** construct launches a single kernel, the **kernels** construct launches multiple kernels. Our current compiler translates a **kernels** region to some separated kernels, in the same manner as for GPU. We will modify our compiler to translate the region to the single kernel when the target is PEZY-SC. In the kernel, our compiler automatically inserts sync() or flush() at the ends of each loop parallelized among gangs, not breaking the semantics of the OpenACC program.

For explicit thread switching, we propose an additional directive corresponding to chgthread(). Another method is for our compiler to automatically insert chgthread() at appropriate points, such as at the end of a loop body, but it is not always effective because it may lead to additional overhead due to thread switching or cache miss. Therefore, it is preferable to give an API for programmers to specify thread switching explicitly by using some directives. As there is no OpenACC directive that corresponds this, we will introduce the additional directive to OpenACC. In addition, our compiler will replace the directive to chgthread() when the target is PEZY-SC, or ignore it.

Although we did not exploit the hierarchy of PEs on PEZY-SC in this study, we will utilize that by also using worker level parallelism in OpenACC. For example, it is considered to map gang to City, worker to PE, and vector to thread.

6.2   Comparison with OpenMP

OpenMP supports offloading since version 4.0, and that is similar to OpenACC. Even if we implement an OpenMP compiler for PEZY-SC, we will obtain almost the same performance and productivities for the benchmarks.

However, some difference between OpenMP and OpenACC may affect performance. OpenMP parallel construct can be multiple nested; whereas OpenACC has only three-level parallelism. Therefore, if we describe five-nested parallel constructs, they correspond to all levels of PEZY-SC hierarchy one-to-one. Further, OpenMP provides barrier and flush directives which OpenACC does not. The directives correspond to sync and flush functions in PZCL, respectively and allow programmers to synchronize threads and flush cached data at each level of the hierarchy. However, the correspondences between OpenMP parallel constructs and the hierarchy levels are implicit when using less than five nested parallel constructs especially. In OpenACC, programmers can clarify parallelisms by using gang, worker, and vector clauses.

Therefore, specifying parallelism level extension for parallel construct can be considered for OpenMP, and more parallelism levels and synchronization and flushing directives extension can be considered for OpenACC.

7   Conclusion

In this paper, we preliminarily designed and implemented an OpenACC compiler for PEZY-SC to improve productivity. The compiler is based on our Omni OpenACC compiler, and we implemented it to translate OpenACC code to PZCL for PEZY-SC. In the evaluation, the performance of the OpenACC version was over 98 % at N-body and up to 88 % at NPB-CG of that of the PZCL version. At NPB-CG, some optimizations such as kernel merging and explicit thread switching were effective for improving performance. From the viewpoint of productivity, OpenACC outperforms PZCL because OpenACC allows programmers to offload work to accelerators by adding directives to the serial version of code, and the SLOC of OpenACC version are less than half of the PZCL version at both N-Body and NPB-CG.

In our future work, we will optimize our compiler using PEZY-SC-specific features. We plan to improve the translation of kernels construct and introduce an additional directive for thread switching.

Acknowledgment. The present study was supported in part by the JST/CREST program entitled "Research and Development on Unified Environment of Accelerated Computing and Interconnection for Post-Petascale Era" in the research area of "Development System Software Technologies for post-Peta Scale High Performance Computing".

References

1. The green500. http://www.green500.org
2. Khronos Group. OpenCL - The open standard for parallel programming of heterogeneous systems. https://www.khronos.org/opencl/
3. OpenACC-Standard.org. OpenACC Home. http://www.openacc.org
4. Tabuchi, A., Nakao, M., Sato, M.: A source-to-source OpenACC compiler for CUDA. In: an Mey, D., et al. (eds.) Euro-Par 2013. LNCS, vol. 8374, pp. 178–187. Springer, Heidelberg (2014)
5. NASA Advanced Supercomputing Division. NAS Parallel Benchmarks. http://www.nas.nasa.gov/publications/npb.html
6. Reyes, R., López-Rodríguez, I., Fumero, J.J., de Sande, F.: accULL: an OpenACC implementation with CUDA and OpenCL support. In: Kaklamanis, C., Papatheodorou, T., Spirakis, P.G. (eds.) Euro-Par 2012. LNCS, vol. 7484, pp. 871–882. Springer, Heidelberg (2012)
7. Tian, X., Xu, R., Yan, Y., Yun, Z., Chandrasekaran, S., Chapman, B.: Compiling a high-level directive-based programming model for GPGPUs. In: Caşcaval, C., Montesinos-Ortego, P. (eds.) LCPC 2013. LNCS, vol. 8664, pp. 105–120. Springer, Heidelberg (2014)
8. Lee, S., Vetter, J.S.: Openarc: open accelerator research compiler for directive-based, efficient heterogeneous computing. In: Proceedings of the 23rd International Symposium on High-performance Parallel and Distributed Computing, HPDC 2014, New York, NY, USA, pp. 115–120. ACM (2014)
9. University of Delaware and LLNL. RoseACC. http://roseacc.org/
10. GCC. OpenACC - GCC Wiki. https://gcc.gnu.org/wiki/OpenACC
11. RIKEN AICS and University of Tsukuba. Omni Compiler Project. http://omni-compiler.org
12. Warren, M.S., Salmon, J.K., Becker, D.J., Goda, M.P., Sterling, T., Winckelmans, W.: Pentium pro inside: I. a treecode at 430 gigaflops on asci red, ii. price/performance of $50/mflop on loki and hyglac. In: ACM/IEEE 1997 Conference on Supercomputing, p. 61, November 1997

Performance Evaluations
and Optimization

Evaluating OpenMP Implementations
for Java Using PolyBench

Xing Fan[(✉)], Rui Feng, Oliver Sinnen, and Nasser Giacaman

Department of Electrical and Computer Engineering,
University of Auckland, Auckland, New Zealand
{fxin927,rfen995}@aucklanduni.ac.nz,
{o.sinnen,n.giacaman}@auckland.ac.nz

Abstract. This paper proposes a benchmark suite to evaluate the performance and scalability of (unofficial) OpenMP implementations for Java. The benchmark suite is based on our Java port of PolyBench, a Polyhedral Benchmark suite. We selected PolyBench instead of other existing benchmarks, like JGF, as it allows us to run and use the OpenMP C version as a performance and scalability reference. Further, PolyBench was conceived as a benchmark suite to analyse the optimisation capabilities of compilers. It is interesting to study these capabilities in the OpenMP context of a dynamically compiled language like Java in comparison to the statically compiled C. We apply the benchmark suite to two Java OpenMP implementations, Pyjama and JOMP, and compare with C code compiled by GCC, optimised and unoptimised. The sometimes surprising and unexpected results shed light on the appropriateness of Java as an OpenMP platform, the areas for improvement and the usefulness of this benchmark suite.

1 Introduction

Now that multi-core processors have become the norm in mainstream consumer devices, parallel programming needs to support the software developers of these parallel computing systems. This new domain brings distinct differences compared to the traditional fields of parallel programming. Here, the applications are no longer running on a dedicated, let alone known, target system [12]. High-level object-oriented languages, such as Java, dominate the programming scene [9,18]. This is easy to see why, considering the unprecedented high number of smartphone and tablet apps. For parallel programming to be embraced by this mainstream software development community, parallel tools and libraries need to be in the spirit of these languages [11]. Although most of these languages inherently support multi-threading though their libraries, these solutions lack the intuitive and elegant approach of OpenMP.

OpenMP has long served the traditional parallel computing community with its constant adaption in response to the newest hardware technologies, as well as promoting programmer productivity. In recognition of Java's popularity in the programming arena, numerous efforts have proposed a Java version of OpenMP

N. Maruyama et al. (Eds.): IWOMP 2016, LNCS 9903, pp. 309–319, 2016.
DOI: 10.1007/978-3-319-45550-1_22

[6,10,13,14,19]. As future efforts continue in this direction, having a standardised empirical evaluation grows in importance. This will provide the researchers and developers of Java OpenMP technologies with an accepted approach to present their development. PolyBench [15] is such a respected benchmark suite that helps developers to consistently validate their compilers, written in C. While one aspect of the focus here is that a Java PolyBench port, more important is the characteristic differences between a statically compiled language and a dynamically compiled language. This will set the scene for better insight into Java's future aptitude as a viable OpenMP language.

The optimisation mechanisms of Java and C are very different. The portability qualities of Java has contributed to its popularity in mainstream software development. Java source code is compiled to Java bytecode, which is in turn interpreted by the Java Virtual Machine (JVM) using Just-In-Time (JIT) compilation. As a consequence, a Java program's optimisation is undertaken at runtime by the JVM to pursue better performance. This mechanism is very different from the execution of C/C++ programs, where optimisation occurs in the compilation stage. Although the performance of a benchmark will depend on many factors including hardware architecture, operating system, and specific benchmark characteristics, it is still beneficial to understand how the optimisation differences of these languages differ in the context of a parallel programming environment.

The remaining part of this paper is organised as follows. Section 2 presents related work, while Sect. 3 discusses the methodology and guideline of the benchmark suite. Section 4 describes the experimental setup, with performance results presented in Sect. 5 before concluding in Sect. 6.

2 Related Work

This section discusses related work in regards to Java OpenMP efforts and benchmarks.

2.1 OpenMP for Java

A number of efforts have been striven to infuse the philosophy of OpenMP into Java. JOMP [6] is a source-to-source compiler which transforms OpenMP-like directives in Java code into multi-threaded Java code executed using native Java threads. JaMP [13] is a distributed shared memory implementation that uses the Jackal framework to translate the sequential code to parallel version. JMP [10] is a Java library implementation simulating an OpenMP-like runtime support. AOmpLib [14] is an aspect-oriented library that imitates OpenMP for Java using AspectJ. Pyjama [19], like JOMP, provides a source-to-source compiler to convert sequential Java code annotated with OpenMP into multi-threaded Java code. Pyjama provides extensions for features to support event-driven applications, especially for the development of interactive graphical user interface applications.

2.2   Benchmarks

Java Benchmarks. The SPECjbb benchmark suite [1] is typically used to evaluation the server-side Java performance in different systems. At the same time, numerous Java benchmarks have been developed to test the performance of the JVM, e.g. Decapo [5], Java Grande Forum Benchmarks [7,8]. Some benchmarks specially focus on Java parallelisation [17] or multi-threading [16].

Parallel Processing Benchmarks. There are also many benchmark suites which are designed to evaluate the performance of parallel processing although they are not written in Java. For example, SEPComp [2] is an OpenMP code based benchmark suite which is used to evaluate high-performance multi-core systems. The PARSEC benchmark suite [3,4] implements a series of state-of-art multi-threading applications for evaluating Chip-Multiprocessors.

3   PolyBench for Java OpenMP

Even though it is reasonable that the performance of Java is not as competent as C/C++, referencing the performance of C/C++ OpenMP could help better understand Java OpenMP performance. Therefore, the methodology of this work is converting pre-existing C/C++ OpenMP benchmark cases to Java code implementing OpenMP. The major benchmark suite selected in this work is PolyBench, a benchmark suite developed for the polyhedral community that is used by many members of the community [20]. Because most of the benchmarks focus on linear algebra, data mining, medley and stencils problems that are parallelisation candidates, PolyBench has drawn the attention of the parallel processing community. The reason PolyBench is chosen is because the benchmarks simulate real world problems, and all of them contain massive numerical operations and iterations. The performance of these kernels can be improved with parallelisation, especially as they include large amounts of for-loops that are perfect candidates for the OpenMP programming interface.

There is a total of 30 available benchmark cases in the PolyBench suite. The original kernels are written in C with OpenMP pragmas, which may then be compiled by OpenMP-supported C/C++ compilers. Each kernel is then ported to Java, with OpenMP directives injected that conform to the requirements of the available Java OpenMP compilers. With the object-oriented nature of Java, each Java kernel exists as an independent Java class. In order to compare the performance under the same criteria, every Java implementation uses exactly the same directives and schedule clauses as its paired C implementation counterpart. The kernels implemented are listed in Table 1. The kernel naming follows the following convention: the first letter "P" stands for PolyBench while the second letter "L", "D", "M", "S" stand for linear-algebra, datamining, medley or stencils respectively, followed by the original benchmark name in PolyBench/C.

Table 1 lists all the ported and parallelised benchmarks with their short description.

4 Evaluation

This section details the experimental setup and the results are presented and discussed in the next section.

Compilation. The OpenMP C code can be compiled by any C compiler which supports OpenMP. In this experiment, GCC v4.8.4 is used to compile all C benchmarks. With regard to Java code, this experiment uses two different Java implementations of OpenMP – Pyjama (v1.5.4b) and Jomp (v1.0b) respectively to parallelise the Java OpenMP benchmarks.

Table 1. List of implemented PolyBench benchmarks, with their sequential execution times (ms).

Benchmark	Description	Execution Time (ms)		
		Java	C-o0	C-o3
PL2mm	Multiplication of 2 matrix	27029	169783	92043
PL3mm	Multiplication of 3 matrix	40199	248351	138448
PSadi	Alternating direction implicit solver	3787	7116	4437
PLatax	Matrix transpose and vector multiplication	112	294	72
PLbicg	BiCG sub kernel of BiCGStab linear solver	106	259	74
PLcholesky	Cholesky decomposition	387	1273	338
PDcorrelation	Correlation computation	6621	10100	4511
PDcovariance	Covariance computation	6577	9908	4525
PLdoitgen	Multi-resolution adaptive numerical analysis	677	3500	975
PLdurbin	Toeplitz system solver	574	406	361
PLdynprog	2-D Dynamic programming	1073	2809	725
PSfdtd_2d	2-D finite different time domain kernel	1298	1956	1317
PSfdtd_apml	FDTD using anisotropic perfectly matched layer	2705	3305	2320
PMfloydWarshall	Floyd– Warshall algorithm	5138	13622	5074
PLgemm	Matrix multiplication and addition	13138	85859	45437
PLgemver	Vector multiplication and matrix addition	479	688	320
PLgesummv	Scalar, vector and matrix multiplication	130	258	105
PLgramschmidt	Gram-Schmidt decomposition	1780	2246	2078
PSjacobi_1d_imper	1-D Jacobi stencil computation	38	21	3
PSjacobi_2d_imper	2-D Jacobi stencil computation	331	461	321
PLlu	LU composition	1277	3785	1245
PLludcmp	LU decomposition	3435	4000	2080
PLmvt	Matrix vector product and transpose	384	447	229
PMreg_detect	2-D image processing	86	218	47
PSseidel_2d	2-D Seidel stencil computation	508	722	421
PLsymm	Symmetric matrix-multiply	17547	70971	46419
PLsyr2k	Symmetric rank-2k operations	5981	22400	6380
PLsyrk	Symmetric rank-k operations	2902	12353	2905
PLtrisolv	Triangular solver	50	73	25
PLtrmm	Triangular matrix-multiply	1393	5994	1442

Table 2. Four types of compilation of OpenMP code.

Name	Compilation
C-o0	`gcc -O0 -fopenmp -DPOLYBENCH_TIME -I benchmark.c -o benchmark`
C-o3	`gcc -O3 -fopenmp -DPOLYBENCH_TIME -I benchmark.c -o benchmark`
Jomp	`java -cp jomp1.0b.jar jomp.compiler.Jomp benchmark.jomp`
Pyjama	`java -jar Pyjama-v1.5.4.jar benchmark.pj`

The compilation details are listed in Table 2. Since the optimisation of C code only happens at the compilation stage, two different optimisation levels were used to compile the C code. More specifically, flag -O0 indicates no optimisation at all. Flag -O3 triggers very salient static code optimisation to improve the efficiency of the C program, including vectorization.

In contrast, the compilation from Java source code to Java bytecode is not given any optimisation option and the virtual machine does so many just-in-time optimisations at runtime.

Execution. All the benchmarks are executed on a 16-core 2.4 GHz SMP machine (4 quad-core Intel Xeons E7340) with 64 GB memory, running under Ubuntu Linux 12.04 LTS and Java HotSpot 64-Bit Server VM (1.8.0_66) is used. With regard to Java benchmark cases, as a matter of fairness, they do not apply any deliberate warm-ups to make Java Virtual Machine discover hot spots, which could lead to better performance. For every benchmark, the same data set is used for all implementations.

The sequential execution times are also listed in Table 1, with the standard data set, as specificed by PolyBench.

It can be observed from Table 1 that for 29/30 benchmark cases, the sequential execution time of Java version is faster than unoptimised C version, and even 8/30 benchmarks are faster than optimised C version, which is somewhat unexpected. According to the execution time of Java, all the benchmark cases are categorised into three groups. There are 8/30 benchmark cases whose execution times are longer than 5 s, and there are 9/30 cases whose execution times are between 1 s and 5 s. All the remaining 13/30 cases have less than 1 s execution times.

5   Results

The absolute running times of all implemented benchmark cases are recorded over different numbers of processors. The speedups of each implementation are calculated according to the execution times. The first observation we made is that the absolute runtimes have a significant impact on the scalability of the Java implementations. We therefore organise the discussion along the benchmark groups (>5 s, 1 s–5 s, <1 s) in the following.

5.1   Long Runtimes

For the benchmarks where Java's execution time is longer than 5 s, Java shows
very good performance and scalability. It is surprising that in some cases, the
Java implementations have very impressive execution times and even better than
optimised C versions. These benchmark cases include PDcorrelation, PL2mm,
PL3mm, PLgemm and PLsymm. For these 5 benchmarks, the Java versions are
significantly faster than C versions, which is more than twice the speed with any
number of threads. The scalability of the Java versions is also comparable to C
versions and even better than C in some cases. Most of these benchmarks are
linear algebra problems and the computational kernels involve large amounts of
manipulations on matrices. A nested loop without any dependency is the best
candidate to be parallelised and reaches good speedup. At the same time, the
long running time could be an important factor that the JVM discovers the hot
spots and optimises the execution.

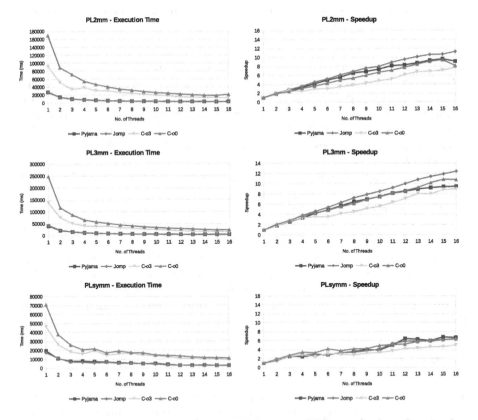

Fig. 1. Selected benchmark cases (PL2mm, PL3mm and PLsymm) where Java implementations have good performance and scalability (comparing to C).

Figure 1 shows three selected benchmark cases which have this type of characteristic. It can be seen that both Jomp and Pyjama have faster speed than both C versions with regard to execution time. When it comes to scalability, all four implementations have similar speedups. For most of the time, Java implementations (either Jomp or Pyjama) lead among the four implementations.

5.2 Medium Runtimes

For the second category, in which the execution time of Java is between 1 s and 5 s, Java OpenMP also shows some performance improvements but not in a prominent way. For many of the benchmark cases in this group, the performance of Java versions is faster than unoptimised C version, but cannot compete with the optimised C version. These benchmark cases include PLtrmm, PLlu, and PLsyrk.

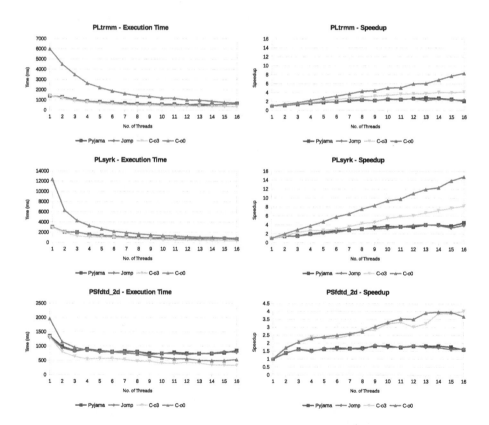

Fig. 2. Selected benchmark cases (PLtrmm, PLsyrk and PSfdtd_2d) where Java implementations have comparable performance with C versions, but scalability is not very good.

Figure 2 illustrates some examples of this situation. Taking PLtrmm for example, the execution times of Jomp and Pyjama nearly overlay with each other, which indicates they have very similar performance. Even though most of the time, the execution of Java versions is faster than unoptimised C, optimised C version always is better than the other three versions. When it comes to speedup, both C versions have better scalability than Java versions. It should be noted that even though Java versions are faster than unoptimised C version, the scalability is poor for both Jomp and Pyjama. For instance, the speedup of Java versions never reaches 3 for benchmarks PLtrmm and PSfdtd_2d. In contrast, both C versions have better speedup than Java.

5.3   Short Runtimes

As for the last group of benchmark cases, where the execution time of Java is lower than 1 s, both Jomp and Pyjama do not have very good execution time, and even worse, Java has longer execution time when the number of threads

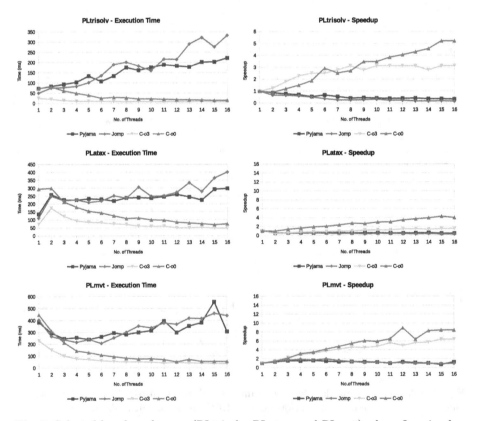

Fig. 3. Selected benchmark cases (PLtrisolv, PLatax, and PLmvt) where Java implementations have bad performance and scalability.

is increased. This type of benchmark indicates that for some situations, Java OpenMP parallelisation even can degrade the performance.

Figure 3 selects PLatax, PSfdtd_ampl and PLmvt to demonstrate this type of benchmark results. Besides the long execution time of Java, the speedups also show the bad scalability of Java parallelisation of these benchmark cases. It seems obvious that the Java execution times are too short to benefit from parallelisation, where C as an OpenMP language is still able to achieve speedup. Lower parallelisation overhead sets the threshold for useful parallelisation lower for C.

5.4   Other Observations

For most of the cases, even though the execution time is not always better than Java and optimised C, unoptimised C version always has better scalability than the three other versions. On the other hand, although Java versions outperform in some of the benchmarks, they do not show very good speedups with regard to scalability.

Non-scalable Benchmark Cases. There are three benchmark cases (PLdyn-prog, PSjacobi_1d_imper and PMerg_detect) that cannot benefit from both C and Java parallelisation. When the number of threads increases, the execution time even gets slower than sequential. This may be due to the nature of these computational kernels and that they are not suitable for OpenMP parallelisation.

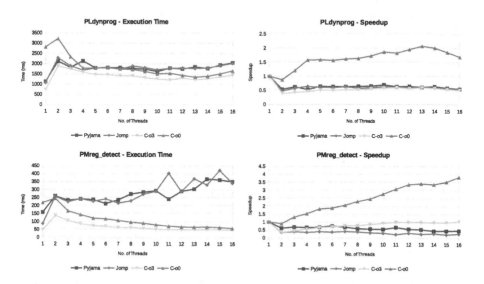

Fig. 4. Benchmark cases (PLdynprog and PMreg_detect) show their unscalability of parallelisation.

Figure 4 shows the results of PLdynprog and PMreg_detect. Nearly all four versions show bad performance and the execution time even grows when the number of threads increases. Even though the execution time of PLdynprog is long enough (around 1–3 s), when the number of threads increases, two Java version and optimised C version degrade the performance, and unoptimised C only gains very low speedup (up to 2).

6   Conclusions

This paper proposed a new benchmark suite to evaluate the performance of OpenMP implementations of Java. It is based on our port of PolyBench to Java, augmented with (Java) OpenMP directives. The choice for this benchmark suite was driven by two criteria: to have an equivalent C implementation that can serve as a performance and scalability reference; and to use code with varying optimisation potential for compilers.

With this benchmark suite we wanted to analyse the appropriateness of Java as an OpenMP platform. We carried out an experimental study applying Poly-Bench to the OpenMP Java implementations Pyjama and Jomp and compared with C code compiled by GCC.

An early observation was that the runtime of some of the benchmarks is too small to allow efficient parallelisation, especially for Java. While this can be seen as a deficit of this benchmark suite, it revealed that Java as an OpenMP platform has a significantly higher parallelisation threshold than C. On the other hand, when the runtimes were long, OpenMP under Java did not only show similar scalability as C, it was surprisingly competitive in regards to the absolute runtime. The difference between the two Java implementations was relatively small with no clear winner, showing similar behaviour at both ends of the spectrum. Overall, the experiments showed that the proposed PolyBench based benchmark suite is an effective tool to analyse Java OpenMP performance.

References

1. Adamson, A., Dagastine, D., Sarne, S.: SPECjbb2005 – a year in the life of a benchmark. In: SPEC Benchmark Workshop (2007)
2. Aslot, V., Domeika, M., Eigenmann, R., Gaertner, G., Jones, W.B., Parady, B.: SPEComp: a new benchmark suite for measuring parallel computer performance. In: Eigenmann, R., Voss, M.J. (eds.) WOMPAT 2001. LNCS, vol. 2104, pp. 1–10. Springer, Heidelberg (2001)
3. Bienia, C.: Benchmarking modern multiprocessors. Ph.D. thesis, Princeton University, January 2011
4. Bienia, C., Kumar, S., Singh, J.P., Li, K.: The PARSEC benchmark suite: characterization and architectural implications. In: Proceedings of the 17th International Conference on Parallel Architectures and Compilation Techniques, pp. 72–81. ACM (2008)

5. Blackburn, S.M., Garner, R., Hoffmann, C., Khang, A.M., McKinley, K.S., Bentzur, R., Diwan, A., Feinberg, D., Frampton, D., Guyer, S.Z., et al.: The DaCapo benchmarks: Java benchmarking development and analysis. ACM SIG-PLAN Not. **41**, 169–190 (2006). ACM
6. Bull, J.M., Kambites, M.E.: JOMPan OpenMP-like interface for Java. In: Proceedings of the ACM Conference on Java Grande, pp. 44–53. ACM (2000)
7. Bull, J.M., Smith, LA., Westhead, M.D., Henty, DS, Davey, RA.: A methodology for benchmarking Java Grande applications. In: Proceedings of the ACM Conference on Java Grande, pp. 81–88. ACM (1999)
8. Bull, J.M., Smith, L.A., Westhead, M.D., Henty, D.S., Davey, R.A.: A benchmark suite for high performance Java. Concurr. Prac. Exper. **12**(6), 375–388 (2000)
9. Carbonnelle, P.: PYPL PopularitY of Programming Language Index (2016). http://pypl.github.io/PYPL.html
10. Cook, R.P.: An OpenMP library for Java. In: Proceedings of IEEE Southeastcon, pp. 1–6 (2013)
11. Geeknet Media: Parallel programing: Goals, skills, platforms, markets, languages (2012)
12. Giacaman, N., Sinnen, O.: Object-oriented parallelisation of Java desktop programs. IEEE Softw. Softw. Multiprocessor Deskt. Appl. Environ. Platforms **28**(1), 32–38 (2011)
13. Klemm, M., Bezold, M., Veldema, R., Philippsen, M.: JaMP: an implementation of OpenMP for a Java DSM. Concurr. Comput. Pract. Exper. **19**(18), 2333–2352 (2007)
14. Medeiros, B., Sobral, J.L.: AOmpLib: an aspect library for large-scale multi-core parallel programming. In: 42nd International Conference on Parallel Processing (ICPP), pp. 270–279. IEEE (2013)
15. Pouchet, L.-N.: Polybench: The polyhedral benchmark suite (2016). http://www.cs.ucla.edu/~pouchet/software/polybench/. [cited May]
16. Smith, L.A., Bull, J.M.: A multithreaded Java Grande benchmark suite. In: Proceedings of the Third Workshop on Java for High Performance Computing (2001)
17. Smith, L.A., Bull, J.M., Obdrizalek, J.: A parallel Java Grande benchmark suite. In: ACM/IEEE Conference on Supercomputing, p. 6. IEEE (2001)
18. TIOBE Software BV: TIOBE programming community index (2016). http://www.tiobe.com/tiobe_index
19. Vikas, N.G., Sinnen, O.: Pyjama: OpenMP-like implementation for Java, with GUI extensions. In: Proceedings of the International Workshop on Programming Models and Applications for Multicores and Manycores, pp. 43–52. ACM (2013)
20. Yuki, T.: Understanding PolyBench/C 3.2 kernels. In: International Workshop on Polyhedral Compilation Techniques (IMPACT) (2014)

Transactional Memory for Algebraic Multigrid Smoothers

Barna L. Bihari[1]([✉]), Ulrike M. Yang[1], Michael Wong[2],
and Bronis R. de Supinski[1]

[1] Lawrence Livermore National Laboratory, Livermore, CA, USA
{bihari1,yang11,desupinski1}@llnl.gov
[2] Codeplay Software, Edinburgh, UK
fraggamuffin@gmail.com

Abstract. This paper extends our early investigations in which we compared transactional memory to traditional OpenMP synchronization mechanisms [7,8]. We study similar issues for algebraic multigrid (AMG) smoothers in *hypre* [16], a mature and widely used production-quality linear solver library. We compare the transactional version of the Gauss-Seidel AMG smoother to an `omp critical` version and the default *hybrid* Gauss-Seidel smoother, as well as the l_1 variations of both Gauss-Seidel and Jacobi smoothers. Importantly, we present results for real-life 2-D and 3-D problems discretized by the finite element method that demonstrate the TM option can outperform the existing methods, often by orders of magnitude, in terms of the recently introduced performance measure of *run time per quality*.

1 Introduction

Transactional memory (TM) is widely recognized as an easy-to-use shared memory synchronization mechanism. However, the next version of the OpenMP specification does not currently seem likely to support it despite previous proposals to do so [9,31], The lack of interest stems partly from limited availability of hardware support but perhaps even more so from the lack of demonstrations that it offers reasonable performance for production applications.

In addition, so far only two major vendors, IBM and Intel have offered a production version of hardware transactional memory (HTM) as part of their memory subsystem, but with very different runtime libraries and API's. The IBM BG/Q systems have an OpenMP extension for TM using directives, while Intel offers locks with hints as part of the Intel or LLVM runtime (see e.g. [3,7]). Both of these HTM versions have been explored by our previous efforts [7–9,26] and resulted in overall positive conclusions. However, in all studies some effort had to be made to explain and conform to the specific syntax, invocation and usage models which were very different on the IBM and Intel systems, thus placing both implementations far from what could be called a "standard".

© Springer International Publishing Switzerland 2016
N. Maruyama et al. (Eds.): IWOMP 2016, LNCS 9903, pp. 320–335, 2016.
DOI: 10.1007/978-3-319-45550-1_23

Most TM studies focus on the design of TM mechanisms and their optimization. Nearly all only consider benchmarks or kernels, particularly when applying TM to scientific computing [3,6–9,26,29,31,33]. For example, our prior work used a small example code to explore TM performance when application semantics allow a degree of nondeterminism. In this work, we consider similar issues for a production code base with over two decades of development and widespread use: the *hypre* linear solver library [16]. Our results demonstrate that TM not only can simplify development but also provide significant performance benefits for mature applications. Overall, we show that TM can outperform alternative methods in *hypre*'s threaded algebraic multigrid (AMG) smoother by up to two orders of magnitude for some 2-D and 3-D problems. These results indicate that the OpenMP arsenal of synchronization techniques should include TM.

The paper is structured as follows. Section 2 covers related work, focused primarily on the current state of the art of TM. Section 3 provides a brief overview of the AMG method and then details how we use TM to simplify its implementation and to improve its performance. Section 4 compares experimental results for five AMG smoothers, including two OpenMP synchronization options that we implement for this work. In Sect. 5 we conclude with a brief review of our results.

2   Transactional Memory State-of-the-Art

Many studies have explored TM programmability and performance compared to locks for a range of benchmarks and kernels including Delaunay triangulation [27], minimum spanning forest of sparse graphs [17], and Lee's routing algorithm [2], among others [15,18,23]. QuakeTM [13], Atomic Quake [34] (using a lock-based version), and SynQuake [20], which use TM to implement the Quake game server [1], provide the most significant application studies. These studies demonstrate that TM can improve performance as well as programmability for production multi-player games; our work provides similar proof for a production scientific computing application.

Other studies have investigated the usability of TM. For example, Rossbach et al. found that programs using fine-grain locking were more likely to contain errors than those using coarse grain locks or TM [25]. Pankratius and Adl-Tabatabai concluded that TM is not a panacea for parallel programming: it still requires good programmers although it has promise compared to fine-grain locking for large and complex parallel programming tasks [24]. While we are not specifically studying programmability, we have found that TM simplifies writing data-race free programs without sacrificing performance.

Substantial recent effort has explored mechanisms to add TM support to C++ [14]. This activity includes participation from HP, IBM, Intel, Oracle and RedHat and has led the C++ Standards Committee to form Study Group 5: Transactional Memory (SG5, for short) [32]. SG5 is now working with the C++ Standards Committee with the goal of creating an acceptable set of transactional language constructs for Standard C++. We have proposed OpenMP pragmas and semantics [30] that are closely related to a recent C++ SG5 proposal [19] and would simplify interoperability with a likely addition to the C++ Standard.

This direction within the C++ community indicates that OpenMP should strongly consider adding TM support, as we advocate in this paper. Indeed, besides this interoperability advantage, having TM also in OpenMP would fill this gap in OpenMP-based threading as well as in retrofitting C or Fortran codes, in addition to having a choice for modern C++.

In addition to our prior work [6–9, 26, 31], others have proposed adding transactional memory support to OpenMP [4, 22]. These efforts have concluded that TM is well suited to a directive-based approach since transactions are naturally represented as sequential code blocks. As already discussed, our work has found that TM can provide competitive performance for toy benchmarks that represent scientific computing patterns found in simple mesh-optimization algorithms [6–9]. Our current work shows that production applications can benefit even more.

3 Applying Transactional Memory to the AMG Smoother

3.1 Brief Review of Algebraic Multigrid Methods

Algebraic multigrid (AMG) methods [28] are well-suited for large-scale scientific applications because they are algorithmically scalable: they solve a sparse linear system $Au = f$ with n unknowns with $O(n)$ computations. They obtain this optimality by reducing error using two separate operations: smoothing and coarse grid correction between successively coarser levels. Coarse grid correction involves restriction and prolongation or interpolation operators between levels. The restriction is generally defined as the transpose of the prolongation.

Smoothers must reduce errors in the directions of eigenvectors. These "smooth errors" can be characterized with $Ae \approx 0$. For an effective AMG method the prolongation operator $P^{(m)}$ that interpolates the approximate error e^{m+1} from the $m + 1$-st level to the mth level must be defined so that the smooth errors on the mth level are approximately in the range of $P^{(m)}$. Simple pointwise smoothers, such as Jacobi or Gauss-Seidel, or their combinations, reduce smooth errors associated with large eigenvalues rapidly. Reducing errors associated with small eigenvalues can be more time consuming. Algebraic multigrid (AMG) does not require an explicit grid. Instead, coarse grid selection and the generation of interpolation and restriction operators only depend on the matrix coefficients.

AMG consists of two phases: setup and solve, as shown in Fig. 1. The primary computational kernels in the setup phase are the selection of the variables for the coarser grids, the definition of the interpolation ($P^{(m)}$) and restriction ($R^{(m)}$) operators, and the creation of the coarse grid matrix operator $A^{(m+1)}$ for $m = 0, 1, ..., L$, where $L + 1$ is the number of levels. The variables for the $(m + 1)$st level as well as the entries in $P^{(m)}$ and $R^{(m)}$ are determined by making use of the coefficients of $A^{(m)}$. These algorithms can be quite complicated.

In the solve phase, a smoother is applied on each level $m = 0, ..., k - 1$, and then the residual r^m is transferred to the next coarser grid, where the

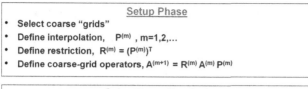

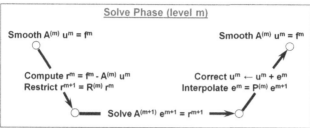

Fig. 1. AMG building blocks.

process continues. On the coarsest level, the linear system $A^{(k)}e^k = r^k$ is solved by Gaussian elimination. The error e^k is then interpolated to the next finer grid, followed by relaxation, which continues to the finest grid. Figure 1 describes the m-th level of the solve phase. The process of starting on the fine grid, restricting to the coarse grid, and interpolating back to fine grid again is called a V-cycle.

The solve phase primarily consists of a matrix-vector multiplication (MatVec) and the smoother. The classical smoother used for algebraic multigrid is Gauss-Seidel, which is highly sequential. Therefore AMG often uses a parallel variant, called hybrid Gauss-Seidel (*HGS*), which can be viewed as an inexact block-diagonal (Jacobi) smoother with Gauss-Seidel sweeps inside each process. In other words, we use a sequential Gauss-Seidel algorithm locally on each process, with delayed updates across processes. One HGS sweep is similar to a MatVec.

For our experiments, we use the parallel AMG code BoomerAMG as a preconditioner to a GMRES solver, both contained in the *hypre* software library [16]. We use HMIS coarsening [11] with extended+i interpolation [10]. Sparse matrices in BoomerAMG are stored in the ParCSR matrix data structure, in which the matrix A is partitioned by rows into matrices A_k, $k = 0, \ldots, p-1$, where p is the number of MPI processes or OpenMP threads. A_k is stored locally as two matrices in sequential CSR (compressed sparse row) format, D_k and O_k. D_k contains all entries in A_k for which column indices point to rows stored on process k. O_k contains the remaining entries, which have column indices that point to rows stored on other processes. Matrix-vector multiplication Ax involves computing $A_k x = D_k x^D + O_k x^O$ on each process, where x^D is the portion of x stored locally and x^O is the portion that needs to be sent by other processes. Both the MPI- and OpenMP-based parallelism for Gauss-Seidel relaxation is accomplished in the same "hybrid" fashion: on node- or thread-boundaries the previous iterate's information is passed and used, while within each node or thread a full Gauss-Seidel iteration is performed [12].

```
· · · · · · · · · ·
#pragma omp parallel for private(i,ii,jj,res) HYPRE_SMP_SCHEDULE
  for (i = 0; i < n; i++)
  {              // start of for-loop threaded over rows
    if (cf_marker[i] == relax_points &&
        A_diag_data[A_diag_i[i]]  != zero)
    {             // start of if-statement
      res = f_data[i];
      for (jj = A_offd_i[i]; jj < A_offd_i[i+1]; jj++)
      {
        ii = A_offd_j[jj];
        res -= A_offd_data[jj] * Vext_data[ii];
      }
#pragma tm_atomic
      {              // start of transaction
// Step 1:   Take weighted-average.
        for (jj = A_diag_i[i]+1; jj < A_diag_i[i+1]; jj++)
        {        // start of averaging for-loop
          ii = A_diag_j[jj];
          res -= A_diag_data[jj] * u_data[ii];
        }         // end of averaging for-loop
// Step 2:   Update current u.
        u_data[i] = res / A_diag_data[A_diag_i[i]];
      }             // end of transaction
    }             // end of if-statement
  }               // end of for-loop threaded over rows
· · · · · · · · · ·
```

Fig. 2. Transactional version of actual code section from *hypre*.

3.2   TM-Assisted Error-Smoothing in AMG

We now describe how we use TM to simplify the implementation of multi-grid smoothing and how our approach can improve its convergence. Multigrid smoothing is symbolically represented by the equation:

$$u_i^{(n+1)} = \frac{1}{A_{ii}}(f_i - \sum_{j=1}^{N} A_{ij}u_j^{(l)}) \qquad (1)$$

where u_i and f_i are the i-th components of the approximation u and of the right hand side f, respectively. Furthermore, A_{ij} represents the j-th component of row i in the matrix A, N is the order of the matrix, n marks the current iteration on u (so $n+1$ is the next), and l is either n or $n+1$, depending on whether that entry has already been updated. Note that only the nonzero coefficients of the matrix A are actually used.

Since $u^{(l)}$ can imply dependences within the straightforward loop-based calculation of $u^{(n+1)}$, threading the computation over index i is non-trivial. However, we can apply the TM-based threading approach that we previously used for mesh smoothing operations [7,8].

Figure 2 shows the relevant *hypre* code section. We add exactly *one* OpenMP directive. In essence, this becomes a simplified version of *HGS* where the inter-thread Jacobi update is eliminated, or rather, replaced by TM. We have write-after-read (WAR) race conditions as a careful analysis of Fig. 2 reveals. Because the value of the other elements of u_data might change during "Step 1", the resulting average could depend significantly on whether the update in "Step 2" uses old or new data. Therefore, the transaction must protect the entire code section that includes both steps, and not just the update operations of u_data in "Step 2". If we protected the latter update only – which, by itself, would be embarrassingly parallel – there would be no conflicts detected, but race conditions outside of this update exist nevertheless. Since "Step 2" depends on the previous averaging operation, we have a write-after-read (WAR) conflict for which we cannot use #pragma omp atomic.

4   Experimental Results

Our experiments evaluate the convergence rate and run time of the algorithm in Sect. 3.2 for two finite element discretizations in 2-D and 3-D [5]. All results use the modification of the BoomerAMG branch of *hypre*, HMIS coarsening [11] with extended+i interpolation [10] and AMG-preconditioned GMRES as the solver. Several existing smoother options provide state-of-the-art comparisons [16].

We stop calculations after a preset iteration count and use the residuals to measure quality instead of allowing the run to converge to a tolerance value. We do not use iteration count for the latter since our metric provides much more accurate timings per unit reduction in residuals (i.e. "quality"). We used the built-in *hypre* timers associated with the solve phase of Fig. 1. We run our experiments on an IBM Blue Gene/Q system using its hardware transactional memory (HTM) support with the TM-related environment variable settings of TM_ENABLE_INTERRUPT_ON_CONFLICT = YES and TM_MAX_NUM_ROLLBACKS=10.

4.1   Problem Descriptions

Both test problems solve the scalar diffusion problem described by (see also [5]):

$$- \nabla \cdot (a(x, y, z)\nabla u) = f. \tag{2}$$

It is discretized on unstructured meshes using the MFEM finite element package [21], which results in matrices that are not diagonally dominant. Both cases use homogeneous Dirichlet boundary conditions. In addition to our current detailed tests, we can also qualitatively compare with results from a prior study [5].

2-D LLNL is a two-dimensional problem on a unit-square discretized into triangular elements with four material subdomains that form the LLNL logo (Fig. 3). The coefficient $a(x, y)$ is 1 in the three L's and 10^{-3} in the outer domain.

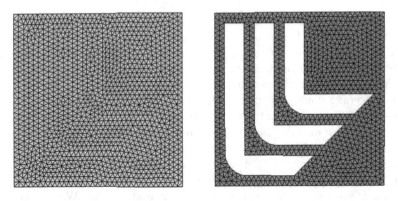

Fig. 3. Original unstructured mesh and cut-outs for multi-material 2-D LLNL mesh.

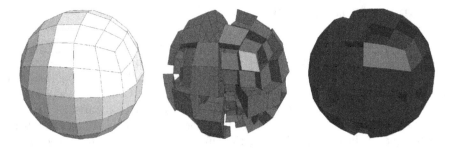

Fig. 4. Coarse version of 3-D sphere mesh and its two material subdomains in color.

3-D Sphere is a three-dimensional sphere discretized with trilinear hexahedral finite elements and two material subdomains that are placed in arbitrary locations. Their material coefficients $a(x, y, z)$ are 1 and 10^3 (see Fig. 4).

4.2   Convergence

We measure convergence as the l_2 norm of the residuals after each GMRES iteration. In addition to our TM algorithm, we run both problems using hybrid Gauss-Seidel, l_1 Gauss-Seidel and l_1 Jacobi, denoted by *HGS*, *L1-GS* and *L1-Jacobi*, respectively. *HGS* is the default option in *hypre* used for problems parallelized both via MPI and OpenMP, while the latter two appeared to remedy some shortcomings of *HGS* observed in prior work [5]. They represent a fair comparison as they are often used as AMG smoothers in conjunction with GMRES to solve non-symmetric problems. We also run a version of the algorithm in Sect. 3.2 that replaces `#pragma tm_atomic` with the OpenMP standard `#pragma omp critical` (called *critical*), which is the only OpenMP synchronization mechanism that is comparable to TM.

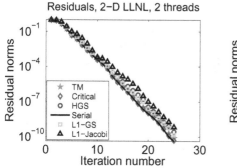
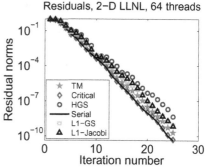

Fig. 5. Convergence on 2 threads, LLNL.   **Fig. 6.** Convergence on 64 threads, LLNL.

2-D LLNL: We stop this calculation at 25 iterations. The serial solution, which should be optimal in some sense, serves as our reference in all plots. Figure 5 shows that differences in convergence of the six different smoothers already emerge with 2 threads. As expected, *L1-Jacobi* is the slowest to converge, while *TM* and *critical* are almost indistinguishable from *serial*, with *L1-GS* and *HGS* being somewhere in between. 64 threads results in a larger spread between the different methods and *HGS* becomes the slowest to converge, with *L1-GS* approaching *L1-Jacobi*, which, of course, is embarrassingly parallel and therefore invariant to thread count (Fig. 6). As initial evidence that synchronization matters as the thread count increases, *TM* and *critical* are the closest to *serial*, the latter being the overall fastest converging. While we do expect *TM* and *critical* to be close to each other in terms of convergence, the inherently non-deterministic and iterative nature of these algorithms will result in slight differences from run to run even within the same synchronization method. However, the convergence of neither *TM* nor *critical* changes significantly with thread count. On the other hand, at 25 iterations we observe two orders of magnitude difference in the residuals of *HGS* with 64 threads and *serial*, which is consistent with prior results [5]. The convergence plots for other thread counts (not shown) are in between the 2 and 64 ones.

3-D Sphere: We stop the calculation at 30 iterations. This problem exhibits a much more dramatic change with increasing thread count so we show plots for 2, 4, 8 and 64 threads. While on one thread all of *TM*, *critical*, and *HGS* are identical to *serial* (not shown), 2 threads already results in a substantial difference between *HGS* and those other options. Its convergence deteriorates by orders of magnitude, approaching that of *L1-Jacobi* (Fig. 7). *HGS* convergence continues to deteriorate as we increase the thread count to 4 (Fig. 8) and it stops converging altogether for 8 threads (Fig. 9); the 64-thread case is similar (Fig. 10).

For all thread counts the convergence of *L1-GS* remains in between *serial* and *L1-Jacobi*, with small deteriorations with increasing number of threads, as

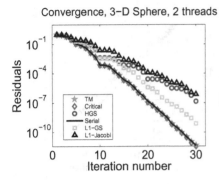

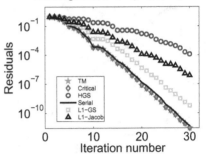

Fig. 7. Convergence, 2 threads, sphere.   **Fig. 8.** Convergence, 4 threads, sphere.

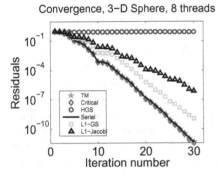

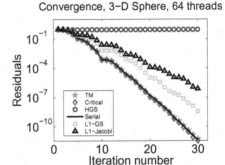

Fig. 9. Convergence on 8 threads, sphere.   **Fig. 10.** Convergence, 64 threads, sphere.

Figs. 7, 8, 9, 10 show. The performance of *TM* and *critical* remain the same in all cases: very close to that of the serial version, showing the value of synchronization in these iterative algorithms. The most surprising result is the significant improvement of *HGS* from the addition of TM, which, in effect, made the difference between non-convergence and convergence.

4.3   Transactional Memory Statistics

The rest of this section focuses on the 3-D sphere problem since it is the larger and therefore more challenging one. An important issue for TM algorithms is how many times the TM subsystem rolled back transactions. At the end of each call to the smoother we use the `tm_print_all_stats()` utility to output the TM-report. Figure 11 shows that these numbers exhibit an uneven but regular pattern for each thread count. Recall from Sect. 3.1 that smoothing is invoked on each level of matrix resolution, and, therefore, both the number of non-zero entries that are averaged and the number of entries that are updated are different on each level.

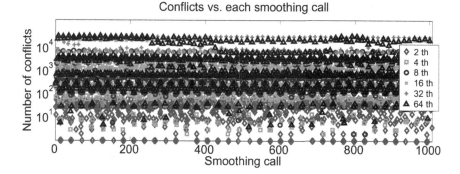

Fig. 11. Rollbacks per call to the smoother for sphere, on 2 through 64 threads.

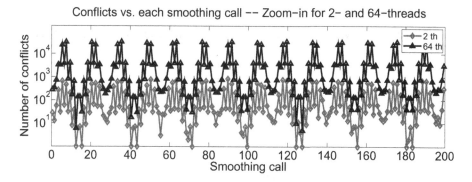

Fig. 12. Zoom-in of rollbacks per call to the smoother for sphere, on 2 and 64 threads.

Thus, the number of transactions and the number of rollbacks varies with the level m. While Fig. 11 is extremely busy, one can already notice a cyclic pattern for some thread counts. This pattern becomes more obvious after simplifying the figure by zooming in and connecting the symbols for only two characteristic thread counts at the two ends of the spectrum: at 2 and 64 threads (see Fig. 12). These patterns reflect AMG's cyclic nature described in Sect. 3.1.

Figure 13 depicts the per-thread breakdown of the total number of conflicts for the entire calculation. Since the BG/Q has 16 physical cores and each core can execute up to four hardware threads, this figure also shows the assignment of threads for the different thread counts from 2 to 64. According to this figure the total number of conflicts per thread has a relatively even pattern between threads although in general the number of rollbacks is highly dependent on the ordering of the original finite element mesh and it can vary greatly between different threads. The total number of rollbacks versus thread count curve shows a monotonic increase that tapers off at 32 threads (Fig. 14). This may possibly

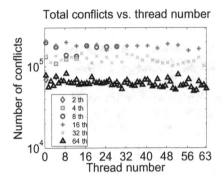

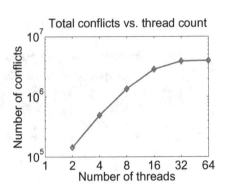

Fig. 13. Rollbacks per thread number for sphere, on 2 through 64 threads.

Fig. 14. Total number of rollbacks per thread count for sphere.

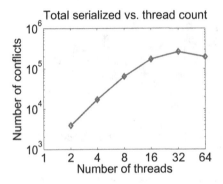

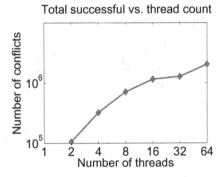

Fig. 15. Total number of serialized transactions per thread count for sphere.

Fig. 16. Total number of successful rollbacks per thread count for sphere.

be due to having only 16 physical cores on each node, so at 32 and 64 threads each core has more than one thread assigned to it.

In addition to the number of rollbacks, IBM's TM statistics routine also outputs the total number of transactions as well as the number of times loops were serialized because the number of rollbacks on the same transaction exceeded the preset maximum allowed; the latter is the aforementioned environment variable TM_MAX_NUM_ROLLBACKS which we had set to 10 for all experiments. The per-smoothing-call conflict count patterns of serialized transactions (not shown) is similar to those of Figs. 11, 12. The total number of serialized transactions is shown in Fig. 15 with a similar trend to that of Fig. 14 except at 64 threads where there is slight decrease.

If we now define T as the total number of transactions, C as the number of rollbacks (or conflicts), S as the number of serialized transactions, and M as the maximum number of rollbacks allowed, we have:

$$N = C - SM, \tag{3}$$

where N is now the number of *successful* (or non-serialized) rollbacks that did not result in serialization; that is, they eventually succeeded. The total number of successful rollbacks is shown in Fig. 16 with a monotone increase all the way to 64 threads. Note that the number of successful rollbacks will still include multiple rollbacks on the same update and therefore will greatly exceed the number of actual memory locations which are updated in a transactional manner. Nevertheless, N is but a small percentage of the total number of transactions; even at 64 threads, for example, N/T is about 4 %. If we assume a statistically even distribution of multiple rollbacks $(1, 2, ..., 9$ in our case) on the same conflicted transaction, there would be an average of $M/2$ rollbacks for each of those locations. Therefore, the average number $\bar{N}$ of conflicted but successfully executed transactions becomes:

$$\bar{N} = \frac{N}{\frac{M}{2}} . \tag{4}$$

$\bar{N}$, together with the serialized transactions, gives the total number of transactions with conflicts $P = \bar{N} + S$. Now the "rolled-back transaction rate" U can be defined as the percentage of transactions that had at least one rollback and was either successful or serialized:

$$U = \frac{P}{T} = \frac{\bar{N} + S}{T} . \tag{5}$$

Plotting this rate for each thread count reveals that even at 64 threads it is only slightly more than 1 % (see Fig. 17) implying that 99 % of transactions were executed without rollbacks. It is indeed remarkable that correcting a small

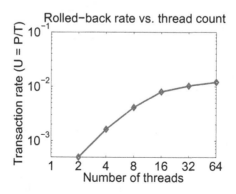

Fig. 17. "Rolled-back" transaction rate per thread count for sphere.

fraction of variables with up-to-date information results in the dramatic improvements of overall convergence shown in Subsect. 4.2.

4.4   Timed Performance

Strong Scaling: Given the limited memory capacity of a BG/Q node and our emphasis on OpenMP threading, we show results for strong scaling only. Figure 18 shows relatively linear scaling for *TM* on up to 16 threads, for *L1-Jacobi* on up 32 threads, and for *L1-GS* and *HGS* (virtually on top of each other) on all thread counts; *critical*, on the other hand, does not scale at all, an expected result. However, the same figure also shows that, on a per-run (30 iterations) basis, *critical* is faster than *TM* on 1- or 2 threads, and *L1-Jacobi*, *L1-GS* and *HGS* are up to an order-of-magnitude faster than *TM* on all thread counts. However, these raw timings do not consider quality of solution.

Time-to-quality: We slightly modify our performance measure introduced in [8] to define "run time per quality" $t_q^{(n)}$, (assuming $q^{(n)}$ is the inverse of the l_2-norm of the residual $r^{(n)}$) at each iteration n:

$$t_q^{(n)} = \frac{t^{(n)}}{q^{(n)}} = t^{(n)} r^{(n)}. \tag{6}$$

The results in Fig. 19 for this performance measure show several orders of magnitude difference between the various smoothing methods. As already indicated by Figs. 9, 10, *HGS* does not converge past four threads, thus its $t_q^{(n)} \to \infty$, despite its near perfect scaling shown in Fig. 18. On the other hand, *critical* has strong performers in Fig. 19 even though it does not scale at all. The best performance is offered by *TM* on 8 through 64 threads, with its 32-thread $t_q^{(n)}$ being the overall best performer for this problem.

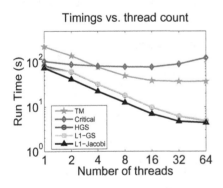

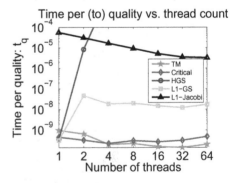

Fig. 18. Strong scaling for sphere, on 1 through 64 threads.

Fig. 19. Time per quality for sphere, on 1 through 64 threads.

As with the simpler mesh optimization problem [7,8], even though some methods may be more expensive on a per-iteration basis, if they converge faster they may end up being more efficient overall since fewer iterations are needed to achieve convergence, and the CPU-time to solution can actually be shorter.

5 Concluding Remarks

Building upon our prior work [5,7,8], we studied two different OpenMP synchronization constructs in the context of iterative AMG smoothers with emphasis on transactional memory as a promising mechanism to resolve write-after-read memory conflicts. On each thread count we conducted detailed studies of the behavior of residuals, TM statistics, strong scaling, as well the overall "price/performance" of each method considered. Using our figure of merit [8], we concluded that TM outperformed the alternatives currently offered in Boomer-AMG and *hypre* often by orders of magnitude. In all of our tests, OpenMP synchronization made a significant difference in reducing the residuals for a given CPU time. Surprisingly, OpenMP critical performed well under this metric.

In our future work, we plan to use TM for other GS-flavored methods, such as l_1 GS and l_1 symmetric GS. These implementations will allow explorations for other classes of solvers, such as conjugate gradient.

Acknowledgments. The authors thank the anonymous reviewers for their constructive comments. We are also grateful to Lori Diachin of LLNL for the many discussions and ideas on this subject matter and for her continuing support of this research. Finally, we thank Tzanio Kolev of LLNL for his help in generating the relevant matrices using MFEM.

This article (LLNL-PROC-528852) has been authored in part by Lawrence Livermore National Security, LLC under Contract DE-AC52-07NA27344 with the U.S. Department of Energy. Accordingly, the United States Government retains and the publisher, by accepting the article for publication, acknowledges that the United States Government retains a non-exclusive, paid-up, irrevocable, world-wide license to publish or reproduce the published form of this article or allow others to do so, for United States Government purposes.

References

1. Abdelkhalek, A., Bilas, A.: Parallelization and performance of interactive multiplayer game servers. In: IPDPS (2004)
2. Ansari, M., Kotselidis, C., Jarvis, K., Lujan, M., Kirkham, C.: Watson, I.: Lee-TM: a nontrivial benchmark for transactional memory. In: ICA3PP (2008)
3. Bae, H., Cownie, J., Klemm, M., Terboven, C.: A user-guided locking API for the OpenMP* application program interface. In: DeRose, L., de Supinski, B.R., Olivier, S.L., Chapman, B.M., Müller, M.S. (eds.) IWOMP 2014. LNCS, vol. 8766, pp. 173–186. Springer, Heidelberg (2014)
4. Baek, W., Minh, C.C., Trautmann, M., Kozyrakis, C., Olukotun, K.: The OpenTM transactional application programming interface. In: PACT, pp. 376–387 (2007)

5. Baker, A.H., Falgout, R.D., Kolev, T.V., Yang, U.M.: Multigrid smoothers for ultraparallel computing. SIAM J. Sci. Comput. **33**, 2864–2887 (2011)
6. Bihari, B.L.: Applicability of transactional memory to modern codes. In: ICNAAM, pp. 1764–1767. APS, Rodos, Greece (2010)
7. Bihari, Barna L., Bae, Hansang, Cownie, James, Klemm, Michael, Terboven, Christian, Diachin, Lori: On the algorithmic aspects of using openmp synchronization mechanisms II: user-guided speculative locks. In: Terboven, C., et al. (eds.) IWOMP 2015. LNCS, vol. 9342, pp. 133–148. Springer, Heidelberg (2015). doi:10.1007/978-3-319-24595-9_10
8. Bihari, B.L., Wong, M., de Supinski, B.R., Diachin, L.: On the algorithmic aspects of using OpenMP synchronization mechanisms: the effects of transactional memory. In: DeRose, L., de Supinski, B.R., Olivier, S.L., Chapman, B.M., Müller, M.S. (eds.) IWOMP 2014. LNCS, vol. 8766, pp. 115–129. Springer, Heidelberg (2014)
9. Bihari, B.L., Wong, M., Wang, A., de Supinski, B.R., Chen, W.: A case for including transactions in OpenMP II: hardware transactional memory. In: Chapman, B.M., Massaioli, F., Müller, M.S., Rorro, M. (eds.) IWOMP 2012. LNCS, vol. 7312, pp. 44–58. Springer, Heidelberg (2012)
10. De Sterck, H., Falgout, R.D., Nolting, J.W., Yang, U.M.: Distance-two interpolation for parallel algebraic multigrid. Numer. Linear Algebra Appl. **15**, 115–139 (2008)
11. De Sterck, H., Yang, U.M., Heys, J.J.: Reducing complexity in parallel algebraic multigrid preconditioners. SIAM J. Matrix Anal. Appl. **27**, 1019–1039 (2006)
12. Falgout, R.D., Jones, J.E., Yang, U.M.: Pursuing scalability for hypre's conceptual interfaces. ACM Trans. Math. Softw. **31**, 326–350 (2005)
13. Gajinov, V., Zyulkyarov, F., Unsal, O.S., Cristal, A., Ayguade, E., Harris, T., Valero, M.: QuakeTM: parallelizing a complex sequential application using transactional memory. In: ICS, pp. 126–135 (2009)
14. Transactional Memory Specification Drafting Group. Transactional language constructs for C++, May 2014. https://sites.google.com/site/tmforcplusplus/
15. Guerraoui, R., Kapalka, M., Vitek, J.: STMBench7: a benchmark for software transactional memory. In: EuroSys, pp. 315–324 (2007)
16. hypre: High performance preconditioners. http://www.llnl.gov/CASC/hypre/
17. Kang, S., Bader, D.A.: An efficient transactional memory algorithm for computing minimum spanning forest of sparse graphs. In: PPoPP, pp. 15–24 (2009)
18. Kestor, G., Stipic, S., Unsal, O., Cristal, A., Valero, M.: RMS-TM: a transactional memory benchmark for recognition, mining and synthesis applications. In: Proceedings of 4th ACM SIGPLAN Workshop on Transactional Computing TRANSACT (2009)
19. Luchangco, V., Wong, M.: Transactional Memory Support for C++, February 2014. http://www.openstd.org/jtc1/sc22/wg21/docs/papers/2014/n3919.pdf
20. Lupei, D., Simion, B., Pinto, D., Misler, M., Burcea, M., Krick, W., Amza, C.C.: Transactional memory support for scalable and transparent parallelization of multiplayer games. In: EuroSys, pp. 41–54 (2010)
21. MFEM: Modular parallel finite element methods library. http://mfem.googlecode.com
22. Milovanović, M., Ferrer, R., Unsal, O.S., Cristal, A., Martorell, X., Ayguadé, E., Labarta, J., Valero, M.: Transactional memory and OpenMP. In: Chapman, B., Zheng, W., Gao, G.R., Sato, M., Ayguadé, E., Wang, D. (eds.) IWOMP 2007. LNCS, vol. 4935, pp. 37–53. Springer, Heidelberg (2008)
23. Minh, C.C., Chung, J., Kozyrakis, C., Olukotun, K.: STAMP: stanford transactional applications for multi-processing. In: IISWC, pp. 315–324 (2008)

24. Pankratius, V., Adl-Tabatabai, A.: A study of transactional memory vs. locks in practice. In: SPAA, pp. 43–52 (2011)
25. Rossbach, C.J., Hofmann, O.S., Witchel, W.: Is transactional programming actually easier?. In: PPoPP, pp. 47–56 (2010)
26. Schindewolf, M., Gyllenhaal, J., Bihari, B.L., Wang, A., Schulz, M., Karl, W.: What scientific applications can benefit from hardware transacional memory?. In: SC12 (2012)
27. Scott, M.L., Spear, M.F., Dalessandro, L., Marathe, V.J.: Delaunay triangulation with transactions and barriers. In: IISWC (2007)
28. Stüben, K.: An introduction to algebraic multigrid. In: Trottenberg, U., Oosterlee, C., Schüller, A. (eds.) Multigrid, pp. 413–528 (2001)
29. Wang, A., Gaudet, M., Wu, P., Ohmacht, M., Amaral, J.N., Barton, C., Silvera, R., MIchael, M.: Evaluation of blue gene/Q hardware support for transactional memories. In: PACT (2012)
30. Wong, M., Ayguadé, E., Gottschlich, J., Luchangco, V., de Supinski, B.R., Bihari, B., other members of the WG21 SG5 Transactional Memory Sub-Group: Towards Transactional Memory for OpenMP. In: DeRose, L., Supinski, B.R., Olivier, S.L., Chapman, B.M., Müller, M.S. (eds.) IWOMP 2014. LNCS, vol. 8766, pp. 130–145. Springer, Heidelberg (2014)
31. Wong, M., Bihari, B.L., de Supinski, B.R., Wu, P., Michael, M., Liu, Y., Chen, W.: A case for including transactions in OpenMP. In: Sato, M., Hanawa, T., Müller, M.S., Chapman, B.M., de Supinski, B.R. (eds.) IWOMP 2010. LNCS, vol. 6132, pp. 149–160. Springer, Heidelberg (2010)
32. Wong, M., Gottschlich, J.: SG5: Software Transactional Memory (TM) Status Report. http://www.open-std.org/jtc1/sc22/wg21/docs/papers/2012/n3422.pdf, September 2012
33. Yoo, R., Hughes, C., Lai, K., Rajwar, R.: Performance evaluation of Intel transactional synhcornization extensions for high-performance computing. In: SC13 (2013)
34. Zyulkyarov, F., Gajinov, V., Unsal, O.S., Cristal, A., Ayguade, E., Harris, T., Valero, M., Quake, A.: Using transactional memory in an interactive multiplayer game server. In: PPoPP, pp. 25–34 (2009)

Supporting Adaptive Privatization Techniques for Irregular Array Reductions in Task-Parallel Programming Models

Jan Ciesko[1]([⊠]), Sergi Mateo[1,2], Xavier Teruel[1], Xavier Martorell[1,2],
Eduard Ayguadé[1,2], and Jesus Labarta[1,2]

[1] Barcelona Supercomputing Center, Barcelona, Spain
{jan.ciesko,sergi.mateo,xavier.teruel,xavier.martorell,
eduard.ayguade,jesus.labarta}@bsc.es
[2] Universitat Politècnica de Catalunya, Barcelona, Spain

Abstract. Irregular array-type reductions represent a reoccurring algorithmic pattern in many scientific applications. Their scalable execution on modern systems is not trivial as their irregular memory access pattern prohibits an efficient use of the memory subsystem and costly techniques are needed to eliminate data races. Taking a closer look at algorithms, memory access patterns and support techniques reveals that a one-size-fits-all solution does not exist and approaches are needed that can adapt to individual properties while maintaining programming transparency. In this work we propose a solution framework that generalizes the concept of privatization to support a variety of techniques, implements an inspector-executor to provide memory access analytics to the runtime for automatic tuning and shows what language extensions are needed. A reference implementation in OmpSs, a task-parallel programming model, shows programmability and scalability of this solution.

Keywords: Array reduction · Privatization · Inspector-executor · OmpSs · OpenMP

1 Introduction

The widening gap between processor and memory speeds periodically brings up the discussion on how to improve scalability of algorithms that hit the memory wall exceptionally fast such as scatter-updates. At the core of the problem are high memory access latencies that become dominant as a result from the caching and bandwidth inefficiencies of these algorithms. Further, techniques are needed to ensure correctness by avoiding data races that occur because of concurrent accesses of overlapping memory regions. Among these techniques only a single generally applicable solution exists, namely access synchronization. Synchronization uses software and hardware assisted techniques to implement atomicity of the update operation (read-modify-write) with overheads that differ

© Springer International Publishing Switzerland 2016
N. Maruyama et al. (Eds.): IWOMP 2016, LNCS 9903, pp. 336–349, 2016.
DOI: 10.1007/978-3-319-45550-1_24

```
1 int  i ,  res [S];
2 ...
3 while(simulation_runs()){
4    ...
5    for(i=0;  i<N;  i++){
6      res[f(i)]++;
7    }
8 }
```

Fig. 1. Structure of a typical scientific application with an array reduction in a global simulation loop

between processor architectures. Synchronization constructs are typically members of either the language or runtime specification of a programming model and therefore easy to use but unfortunately do not deal with the issue of poor locality of these algorithms.

A special case occurs when the scatter-update implements an iterative function that is associative, commutative and has no control dependency between loop iterations. These algorithms are called reductions and allow a whole set of additional techniques to improve performance and scalability. An irregular array-type reduction is defined as

$$for\ i\ over\ iters :$$
$$j = f(i);$$
$$a[j] = op(a[j], expression)$$

(1)

where i is an induction variable, $iters$ is an iteration space, and where a is a reduction variable with op being an algebraic monoid. Figure 1 shows a schematic representation of a typical occurrence where a global loop drives the progress of a simulation and performs an array reduction in each step. Figure 2 shows two examples of such kernels from the LULESH [1] and SPECFEM3D [8] applications.

Main implications of the mathematical properties of reductions are two-fold: firstly, the order of memory accesses does not matter anymore which allows concurrent executions without maintaining a constant execution order of tasks or loop iterations and the existence of the neutral element allows the use of scratch data to temporarily store intermediate results. This led to the development of different support techniques [2] that can be grouped into two strategies: access redirection, also called privatization and iteration ordering. Access redirection is a strategy where accesses are redirected to a scratch memory while leaving the iteration space untouched. The scratch memory is either a thread-private copy of the original data (replication) or any other private storage that serves the same purpose but for performance reasons implements an alternative memory layout (AML). We call techniques that use such an alternative memory layout *AMLs*. Ordering is a strategy that avoids redirection and reorders iterations to obtain a desired memory access pattern instead, thus creating an alternative iteration space (AIS).

Interestingly, techniques implementing access redirection can be improved if information about the memory access pattern of the reduction kernel is provided to them. In addition, for AIS implementations, this information is always required.

```
1 ...
2 for ( Index_t k=0 ; k<numElem ; ++k )
3 {
4    const Index_t* const elemToNode = domain.nodelist(k);
5    ...
6    for ( Index_t lnode=0 ; lnode<8 ; ++lnode ) {
7       Index_t gnode = elemToNode[lnode];
8       domain.fx(gnode) += fx_local[lnode];
9       domain.fy(gnode) += fy_local[lnode];
10      domain.fz(gnode) += fz_local[lnode];
11   }
12 }
```

(a) IntegrateStressForElems(), LULESH

```
1 //scatter(...)
2 int i,j,k,iglob, elem;
3    for (elem=0; elem<actual_size; elem++) {
4       for (k=0;k<NGLLZ;k++) {
5          for (j=0;j<NGLLY;j++) {
6             for (i=0;i<NGLLX;i++) {
7                iglob = ibool[elem][k][j][i];
8                accel[iglob][X] += sum_terms[elem][k][j][i][X];
9                accel[iglob][Y] += sum_terms[elem][k][j][i][Y];
10               accel[iglob][Z] += sum_terms[elem][k][j][i][Z];
11            }
12         }
13      }
14   }
15 }
```

(b) Scatter(), SPECFEM3D

Fig. 2. Kernels performing irregular array-type reductions in scientific applications

This creates the demand for programming models that are capable of inspecting dynamic properties and switching to optimized execution at a certain point in time. This execution model is called inspector-executor and works for cases where the executor can be run multiple times such that the benefit hides the cost of inspection. Adding inspector-executors to parallel programming models is not trivial since syntactical means are needed to express *what* variable to target, *when* to inspect and *how* to optimize.

In this work we present the OmpSs Reductions Model (OmpSs-RM). It aims to enable generic support of AMLs for improved scalability of irregular array-type reductions. OmpSs-RM consists of a common interface, an inspector-executor and language support. The common interface allows vendors to implement any privatization technique including AMLs with custom initializer and reducer functions. The OmpSs inspector-executor tracks memory accesses and exposes access statistics to techniques that require them for tuning. Further we show which language constructs are needed to support AMLs as well as inspector-executors. To show-case this solution, we added an AML example implementation to OmpSs called binning [4]. Results show that binning with selective privatization based on statistical data provided by the inspector achieves a substantial performance increase compared to other techniques.

The rest of the paper is structured as follows. Section 2 introduces the idea of AMLs. Section 3 discusses runtime support for AMLs and inspector-executors in OmpSs. Section 4 discusses language support. Section 5 presents a case study and performance evaluation. Section 6 gives an overview on related work and Sect. 7 concludes this work.

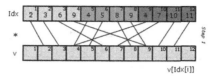

Fig. 3. Access pattern in irregular array reductions

2   Generalization Through AMLs

The most common technique to support reductions is data replication. This technique falls into the category of access redirection where memory accesses to the original reduction variable are replaced by accesses to thread-private copies of the original data in each task. While replication is an efficient technique for scalar data types, it quickly reaches scalability limitations due to the excessive memory consumption as well as the need to initialize and reduce duplicate copies. Further this technique does not optimize for locality since the memory access pattern remains unchanged. As it is an approach that puts minimal demands on language and runtime support, it is the most widely used technique to parallelize reductions in programming models today. Figure 3 shows a visual representation of an irregular array reduction where an output array v is indexed by values stored in an index array Idx and each connecting line represents a memory access. Figure 4 shows the resulting access pattern using replication, where each task processes a set of iterations and updates its own local copy (step 1). All private copies are reduced once all participating tasks have finished (step 2). In task-parallel programming models, this is typically the case when the scope of a reduction ends [5].

Other techniques exist that follow the same idea of access redirection but implement an optimization strategy to improve data access locality of irregular array reductions. Representative approaches for this group are caching [3] and binning [4]. Software caches are useful in distributed memory scenarios where the cost of communication between nodes is higher than the processing overhead on the local node and where the problem is at least partially cache-friendly. Binning redirects accesses into bins that correspond to memory regions of original reduction array. Once a bin is filled, it is reduced to the corresponding memory location. The proximity of data within a bin results in an improved locality during the reduction phase. These techniques have three characteristics in common:

- Implementation of an alternative memory layout (AML) to accommodate thread-private data structures of a particular approach and to minimize the memory footprint
- Implementation of a custom initializer and reducer
- Implementation of a GET-method that returns a pointer to a private storage that accommodates at least one reduction array element

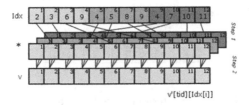

Fig. 4. Data replication that redirects accesses into full array copies

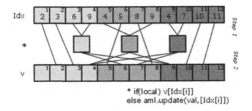

Fig. 5. Access redirection to an AML with selective privatization allows to bypass memory accesses in certain cases

In terms of AMLs, array replication is a case where the initializer and reducer methods operate on array copies and the GET-method is obsolete as the [ ] operator can be used instead. Figure 5 shows the generalization of access redirection where accesses to the original reduction variable are redirected to an AML object. Particular interface definitions as used in our reference implementation are shown below.

– void initializer(AML_T * priv, void * global)
– void reducer (AML_T * priv, void * global)
– void * get (void * address, void * global, analytics_info_t * a)

This interface allows runtimes to allocate any private storage of the size of an AML (*sizeof(AML_T)*) and to invoke the initializer and reducer for each thread-private copy. The initializer method accepts a reference to an allocated thread-private storage as well as a reference to a global object. The global object is typically either a pointer to global reduction variable or any other structure containing additional information needed by the initializer such as size information. Similarly, the reducer function receives a pointer to a an AML as well as pointer to a global data structure containing further information if required by the reducer. The GET-method (*get*) returns a pointer to a private storage location to store a single target array element. It accepts a global object and an analytics object. The analytics object is computer by the inspector-executor on a phase switch. An example implementation is shown in the next section.

Figure 6 gives an overview on how algorithms, parallelization strategies and techniques are related to each other. Further it shows which techniques require an inspector-executor as well as their support in the OmpSs reduction model.

3   Runtime Support

Our OmpSs-RM implementation consists of three components: an example AML implementation, a set of support classes that implement the inspector-executor and a collection of APIs to interface with the programming model runtime. We explain each component in the next section.

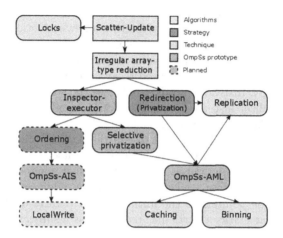

Fig. 6. Landscape of algorithms, parallelization strategies and techniques (Color figure online)

```
1 //AML interface
2 inline void * AML_GET (void * adr, AML_t * aml, analytics_t * mal);
3 void AML_init (AML_t * priv, reduction_info_t * info);
4 void AML_red (AML_t * in, reduction_info_t * info);
```

Fig. 7. Interface to our AML object that implement binning with selective privatization

The following work was implemented in the OmpSs [6] programming model. OmpSs (Omp Superscalar) is a task-parallel, data-flow aware parallel programming model developed at the Barcelona Supercomputing Center. Its proximity to the language specification of OpenMP [9] makes is relevant to runtime developers working on comparable implementations.

3.1   Handling AMLs by the Compiler

Our sample AML implements binning with selective privation through the aforementioned interface methods and its source code is located in a header file. During compilation, this header is inserted into the user application and accesses to the original reduction variable are replaced by calls to the GET-method. Encapsulating AMLs into header files is a design that offers support for any other user or vendor provided AML implementations without the need to recompile the programming model runtime. Further, due to the frequent accesses to the GET-method, its in-lining into intermediate code reduces the overhead of stack operations. Figure 7 shows the particular interfaces used to support AMLs in OmpSs.

3.2 Handling AMLs by the Runtime

The runtime support for OmpSs-RM builds on top of the existing reduction support where the runtime is capable of registering a new reduction and allocating, initializing and reducing private storage. For the additional support of AMLs, the runtime needs to distinguish between the use of AMLs and replication. In case of on AML, the runtime is required to avoid the allocation and initialization of an array copy. Instead it needs to allocate the size of the AML type and call the AML initializer instead. This allows AMLs to allocate and initialize any arbitrary memory layout by themselves. Similarly, in case the runtime decides to reduce private copies, it is required to call the reducer function of the AML instead of attempting to reduce the private memory itself.

Therefore whenever the OmpSs front-end compiler generates a method call to the runtime that registers a new AML reduction, additional parameters are passed. They include pointers to the initializer and reducer of the AML object as well as a flag that marks a particular reduction as a subject to the inspector-executor.

3.3 Handling Inspector-Executors

The inclusion of the inspector-executor into a parallel programming model requires the following feature sets.

Scope, Granularity and Invariance. Firstly it is required to establish a region where the inspection can take place and where the application of the executor is valid. We call this region an optimization frame. In case of a reduction, an optimization frame corresponds to the scope of a reduction computation. Further, a definition of granularity is required. In our case the inspector-executor is created for each individual task that participates in the reduction computation. Finally, since any statistical data created by the inspector for a particular task needs to be applied on the same task instance in the future, the runtime is required to track task instances. In case the optimization frame is identified by a hash value generated by any set of instance invariant values (such as function pointers), then particular task instances can be tracked by a simple counter that is incremented on every instantiation of a participating reduction task. This assumes that neither the creation order of tasks nor the memory access pattern of the reduction kernel change between the inspection and execution phases.

```
1 while (...){
2     frameID = instance_invariant_identifier;
3     handle_optimization_frame(ID) //compute anltcs
4     task = new reduction_task(frameID,taskcode,...)
5     task.run();
6 }
7 ...
8 taskcode(...){
9     void * v_priv; red_info_t * i; analytics_t * a;
10    v_priv = get_thread_storage(v);
11    i      = get_red_info(v);
12    a      = get_analytics(v, a->instanceID);
13    for(...) {
14        j = f(j);
15        if(!a->ready)
16            inspect(&v[j],v , a, a->frameInstanceID);
17        (*aml_get(&v[j], v_priv, i, a))++;
18    }
19 }
```

Fig. 8. A simplified, intermediate code shows the support of AMLs and inspector-executors in OmpSs

Implementation of the Inspector. The OmpSs-RM inspector is located in a header file that is inserted into the intermediate code and implements a logger method (log). This method receives the address of the currently accessed memory location and is called from within an AML's GET-method. Every time the runtime registers a new reduction, a global inspector manager is created for that particular reduction. Participating tasks register their inspectors in the inspector manager. At the end of an optimization frame, the manager passes all logs from all inspectors to an analytics object for processing and sets a ready flag. This completes the inspection phase.

Code Generations. Figure 8 shows a simplified, intermediate code where an instance-invariant identifier (*frameID*) is created to identify an optimization frame and that is subsequently passed to all participating task. By doing so, all tasks sharing one identifier are associated to one optimization frame. Once a task instance is created, the frame identifier is used to generate a new unique identifier for that particular task instance (*instanceID*). In OmpSs and for the context of reductions, the frame identifier is computed as an *xor* between the reduction target address and value of the reducer function pointer. The instance frame identifier for each particular task is created again as an *xor* between frame identifier and a task creation counter. In case of nesting, new identifiers are created for each nest. Optimization frames across nesting levels are not supported. The intermediate task code in Fig. 8 (line 8) shows the triplet of runtime library calls to acquire a private thread storage (*get_thread_storage*), a reduction information object containing additional information about the reduction (*get_red_info*) and access analytics (*get_analytics*). In the kernel loop itself, occurrences of the reduction target variable are replaced by a call to the GET-method as well as each access to the original reduction variable is inspected in cases where the analytics object is not ready yet.

Figure 9 shows the compilation process with the OmpSs front-end compiler (mcxx) and code organization as used in our implementation.

4   Language Support

To program with OmpSs-RM, we require three additional information from the developer. Firstly, the developer is required to express the intention to use an AML. This step is necessary in order to preserve consistency as with AMLs, the scratch memory is not necessarily a replica of the original data anymore. For this purpose, we propose the extension of the reduction clause by the additional parameter $MODE$, where mode is an identifier of a vendor provided privatization technique. We define a reduction clause using the mode identifier as

$$reduction\ (id : target : mode)$$

where $reduction$ corresponds to the OpenMP reduction clause, id is an operator and $target$ a variable identifier.

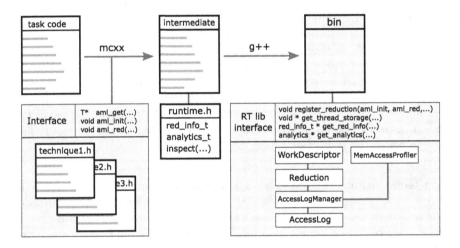

Fig. 9. Code organization in OmpSs

Further, in order to enable AMLs that require an inspector-executor, we propose the addition of the $invariant(target)$ clause. The invariant clause defined over a target specifies that the access pattern of the target as well as the calling order within the scope of a reduction are invariant. This step is important to guarantee that the inspector-executor is always applied to the matching function and that optimization results obtained during the inspection phase are still valid for subsequent function calls or task instances. It is defined as

$$reduction\ (id : target : mode)\ invariant(target)$$

Lastly we propose the addition of the $loopstep$ pragma. This pragma declares the encountering region as an optimization frame and is used to differentiate between inspection and execution phases. It is defined as

$$\#pragma\ omp\ loopstep$$

On encountering a loopstep pragma, the runtime may transition from executing an instrumented code (inspector) to an optimized code version. The pragma applies to all targets that were declared in the invariant clause in the same region. Figure 10 shows an example of an array reduction using the proposed language extensions where MODE is set to selective privatization (*SP*).

Restriction. A variable that is declared as a reduction target with a MODE set to an AML may not be passed to an external function or library due to mismatching memory layouts.

```
1
2 /*region*/
3 while(simulation_runs()){
4   #pragma omp parallel for reduction (+:v:SP) invariant (v)
5   for(int i = START; i < END; i++) {
6     j = f(i);
7     v[j]++;
8   }/*end of reduction*/
9   #pragma omp loopstep
10 }/*end of optimization frame for v*/
```

Fig. 10. OmpSs implementation of a reduction kernel showing the proposed language extensions

5   Case Study

Our work on OmpSs-RM was largely motivated by LULESH, a seismic simulation code that contains irregular array-type reductions. Inspecting its memory access pattern in the inspector phase of execution revealed a linear access pattern with very small overlaps for boundary iterations. The inspector used in this case records histograms over addresses, over distances between memory accesses and over the rate of distance changes. Figure 11 shows a visual output of the inspection phase as seen by a single task. It shows the histograms of memory accesses over different memory regions (bins) as well as the average access distance between bins. In this case only two tasks participated in the computation with each task accessing half of the reduction array. The average access distance between regions is zero, indicating a linear or close to linear access pattern.

5.1   The Choice of AML

The linear memory access pattern makes LULESH a perfect candidate for selective privatization. Due to the fact that the majority of accesses is performed within the owned memory region of the executing task, access redirection can be avoided for most memory accesses. Those memory accesses updating memory outside the owned regions are redirected to bins (binning). Bins implement linear buffers of small sizes without the memory overheads associated with array replication.

5.2   Performance Results

Figures 12 and 13 show scalability results of two Lulesh reduction kernels implemented with different techniques and running on two different systems. On the Intel XEON system, the OmpSs AML implementation with binning and selective privatization achieved the highest speedup compared to implementations with atomics, replication (PRIV) as well as a manually optimized implementation (ORIG). In the manually optimized code, the implementer assumed that each task will only access index+8 positions, therefore for any number of threads, a maximum of 8 private copies are created. Further the manual implementation implements a concurrent initializer and reducer. On the POWER8 system, the OmpSs implementation performed comparably to the manually optimized code. For completeness we added a performance chart showing a version without any support technique (RACE).

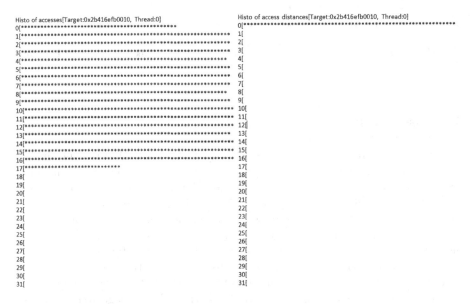

Fig. 11. Linear access pattern detected during the inspection phase of a reduction kernel in LULESH showing histograms over 32 bins and rates of change(right)

System Configuration. Benchmark results were obtained on a node of the MareNostrum supercomputer equipped with a 2-way Intel XEON E5-2670 CPU with 8 cores each and a 4-way IBM POWER8 system equipped with 6 cores each and 8 native treads per core. On the POWER8 system, a thread striding offset of 8 was used in order to distribute small thread counts evenly across all sockets and cores. for smaller thread counts, this placement allows threads to utilize entire caches and memory bandwidth exclusively which explains the early performance spikes in Fig. 13.

6   Related Work

First work giving an overview of support techniques for irregular array reductions was conducted by *Han* and *Tseng*[7]. Their work discusses each approach as well as their implications on performance in respect to key algorithmic properties. A decision framework based on algorithmic properties was presented by *Yu* and *Rauchwerger* [11]. In their work they identified a multitude of different static and dynamic properties of reduction kernels that allowed them to develop a decision tree. Using that tree, a runtime system could select a technique for a particular problem. This work led to the publication by *Yu, Dang* and *Rauchwerger*[10] where the decision making process was further formalized by introducing a pattern descriptor and a decision tree learning algorithm. In this work we took the ideas on reduction parallelization techniques as well as inspec-

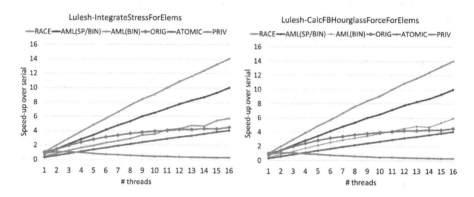

Fig. 12. Performance scalability of two reduction kernels in LULESH showing performance gains obtained by binning and selective privatization in OmpSs on a 2-way Intel Xeon E5 processor (Color figure online)

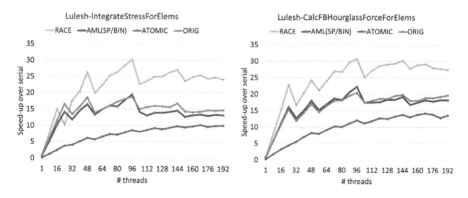

Fig. 13. Performance scalability of LULESH obtained on a IBM POWER8 system shows comparable performance to a manually optimized concurrent implementation (Color figure online)

tion of dynamic kernel properties to derive a proposal towards their adoption into popular task-parallel programming models. While we did not experiment with automatic switching between parallelization approaches, we believe that it is feasible to implement an AML initializer that can configure itself following a decision tree and access analytics obtained from an inspector.

7 Conclusion

In this work we presented how adaptive techniques for irregular array reductions can be integrated into a task parallel programming model. Further we showed which runtime features as well as language constructs are needed to allow the use of reduction techniques implementing an alternative memory layout (AML). We believe that specifying a common interface for initialization, reduction and memory accesses offers implementors a convenient way to implement new techniques that adapt to algorithmic and system properties. The inclusion of inspector-executors provides new capabilities to programming model runtime systems of which adaptive reduction support is an example. Benchmarking results show that knowledge about dynamic properties of an algorithm leads to better performance results. We are interested to explore the support of techniques that implement alternative iteration spaces (AIS) in the context of worksharing constructs in the future.

Acknowledgment. This work has been developed with the support of the grant SEV-2011-00067 of Severo Ochoa Program, awarded by the Spanish Government and by the Spanish Ministry of Science and Innovation (contracts TIN2012-34557, and CAC2007-00052) by the Generalitat de Catalunya (contract 2009-SGR-980) and the Intel-BSC Exascale Lab collaboration project.

References

1. Hydrodynamics Challenge Problem, Lawrence Livermore National Laboratory. Technical report LLNL-TR-490254
2. A comparison of parallelization techniques for irregular reductions. In: Proceedings 15th International Parallel and Distributed Processing Symposium, p. 8, April 2001
3. Ciesko, J., Bueno, J., Puzovic, N., Ramirez, A., Badia, R.M., Labarta, J.: Programmable and scalable reductions on clusters. In: 2013 IEEE 27th International Symposium on Parallel Distributed Processing (IPDPS), pp. 560–568, May 2013
4. Ciesko, J., Mateo, S., Teruel, X., Beltran, V., Martorell, X., Labarta, J.: Boosting irregular array reductions through in-lined block-ordering on fast processors. In: High Performance Extreme Computing Conference (HPEC), pp. 1–6. IEEE, September 2015
5. Ciesko, J., Mateo, S., Teruel, X., Beltran, V., Martorell, X., Badia, R.M., Ayguadé, E., Labarta, J.: Task-parallel reductions in OpenMP and OmpSs. In: DeRose, L., de Supinski, B.R., Olivier, S.L., Chapman, B.M., Müller, M.S. (eds.) IWOMP 2014. LNCS, vol. 8766, pp. 1–15. Springer, Heidelberg (2014)

6. Duran, A., Ayguadé, E., Badia, R., Labarta, J., Martinell, L., Martorell, X., Planas, J.: Ompss: a proposal for programming heterogeneous multi-core architectures. Parallel Process. Lett. **21**(02), 173–193 (2011)
7. Han, H., Tseng, C.W.: A comparison of parallelization techniques for irregular reductions. In: Proceedings of the 15th International Parallel & Amp; Distributed Processing Symposium, IPDPS 2001, p. 27. IEEE Computer Society, Washington, DC, USA (2001). http://dl.acm.org/citation.cfm?id=645609.662492
8. Komatitsch, D., Tromp, J.: Introduction to the spectral-element method for 3-D seismic wave propagation **139**(3), 806–822 (1999)
9. OpenMP Architecture Review Board: OpenMP Application Program Interface Version 4.0, July 2013
10. Yu, H., Dang, F.H., Rauchwerger, L.: Parallel reductions: an application of adaptive algorithm selection. In: Pugh, B., Tseng, C. (eds.) LCPC 2002. LNCS, vol. 2481, pp. 188–202. Springer, Heidelberg (2005)
11. Yu, H., Rauchwerger, L.: Adaptive reduction parallelization techniques. In: ACM International Conference on Supercomputing 25th Anniversary Volume, pp. 311–322. ACM, New York, NY, USA (2014). http://doi.acm.org/10.1145/2591635.2667180

Author Index

Printed in the United States
By Bookmasters